THE VIVARIUM,

BEING A PRACTICAL GUIDE TO

The Construction, Arrangement, and Management of Vivaria,

CONTAINING

FULL INFORMATION AS TO ALL REPTILES SUITABLE AS PETS, HOW AND WHERE TO OBTAIN THEM, AND HOW TO KEEP THEM IN HEALTH.

Illustrated.

By

THE REV. GREGORY C. BATEMAN, A.K.C.

Author of " The Fresh Water Aquarium," &c.

PREFACE.

Up to the present time there has been no reliable work on the management of the many attractive batrachians, reptiles, etc., that can be readily kept in confinement. Yet there are no more charming and interesting pets than such as can be included in an amateur's Vivarium. For these reasons this book has been written, and readers may rely on the information given in the following pages being the outcome of practical experience, the result of my having kept these interesting and extraordinary animals for very many years.

For information concerning some of the animals of which this book treats I am much indebted to the writings of Dr. Günther, Mr. Boulenger, Dr. Stradling, and others, and to the obliging keeper of the Reptile House at the Zoological Gardens, London, Mr. J. Tyrrell.

G. C. B.

Jacobstowe Rectory, North Devon.
July 28*th*, 1897.

THE VIVARIUM.

CHAPTER I.

INTRODUCTORY.

YEARS ago I built a large aquarium on the outside window sill of one of the first rooms I could ever call my own, and it was pleasanter (so I thought) to look into it and watch the fish of various colours and shapes swimming among graceful water-weeds than into the little strip of not very interesting town garden belonging to my landlady. But, alas! my satisfaction in my device was short-lived, for I had made the aquarium upon wrong principles: the wood warped, the glass cracked, and my tank was ruined. It had cost me not a little time and trouble to make, and I somewhat sadly contemplated the wreck as I ate my solitary breakfast. I did not like to remove it and confess to complete failure, and while thinking the matter over, it occurred to me that I would turn the affair into a fernery. I had always been fond of Ferns, and a fernery would not only be a source of interest and amusement, but it would also hide the rather depressing view from the window. So, at my first leisure, I removed the fish and aquatic plants to an aquarium inside the room, and commenced the work of turning the leaking tank into a fern-case.

The thing was done, and the Ferns grew and flourished, and it was no inconsiderable pleasure to attend to their wants and watch their growth. Every morning, as I came down to breakfast, I could see some change and progress. Soon, however, I began to think that the fernery would be far more attractive were it to contain animal, as well as plant life. Presently, therefore, I had a small tank made, fixed it in the soil among the ferns, and thus formed a tiny pond. I then procured some Lizards, and as they seemed to live quite happily in the case, basking wherever they could manage to get a gleam of sunshine, I added a few Slow-worms, and afterwards two or three Water-tortoises. Thus, gradually, I was led to keep and find pleasure in Reptiles.

Many people have really a repugnance for these creatures, and so might I have had had it not have been for the experience related above. They seem to shudder at the very name of Reptile. Why? For the most part these animals are perfectly harmless, some of them exceedingly beautiful, and many wonderfully quaint and curious. This repugnance, I think, comes rather of training than of instinct. A man who dreads them does so not instinctively, but because his parents and fore-parents dreaded them before him, and he has always, or nearly always, heard them spoken of with disgust. This disgust, hatred, or dread of Reptiles probably originated partly through our ancestors' natural distrust of the unfamiliar, and partly because some of these animals were known to have the power of giving most deadly wounds.

As an illustration, I venture to mention that some time ago a foolish nurse frightened my little daughter by talking to her of the dreadfulness of Snakes, and the consequence was that the child frequently cried out in terror at night, dreaming of Snakes. But her fear of these animals was quickly dispelled when I showed her, and let her handle, a young Green Snake (*Tropidonotus natrix*), somewhat longer than an ordinary penholder, and not quite so thick. A few weeks after this, a parishioner brought me an unusually large Slow-worm (*Anguis fragilis*), and as I was away from home at the time, handed it over to the care of my small son, who put it into a bottle and placed it in my study. Soon it was discovered that the creature had escaped and was roaming over the floor of the room. While the servants were discussing what was to be done, my little daughter, not five years old, went of her own accord into the study, and looking about, saw the Reptile, gently picked it up, and returned it to the bottle, where I found it on my return.

This somewhat trivial circumstance is mentioned simply to remind how easily children may be taught to have a horror of Reptiles, and how easily that horror may be dissipated by proving to them there is nothing repellent and dangerous in harmless animals of this kind. Of course, those who live in England should be taught to recognise the Viper (*Pelias berus*).

Reptiles are exceedingly interesting, wonderfully varied, very soon get tame, and are, perhaps, far more easily kept in a contented and healthy condition in confinement than any other animal. Other pets suffer severely if neglected for a day or even part of a day, but Reptiles are as wonderful in their powers of fasting as in their powers of feasting. A small Snake, for instance, will eat at one time, and without division, an animal so large that to the uninitiated it would seem an utter impossibility, and yet the same Snake might fast for a whole year and suffer no injury.

Some Reptiles and Batrachians only feed at night, others only in the daytime; some prefer shade, others sunshine; some lay eggs, others produce their young alive; some are delicate and short-lived, while others are so robust as to exist for more than a hundred years; some will die upon receiving the slightest blow, while others will not only survive mutilation, but will even reproduce a limb nearly as often as it is amputated; some live altogether in water, others will never voluntarily enter it; some are famous climbers, even scorning the laws of gravitation, while others cannot climb at all; some seem to possess all the colours of the rainbow, while others are of the soberest tints; some have the power of making noise out of all proportion to their size, and others have no voice of which man knows; some have the softest skin, but others are covered, both above and below, with very hard shell; some can give most deadly wounds, while others can give no wounds at all; some ———. But enough, I think, has been said, awkwardly no doubt, but I hope briefly, to remind one that, at any rate, there is much that is interesting, curious, wonderful, and instructing in these creatures, which are so often dreaded and ignored.

The ignorance displayed by the general public in respect of

Reptiles and Batrachians has given rise to many extraordinary mistakes concerning them. For example, that Snakes sting by means of their harmless tongues—called in Devonshire "spears"—that they have the power of fascinating their prey, and that they will, as a rule, go out of their way to attack man, that the Salamander can live in fire, and that the Toad (*Bufo vulgaris*) has the power of inflicting deadly wounds. In England the harmless Slow-worm (*Anguis fragilis*) is often considered far more deadly than the Viper (*Pelias berus*). These and other delusions will be spoken of when the various animals are described. A writer in *Science Gossip* says truly that "there is more romance amongst us and less sound knowledge with regard to Reptiles than other of the objects of natural history."

Formerly, Batrachians, such as Frogs, Toads, and Newts, were spoken of as Reptiles, but now they are placed in a separate class.

The *Vertebrata*, or those animals which possess a backbone, are divided into five classes :
1. *Mammalia*, or Men and Beasts.
2. *Aves*, or Birds.
3. *Reptilia*, or Tortoises, Lizards, etc.
4. *Batrachia*, or Frogs, Toads, Newts, etc.
5. *Pisces*, or Fishes.

Birds and Reptiles have been also grouped under the common title of *Sauropsida* (from *sauros*, a lizard, and *opsis*, appearance); while the Batrachians and Fishes are placed under that of *Ichthyopsida* (from *ichthys*, a fish, and *opsis*, appearance). Thus it is seen that Reptiles are considered to be allied to Birds, and the Batrachians to Fishes.

Reptiles themselves, according to Dr. Günther and other great authorities, are at present divided into the following ten Orders, of which five are now extinct :—
1. *Ichthyopterygia* (*ichtys*, a fish ; *pteryx, pterygos*, wing—or fin-like).—Extinct Sea Reptiles, with a whale-like naked body, having four paddle-like limbs and a long tail.
2. *Anomodontia* (*anomos*, lawless ; *odous, odontos*, a tooth).—Extinct Lizard-like Reptiles, some being toothless, others possessing "long ever-growing tusks and other smaller teeth."
3. *Dinosauria* (*deinos*, terrible ; *sauros*, a lizard).—Extinct huge Lizards, of terrible appearance. Some of them more than

INTRODUCTORY. 5

70ft. in length, exceeding in size any land animals. Some were fitted for a terrestrial life, others for an aquatic. Most of them were herbivorous, few carnivorous.
4. *Ornithosauria* (*ornis*, *ornithos*, a bird; *sauros*, a lizard).— Extinct flying Reptiles.
5. *Crocodilia* (*krokodeilos*, a crocodile).—Crocodiles, Alligators, etc.
6. *Sauropterygia* (*sauros*, a lizard; *pteryx*, *pterygos*, wing—or fin-like).—Extinct Sea Reptiles, having a small head, a long neck and tail, a naked skin, and four paddle-like limbs.
7. *Rhynchocephalia* (*rhynchos*, a beak; *kephale*, a head).—Lizard-like Reptiles, of which there is only one living representative, viz., the *Hatteria*.
*8. *Lacertilia* (*lacerta*, a lizard).—Lizards.
*9. *Ophidia* (*orphis*, a serpent).—Snakes.
10. *Chelonia* (*chelone*, a tortoise).—Tortoises and Turtles.

The Batrachia are arranged in four Orders, of which one is extinct:
1. *Ecaudata.*—Those Batrachians, such as Frogs and Toads, which lose the tail of tadpolehood before they reach maturity.
2. *Caudata.*—Those Amphibians, such as the Newts, which retain the tail throughout life.
3. *Apoda* or *Ophimorpha.*—Batrachians of a snake-like appearance — e.g., the Cœcilla.
4. *Labyrinthodonta.*—The animals belonging to this order are extinct. They were crocodile-like Batrachians upwards of 12ft. in length. Their curious and beautiful teeth have given them the above title.

Reptiles may be defined as cold-blooded, oviparous, or ovoviviparous vertebrate animals, breathing by means of lungs. Their bodies, which go through no transformation at any portion of their lives, are covered with scales or shelly plates.

Batrachians, or Amphibians, are also, as the Reptiles, cold-blooded, oviparous or ovoviviparous, vertebrate animals; but, unlike the Reptiles, they commence their life in the water, breathing there by means of branchiæ, or gills, and undergo a transformation.

As Reptiles and Batrachians are cold-blooded animals they are

---

*These two orders are now, by some authorities, considered as one under the title of *Squamata*, or scale-covered reptiles (*Squama*, a scale).

dependent to a very great extent upon external heat for that of their bodies. For instance, if a cold Snake be wrapped up in unwarmed blankets it will remain cold, for it is able to generate very little or no heat of its own; but on the other hand, if a cold, healthy man be enveloped in unwarmed blankets he will soon become quite hot, which would never happen in the case of the Reptile. Reptiles and Batrachians, therefore, are not found in the Arctic or Antarctic regions, but in the tropical and subtropical countries they are in the greatest variety and abundance.

Most Reptiles and Batrachians spend the cold months of the year in a state of torpor, commonly called hibernation; while a few of them, in very hot climates, estivate, that is, they remain more or less dormant during the greatest and driest heat of the summer.

The late Mr. Thomas Bell, in the introduction to his "History of British Reptiles," well says that "the phenomena of hibernation are amongst the most remarkable and interesting which occur in the history of animals." Both the low temperature of winter and the absence of suitable food tend to cause this hibernation. During hibernation the respiration is very slow, and apparently ceases, digestion is at a standstill, and insensibility is all but complete.

In our own, and other countries, as winter approaches, most of the insectivorous birds are able to migrate to warmer climates and more abundant food; but as Reptiles and Batrachians, in common with the Squirrel, the Bat, the Dormouse, and some other animals are unable to cross the seas, they are obliged to retire to their various hibernacula, or winter quarters, which they make according to their species and needs under ground, under stones, under heaps of rubbish, in clefts of rocks, in crevices of banks, in the mud at the bottom of ponds, in nests of their own construction, in the hollow of trees, and similar places. The state of torpidity, however, of the cold-blooded Reptiles and Batrachians is more complete during hibernation than is that of the warm-blooded animals, such as those which have been mentioned above.

MM. Duméril and Bibron, in their great work upon Reptiles and Batrachians (completed in 1854), described no less than 121

Chelonians, or Tortoises, 468 Saurians, or Lizards, 586 Ophidians, or Snakes, and 218 Batrachians. This will give one some idea of the great variety of these creatures. Since 1854, however, a period of forty years, a great addition has been made to our knowledge of these animals. For example, it may be mentioned that something like 1700 different kinds of Lizards, 1800 different kinds of Snakes and 300 different kinds of Tortoises are now known to science; and, perhaps, our knowledge of the Batrachians has increased with quite as great strides.

CHAPTER II.

HOW TO MAKE VIVARIA.

AS the Reptiles and Batrachians which may be kept successfully in confinement are so different in form and habit, it is necessary to describe a variety of Vivaria, or cases.

Handsome Vivaria may be readily bought in London, and other large towns, but they are rather expensive and not always suitable for their purpose. If money, indeed, be not an object, it is wise to choose those Vivaria which are constructed most like the ones in use in the beautiful and well-kept Reptile House in Regent's Park. Such cases would in all probability be well worth the money given for them. However, very convenient Vivaria for Reptiles and Batrachians—and by no means unsightly—may easily and cheaply be made by an ordinary amateur carpenter. It is proposed to give in this chapter directions for the building of such; and I will try to write as simply and as plainly as I can, in order that a young schoolboy may, if he think fit, readily understand how to construct, without difficulty, a suitable case for his Reptilian pets.

Fig. 1 represents a very useful summer case for either Snakes (not those that eat mice) or Lizards. It is made of well-seasoned match-boarding, glass, and canvas. This kind of wood is recommended because of the readiness with which it is jointed, and the grooves with which it is provided are very convenient for the reception of the glass.

The following are good dimensions for such a Vivarium as this: 3ft. 6in. long, about 20in. wide (or three boards wide), and

2ft. high; but if it is not made according to these sizes, it should be of this proportion. For the back, laths of wood 2in. wide are sawn and made into a frame of the required length and breadth, and over it is carefully and evenly nailed the canvas. This material, strong and clean-looking, may be cheaply bought of most drapers. There are several ways in which the canvas may be affixed to the wood, but the following I have found the simplest and best: Narrow strips of stout and finely perforated zinc are cut into lengths of not less than 1ft. These strips should

FIG. 1.—SNAKE OR LIZARD CASE FOR SUMMER USE.

be so narrow that there is down their centre only one row of perfect holes. They are nailed over the canvas, along the edges, after it has been cut to size, by means of those black pintacks which are generally used by haberdashers and upholsterers, and which may be put 1in. apart. Of course, care must be taken that the heads of the nails are larger than the holes in the zinc. The two ends and the top of the case should be made in the same way. In one of the ends (Fig. 2) there is a wooden door. A is a narrow wooden crosspiece; below it the door is hung by means of two slender French nails, which run through the frame-work at either side of the door, and is securely fastened at the bottom by the help of two buttons, or little hooks and eyes. The door falls against a strip of wood fastened on the inside. This opening is very useful for the purpose of cleaning out the Vivarium, and for introducing food and water.

The front of the case is also made by means of a frame; but each lath is so cut that there is a groove on the inside. The lower and end pieces are nailed or fastened together, and the glass, stout window-glass, cut the right size, is gently slipped into the grooves ready to receive it, and then the top lath is carefully and firmly affixed in its place. The bottom of the case is formed by nailing together three pieces of match-boarding, cut the proper length.

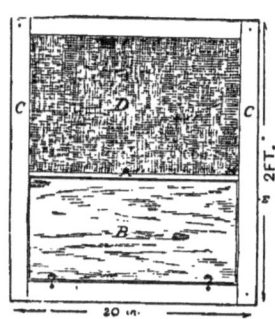

FIG. 2.—END OF VIVARIUM.
A, Strip of Wood; B, Door; C, Sides of Frame; D, Canvas; E, Positions of Wire Nails used as Hinges.

The back and the front are now screwed on to the ends, and the bottom on to the frame thus constructed. The top is fastened with three strong hinges to the upper side of the back, and is thus made to open and close like the lid of a box. It is very necessary to see that the lid lies so nicely in its place that even a fly would have difficulty in crawling between it and the rest of the case. The lid is made secure by means of hooks and eyes. If preferred, a small beading may be nailed to the front of the case and so improve its appearance.

The Vivarium is now almost completed and can be painted according to taste with Aspinall or other suitable colouring. This kind of case is very strong and light, and can be unscrewed at any time and packed away when not wanted. It is suitable for placing in a sunny window, as the canvas does not impede much light, and yet effectually prevents curious people without from looking into either the case or the room.

A branch of a tree (Fig. 1) ought to be fixed in such a way that the inmates of the case may climb upon it for sunning purposes, and the bottom of the Vivarium should be covered with clean and fine gravel. In the lid there is a glass funnel through which flies, etc., may be dropped, but by means of which nothing can escape. This case is, perhaps, more suitable, with certain exceptions, for Snakes than Lizards, as the latter are apt to climb up the canvas and so escape when the lid is unwarily opened. I am indebted to an excellent series of articles, published in the *Zoologist* for 1882-83, on "The Treatment of Snakes in Captivity," by Dr. Stradling, for my knowledge of the usefulness of canvas in the construction of Vivaria.

The Vivarium (Fig. 1), could, of course, be made of glass instead of canvas, and though, perhaps, it would then be more useful, it would, at the same time, be more expensive to construct, and heavier to move. If glass be used, any kind of small Snake may be kept in the case, and Lizards would not be able to escape when the lid is opened. I have never found these latter animals get their claws caught in the canvas. The illustration shows the Vivarium in use as a kind of fernery for Frogs, Toads, Newts, Slow-worms and the like. A board about 4in. wide, is

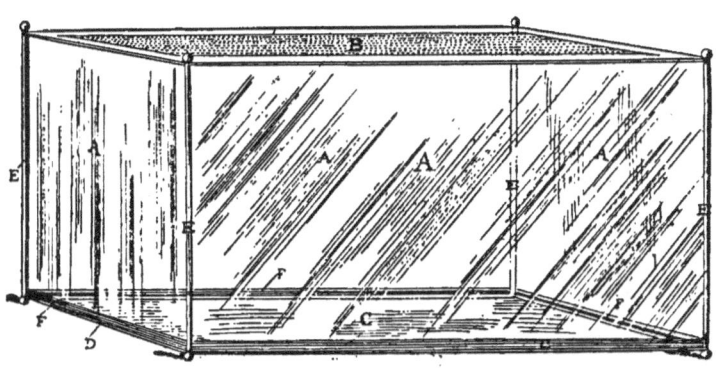

FIG. 3.—SNAKE OR LIZARD GLASS CASE FOR SUMMER OR WINTER USE.
A, Glass Sides; B, Perforated Zinc Top; C, Drawer; D, Perforated Zinc Bottom E, Round Grooved Wooden Uprights.

placed along the back, inside, to keep the mould from touching the canvas, and some holes have been made in the bottom to admit of drainage.

Fig. 3 represents a case suitable for Snakes, Lizards, or Batrachians, during either summer or winter. In the latter season, this Vivarium can easily be heated—directions for which will be given presently. This case, of course, can be constructed more or less elaborately; but if the following directions are carried out, it may be easily and inexpensively made. Slender well-seasoned broomsticks will do excellently for the pillars, especially if the case is to be of good dimensions. The Vivarium can be built of any reasonable size, but its proportions should somewhat correspond to those of Fig. 1. After the pillars have been cut of the desired length they ought to be grooved for the glass. The two grooves in each pillar must run lengthwise and at right angles to each other. The grooves can be made with a carpenter's ordinary plough, or with the help of chisels and a saw. The pillars, if preferred, may be 1in. square, instead of round, or they can be made of stout zinc.

Two wooden frames like Fig. 4 ought now to be prepared for the top and the bottom of the case. They may be mitred, or fastened together in some simpler manner, according to taste and skill. These frames are to be held in their places by the four pillars (see Fig. 3), which are attached to them by means of screws running through the top and bottom frames respectively, at (A) Fig. 4.

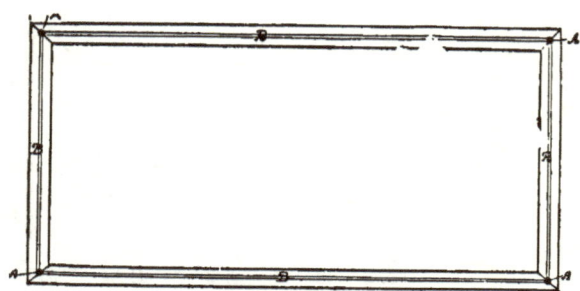

FIG. 4.—FRAME FOR EITHER THE TOP OR BOTTOM OF VIVARIUM (FIG. 3).
A, Holes through which Screws run for the purpose of Holding the Pillars; B, Grooves to receive either bottom or top edges of the Glass Sides.

If it is decided to form the pillars of zinc, the metal must be cut into strips the necessary length according to the desired height of the case, and about 1½in. wide. The zinc strips should then be bent exactly in the middle, lengthwise, at right angles (see Fig. 5). One piece of zinc, thus prepared, should be nailed by means of wire nails (or screws, if at any time it should be desired to take the case to pieces) at each corner of that frame which is chosen for the bottom, and then the opposite ends of the zinc should be fastened similarly to the other frame.

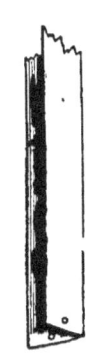

FIG. 5.—PART OF ZINC PILLAR FOR VIVARIUM SHOWN AT FIG. 3.

A sheet of finely perforated zinc ought to be nailed over the inside of the bottom frame, running as closely as possible to the grooves prepared for the glass. The glass sides are put in their places before the pillars are fastened to the upper frame.

The glass side in front may be made to slide up; for this purpose the groove in the upper frame should be cut quite through, and in order that the glass may the more readily be lifted, it ought to be so broad that its upper edge will stand ½in. above the frame at the top. The sliding side is convenient when the case has to be provided with fresh sand or gravel, and it also will keep the wooden drawer in its place.

At F, Fig. 3, there are narrow strips of wood to prevent spaces being left between the edges of the drawer and the sides of the case. These strips need be no deeper than the drawer, and the latter should be made to fit quite closely to them. If zinc is used for the pillars, the glass sides may be fastened in their places by means of the following cement: One part each of plaster of Paris, litharge, and fine white sand, and one-third part of finely-powdered resin. These ingredients should be well mixed into a putty with boiled oil and driers. Cement, however, must not be employed if it should be wished at any time to take the case to pieces. Instead of the cement, four narrow pieces of wood, one for each corner, about ½in. by ½in., running from the top frame to the bottom and fastened at both ends by screws passed through the frames, can be used. These, if placed quite in the corners, will hold the glass very firmly. The outside edges of the frames, if the pillars are of zinc, may be covered with narrow strips of the same metal. When zinc pillars are used no grooves need be made in the upper and lower frames for the glass sides.

As a rule, the inmates of a Vivarium should be attended to from the top, and for this purpose the case ought to be provided

14   THE VIVARIUM.

with an easily movable lid. This lid can be made by forming four narrow pieces of wood into a frame which will fit exactly into the top of the case, and over this frame securely nailing a sheet of finely perforated zinc. The little pin tacks, already

Fig. 6.—A Snake Case and a Lizard Case, both heated by the same Lamp.

spoken of, placed rather closely together, may be used. The zinc ought to be so cut that it will extend a little more than a ¼in. all round. This will prevent the lid from dropping into the case, as well as the animals, or even a fly, from getting out. Four

HOW TO MAKE VIVARIA. 15

little buttons running over the extending zinc will hold the lid quite securely. The drawer, which may be dispensed with, should be made of wood.

When Reptiles and Batrachians are not allowed to undergo their natural hibernation, they must be provided with artificial heat, which may easily be supplied with little trouble and at a trifling expense. Fig. 6 represents a winter case for Snakes and another for Lizards, both heated by the same lamp.

A cylindrical zinc or tin boiler (Fig. 7), about two-thirds of the length of the Vivaria, is enclosed in the case B, Fig. 6. This boiler may be made without difficulty by taking two empty Sanitas or other tins of a suitable size, and driving the opening of one into the opening of the other, and soldering them together. If the tins are about 9in. long, and 3½in. in diameter, they will be quite large enough to heat properly cases of the size of those represented in Fig 6. An Aspinall tin (which can be made clean by placing it for a time in very hot water and soda) will do capitally for the smaller boiler. The top of D, Fig. 7, should be well below that of A. The lid of the smaller boiler must be soldered in its place. B, Fig. 7, is a leaden pipe for filling the boilers. As there is no other opening to the boilers, a little care is required to fill them properly with water. But this can easily be done by means of a small india-rubber siphon of a diameter considerably less than that of the pipe; this will allow the air to escape as the water runs in. While the boiler is in use, a little water should in this way be added occasionally to make up for loss.

FIG. 7.—A, ZINC OR TIN BOILER; B and C, ½in. Gas-pipes, soldered in to the Boiler; D, a much smaller Boiler, joined to the larger by means of two short pieces of Gas-pipe.

Fig. 8 represents the interior of B, Fig. 6, when the boiler is in its place. The bottom of A, Fig. 6, and the top of C, Fig 6, are made of finely-perforated zinc. A fits *exactly* into the top of B, resting there on little ledges which are nailed inside, and B stands evenly upon the top of C. And in order that there may be no unnecessary loss of heat, the edges of C at the top are covered with felt. A door made of perforated zinc, (see D) is useful for both ventilation and the regulation of heat. The backs and sides (within) of the cases A and C, are covered with paper of a suitable tint, or painted. The outsides of the cases, the backs, top, and sides are protected with felt of some pleasing colour. And a curtain of the same material is arranged to fall over the front of the cases on very cold nights. Strips of felt ought also to be nailed on the edges of the cases (E) to prevent the escape of heat between them and the glass.

The glass fronts of these Vivaria are made to slide to and fro. The glass will not jam in the grooves if the gravel which covers the bottom of the cases be of the size of peas. If sand or unsifted gravel be used, some of it is sure to get into the lower grooves and cause the glass occasionally to stick. To prevent this, the grooves at the bottoms of the cases ought to be so formed that any sand or gravel which may be thrown into them will drop away from the glass. This can be done by making each groove of two laths of about ¼in. thick. The laths are kept at the right distance apart by means of little strips of wood which run perpendicularly from the bottom of each lath to within a ¼in. of the top of each. To these strips the laths are nailed. The ends of the strips of wood over which the glass sides run should be slightly rounded at the corners to prevent unnecessary friction.

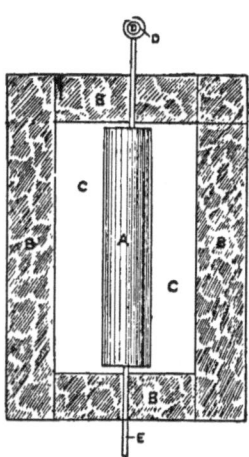

FIG. 8. — INTERIOR OF THE BOILER CASE. A, Larger Boiler; B, Sawdust to prevent unnecessary loss of Heat; C, Opening through which the Heat can both Ascend and Descend; D, Small Boiler; E, Filling Pipe.

These strips may be placed about every 4in. The bottom of the groove being open, all sand, gravel, and moisture will drop through or down; and the glass sides always run freely and easily. The upper grooves may, of course, be formed in the ordinary way.

These cases (Fig. 6) are made to stand on a table or some similar support, and face a sunny window. When the water in the boiler becomes quite hot, a very little flame is sufficient to keep it at the necessary temperature. If the air in the Vivaria becomes too hot, the curtain or piece of felt which is cut to lie over D, Fig. 6, can be turned back, and the flame of the lamp lowered. The lamp, if desired, can be hidden from sight by a little wooden or metal screen, made to slide over it. I believe, after many experiments, that cylindrical, and not too large, boilers are the best kind to use for such a purpose as the above. In summer, when no artificial heat is required, these cases can easily be detached and used separately, and the boiler, etc., put away for another winter.

The boiler case (Fig. 8), should have a wooden bottom, covered inside thickly with sawdust or folded paper, when it is intended to be used for heating only one Vivarium, e.g., one like that represented by Fig. 3. And unless gas be convenient as a source of heat, it ought to be provided with legs or a stand, so that a small lamp may be placed beneath the outside boiler. Of course, it could easily be arranged that the boiler case, the bottom being left open and the top enclosed, should be placed above the single Vivarium (it being provided with a perforated zinc top), and then there would be no need of a stand or legs. This device has its advantage, since the Lizards or Snakes within the case would be tempted to spend a great portion of their time upon the branches of the tree, and so be well exposed to view, and more likely to become very soon quite tame.

Fig. 9 is a Fernery and Vivarium combined. It is fairly easily made, and if well done, well arranged and cared for, is very ornamental and interesting. Certain Reptiles and Batrachians will live all the year round in it, apparently happy and contented. The bottom (A) is made of wood and lined with zinc, or covered inside thickly with pitch. It is provided, at some convenient spot, with a small pipe used for drainage purposes. The framework for the glass can be made of either wood or zinc as described for Fig. 3. That portion of the top of this Vivarium, marked G, is covered with perforated zinc for ventilation. B is a sheet of glass made to slide completely over the zinc, so that all outside air, when necessary, may be excluded. If the Vivarium must be so placed that the sliding sheet of glass (B) would be in the way when open, it (the glass) should be placed in a frame and made to work on hinges at H and I, and little stays affixed at J and K, to keep it, more or less, open as required. The ends L and M ought to be made to work as doors, in order that any portion of the interior of the case may easily be reached.

With the exception of the frame, the Vivarium is all of stout glass. D is an arch made of brick, stone, or coke, fastened together with Portland cement, and when finished, covered with

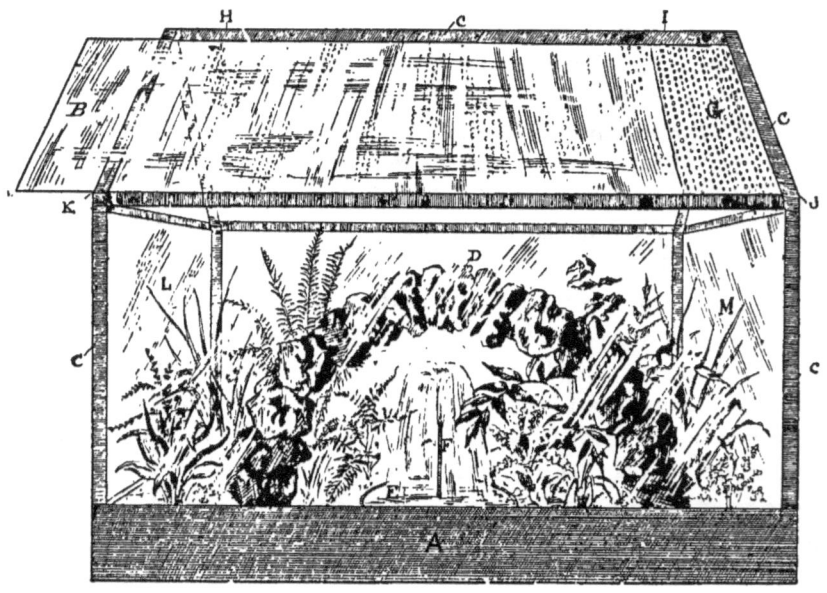

Fig. 9.—Fernery, with Fountain and Arch, very suitable for some Reptiles and Batrachians.

a thin coating of the same, sprinkled with coarse sand. If no fountain be made to play underneath, it need not be so high as represented in the illustration. The arch will probably take several days to construct, as the hardening of the cement must be waited for. E is a tank sunk nearly level with the soil inside the Vivarium, and is provided with an overflow pipe. F is a fountain which may be connected with some permanent supply of water or with an elevated tank, hidden out of sight, and which of course must be from time to time filled with water. However, neither a fixed interior tank nor a fountain is necessary, though they have many advantages. The soil, drainage, and the planting of ferns and the like, will be described later on. The Vivarium should be painted with Aspinall, or some similar colouring.

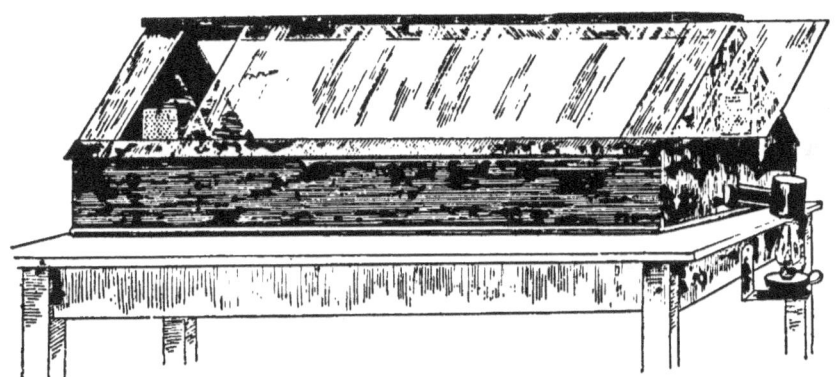

FIG. 10.—VIVARIUM FOR TORTOISES, ALLIGATOR, BULL-FROGS, &c.

The case which is illustrated in Fig. 10 is suitable for Tortoises, a small Alligator or Crocodile, Bull-frogs, or animals which occasionally need water kept at a temperature higher than that of the outside air. By means of a little paraffin lamp, the water in the tank within the case can be maintained at a heat of about

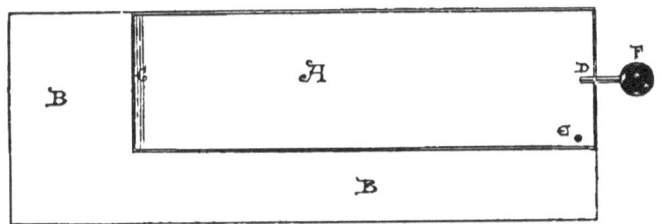

FIG. 11.—PLAN OF THE INTERIOR OF FIG. 10.
A, Tank; B, Platform; C, Wooden Ladder; D, Pipes connected with Outside Boiler; E, Emptying Pipe; F, Small Boiler.

80deg. Fahr. The platforms (Fig. 11) are level with the top of the tank. The Vivarium should be made according to the size of the animals to be kept in it. There is glass both in front and at the back. The front piece is arranged to slide to and fro; and

c 2

20 THE VIVARIUM.

air is admitted through the little perforated zinc doors at each end. This Vivarium is very useful for keeping amphibious animals throughout the winter when it is not intended to allow

FIG. 12.—VIVARIUM FOR A CHAMELEON.

them to hibernate. A small Alligator or Crocodile will do well in such a tank as this, which is easy to make, and, because of the position of the glass, very easy to see clearly into. Of course, if not wanted, the heating arrangement can be dispensed with.

Fig. 12 represents a Chameleon case for winter use. The lower part is provided with a boiler which is surrounded by thick layers of sawdust to prevent unnecessary loss of heat (see Fig. 8), and the bottom of the wooden case, which contains the boiler, is also thickly covered with sawdust or several folds of paper. The boiler itself need not be larger than a ½lb. coffee canister, and is provided with a small outer boiler and a filling pipe, which latter extends for an inch or two beyond the side which is remote from the lamp (see Fig. 7). The exposed end of the filling pipe ought to be covered with a felt coat to prevent loss of heat. The bottom of the upper part of this Vivarium is covered with finely-perforated zinc, through which the heat ascends from the boiler. The top of the case is made of wood, and should fit so nicely that a small fly cannot escape between it and the sides of the Vivarium. There are some round holes in the lid which are also covered with perforated zinc and are provided with lids of wood or zinc so that the heat within can be regulated. One hole, though supplied with a lid, has no perforated zinc. This is used for the admission of food to the Chameleon. In such as case as this I have kept, without any difficulty, a Chameleon in perfect health and appetite throughout a cold autumn, winter, and early spring, by far the most trying portion of the year for such Reptiles, which, as a rule, succumb to our English winters. Of course, except during summer, the little lamp must be kept lighted day and night. A Vivarium for a Chameleon ought not to be less than 14in. long, 12in. wide, and about the same high.

Fig. 13 is an arrangement for Newts during their breeding season. In the glass tank they may easily be seen laying and depositing their eggs; and they can, when they like, leave the water and retire into seclusion. The Aquarium, which is an inverted propagating-glass, stands on a square board raised a little above the table upon which it is placed. In the centre of the board there is a round hole, big enough to receive the knob of the glass. Another square board, rather smaller and thinner than the lower one, is prepared with a hole sufficiently large to receive *exactly* the top of the glass when inverted (see illustration). There must be no space between the glass and the edges of the larger hole or the Newts will escape. Instead of this board, a piece of zinc may be used. The board or zinc is supported by four wooden legs (Fig. 13), of the right height. The legs rest on the lower board. The upper part of the Vivarium may have two of its sides of glass and two of wood, as in the illustration, or all of glass. The glass sides are held in position by either grooves in the upper part of the legs, or by little zinc clips (see Fig. 13), attached to them.

The top is covered in with a lid of wood, in the centre of which is a round hole, of about 2in. in diameter, which is necessary

Fig. 13.—Vivarium for Newts during their Breeding Season.

for ventilation, and useful for dropping worms and meat through into the water for the Newts. The platform surrounding the top of the tank should be covered with clean and fine gravel. With some suitable plants in the water, and pieces of cork on the platform, the Vivarium is complete. I have kept successfully in such an arrangement as this, several different kinds of European Newts. The whole thing when well made and cared for, is both ornamental and interesting. In the usual kind of

Vivarium the Newts cannot be seen properly when in the water where they always exhibit themselves to the greatest advantage. The hole in the centre of the lid need not be covered, for the Newts, though excellent climbers, cannot escape. The larger the Aquarium is, the better.

Fig. 14 is the representation of a case which is useful for Water-Tortoises, Frogs, Toads, Newts, and Salamanders. It is provided with a rather large tank. The vessel which forms the tank is shaped by pressure in tin, and can be bought of an ironmonger for a few pence. It is made with a lip which prevents it from slipping through the hole which is cut in the

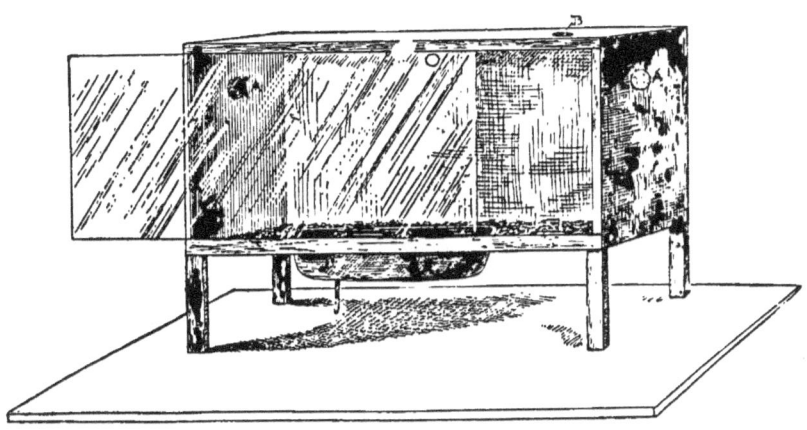

FIG. 14.—CASE FOR TORTOISES, FROGS, TOADS, NEWTS, SALAMANDERS, &c.
A, Holes, covered with Zinc, for Ventilation; B, Opening for dropping Food into the Case.

floor of the Vivarium for its reception. There are two advantages in arranging the tank like this: the water is easily accessible to the Reptiles within the case; and in winter it may be kept warm by placing a lamp beneath the tank. It is provided with a pipe by which it can be emptied. The interior of the tin ought to be painted with Brunswick black, to prevent leakage through rust.

In a tank similarly arranged, but very much larger, I keep an Alligator, and the water is easily maintained at the proper heat by a very small flame. The lower groove in which the glass front slides (Fig. 14), should be open, as already described, to prevent all chance of jamming caused by pieces of gravel.

Fig. 15 shows a Vivarium made entirely of glass, except the bottom and back, which are of wood. The glass sides and top are held in position by means of pieces of fine and strong wire which run through small holes bored in the glass. The holes can be made by the help of a little brace and bit, using as a lubricant spirits of camphor and spirits of turpentine. In each sheet of glass, except the lid and in that only two, four holes should be pierced at the distance of at least 1in. from the edge, two holes

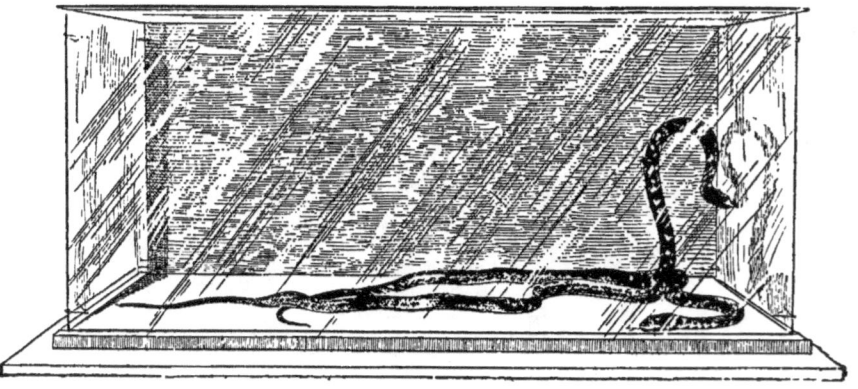

FIG. 15.—USEFUL VIVARIUM, MADE ALL OF GLASS, EXCEPT THE BACK AND BOTTOM.

at the top, one on either side, and two at the bottom in the same position. The top opens and closes like the lid of a box, and is fastened to the wooden back by means of small hinges made of wire. The lid should be about 1in. longer than the length of the case. A little wooden ledge runs outside the glass sides at their base, against which the sides are pressed and held firmly by a board which exactly fills the area of the interior of the case. This makes a capital case for small lizards which love and require plenty of light and sun. The little creatures, though excellent climbers, cannot escape when the Vivarium is opened. Two very beautiful Leopard Snakes (*Coluber leopardinus*), were placed in the case just before it was photographed and are thus represented in the illustration.

The little case of which Fig. 16 is an illustration, is very easily and quickly made. It is useful for small Skinks, Geckos, and the like. The piece of cork (see Fig. 16), under which the Reptiles will retire can be raised without disturbing them by means of the piece of wire which runs from it through the top of the case. The glass sides will move up or down, and are kept firmly in their places by wire buttons and staples (see A). In the upper part of the Vivarium there is a round hole, covered with a

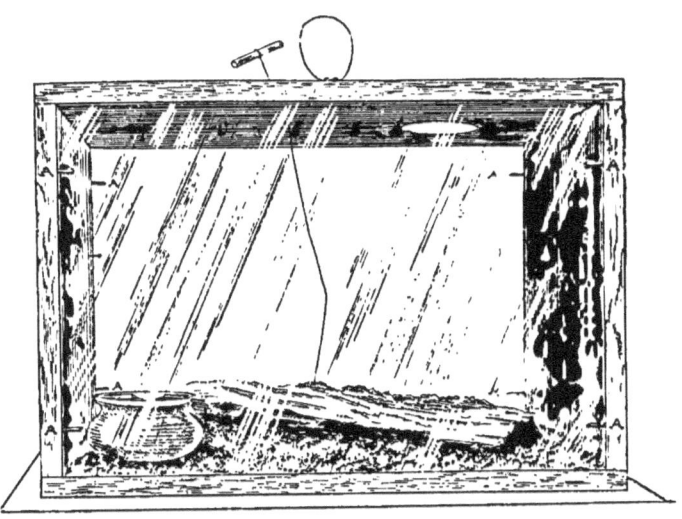

FIG. 16.—SMALL VIVARIUM, MADE OF FOUR PIECES OF WOOD AND TWO PIECES OF GLASS.

lid through which food can be dropped. A handle fastened to the top completes the case.

Fig. 17 is a Vivarium made out of a suitable box for Geckos, Skinks, Lizards, and tiny Snakes. The glass front rests against rabbets, or wooden ledges, and is held in its place by wire buttons, or clips of wood, and can easily be removed for cleaning purposes. In the top there is a round opening through which a hand and arm can be inserted, and is closed by means of a sliding piece of glass. The cork can be lifted for the inspection of the Reptiles, as described above. At one side, at the bottom, there is a little trough which slides from without into its place and is kept there by a button. Hanging over the opening A (inside) made to receive the trough is a small zinc door, which falls down and closes the opening when the trough is removed to be cleaned and refilled, but is raised horizontally when the vessel is returned to its former position. Such an arrangement as this will tend to prevent the escape of the inmates of the case. The interior should be coloured with distemper of some suitable tint, and the outside painted with Aspinall or a similar preparation. This case is intended to face the sun.

Fig. 17.—Small Vivarium for Geckos, Skinks, and the like.

Of course, the various Vivaria which have been described in this chapter are capable of many modifications and improvements. In making such articles it is always wise and kind to provide for the especial needs of the animals for which a particular case is intented, *e.g.*, a case for Lizards should be so arranged that its inmates can have access to the rays of the sun, and to some covering under which they can retire ; that for Batrachians should be supplied with plenty of clean water, shade, and some sun ; that for Snakes, gravel, a tree, and bathing water ; that for Skinks, sand, a hiding-place, and as much sun as possible. On no account should animals be placed in the same case with others of which naturally they would live in fear. For example, Frogs and Toads should not be confined with certain Snakes, nor Lizards and Newts with Bull-frogs, nor Alligators with small fresh-water tortoises.

In the construction of Vivaria, all chance of the captive's escape should be avoided as far as possible. For it is rather mortifying to realise the loss of a valuable Snake, or of a favourite Lizard ; nor does one get much encouragement in a hobby of this kind should he be often obliged to ask the ladies or servants of his home if they may happen to have seen anything of the missing Reptiles.

It is well to keep in each case a little thermometer, which can be bought for sixpence.

CHAPTER III.

PLANTS SUITABLE FOR VIVARIA.

CERTAIN plants in certain Vivaria are both useful and ornamental; nevertheless plant life in the Vivarium is of only secondary importance.

A Fern-case properly made and furnished is a very suitable habitation for some Reptiles and Batrachians. The ferns provide the animals with convenient retiring places and pleasant shade, and the latter are of benefit to the former by freeing them of injurious insects, and the two together, Ferns and Reptiles, are a very interesting possession. Ferns should, as a rule, have an abundance of light, and yet they ought to be shaded to a great extent from the direct rays of the sun. If Lizards, however, are kept in a Fern-case it should be arranged that the sun can shine as long as possible upon some portion of the case which is accessible to the Lizards. For this purpose, an arch is useful (See Fig. 9, p. 18), for upon it the Reptiles can climb and bask in the rays of the sun, which do not reach the ferns below. It is not a difficult matter, of course, to supply the necessary shade.

All Fern-cases must be well-drained and well-ventilated—the means of ventilation being under good control. If a Fern-case be built like that represented by Fig. 9, the bottom of it, to the depth of about three inches, should be covered with cinders, pieces of brick, coke, or stone, broken to the size of a pigeon's egg, and to prevent the mould from being washed down among the stones and the like, they ought to be protected by a layer of moss, cocoa-nut fibre, or a sheet of perforated zinc cut the

FIG. 18.—ADIANTUM FORMOSUM.

proper size. All surplus water can then be easily drawn off by means of the pipe already mentioned.

The soil of the Fern-case is a very important matter, as far as the health of the Ferns is concerned. Any kind of earth will not do. Properly prepared mould may be readily and cheaply bought in most large towns. The following mixtures have been recommended as forming soils in which ferns will grow well: (i.) Two parts peaty soil, and one part cocoa-nut fibre. (ii.) Peat, turfy loam, and coarse sand well mixed. (iii.) Fibrous bog-mould, sand, and small pieces of porous stone, mingled together. (iv.) Equal portions of coarse fibrous loam, good fibrous peat, leaf-mould, and silver sand, to this may be added charcoal and sandstone, broken up in small pieces. (v.) Good loam, leaf-mould and river or coarse silver sand. Naturally, different ferns sometimes require slightly different soil. It is never wise to plant ferns very closely together, plenty of space should be allowed for their growth.

The undermentioned ferns are suitable for such a Fern-case as the one referred to: The British Maidenhair (*Adiantum capillus-*

FIG. 19.—ASPLENIUM FONTANUM.

veneris); the Plumed Maidenhair (*Adiantum formosum*, Fig. 18); the Fountain Spleenwort (*Asplenium fontanum*, Fig. 19); the Black Maidenhair Spleenwort (*Asplenium adiantum-nigrum*);

the Wall Spleenwort (*Asplenium trichomanes*, Fig. 20); the Sea Spleenwort (*Asplenium marinum*); the Green-stalked Spleenwort (*Asplenium viride*); the Wall Rue (*Asplenium ruta-muraria*); the Forked Spleenwort (*Asplenium septentrionale*); the German Spleenwort (*Asplenium germanicum*); the Large-leaved Cyrtomium (*Cyrtomium falcatum*); the Comely Hare's-foot Fern (*Davallia decora*); the Graceful Hare's-foot Fern (*Davallia elegans*); the Blackened Boss Fern (*Lastrea atrata*); the Prolific Boss Fern (*Lastrea prolifica*); the Opaque Boss Fern

FIG. 20.—ASPLENIUM TRICHOMANES.

(*Lastrea opaca*); the Alpine Hard Fern (*Lomaria alpina*); the Climbing Fern (*Lygodium scandens*); the Palmate Climbing Fern (*Lygodium palmatum*); the Elk's-horn Fern (*Platycerium grande*); the Common Polypody (*Polypodium vulgare*); the Irish Polypody (*Polypodium v. semilacerum*); the Welsh Polypody (*Polypodium v. cambricum*); the Six-angled Polypody (*Polypodium hexagonopterum*); the Saw-leafed Bracken (*Pteris serrulata*); the Slender Bracken (*Pteris scaberula*); the Crisped Hart's-tongue (*Scolopendrium vulgare crispum*); the Endive-leafed Hart's-tongue (*Scolopendrium v. laceratum*); the Branched Hart's-tongue (*Scolopendrium v. ramosum*).

PLANTS SUITABLE FOR VIVARIA. 33

Besides the above evergreen Ferns, foreign as well as English, there are others more beautiful and perhaps more suitable for some Vivarium Fern-cases, *videlicet*, the deservedly popular Filmy Ferns. These Ferns are "membrane-leaved," hence their generic name of *Hymenophyllum*. They especially flourish in the moist atmosphere of a closed Fern-case, and therefore only those animals which thrive best in similar surroundings should be placed among them. The following Filmy Ferns are recommended:

FIG. 21.—TODEA PELLUCIDA.

The Tunbridge Filmy Fern (*Hymenophyllum Tunbridgense*); the Wilson's Filmy Fern (*Hymenophyllum Wilsonii*); the Transparent Filmy Fern (*Todea pellucida*, Fig. 21); The Beautiful Filmy Fern (*Todea superba*, Fig. 22); the Killarney Fern (*Trichomanes radicans*). Some of the Selaginellas will grow and look very well among the Ferns, such as *Selaginella denticulata*, *S. involens*, *S. apoda*, *S. Cæsia*, *S. Krauseiana*, and also their

D

near relatives the Club Mosses, or Snake Mosses, as they are sometimes called, *e.g.*, *Lycopodium selago*, the Fir Club Moss; *Lycopodium clavatum*, the Common Club Moss; *Lycopodium alpinum*, the Alpine Club Moss; and the like. A few of our beautiful Mosses will grow well in a Fern-case, if carefully managed, for example, *Funaria hygrometrica*, *Tortula muralis*, *Sphagnum cymbifolium*, and *S. acutifolium*.

FIG. 22.—TODEA SUPERBA.

In some Vivaria, which ought to be kept, because of the animals they contain, in a drier condition than an ordinary Fern-case should be, certain of the Houseleek family will be useful, of which the following may be mentioned: *Sempervivum anomalum*, *S. arachnoideum*, *S. arenarium*, *S. calcareum*, *S. ciliatum*, and *S. tectorum*. The same may be said of the beautiful Saxifrages: *Saxifraga incrustata*, *S. pyramidalis*, *S. aquatica*, *S. umbrosa*

London Pride or None So Pretty), *S. granulata, S. hypnoides-* (Ladies Cushion), *S. crassifolia,* and others. Nor, for a similar purpose, should the charming little Stonecrops be overlooked, of which may be suggested: the Common Roseroot (*Sedum rhodiola*), the Tuberous Stonecrop (*S. telephium*), the Evergreen Stonecrop (*S. anacampseros*), the Bitter Stonecrop or Wall-Pepper (*S. acre*), the White Stonecrop (*S. album*), and the like. Certain of the Ivies grow exceedingly well in Vivaria, particularly the common sort (*Hedera hebix*).

The Spiderworts (*Tradescantia*) are favourite plants for Reptilian cases. They seem to grow without difficulty almost anywhere. Their flowers though not large are pretty, and their foliage is both various and beautiful. A tiny piece of the plant

FIG. 23.—AN ORDINARY SLATE AQUARIUM CONVERTED INTO A VIVARIUM FOR BATRACHIANS.

A, Slate; B, Glass Sides; C, Iron Rods for holding Case together; D, A Bed of Gravel, sloping from 4in. deep at one end to ½in. at the other; E, Water about 3in. deep.

broken off and placed in the ground will quickly take root and flourish. There are several different kinds, of which these undermentioned may be enumerated: *Tradescantia congesta, T. subaspera, T. virginica,* of which there are many varieties (this perhaps is the most common of the Spiderworts), and *T. zebrina.*

For those Vivaria in which Tree and other slender Snakes are kept, Orange and Lemon trees, Fuchsias, Geraniums, Myrtles, and the like are suitable, and in the branches of which these beautiful Snakes will climb, bask, and sleep.

Fig. 23 represents an Aquarium turned into a case for Batrachians. In such a Vivarium as this several different kinds of

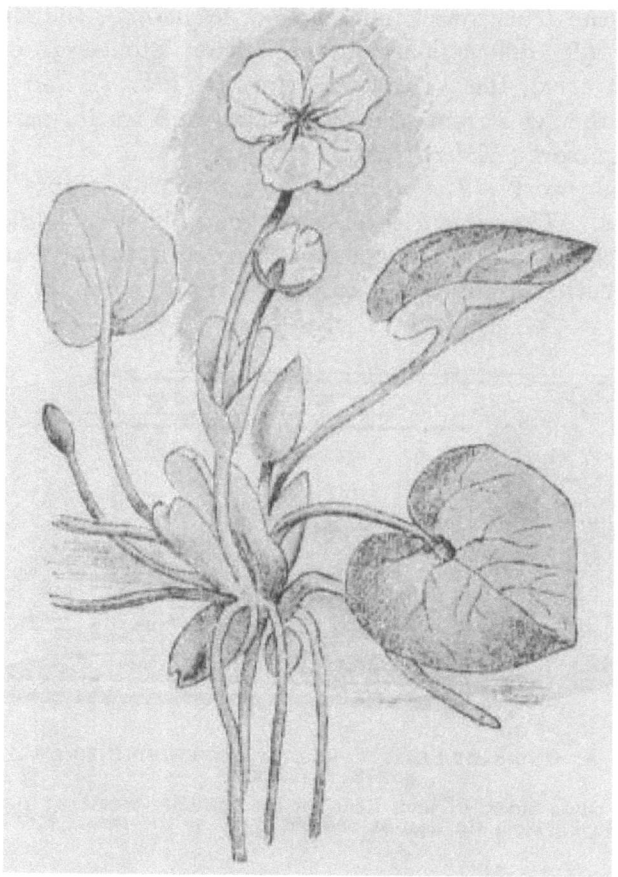

FIG. 24.—FROG-BIT (*Hydrocharis morsus-ranæ*).

aquatic or semi-aquatic plants can be grown. The gravel is made to slope from about 4in. deep at one end to about ½in. deep at the other. The water should be allowed to stand at a depth of about 3in. There will be then a uniform depth of some 3in. of water in the Vivarium, though there will seem to be, at one end only, a small pond with a sloping side. In this Vivarium the following plants may be successfully grown: The Frog-Bit (*Hydrocharis morsus-ranæ*, Fig. 24), this must float on the surface of the water; the Water-Soldier (*Stratiotes aloides*, Fig 25), in or on

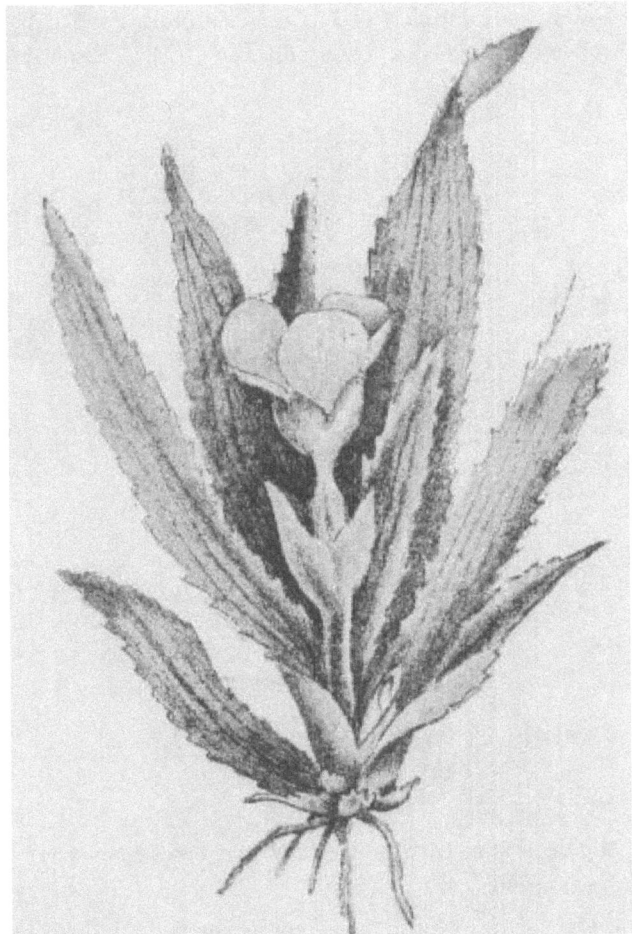

FIG. 25.—WATER SOLDIER (*Stratiotes aloides*).

the water; the Vernal Water Starwort (*Callitriche verna*, Fig. 26); the Water Crowfoot (*Ranunculus aquatilis*, Fig. 27); Ivy-leaved Crow-foot (*Ranunculus hederaceus*); the Buck-bean

(*Menyanthes trifoliata*), which should be a small plant; the Brooklime (*Veronica beccabunga*, Fig. 28); the Water-mint (*Mentha sylvestris*); Watercress (*Nasturtium officiale*); the Greater Duck-weed (*Lemna polyrhiza*, Fig. 29); the Thick Duck-weed (*Lemna gibba*, Fig. 30); the Lesser Duck-weed (*Lemna minor*, Fig. 31); the Ivy-leaved Duck-weed (*Lemna trisulca*, Fig. 32). Except the first

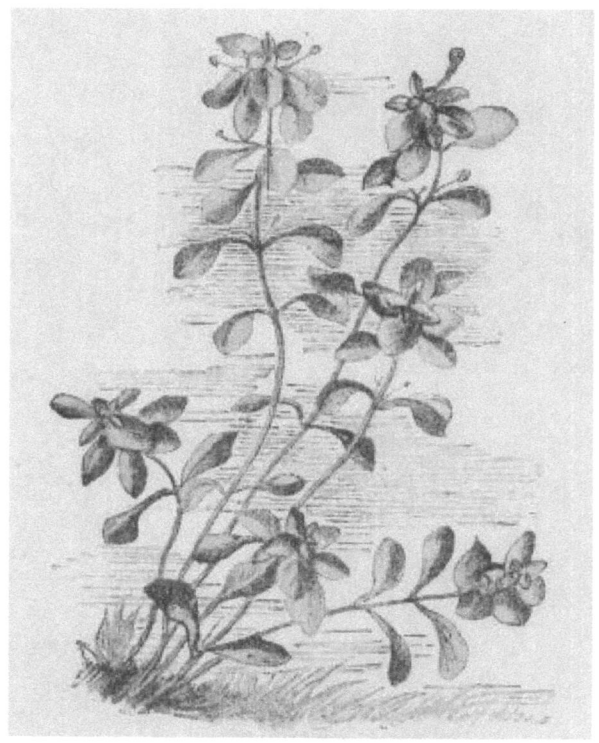

FIG. 26.—VERNAL WATER STARWORT (*Callitriche verna*).

two of the above plants and the Duck-weeds, all may be planted anywhere in the Vivarium.

This case is very suitable for such Batrachians as Frogs, Toads, Newts, Axolotls, and the like. A tank 3ft. long, 2ft. wide, 16in. deep, is a very good size for such a purpose as this. Water-Tortoises might be kept in this Vivarium, but they will frequently disarrange the gravel not a little. At the pond end of the tank there should be a pipe and plug so that water may be occasionally drawn off and replaced with fresh.

It goes without saying that a Vivarium is the more interesting when plants and animals are living and thriving together. As a rule, this can be generally managed. Not only should the plants be chosen for the animals, but also for the cases. Plants generally do best in those Vivaria which have either two or four

FIG. 27.—WATER CROWFOOT (*Ranunculus aquatilis*).

sides made of glass or two or three sides of canvas as well as the glass side or sides. Care should be taken that the pot and the plant, or tree, which it contains do not take up too much room in the Vivarium. Sometimes, it is a good plan to get rid of the pot, as it were, by placing the case on short legs, and cutting a round hole in the centre of its floor sufficiently large to receive, and just hold tightly the pot near its rim. The plant will then have all the advantage of the pot and the Vivarium none of its disadvantages. Of course the rest of the bottom of case must be covered with mould, sand, gravel, or moss, according to the animals which the case is to contain.

In summer, a Vivarium like Fig. 12 may have the boiler withdrawn, and the space which it occupied filled with suitable mould

FIG. 28.—BROOKLIME (*Veronica beccabunga*).

in which certain plants may be grown. A small ordinary flower-pot can be made both ornamental and useful in a Vivarium by tastefully covering its sides, by the help of Portland cement, with small pieces of coke, and then dipping the whole in liquid cement of the consistency of cream. The pot will then hold the plant, have the appearance of rock-work, and provide climbing facilities and shade for the Reptiles.

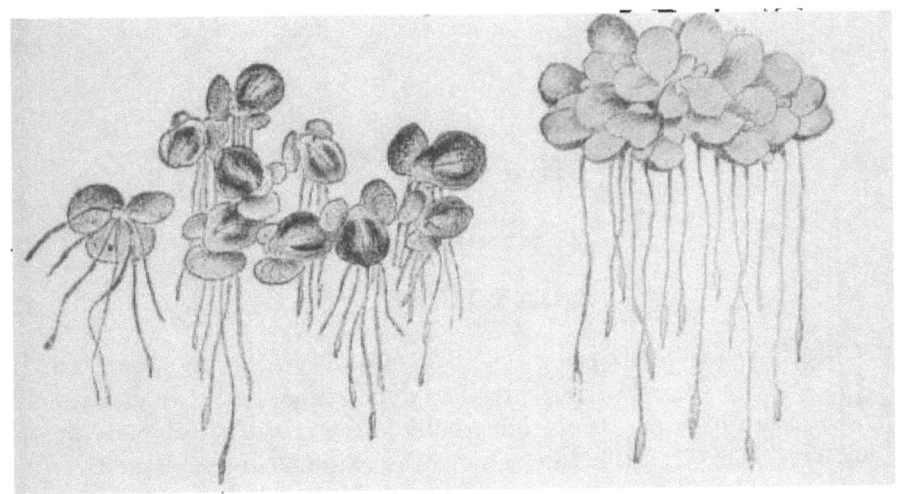

FIG. 29.
GREATER DUCK-WEED (*Lemna polyrhiza*).

FIG. 30.
THICK DUCK-WEED (*Lemna gibba*).

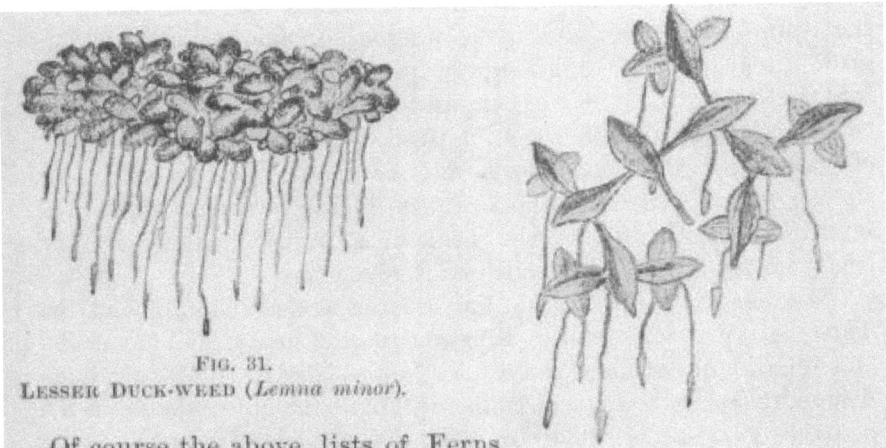

FIG. 31.
LESSER DUCK-WEED (*Lemna minor*).

FIG. 32.—IVY-LEAVED DUCK-WEED (*Lemna trisulca*).

Of course the above lists of Ferns and other plants could be considerably lengthened, but I hope enough names have been given to enable a novice in these matters to obtain some idea of what kind of Fern or plant he should place in his case.

CHAPTER IV.

TORTOISES.

THE general shape of a Tortoise is fairly familiar to nearly everybody. It is well called a "Bucklered Reptile" for it is effectually protected by a case or buckler. This buckler, in which the animal lives, somewhat in the same way as a snail does in its shell, is a very curious contrivance. The upper part of it, the carapace, is chiefly formed by the dilation and union of the bones of the spine and ribs, and by a number of bony plates which grow in the skin; the lower part, the plastron, consists for the most part of the expansion and joining together of certain dermal or skin bones. Most Tortoises have the power of withdrawing the head, legs, and tail under the protection of their shell. The Chelonians are toothless, and their jaws bear no little resemblance to the beak of a parrot. They all lay eggs, mostly with a hard, calcareous covering.

No other vertebrate animal has greater tenacity of life than the Tortoise. For example, it is said that the heart of a beheaded Chelonian will continue to beat for hours after all blood has been drained from its body. It is also recorded that M. Redi deprived a Land Tortoise of its brain, and the creature on being set at liberty crawled about as if it had hardly been injured at all, the only difference in its appearance was the persistent closing of its eyes. After the operation, it continued to live for nearly eight months. Another Chelonian existed for twenty-three days after it had been decapitated.

Tortoises have been divided into the following four families: (1) *Testudinidæ*, or Land Tortoises, which have feet formed for walking and have no webbing between the toes. (2) *Emydidæ*, or Freshwater Tortoises, sometimes called Marsh Tortoises and Terrapins. These possess feet adapted for both walking and swimming, the toes being slightly webbed. (3) *Trionychidæ*, or Freshwater Turtles, also known as River and Soft Tortoises. These have feet far more webbed than those of the preceding family. (4) *Cheloniidæ*, or Sea Turtles, whose feet are fin-shaped.

The above is not the most scientific division, but it is perhaps the simplest, and, at any rate, the most suitable for our purpose, since it is founded chiefly upon the manner of life of the creatures, rather than upon their difference of structure. Though representatives of all these families just mentioned can be kept in confinement, the members of the former two only come within the limits of this book.

Tortoises are interesting animals and give very little trouble when kept in captivity. As none of these Reptiles are now indigenous to Britain, their presence in this country is due to importation. The most commonly imported Chelonians are the European Land Tortoises. They are brought into England in great numbers, and, consequently, are very inexpensive to buy. The twisted appearance of their front legs has given the general name of Tortoise to all their relatives (from the French *tortis*, fem. *tortisse*, twisted, which comes from the Latin *torqueo* (*tortum*) "I twist").

The Greek Tortoise, which is illustrated at Fig. 33, was probably one of the first Reptiles in which the English began to take an interest, to keep in confinement, and ventured to treat as a pet. The late Mr. Frank Buckland speaks of a ship's cargo of them. In London they, with other Land Tortoises, may sometimes be seen covering the platform of a costermonger's barrow. And there nearly every bird-dealer offers, during the spring and summer months, numbers of these creatures for sale, keeping them frequently for the time being in a pigeon or fowl's pen, where they spend their days, either in apparent apathy, or in trying to climb and crawl over each other. In the larger dealers' establishments, occasionally, they may be found crowding, as thickly as possible, the floor of some upper room. A seller of these Reptiles, the other day, headed his advertisement with the announcement "10,000 Tortoises." One naturally wonders what becomes of all these creatures. They do not easily die, and the English people are said not to eat them, though in other countries they are looked upon as a useful food.

Tortoises will live for a very long time in confinement. The celebrated Tortoise, mentioned frequently in the Natural History of Selborne, came into Mr. White's possession forty years after its importation into this country.

Mr. Murray, author of "Experimental Researches," says that "from a document belonging to the archives of the cathedral, called the *Bishop's Barn*, it is well ascertained that the Tortoise at Peterborough must have been about 220 years old. Bishop Marsh's predecessor in the See of Peterborough had remembered it above sixty years, and could recognise no visible change. He was the seventh bishop who had worn the mitre during its sojourn there. If I mistake not, its sustenance and abode were provided for in the document. Its shell was perforated in order to attach it to a tree, etc., to limit its ravages among the strawberry borders." It is also recorded that "this animal moved with apparent ease, though pressed by a weight of 18st.; it weighed 13½lb."

It seems to be no very unusual thing for a Tortoise to live for more than 100 years. Dr. Günther, in 1875, described in the July number of *Nature* a pair of Aldabra Land Tortoises, which had been deposited in the Zoological Gardens. The male weighed 800lb.; its carapace in a straight line measuring, in length, 5ft. 5in., and in breadth, 5ft. 9in.; and the circumference of the shell was as much as 8ft. 1in. This Tortoise, a male, was known to have been in the Seychelles for about seventy years. When it died, some ten years after its arrival in this country, it was still growing. Dr. Günther, elsewhere, speaking of these very interesting gigantic Tortoises, which used to live in great numbers in the Mascarene and Gallapagos Islands, says that they are now on the verge of extinction or have actually become extinct.

Land Tortoises will not only live for a very great number of years in English gardens, but will also, under favourable circum-

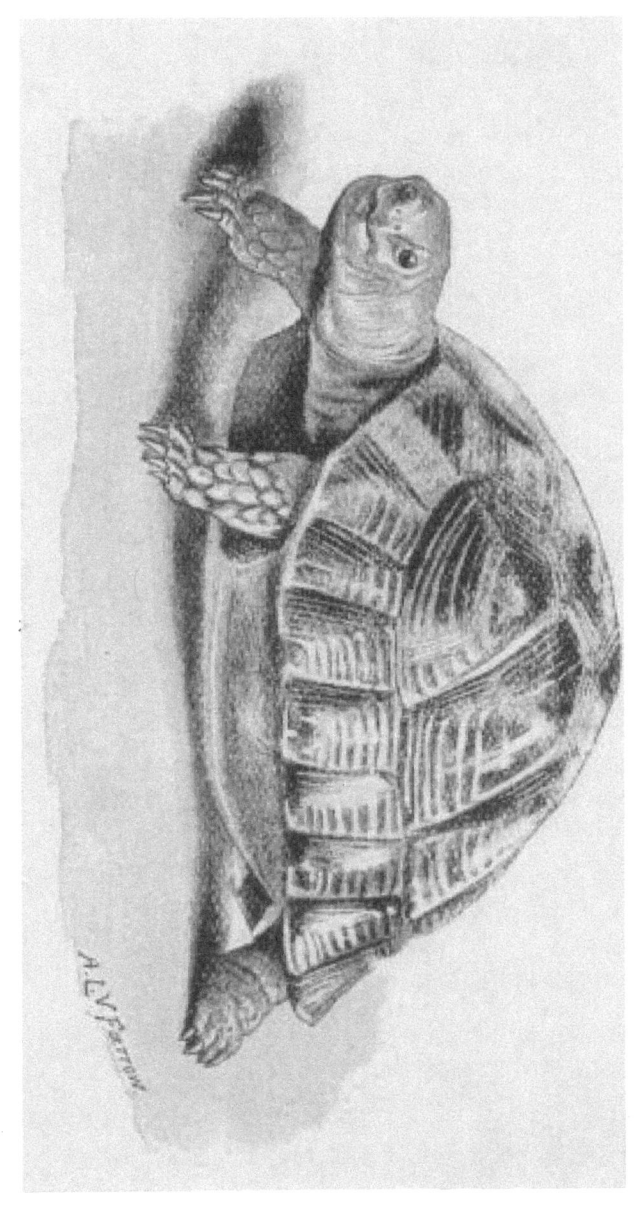

FIG. 33.—GREEK TORTOISE (*Testudo Graeca*).

stances, breed there. If it is wished that they should propagate their kind, a pair, at least, of the same species should be chosen, the female larger than the male. In many species of Tortoises the male may be known by its concave plastron, and by its longer tail. When the female wishes to lay her eggs, with her powerful feet she will probably scrape a hole in the earth to a depth of from 4in. to 6in. and about the same in diameter, and then after depositing her eggs in the little pit she has made, will cover them up, flattening the ground above them so neatly, that, unless the exact place is known, it will be no easy matter to find where she has hidden her treasures. As soon as the eggs are laid they should be unearthed and gently re-buried in fine, loose, moist sand, and put under the influence of heat, not less than 75deg. and not greater than 90deg. A forcing frame, or some such contrivance, will do well for this purpose. The eggs ought to hatch in from eight to ten weeks (the eggs of Freshwater Tortoises take much longer) according to the regularity and the amount of heat by which they have been surrounded. The young should be kept, for some little time, in the same place in which they were hatched; that is to say, until they have got into the habit of feeding freely, and then they may be gradually brought to endure a colder temperature.

Tortoises will not hibernate if kept in a warmed greenhouse during the winter months, and provided during that time with a regular supply of suitable food. This applies to both Land and Water Tortoises. The former eat lettuces, cabbages, lucerne, grass, dandelions (particularly the flowers), spiræa, gooseberries, strawberries, currants, peas, and similar food. They dislike rain, and do not care to remain for long in very hot rays of the sun. They soon become tame, and many will learn to know the person who provides them regularly with food. Their eyesight is very keen, but their ears seem to be anything but acute. They are strangely persevering and by no means void of intelligence. I have tried to see if one would walk off a table (I should have caught him had he fallen), but as soon as he got near enough to look over the edge he altered his direction; this he always did.

Dr. Günther says that Land Tortoises are the worst swimmers of all the Reptiles except the Chameleon. Small Land Tortoises do very well in a Vivarium with Snakes, but they should then be provided with means of retiring into shade. Water ought to be so placed that they can drink it without difficulty.

When at liberty in an English garden they hibernate, by burying themselves, about the beginning of autumn, either in the ground or under a heap of rubbish, where they will remain, unless disturbed, until the latter part of the following spring. Soon after leaving their winter quarters they recommence to feed. A few days, however, generally elapse before they recover their appetite. This may be due to the fact that the meal they partook of just before hibernation is still undigested. The late Mr. Thomas Bell, in his "History of British Reptiles," says that he has "known a Tortoise, which had fed largely upon grass immediately before it became torpid, retain the grass unchanged in the stomach during the whole of the winter, so that on opening the body after its death, which took place immediately on its awaking in the spring, and before it had any access to food, the stomach was found filled with a large quantity of grass wholly undigested."

Perhaps in this country, the most readily obtained Land Tortoises and the most suitable for confinement here, are those which belong to Europe, e.g., *Testudo Graeca, T. mauritanica,* and *T. marginata.* The last-mentioned, the Margined Tortoise, though when fully grown does not exceed a foot in length, is the largest of the three. This Reptile may be distinguished from its near relative, *T. mauritanica,* by the flattened and *extended hind margin* of its carapace; hence its specific name. The Greek Tortoise can be known from either of the other two, by remembering that its tail is long and fitted with a kind of nail or claw at its end, while theirs is so short that it hardly reaches beyond the covering of the carapace. Again, *T. mauritanica* and *T. marginata* have a single caudal plate, or only one plate just over the tail, and a plastron which is movable behind; but *T. graeca* has a double caudal plate and a plastron which is immovable behind.

Of course, other Land Tortoises, besides those which are indigenous to Europe, are often imported into this country, but then their price is higher than that of the European Chelonian. There are numerous species of Land Tortoises. The Moorish Tortoise

(*T. mauritanica*) and the Greek Tortoise are imported into this country in great numbers from Africa. They frequently arrive packed in barrels. Many people buy these Reptiles under the idea that they will eat the slugs of their kitchen gardens, and then are made a little unhappy by discovering that they are eating or destroying, instead, their finest lettuces and their choicest strawberries. Their ravages, however, may be entirely prevented by boring a small hole in the hinder margin of their carapace, through which one end of a piece of string may be fastened, while the other end is made secure to a stick driven into the ground, or to a staple in either a tree or wall. A small swivel will lessen the chance of the twisting of the cord. I have at present an American Freshwater Tortoise, which has a hole already bored in its shell, so that in all probability it has been tethered near or in its native stream or pond.

Two 11in. boards placed on their edges at right angles in a corner of a sunny part of a walled garden, and an inverted box with an end knocked out, covered with a large slate, or some such contrivance, as a shelter from rain and cold, will make a very convenient open-air Vivarium for Land Tortoises. Land Tortoises do no good in a garden, but if one of the above methods of limiting their wanderings be adopted they will do no harm. They are interesting creatures, and well worth the very little trouble they necessitate. Mine, however, have their liberty and do on the whole no very appreciable damage. In many countries, the Land Tortoises and their eggs are considered a useful article of food.

The *Emydidæ* or Freshwater Tortoises are chiefly distinguished from the fore-mentioned by their flatter appearance, by the webbing of their feet, and by the greater length of the nails of their toes. However, there is no distinct line of demarcation between the two families. Some of the Water Tortoises live quite as much out of the water as in. All of them are amphibious, and though they can swim with considerable activity, they are better walkers on land than any of the *Testudinidæ*.

All the Terrapins are carnivorous with the exception of the Batagurs and Dermatemys, which are herbivorous. They feed when at liberty upon worms, fish, frogs, newts, insects, and the like; but in captivity, in addition to these foods, they will eat pieces of raw meat, mice, and young birds. Many of these Tortoises will pass even more of their time upon land than in the water. They prefer in confinement that water in which such plants as the Duck-weed (*Lemnæ*) are growing. They are naturally timid animals, and are evidently more at ease and at home when under the protective covering of the aquatic weed. I have noticed that when Freshwater Tortoises refuse to remain in the water (if they can help doing so) and try to hide themselves on land under some plant, rock, or piece of cork, they will leave voluntarily such covert on shore and return to the water should a few handfuls of duckweed be thrown upon its surface. There among the *Lemnæ* they will live apparently quite contentedly, frequently floating with their heads well above the weed, but ready to dive down and swim away on seeing that which alarms them.

While at liberty they hibernate in the holes of muddy banks, under heaps of rubbish, or in the mud at the bottom of ponds. In confinement they will forego hibernation when kept during the winter in a heated Vivarium and warm water. If they are wished to hibernate, they may, provided that they have been feeding well for some weeks in early autumn, be packed, surrounded by moss, in a small box, and put away in a cool place where frost cannot reach. And in spring when restored to their Vivarium they will, if all things have gone well with them, rouse from their torpor and soon recommence to eat.

Some of the *Emydidæ* might be naturalized in England. Occasionally certain of these Tortoises on escaping from confinement have been found years afterwards, alive and healthy, in some pond, river, or canal. Indeed, the Mud Tortoise (*Emys. lutaria*) which is illustrated at Fig. 34, at least, used to be indigenous to this country, its remains having been found in peat in England. The greater proportion of the 300 different Chelonians are Freshwater Tortoises. North America is particularly rich in the *Emydidæ*; there are none at all in New Zealand.

The Terrapins and their eggs are frequently eaten by the natives of those countries in which they are found. As a rule, however, their flesh has not a pleasant flavour, owing to the carnivorous habits of the Reptiles. Some of them, *e.g.*, the Mud Tortoise (*E. lutaria*), are occasionally induced to feed upon

FIG. 34.—MUD TORTOISE (*Emys lutaria*).

grain, it is said, and then the animals are much more highly prized as food for man. As with the *Testudinidæ*, perhaps, the most suitable *Emydidæ* for confinement in Britain are those which belong to Europe. Probably the Terrapins which are commonest in this country are the Mud Tortoises (*E. lutaria*). They are sometimes sold as cheaply as 3s. 6d. a dozen, and frequently so small in size that their carapace is not of so great a diameter as half-a-crown. With care and gentle treatment they can soon be induced to feed upon pieces of raw meat, worms, and tiny fish. In common with other Terrapins they seize their food in a dog-like fashion, seeking the assistance of their fore-feet in the tearing of their prey and in the guiding of it into their mouths.

It is cruel to keep these and other Freshwater Tortoises always in the water. They should be able to land and retire under cover whenever they wish. Small specimens of the *Emydidæ* may be kept in a tank with fairly-sized fish, provided that they have the facility just mentioned. But they should not, as they are timid Reptiles, be associated with animals of which they would live in continual fear, though they might suffer no harm from them. For example, it is not kind to place small Terrapins in the same Vivarium with young Alligators or Bull-frogs. Such cases as those represented by Figs. 10 and 14 (pp. 19 and 23), are suitable for Freshwater Tortoises.

During the summer months, many of the *Emydidæ* may be kept in small ponds in gardens. To prevent them from straying away and being lost the water should be surrounded with some 1in. meshed wire-netting. The net need not be more than 1ft. deep. Considering their build, they can climb, by the help of their sharp claws, in a rather surprising way over rocks and the like. A tub about 6in. or 8in. deep, and not less than 2ft. 6in. in diameter, also surrounded with wire-netting, and placed in a sunny place in the garden, makes a capital habitation for them during the hot weather. A stone which protrudes a little above the surface of the water, and upon which they can climb for sunning purposes, should be placed in the centre of the tub. Nor should the duckweed be forgotten. If possible, the Tortoises ought to have access to some sand or light soil in which, if they wish, they can deposit and bury their eggs.

The following Terrapins are suitable for confinement in this country. The Mud Tortoise (*E. lutaria*), already referred to, is a very pretty and lively little creature. Its carapace, which is black and marked with yellow rays, is oval and rather flat. The plastron, which is movable both in front and behind, is attached to the carapace by means of cartilage. The tail is long and round and tapers to a point. It is said that the tails of the males are thicker at their base and shorter than those of the females. When full grown, these Tortoises are about 10in. long. They are found in Greece, Italy, Switzerland, Spain, Algiers, the South of France, Hungary, Germany, in the Crimea, etc.

The Caspian Terrapin (*E. caspica*) owes its specific title, as will be naturally concluded, from its inhabiting the neighbourhood of the Caspian Sea. Canon Tristram says that it is very common in "all the streams and marshes" of the Holy Land, "and especially in Lake Huleh (the Waters of Merom)." In the adult animal the oval carapace is smooth, but in the young there are three ridges, or two grooves, running the length of the shell. The colour of the back is a light olive, reticulated with pale yellow lines edged with black. The tail is long, round, and pointed. The plastron is black, dotted with yellow spots, which increase in size as the animal grows. It has rather an unpleasant smell. This Reptile is sometimes more than 1ft. in length.

E. sigriz has no little resemblance to the Caspian Terrapin. It differs, however, in wanting the three ridges and the reticulation of the carapace. In the centre of each plate there is a spot of yellow surrounded by black. The plastron is of a brownish colour, and has a light yellow band along the margin. This Tortoise is considerably smaller than *E. caspica*. It is found in Spain, Morocco, and Algeria.

Besides the European Terrapins, the Carolina Box Tortoise (*Cistudo Carolina*), which is illustrated at Fig. 35, and the Chicken Tortoise (*E. reticulata*), both from North America, and several others may be kept easily in captivity in this country. The Carolina Box Tortoise is a beautiful Terrapin, but it decidedly prefers dry land to water. It and its near relatives are called Box Tortoises, because, with the assistance of their plastron, which is movable both before and behind, they are able

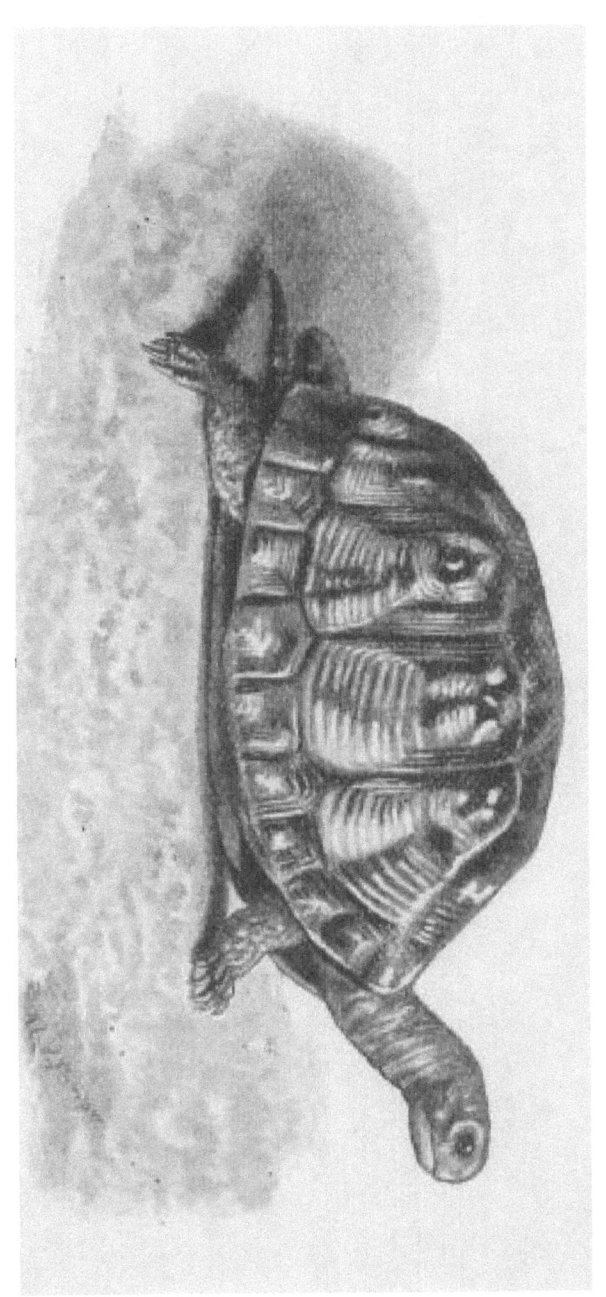

FIG. 35.—CAROLINA BOX TORTOISE (*Cistudo Carolina.*)

to shut themselves up as it were in a box. The carapace is dark brown and is spotted or striped with yellow; the sternum is of a yellowish-brown colour. It will eat its animal food either dead or alive, and is not averse to making a meal of ripe fruit.

The Long-necked Tortoise (*Chelodina longicollis*) of Australia is a very interesting tortoise, and has recently been imported into this country in considerable quantities. This Terrapin lives exceedingly well in confinement, where it soon becomes quite tame.

The Chicken Tortoise (*E. reticulata*) receives its specific name from the reticulated appearance of its carapace. The lines which form the network are yellow. When full-grown, it is about 9in. long. Terrapins from hot countries, such as India, should always be kept in those Vivaria that have a provision for heating the water. If this cannot conveniently be done, it is wiser and kinder to be content with those that come from a more temperate climate.

Freshwater Tortoises have a curious habit of leaving the air-bladders of the fish they have eaten floating upon the surface of the water. Such signs of a Terrapin's meal first taught me that it was not wise to keep a good-sized *Emys* in the same tank with small fish. Mr. Bell records that "it is said that people are wont to judge of the quantity of Tortoises to be found in a lake or pond by the number of air-bags which are seen swimming on the surface of the water."

CHAPTER V.

CROCODILES.

NOT long ago, a lady, who was visiting England for the first time, said to a brother clergyman and me: "I admire your beautiful county of Devonshire very much indeed." And in reply to a question from one of us, continued: "Yes, I have made many excursions in this neighbourhood. Yesterday, for instance, my daughter and I started from our head-quarters on a walking expedition, and we passed through one pretty village and came to a second, where the church and the rectory are quite close to each other, making together a very pleasant picture."

Naturally, as we both lived near at hand, we inquired the names of the villages. The lady did not know, but she had asked who lived in the rectory, which was close to the church. The name of the clergyman she had forgotten, but she remembered that she had been told that among other curious pets he kept a tame Alligator. "This," she said, "excited my interest, for I am very fond of all animals, and so my daughter and I walked round the garden wall, looking for a chink through which we hoped to catch a glimpse of the strange beast, but fearing all the time to hear the scolding voice of some crusty old naturalist ordering us off, and reproaching us for our temerity." We both laughed, and I was obliged to confess to being the "crusty old naturalist" who owned the Alligator.

It is not remarkable that the lady should have noticed so unusual a pet as an Alligator. However, though uncommon now as a pet, he is a very interesting one, and also a very ancient one. In olden days, the Egyptians used not only to worship these animals, or rather their near relatives the Crocodiles, but to keep them as pets which they treated with every reverence and care, decking them with golden earrings, studded with rare jewels, and placing bracelets of the same precious metal round their forefeet. They really dreaded the monsters, and did whatever they could to "propitiate" them.

In the ruins of Egyptian temples mummies of Crocodiles are occasionally found in an excellent state of preservation.

Almost every schoolboy knows that some of the Roman Emperors used to introduce into the amphitheatres, for the purpose of gratifying their own and their subjects' love of excitement and bloodshed, almost every kind of wild beast: lions, tigers, bears, and the like, and among them, sometimes Crocodiles. Thirty-six of these huge Reptiles were, at the expense of the Emperor Augustus, turned at once into the circus and slain by the gladiators.

One can hardly help remarking here upon the skill of the old hunters, who lived hundreds of years before the time of railways and steamboats, and yet were able to bring to Rome these fierce and, very often, rare animals. The successful capture and transportation of wild beasts is by no means an easy matter even in our own day.

The father of historians, Herodotus, recorded a fact of natural history in regard to the Crocodile which has often been scoffed at and derided, namely, that the interior of this Reptile's mouth is frequently covered with a kind of leech which troubles it not a little. And though all birds, as a rule, fly from this animal, there is one which even ventures to enter its open mouth, and to feed upon the leeches there, and so frees the Crocodile of its tormentors. The huge beast shows its gratitude for such a service by never hurting the bird. Many of the naturalists of the present day consider that this assertion of Herodotus is correct in the main.

Mr. John M. Cook, in a letter which was published in the *Ibis*, gives an interesting account of seeing the Crocodile-bird at work. This bird, which is known locally as the "Zic-zac," is the Spur-winged Plover (*Hoplopterus spinosus*).

In some countries Crocodiles are eaten. Certain of the casteless natives of India will even devour with eagerness the flesh while raw. This strange food, when cooked, has been said to taste like veal and like tough lobster. The late Mr. Frank Buckland, in his "Curiosities of Natural History," speaks of his father and a friend tasting a piece of roast Crocodile, and describes, in an amusing manner, how the old servant William, who lived at the Anatomy School, Christchurch, Oxford, imitating their example, ate not only a small portion of the Reptile, but made a hearty supper of Crocodile steak, and consequently roused his household in the middle of the night by crying out in pain, "Oh! that Crocodile! that Crocodile!"

The following is a classification of the order *Crocodilia*:

FAMILY.	GENUS.
Crocodilidæ	Crocodilus
Garialidæ	Garialis / Tomistoma
Alligatoridæ	Alligator / Caiman or Jacare

The chief differences between Crocodiles and Alligators are: The head of a Crocodile is longer and narrower than that of an Alligator. The teeth of the latter are much more unequal in length than are those of the former. When an Alligator's mouth is closed the canine teeth enter cavities in the upper jaws, and thus are nearly, if not quite, hidden from view; while those of the Crocodile are more or less exposed, under the same condition, as they are only received into a notch or groove. An Alligator's legs are comparatively round and smooth, while a Crocodile's are rough and ragged; and the feet of the latter are more webbed than those of the former. Crocodiles are sometimes seen in the sea, but Alligators, I believe, never. Crocodiles are natives of both the New and the Old World; but Alligators, with an exception or two, are confined to America. An Alligator, however, has somewhat recently been discovered in Central China.

The Garial, which has a much larger and slimmer head than a Crocodile, is chiefly found in the Ganges.

The Tomistome, an inhabitant of Borneo and the surrounding islands, has even a more pointed face than the Garial, and there is a difference between these two Reptiles in the arrangement of their teeth.

A Caiman's dorsal and ventral bony plates are articulated together, an Alligator's are not. The latter has smooth and fleshy eyelids, but those of the former contain a bony plate.

The Jacare is said to differ from the Caiman and the Alligator in having wrinkled eyelids instead of smooth ones, and also in possessing a ridge of bone between the eyes. But, after all, there is a very close likeness between Alligators, Caimans, and Jacares; and it much simplifies matters to divide the *Crocodilia* into Crocodiles and Alligators.

The Crocodiles of India sometimes grow to a length of 26ft., and even more than that, according to some writers. In their native waters they are exceedingly dangerous to both man and beast; by a stroke of their very powerful tail they frequently knock their victims into the water, and they are thus completely at their mercy. The only hope, as a rule, that a man has under such terrible circumstances is to force his fingers into the brute's eyes. This also applies to Alligators. Many people have lost their lives through incautiously entering the water or walking upon its banks where these reptiles abound.

In India, sometimes, when Crocodiles have been slain, a *post-mortem* examination shows, by revealing various articles of native jewellery, that he has been preying upon human victims. For instance, Mr. Buckland, a cousin, I believe, of the late Mr. Frank Buckland, writing in a recent number of *Longman's Magazine*, says, in a very interesting article upon these creatures: "It may seem incredible, but at one of the bathing-places of the city of Cuttack a large Alligator (Crocodile) was killed, and when it was cut open the silver and gold and brass ornaments that the women wear which were found in its belly were enough to show that it must have carried off and killed upwards of thirty grown-up women. . . . The head of an Alligator (Crocodile) is in the shape of a triangle, and the base of the triangle in this Alligator was 38in. on the bone, so that when covered with skin, and flesh, and muscle, it must have looked larger."

Men have been known to hunt and kill Crocodiles just simply for the purpose of possessing whatever gold and silver ornaments they may happen to find within the Reptiles. Frequently a Crocodile or an Alligator haunts a particular portion of a river, and seems to look upon all the neighbourhood within certain limits as belonging to himself, nor will he brook any intrusion upon the part of his fellow Crocodiles or Alligators. Should he die, however, another is sure to take his place.

When one of these Reptiles is floating quietly in the water, with only his eyes and nostrils just above its surface, he is very likely to escape the observation of the unwary; hence it is that so many people fall victims to these hungry beasts.

Every member of the Crocodilia possesses three eyelids to each eye. The nictitating eyelid is closed when the animal goes under water, and prevents that element from entering the eye; but, being transparent, allows the Reptile to see. I have noticed that this membrane is also frequently drawn over the eyes as the creature basks in the sun. While under water, besides closing the nictitating eyelids, it covers its nostrils by means of valves provided for that purpose, and folds a flap or lid of skin over the entrance to each ear. In addition, when this creature has seized a victim with its long, sharp, and conical teeth, and dragged it under water to drown it, it is able, by using certain membranes, to prevent the water from running down its own throat.

The *Crocodilia*, because of the narrowness of their throat, are obliged to tear their prey to pieces before swallowing it; hence they frequently break or wear away their teeth. However, they do not suffer from the loss owing to an interesting provision of nature. Each tooth is hollowed at its base and so is able to receive the germ of a new tooth. And between the germ and the tooth in use, there is a third, which is sheathed in the latter, covers the former, and is ready for work as soon as required.

According to the country, some Crocodiles and Alligators hibernate in the winter, and others estivate, in mud, during the drought of summer.

All the *Crocodilia* are oviparous, and the hard calcareous eggs which they lay are very small (not larger than those of the turkey) in comparison with the ultimate size of the animals which are to come from them. For instance, Dr. Günther, in "The Reptiles of British India" says that "Jerdon has reported a case in which an egg of *Crocodilus porosus*, brought from the fort ditch at Vellore to Walter Elliott, Esq., was hatched in the Government House compound, and in eight years had increased to the length of 8ft. or 9ft. becoming so powerful as to destroy a full-grown buck antelope which had come to drink at the tank."

Some of the *Crocodilia* deposit their eggs in the sand on the banks of the water in which they live; while others place them in layers in a kind of nest formed of vegetable substances, the fermentation of which generates a heat suitable for hatching them. The female Alligator seems to keep a watchful eye upon the locality of her treasures, and also shows a certain amount of care for the little ones when they appear. Indeed, it has been said that, like the viper and some other snakes, she will open her mouth and allow her young to enter it and thus shield them from threatened danger.

Crocodile and Alligator eggs can be hatched either in an incubator or under a hen. The little Reptiles at first are not much more than 6in. long. They may be reared by hand without difficulty. If at first they refuse to feed, minced raw meat must be pushed down their throats two or three times a week.

A young Alligator or a young Crocodile is a very interesting possession, as I have said, the former being the hardier of the two. It is an unusual pet, indeed, and likely to be remarked upon. People never seem to think that such an animal can be less than a dozen feet in length, and comparatively harmless. "Are you not afraid that the dreadful beast will hurt or kill your children?" is a remark I have heard. A M.F.H. said to me the other day: "I hear you keep an alligator?" "Yes," I replied. "Do you wish to hunt him?" "Oh, no," retorted he, jokingly. "I am afraid he would hunt me!"

When anyone is desirous of keeping in confinement such an animal, he should procure it when it is between 1ft. and 2ft. 6in. in length. These Reptiles can occasionally be bought cheaply in London or Liverpool. They soon learn to know their fosterer, and if kindly treated come at his call. When placed in a large and properly-heated tank, they grow rapidly and seem to lose their naturally fierce disposition. In the central tank of the Reptile House, Regent's Park, London, there used to be a large Alligator

—or, at any rate, large for a captive one—but so gentle that it would allow its keeper to mount its back, and I understand the keeper had been photographed in that position. This Alligator, which is now dead, was only 1ft. long when it made its first appearance in the Reptile House, but in about nine years it had grown to a little more than 11ft. in length, and was in other respects a very well-developed animal. I have seen it stated somewhere, that if a young Alligator or Crocodile be kept in a small tank, it will not grow much, if at all.

My own Alligator knows me quite well. At my approach he climbs upon the platform at the side of his tank, and makes a curious low call to attract my attention. He hisses loudly at strangers, and when he is angry he gives a kind of grunt-like bark. Occasionally he produces a noise which may be likened to a roar; indeed, a full-grown Alligator is no mean rival of the lion in the matter of roaring. Crocodiles, I think, do not roar.

The temperature of the water of an Alligator's tank should not, as a rule, be allowed to sink lower than 75deg. Fahr., nor to rise above 85deg. In very hot weather, however, it is not necessary to heat it artificially, provided that the tank be situated in a greenhouse or some such building.

A small Crocodile or Alligator may be kept in a Vivarium like that represented by Fig. 10 or by Fig. 14. In the latter case, a small lamp must be placed beneath the tank itself. If the lamp be allowed to go out in cold weather the Reptile will become more or less torpid, and will not feed. Once when I was suffering from an attack of the common enemy, influenza, the gardener, who during my illness was caring for the animals, sent word to me one day that the Alligator was ill and would not eat. As soon as I could I went to see what was the matter, and found that the water in the tank had been allowed to get so low that it could not circulate with the water in the little outer boiler, and the poor beast was in a state of torpidity through cold, the weather being very bitter at the time. Directly the water was restored to its proper temperature, the Reptile recovered its liveliness and his appetite.

The tank should be cleared out as often as necessary—about once a week perhaps—by means of the exit-pipe affixed for the purpose, the dirty water being replaced by clean of the right temperature. The platform ought to be scraped and sprinkled with clean sand. The whole operation need not take more than a few minutes.

Unlike many other Reptiles, the *Crocodilia* (see Frontispiece) will feed readily on dead food, such as raw meat and fish. They are exceedingly fond of the latter. Large worms form a very suitable food for young animals of this kind. The throat of this Reptile is small, and consequently there is a danger of death from choking; the meat, dead mice and birds, therefore should be cut into suitable-sized pieces. An Alligator less than 2ft. long ought not to have any single portion of food given to it bigger than a walnut. And it is wise to allow some of the fur or feathers to remain upon the mice or birds: this is natural, and good for digestive purposes. As a Crocodile or an Alligator swallows the morsel given to him, or seized by him, he lowers his mouth beneath the surface of the water. When I throw a dead minnow or other small fish to my Alligator, he will probably take it by the middle of its body; it will thus be crosswise in his mouth, and in this position he cannot swallow it, but he gets out of the difficulty by throwing the fish up in the air, turning it as he does so, and, deftly catching it, receives it with its head or tail pointing to his throat, when the completion of the business is simply a matter of pleasure to him. In the same way his full-grown relatives act when in their native haunts they seize some unfortunate pig or dog. These Reptiles also occasionally use one of their hind feet to place their food in a suitable position for swallowing.

The *Crocodilia* are by no means devoid of a certain amount of intelligence. For instance, my own Alligator knows strangers from friends, he recognises the tin in which his food is kept and, on seeing it, instantly makes preparations for taking a meal, *i.e.*, he climbs upon the platform of his tank, opens his mouth widely, and utters the low call of which I have spoken. He understands, apparently, what is happening when I change his water, for he crawls out of the way of the cold water with which I swill the bottom of the tank; but directly I begin to refill the tank he gets into such a position that the warm fresh water, coming out of the can, falls upon his back. This not only gives him a good

F

washing, but also seems to cause him great pleasure. I believe, if I had time and inclination, I could train him to follow me like a dog.

Though only a comparatively small beast, he has wonderful power in his tail, and anyone who has once felt its lashing would have little difficulty in realising somewhat the great caudal strength which is possessed by a full-grown beast of the same kind. My Alligator unfortunately, lost his temper when a friend and I one day were trying to photograph him, and, as I was holding him, he whipped my legs with his tail in such a way that I suffered pain from the blows for some little time afterwards, and thought there was some truth in the saying, "If you want to offend your friend, photograph him."

The late Mr. Charles Waterton, in his essay upon "The Caiman," gives this explanation of the origin of the word Alligator: "The Spaniards, on their first arrival in the New World, seeing that the Caiman was an overgrown lizard. . . called it *Una lagarta*, which is the Spanish name for a lizard. . . The British, on hearing the Spaniards exclaim '*Una lagarta*'! when this animal made its appearance, they in their turn called it an Alligator; for so the two Spanish words, *Una lagarta*, sounded in the English ear."

The *Crocodilia* are able to remain for a considerable time under water.

CHAPTER VI.

LIZARDS.

THE Lizards are very interesting, and, as a rule, bear confinement exceedingly well. So great is their variety that it has been necessary to divide them into about 21 families, 330 genera, and 1700 species.

Dr. Günther, in his article on the Lizard in the "Encyclopædia Britannica," says that "Lizards may be described as Reptiles with a more or less elongate body, terminating in a tail, and with a skin either folded into scales (as in snakes) or granular or tubercular." Most Lizards have four legs (*e.g.*, the common English Lizard, *Lacerta vivipara*), a few only two (*e.g.*, the Glass Snake, *Pseudopus pallasi*), and many none at all (*e.g.*, the English Slow-worm, *Anguis fragilis*). Some have extraordinary power of changing colour (*e.g.*, the Chameleons and the Anoles); others are so active as to apparently set the laws of gravitation at defiance (*e.g.*, the Geckos); and there are indeed even so-called flying Lizards (*e.g.*, *Draco volans*).

Most Lizards are carnivorous, and only comparatively a few herbivorous. One Lizard (*Amblyrhynchus cristatus*) enters the sea, and feeds upon seaweed. Some Lizards, like the Monitors, are 6ft. long, while others are smaller than the common English Lizard (*L. vivipara*). There are Lizards of the Skink family which possess bodies of a smooth and polished appearance, and there are Lizards with spine-bearing tubercles, such as the Moloch (*M. horridus*), and the "Californian or Horned Toad" (*Phrynosoma cornutum*).

Lizards are found everywhere in the temperate and tropical parts of the world. They are either oviparous or ovoviviparous, the eggs being covered with a hard or parchment-like calcareous shell. Some Lizards lay about forty eggs, others only one or two, as the Geckos and the Anoles.

The teeth of Lizards are either *pleurodont* or *acrodont*. The pleurodont teeth are those which are attached by their sides to a kind of parapet (on the inside) affixed to the jaws. The acrodont teeth are anchylosed or fastened, not in sockets, to the upper edge of the parapet. Lizards differ from snakes in having, as a rule, eyelids, jaws that do not separate or dislocate at will, and throats that are not extensible.

In many Lizards, such as the Geckos, *Lacertidæ*, and Skinks, the tail is so brittle that it breaks with the greatest ease, though it is reproduced after a time. There is a difference, however, especially in the Geckos, between a tail that has been reproduced, and one that has never been injured. Some Lizards, like the Chameleon, have a prehensile tail.

For their size, most of these Reptiles are wonderfully quick runners, though they are not able to continue their speed for any length of time. If anyone should wish to test their swiftness, let him take a large Continental Sand Lizard, well called *Lacerta agilis*, and place it at liberty in the midle of a large and closely-mown lawn, and then try to catch it. When he has done so, I think he will be disposed to agree with my remark above in regard to the fleetness of these creatures. There are exceptions certainly; for instance, even a Tortoise can out-pace a Chameleon on level ground.

The Lizards, like the Snakes, desquamate, slough, or shed their skins periodically. The former, however, as a rule perform the operation piecemeal; while the latter, though they turn their cast-off coats inside out, leave them, if the animals be healthy, quite entire; and very beautiful objects they are. For some days previous to the shedding of their skin, as it is commonly called, Snakes cease to feed, but Lizards do not seem to suffer much loss of appetite during this period.

As there are so many different kinds of Lizards, it will, of course, be impossible within the limits of these articles to allude to a tenth or even much more than a hundredth part of their number; reference, therefore, will only be made to those which are the most suitable for confinement, the most interesting, or the most easily obtained in this country.

Geckotidæ. — According to a comparatively recent rearrangement of the Lizards, the first on our list will be the family *Geckotidæ*. In this family there are about 57 genera and 270 species. A Gecko may be easily known from other Lizards by its depressed head and body, its short, stout legs, and, generally, disc-bearing feet, its large eye, and, as a rule, vertically contracting pupil, indicating its nocturnal habits, and its tail thick at the base.

Dr. Günther says that "Geckos are found in almost every part of the globe between and near the tropics." Another naturalist remarks that "wherever a Lizard of any other family is found there also will be a Gecko." However, no Geckos are natives of Britain. These creatures are spread over the warm countries of the world in a marvellous way, not only over continents, but also over islands which are far remote from any mainland. They abound in valleys as well as upon the hills, in forests and on the plains, in the busy city, and in the solitary desert. They are natives of Europe, Asia, Africa, America, and Australasia. This very extensive distribution, as well as the formation of their backbone prove them to be of an extremely ancient family.

Geckos live in houses, in ruins, in holes in rocks, in holes in walls, in hollows of trees, under stones, on the ground, and in burrows in banks. They are, though quarrelsome, very gregarious, and may often be seen on some wall or rocky bank in great numbers. They bask in the sun during the day, and become exceedingly lively as night draws on, for they are, with few exceptions, nocturnal in their habits. Those Geckos which may be described as diurnal possess eyes having round pupils.

The Geckos are of a very pugnacious disposition, and constantly fight among themselves. I have seen them, as they basked in the sun, resent, with a curious noise and a short, fierce rush, but returning immediately to their former position, the approach of either a fellow Gecko or a Lizard of some family other than their own. They seem always ready to challenge or fight any Reptile about their own size. They frequently have little pitched battles over their prey.

Geckos are carnivorous, but Dr. Günther says, in his "Reptiles of British India," that "their greediness has developed some intellectual faculties in the House Geckos. Accustomed to be fed at a certain time with rice, etc., these little Lizards will punctually make their appearance and fearlessly take the proffered food." They have, as a rule, keen appetites, and partake of a most varied "bill of fare"—beetles, moths, spiders, cockroaches, mealworms, flies, bees, most other insects, their own shed skins, and even, it is said, their own discarded tail and their own little ones.

Geckos are chiefly famous for two extraordinary accomplishments. One is the utterance of a distinct cry or call, which of course is most unusual among Lizards. The cry, in some species, sounds like "tok-tay," in others like the "click-click" of the horseman. From this strange peculiarity the whole family has received the name of Gecko, "Gecko" being a fair imitation of the call made by some of the species. It is said, that in the stillness of night, the voice of certain Geckos is sufficiently loud to awaken the soundest sleepers. The hollows of the trees in which these cries are frequently made, give a strange resonance to their call, which is chiefly used, it is supposed, by the male to attract the attention of the female. The females, as a rule, lay only one egg at a time, which, in appearance, is like that of other lizards of their own size, being covered with a white, hard, calcareous envelope. Probably each female will produce an egg two or three times during the breeding season. Several females occasionally deposit their eggs in the same hole in the wall or in a similar hiding-place.

At first the young lead a retired life under the shelter of some stone, or in the hollow of a tree, or in a hole in the wall. At any rate, they seem to have sufficient instinct to keep out of the way of their unnatural parents, who, if they happen to meet them, are not able to resist the temptation of devouring them.

The young Geckos literally "come out" and face the dangers of Gecko society when they are little more than half-grown.

There is no danger then of being eaten by their elders. Still, however, they maintain to a certain extent their "retiring disposition," for, should they see that a full-grown Gecko has its eyes upon the same tempting insect as themselves, they will immediately modestly forego all claim to the prospective victim. This conduct on the part of the hobbledehoy (if such a word may be used in this sense) Gecko is very noticeable. His demeanour, however, is not due to any deference on his part, but is just simply a matter of prudence; for when he arrives at a state of complete Gecko vigour, he will fight most fiercely with his seniors over some tempting prey.

The other accomplishment of the Reptiles to which I have already referred, is their extraordinary power of climbing. They seem to set at naught the laws of gravitation; for not only can they ascend with the greatest ease smooth perpendicular walls, but they are also able to run along the ceiling of a room with the facility of a fly. I have seen my own Geckos sleeping, from choice, upon the ceiling of the Vivarium in which they lived. The curious and interesting construction of their feet provides this strange activity. The under-surfaces of their toes are provided with discs, or plates, and Dr. Günther says that "the mechanism resembles in some the adhesive organ of *Echeneis*, or Sucking-fish, in others that of the legs of a fly." Besides these discs, many Geckos have very useful and sharp retractile claws, which enable them to take advantage of any crevice in a wall, or of any roughness on the bark of a tree. Some Geckos have not the discs, but have instead more fully-developed claws. All Geckos cannot therefore climb smooth perpendicular walls or run along ceilings of rooms. There is also a flying Gecko (*Ptychozoon homalocephalum*), the wing-like expansions along the sides of the Reptiles acting as parachutes. No Gecko, I believe, is more than 14in. or 15in. in length; and generally they are much smaller than this.

The tail of these animals is exceedingly brittle, and parts company with the body upon the slightest provocation, so to speak; in fact, these Lizards even appear to have the power of throwing off their tail at will. This curious ability is often a means of escaping death. For instance, when pursued by an enemy they can shake off their tail, thus distracting for the moment the attention of the foe by their discarded wriggling member, and gain the necessary time for making good their escape. A very small blow is sufficient to sever a portion of the tail from the rest of the body. The Gecko is able to reproduce the lost member very rapidly, and perhaps this reproduction will take place several times in the course of a life. The reproduced tail is always different from the original one, being rounder, thicker, and smoother. Sometimes, when a tail has been only partially broken, another end begins to grow from the damaged portion, and the animal soon will have a bifid or forked tail. I have a Lizard at the present time with such a tail.

The Geckos have a short, thick tongue, which is slightly forked. They possess pleurodont teeth, but no teeth on the palate. They spring upon their victims in rather a dog-like fashion; and they have the power of adapting their colour to that of the surface upon which they are at rest. I have sometimes lifted up a piece of cork bark, under which I knew some Geckos were hiding, and failing to find them at once have supposed for the moment that they had escaped, the little creatures having clung closely to the underside of the cork, and their colouring having become almost exactly like that of their shelter. Their colours are brown, grey, yellowish, and sometimes there are beautiful tints of green, red, and blue. The brighter colours generally belong to the males. Nevertheless, as I have said, their colours are more or less changeable, and they are able by this adaptation of colouring to make themselves so inconspicuous that they may both escape the enemy and take their prey more easily. Many of them have the strange habit of licking their own eyes.

The Geckos, generally, do well in confinement, giving hardly any trouble. They may be kept in such a case as that represented by Fig. 17, and they will live with other Lizards of their own size. On fine days they come out of their hiding-places and bask in the sun. The bottom of the case should be covered rather deeply with fine and dry mould; hiding-places in the shape of pieces of cork bark ought to be provided for them, and a little water in a small trough. Care must be taken that they do not escape, for it will be no little trouble to re-catch them. Gentles may occasionally be thrown into the case, and those that are not eaten at once will bury themselves in the mould and re-appear in course of time in the shape of flies. Not many maggots should be provided at once, or there will be more flies together than the Geckos "can make use of," to quote a common Devonshire expression. A few now and then will be more satisfactory. Cockroaches, earwigs, spiders, and mealworms will be readily eaten.

In winter time the Geckos' case should be placed near the hot-water pipes in a green-house, or during that season these Reptiles may be kept in a heated Vivarium like that represented by Fig. 6 or Fig. 12. Personally I have found Geckos hardy and interesting animals, requiring very little trouble, and if cockroaches are their principal food, they (the cockroaches) will, until eaten, live apparently quite happily with the Geckos, even voluntarily taking refuge under the same piece of cork bark. Pieces of bread or sugar should be supplied for the blackbeetles to eat. The contents of one well-stocked beetle-trap will provide a few Geckos with prey for a considerable time. I think that the insects live in no fear of the Reptiles. Cockroaches themselves are also interesting.

Geckos move without making the slightest noise; indeed, they seem to glide in a series of rapid jerks rather than run. As they stop, they constantly raise the head, apparently to reconnoitre, to watch for prey, or to guard against being taken by an enemy. The movements of a Gecko are unlike those of any other animal.

The Geckos are perfectly harmless, though the natives of some countries in which they abound look upon them with fear and disgust, believing them to be poisonous, and that their crawling over the human body will produce leprous sores.

The following Geckos are among the most suitable for confinement in this country :—

1. The Wall Gecko (*Platydactylus muralis*), the Tarentola of the Italians.—The Geckos of this (the broad-fingered) genus have their toes widened throughout their length, and covered beneath with transverse, imbricated scales. All the toes of the feet of this species are nearly equal in length, and only the third and fourth toes of each foot is provided with a claw. The head is depressed, and rather broad behind the eyes. The males have a row of

spines at the base of the tail on each side. If the tail has not been reproduced, there are spines along the whole of its upper surface; but if reproduced, the tail will be thicker, rounder, smoother, and probably without spines. The colour of the animal is various—sometimes light grey above and pinkish-white beneath, and sometimes dark brown, and, occasionally, with light

FIG. 36.—WALL GECKO (*Platydactylus muralis*, Dum. et Bib.).

streaks above and dirty white below. In length, it is from 4in. to 6in., and lives in inhabited houses, ruins, old walls, and the like. This Gecko, which is very hardy, is found in Italy, Spain, South of France, Greece, Sicily, and the coasts of Egypt and Barbary. Fig. 36 represents a Gecko climbing a perpendicular wall, and in the possession of a tail which has been reproduced.

2. The Warty Hemidactyle (*Hemidactylus verruculatus*). The members of this (the half-fingered) genus have the base of each toe, underneath, provided with an oval disc, from the centre of which springs the second joint of the toe, that part of the toe beyond the disc being slender. This species has a claw on every toe: the toes are free and pear-shaped. The males possess femoral pores. The colour of this animal is very like that of the former, with the exception of a little more red in the brown. The length is about 5in. It is found on the shores of the Mediterranean Sea, and is also a hardy species.

3. The European Phyllodactyle (*Phyllodactylus europæus*).—The Geckos of this (the leaf-fingered) genus have claws on all toes, which (the toes) are dilated at their extremities into a subtriangular disc. This species has an oval and depressed head, broader behind the eyes, which are round and large. It has a more distinct neck than is usual with members of this genus. There are no femoral pores. The colour on the back is a dirty pink, covered with spots of a darker shade; beneath the body the colour is a dusky white. It is rather less than 3in. in length. It is found in the South of Europe, and it is not so easily obtained as the foregoing, but is hardy.

4. The Fan-foot (*Ptyodactylus Gecko*, Fig. 37).—The members of this (the fan-footed) genus have toes that are free and slender at the base, but the extremity of each is provided below with a large disc, in front of which a claw is sheathed in a kind of notch. There are no femoral pores. The colour may be described as a red-brown, spotted with white. The colouring, however, varies a good deal. This species is common over North Eastern Africa and South Western Asia.

The other Geckos that may be mentioned are Delaland's Gecko (*Tarentola Delalandii*), the Indian Gecko (*Gecko verus*), and the Ocellated Gecko (*Pachydactylus ocellatus*).

I have bought Geckos in London for half-a-crown each. They are sometimes found in Covent Garden as "stowaways" in boxes of bananas.

Varanidæ.—" Would you like to see him swallow an egg whole, sir?" said the attentive keeper of the Reptile House, Regent's Park, to me one day. Naturally I answered in the affirmative, and watched the animal spoken of. He was looking rather sleepy, and his attitude was far from elegant. Presently, however, his eye brightened, and his long forked tongue commenced to vibrate from his snake-like head, and he quickly became quite alert. He heard something that I could not hear. But as in a second or two a rumbling sound reached my ears, the door at the back of the den suddenly opened and the keeper's head and shoulders appeared in view. The noise, I afterwards discovered, was caused by the moving of the wheeled steps along the corridor behind. The keeper, by means of an iron rod, drove or coaxed the strange beast to the front part of the Vivarium near the glass, and by the help of a cloth dropped a large egg close to him. The animal eagerly and deftly seized the egg, and by a clever toss of his head arranged it lengthwise in his mouth, cracking it slightly as he did so, and swallowed it with evident relish. The feat, however, was not done to the keeper's satisfaction, so another egg was produced which was not even cracked as it slipped down the throat of the big Reptile. The animal who possessed this rather uncommon accomplishment was a large Lizard belonging to the family *Varanidæ*. This clever performer was, if I remember rightly, the Two-banded Monitor (*Varanus salvator*), which had been in the gardens for several years. From time to time I have seen him take many eggs, but the only one I ever saw him crack was the first.

The family of the *Varanidæ*, or of the *Monitoridæ* as it is also called, numbers amongst its members the largest of all the true Lizards, some of them reaching a length of seven feet, and perhaps, occasionally, even more. The *Varanidæ* differ from the rest of their relatives of the order *Lacertilia*, with the exception of the Heloderms, in the formation of their nasal apertures. The Monitors have a long and rather snake-like head covered with very small inimbricate polygonal shields, a long tongue which is deeply forked and sheathed posteriorly, and a long and powerful tail, rounded or compressed according to the manner of life of its owner. The under part of their body is covered with small oblong scales arranged "in crossbands," while those on "the back and tail are rhombic." For their size, they are fiercer, stronger, and braver than any other of the Lizards. Their teeth are acute, compressed, triangular or conical—there are none on

FIG. 37.—FAN-FOOTED GECKO (*Ptyodactylus Gecko*).

the palates. Each foot possesses five toes, armed with sharp and powerful claws. The young of this family are very prettily marked, the markings more or less disappearing with age. The Monitors inhabit the Old World—Africa, Southern Asia, and Australia—in the New World they are represented by the *Iguanidæ*. There is only one genus, which contains about twenty-eight species.

Some of these creatures live in water or in its neighbourhood, others on dry and sandy ground, occasionally quite remote from water. Those Monitors which frequent water have compressed tails, serrated above, by the help of which they are able to swim very quickly. On the slightest alarm they plunge into the water, and often remain for a considerable time beneath its surface. Dr. Günther explains in the following words why these creatures are able to continue under water for so long: " the external nasal opening leads into a spacious cavity situated on the snout; when the animal dives it closes the nasal aperture, and retaining a certain quantity of atmospheric air in that pouch, or rather in the two pouches, it is enabled to remain under water for a prolonged period without the necessity of rising to the surface in order to breathe. It is the same plan of structure as that with which a large northern seal (*Cystophora borealis*) is provided."

The Land Monitors have rounded tails, and live in little caves in the rocks or burrow in the soil; in the vicinity of these they hunt for their food, some of them in the day-time, some in the evening, and others probably during the night. The *Varanidæ* live upon eggs, often those of the Crocodile, Rats, Mice, Lizards, Snakes, Fish, Frogs, Birds, Worms, and Insects. One writer says that he has seen some Monitors pursuing a Fawn, and when they caught it, draw it into the water; and he also records that in the dead bodies of others he has found the remains of Sheep. Dr. Brehm, however, thinks that there must be some mistake here, for he does not believe that these Reptiles would hunt such large animals for the purpose of eating their flesh.

These Lizards on the slightest alarm will, according to their kind, rush to the water or their holes, but should their retreat be cut off they will then fight with great fierceness, sometimes even springing at their would-be captor's face. They are able to give severe wounds not only with their teeth and claws, but also with their tail. When they have once reached their holes, it is no easy matter to withdraw them, for with their great strength of claw they are able to cling with much tenacity to the interior of their refuge. It is beyond the power of one man, even if he has a rope attached to its body, to dislodged a full-grown Monitor when he has "run to earth." Because of a Monitor's very strong claws and its great power of climbing, it is said "that it is actually used by house-breakers in India to surmount obstacles; the robber retaining hold of the creature's tail, while it endeavours to escape it draws him upwards." I dare say that some of my readers will think that this is very like the stories of Baron Munchausen.

Monitors lay from twenty to thirty eggs, which they bury in the sand. These large Lizards have received the name of Monitors because they are supposed to give warning by a loud hiss of the approach of the Crocodile. This, however, is only a delusion, as they are often found living in the same water with the larger Reptiles. The Arabs call this animal *Waran;* hence the generic name of *Varanus*.

The Nile Monitor (*Varanus niloticus*) is about 6ft. in length, of which the tail is one half. This animal is semi-aquatic, therefore it has a compressed tail, keeled at the top. The feet are not webbed, and the toes are unequal in length, the fourth toe being the longest and the fifth the shortest. The Nile Monitor is of dark green colour, and when young it is prettily spotted with yellowish white. It was reverenced by the ancient Egyptians, and is often found engraved upon their ornaments and among their hieroglyphics.

The Ouaran, or Land Monitor (*V. griseus*), was the "Land Crocodile" of the ancients. It chiefly differs from the foregoing in having a rounded instead of a compressed tail. In this species the nostrils are large and placed obliquely near the eyes. There is a streak on each side of its head and neck. This animal is by no means rare in Egypt and Sinai, and extends to the North West of India.

The White-throated Monitor (*V. albigularis*) is another terrestrial species, like the above, and is found in South West Africa.

Though a land Monitor, it frequently lives close to water, and feeds upon frogs, snails, rats, and mice. Like those already spoken of, when alarmed it rushes hastily to its hole in the crevice of a rock, or to a burrow among the roots of some tre., whence it is very difficult to dislodge. Dr. Boulenger describes its colour and markings in the following words: "Greyish brown above, with large round yellow dark-edged spots arranged in transverse series on the back; a dark temporal streak, extending along the side of the neck; tail with alternate brown and yellowish annuli; lower surfaces yellowish."

The Ocellated, or Two-banded Monitor (*V. salvator*), already referred to, is a native of China, Siam, Ceylon, and the East Indian Archipelago. The following is a part of Dr. Günther's description of this species: "Dark brown above, with transverse series of round white spots, snout with three or four white crossbands, a dark-brown streak runs from the eye to the neck, throat, and sometimes the belly, with irregular dark-brown transverse streaks, tail with white rings. All these markings become more and more obscure with advancing age, and finally may disappear entirely." According to the late Dr. Cantor, also quoted by Dr. Günther, the Two-banded Monitor is "very numerous in hilly and marshy localities of the Malayan Peninsula. It is commonly, during the day, observed in the branches of trees overhanging rivers, preying upon birds and their eggs and smaller Lizards, and when disturbed it throws itself from a considerable height into the water; it will courageously defend itself with teeth and claws and by strokes of the tail. The lowest castes of Hindoos capture these Lizards, commonly by digging them out of their burrows on the banks of rivers, for the sake of their flesh, which by these people is greatly relished. Some individuals attain to nearly 7ft. in length."

The Short-toed Monitor (*V. flavescens*) is, according to Dr. Günther, in colour, greenish or brownish olive, with irregular dark markings, which are generally confluent with broad crossbands on the back and tail. This animal is found in Bengal, Penang, East Burmah, etc. Mr. Theobald speaks of these animals as being difficult, when large, to be obtained by Europeans because their flesh is so highly valued by the Burmese and

Karens. They are hunted by dogs which, by means of the scent, track them to their hiding-places in hollow trees. Though a Burman is usually a very lazy man, he is quite ready to undergo the fatigue of cutting down a tree in the hollow interior of which he knows a Monitor to be hiding. These creatures frequently bury their eggs in a deserted White Ant's nest. Their eggs are much relished by the Burmese, and are preferred by these people to those of the ordinary fowl. They are "oily and feculent-looking," but as they have no unpleasant odour they are sometimes eaten readily by Europeans.

Gould's Monitor (*V. Gouldii*) comes from Australia, and is fairly frequently imported into this country. It has two yellow streaks on each side of the neck.

The Gigantic Lace Monitor (*V. giganteus*) of Australia is one of the largest of the Monitors, sometimes attaining the length of 7ft. It is, according to Dr. Gray, "brown, back and tail with cross-bands of large black-edged white spots;" the legs also are spotted with white.

I should not recommend anyone to attempt to keep in confinement a full-grown Monitor, but young ones are quite suitable for such a purpose, and are by no means uninteresting. They are generally hardy and good feeders—taking, as a rule, either live or dead food, preferring, however, the former. Water Monitors, of course, should be provided with a suitably-sized bath, the water of which should be changed every day. Soft water is decidedly better for these animals than hard. Monitors are occasionally sold in London for so little a sum as 5s. each. Those which are firm (*i.e.*, not limp to the touch or listless in appearance, though I have known such to recover their health) and lively should be chosen, and if possible, when they are about 1ft. in length.

It, of course, "goes without saying" that, as a rule, poisonous Reptiles should not be kept as pets, though they are exceedingly interesting. There is the risk of an accident even with the most careful and prudent; and besides this there is the chance of the animal's escape, which is sure to lead to a great deal of anxiety, and perhaps to something far worse than mere anxiety. Though I do not intend in this chapter to say anything about the keeping in confinement of venomous Snakes, I will venture to write a few words about so strange a beast as the one poisonous Lizard. This Reptile is known as the Heloderm (*Heloderma horridum*) and is a native of Central America, Southern Arizona seeming to be the centre of its distribution. It is also called the "Escorpion" and the "Gila Monster."

When Sir John Lubbock presented one of these Lizards to the Zoological Gardens, London, in 1882, not a little excitement was caused among those who were interested in Reptiles. The animal is altogether so different from most other Lizards in its movements and manner of life, and so different from all others in the possession of poison-glands and grooved teeth, that it should have attracted the curious in these things is no matter of surprise. It had, however, been known to science for a very long time, but this was the first, or one of the first, living specimens brought to England.

It is indeed a strange and remarkable animal. Its very appearance is enough to inspire people with an unwillingness to touch it; for it looks dangerous, and is well described as "hideous." Though I do not think that its bite has ever proved fatal to a healthy human being, it is sufficiently poisonous to cause small mammals to die in a minute or two after being bitten. The Heloderm is brown in colour spotted with yellow, and has a heavy, round, useless looking tail, four legs, five apparently weak toes on each foot, armed with curved claws, and a body covered with tubercles; hence its generic name, meaning warty skin.

The monster is heavily and clumsily built, and very inactive, and its power of dealing a dangerous or deadly wound seems to be given it rather as a means of defence than as a means of killing its prey. It is generally a little less than 2ft. in length, though I have seen it described as being 3ft. In captivity it lives for a long time, and feeds upon raw eggs, dead mice, young rats, and uncooked meat. It laps water in a very dog-like fashion.

The Heloderm is tenacious of life, its muscles moving for a long time after it has been beheaded, and it is by no means easily killed by chloroform.

The members of the interesting Teiidæ family are natives of the tropical and sub-tropical parts of the New World. They vary much in form and in scaling. Some of them are 6ft. in length, the tail, however, being longer than the body. These Lizards frequently live in burrows which they make for themselves, or in hollows in trees, and their food consists of fruit, small mammals, frogs, eggs, birds, and small reptiles. They are of a timid nature, but the larger ones will fight very fiercely when cornered, jumping and biting at their would-be captor's face; they will also stand at bay when pursued by dogs. Sometimes, while being hunted they take refuge in water, diving beneath the surface and remaining there for a considerable time.

The Teiidæ are supposed never to ascend trees, but they run along the ground with great rapidity and in a serpent-like manner. They generally lay their eggs, to the number of about fifty, in the nests of the White Ants, from which they have previously driven the lawful owners. By some people the flesh of these Reptiles is highly valued as food; and the natives of those countries in which these animals are found, superstitiously consider that the scales of their tails are useful as a protection against paralysis, and that their fat is serviceable both as a salve and as a poultice.

The Teguexin and its near relatives are said to give warning, by hissing, of the approach of the Alligator, as the Monitors of the Old World are reported to act in regard to the Crocodile. Probably, however, there is no truth in either assertion. These Lizards cannot be kept in captivity as easily as most other Reptiles, for they require almost constant artificial heat, and a regular and plentiful supply of food. Besides in this country they are rather expensive to buy. However, they readily become reconciled to their place of confinement, and if kindly treated, soon learn to know their fosterer, though perhaps they never grow perfectly tame, the least thing sometimes irritating or frightening them.

They have a habit, which is rather attractive, of sitting or reposing with their heads raised and slightly thrown backward. Mr. Boulenger, in his "Catalogue of Lizards," describes thirty-five genera and 108 species of this family.

The Common Teguexin (*Tupinambis teguixin*) is a handsome Reptile, occasionally reaching a length of more than 4ft., of which the tail is about two-thirds. The ground-colour of the upper part of the body is a brownish-green, spotted with greenish-yellow; beneath the body the colour is yellow marked with black. The end of the tail is slightly compressed. There are about forty small femoral pores. In their own country, these animals are looked upon as robbers of hen-houses, stealing both the eggs and the chickens. Good specimens of the Common Teguexin may be sometimes bought for about £2; they are, therefore, rather expensive pets.

In captivity they will eat ripe fruit, raw meat, and dead mice. The food should be supplied daily, for unlike most Reptiles, the Teidæ are unable to fast for any length of time with impunity. They may be kept in a Vivarium like that represented by Fig. 3, p. 11, or by Fig. 6, p. 14. The case ought to be at least twice as long as the animal, and always heated, except during the hottest summer weather. The common Teguexin is also known as the VariegatedLizard, and the South American Sauvegarde. It is found in South America, from the Guianas to Uruguay, but principally in Brazil, living there in the sugar-plantations, and in the woods, being most abundant near the coast. It is also a native of the West Indies.

The Red Teguexin (*Tupinambis rufescens*) is very like the Common Teguexin, but has much smaller scales. The chief colour is a reddish-yellow marked with dark cross-bands. It has fewer femoral pores than its commoner relative. In length it is frequently over 3ft. This Reptile may occasionally be bought in England for from £3 to £8, according to size. For an ordinary Vivarium, it is always wise to buy specimens of all the large Lizards when they are young and small, and, if possible, when they have been known to feed freely in captivity. The Red Teguexin is found in La Plata.

The Dorsal Lizard (*Ameiva dorsalis*, Gray).—The late Mr. P. H. Gosse in his "Naturalist's Sojourn in Jamaica," says that " this animal is one of the most common of the Reptiles in Jamaica, and is as beautiful as abundant. Its colours are striking, but not showy, and its countenance has a very meek expression. All its motions are elegant and sprightly; when it is proceeding deliberately, its body is thrown into latent curves, the most graceful imaginable; but when alarmed, its swiftness is so excessive that it appears as if it literally flew over the ground, and the observer can scarcely persuade himself that it is not a bird. It is very timid, and though its toes are not formed, as in the Geckos and Anoles, for holding on against gravity, I have seen a large Ameiva run with facility on the side of a dry wall, along the perpendicular surfaces of large stones." The colour of this animal is greenish-brown, and there is a light green streak running from the neck along the back, widening as it grows in length; its sides are spotted with dusky white, underneath it is a greenish white.

In all the specimens described above the throat is scaly, and there are two folds in the skin which form a kind of double collar. Both the Red Teguexin and the Dorsal Lizard can be treated in confinement in the same way as is recommended for the Common Teguexin.

The *Lacertidæ* family, which numbers among its members the English and other well-known Lizards, contains about seventeen genera and some ninety-seven species, all of which are natives of Europe, Asia, Africa, and the East Indies; but strangely enough they are not found in the island of Madagascar. They are most abundant in Africa.

The *Lacertidæ* may be roughly described as having the head covered with symmetrical shields; eyes with round pupils and well-developed eyelids; distinct ear-openings; four well-developed limbs, each limb being provided with a foot possessing five clawed toes; a very long, fragile tail, often twice the length of the body; generally femoral pores; teeth that are pleurodont, and hollowed at the base; and a long, flat, forked tongue.

The genus *Lacerta* is the most familiar of the *Lacertidæ*, and of this genus the Eyed Lizard (*Lacerta ocellata*, Fig. 38) is the largest representative, and certainly not one of the least handsome; indeed, the colouring and markings of the young of the species may be justly described as beautiful. *L. ocellata* sometimes reaches a length of 20in., the tail being considerably longer than the rest of the body. Like all the *Lacertæ*, it has a well-marked collar and femoral pores. The rostral scale (that at the end of the nose) enters the nostril. The scales on the back are small and very slightly keeled, but those on the tail are longer,

FIG. 38.—THE EYED LIZARD (*Lacerta ocellata*).

larger, distinctly keeled, and arranged in rings. The scales beneath the body are broader than they are long, if such an expression may be used.

The colouring of this Lizard varies very much with the age of the animal. Mr. Boulenger in his "Catalogue of Lizards" describes the markings and colour in the following words: "Green above, with black dots or network, or blackish-olive with yellowish network; sides with large blue spots—ocelli; lower surfaces uniformly greenish-yellow. Young olive above, covered all over with white or bluish black-edged ocelli, black sometimes forming irregular cross-bands on the back." The ocelli have, of course, given the animal its specific name. The head of the male is larger than that of the female.

I have often thought that the markings of some of these Lizards (*L. ocellata*) might suggest a beautiful pattern for a carpet. The scales and the colouring give the back of the animal a very carpet-like appearance. There are one or two varieties of the Eyed Lizard which bear a very close resemblance to its near relative the Green Lizard (*L. viridis*), and one variety is sometimes called the "Great Green Lizard."

L. ocellata is a very suitable Reptile to keep in confinement. It is hardy, cheap (ranging in price, according to the season and the supply, from 2s. to 8s.), easily tamed, and, what is very greatly in its favour, an eater of dead food. Most Lizards—indeed most Reptiles—will only take living and moving prey.

Though the Eyed Lizard is a very large animal in comparison with the rest of its genus, it does not take advantage of its size, to either bully or to eat its smaller relatives and comrades. However, no doubt, an ill-tempered specimen, and also one that is a cannibal, may occasionally be met with. I have kept a very small Lizard (*L. agilis*) for considerably more than a year in the same Vivarium with a very large Eyed Lizard, and I have often seen it (*L. agilis*) and other small Lizards basking in the sun on the back of their large relative.

L. ocellata will eat mice, live or dead, large worms, cockroaches, mealworms, raw meat, ripe grapes and strawberries, and the like. It is a native of Spain, Portugal, Southern France, and the north-western parts of Italy.

These Lizards are sometimes wild and shy when they are first caught or purchased, and consequently refuse to eat for so long a time that they become very weak and thin. However, to prevent their losing flesh under these circumstances, they must be fed artificially, which may be done in the following way : The animal should be gently and carefully held in the left hand, so that its forelegs are pressed backwards against its sides. In such a position as this, it can neither bite nor struggle very much ; but in its endeavours to bite, it will open its mouth widely and so give an opportunity for inserting, with the right hand and the help of a piece of smooth wood, some raw meat down its very capacious throat. This artificial feeding should be repeated about every third day until the Reptile begins to eat of its own accord. Regular and gentle handling goes a long way towards the begetting of tameness. Of course, care must be taken not to hold the Lizard at all by the tail, or it will probably break.

Eyed Lizards having broken tails can often be bought exceedingly cheaply; and it is quite worth one's while to take advantage of such an opportunity, for the gradual reproduction of the lost member is very interesting to observe.

If kept during the winter in a heated case like that represented by Fig. 6, p. 14, *L. ocellata* will forego its natural hibernation ; but if it is wished that the animal should hibernate, it may, if quite healthy and in good condition, be packed, surrounded by moss, in a wooden box, and placed until the following spring in some cool place which cannot be reached by frost. The day chosen for this "stowing away" should be when the weather is dull and rather cold, and then the Reptile will be in a more or less torpid condition.

Those Vivaria in which this Lizard and its near relatives are confined ought to be provided with plenty of very small and dry gravel, pieces of cork or oak-bark, under which they may hide, and a suitable tree upon which they can climb and bask in the sun. As Lizards do not bathe, the vessel for water need only be small. All Lizards must have as much sunshine as possible, without which they are mostly dull and listless.

I believe that the *Lacertæ* are perfectly contented in captivity when properly cared for. Though these animals are so very fleet and active, they do not seem, when at liberty, as a rule, to range far from their holes or natural homes. I have known escaped foreign Lizards of this genus to keep for weeks in or near the same spot, appearing there with great regularity every bright day, to bask in the sun, and to watch for prey, until, very often, they were finally re-captured. Indeed, if a Lizard's Vivarium be placed with the door open in a retired position on some lawn or in a kitchen garden in all probability the inmates will, provided that they are quite tame, come out of the case in the day-time and roam about in its very near neighbourhood, and return to it at night, or whenever the weather ceases to be fine and sunny.

The Eyed Lizard is oviparous, and occasionally deposits its eggs when in confinement. If the eggs are laid within a reasonable period after the animal's capture, it is quite worth while to attempt to hatch them.

These eggs, as well as those of other Lizards, can be artificially incubated and the young reared without much difficulty. They may be hatched in an ordinary chicken-incubator or in a small tin canister placed in a sufficiently warm situation. The length of time expended in the hatching depends upon the temperature with which the eggs are surrounded. I have found about 96deg. Fahrenheit a suitable heat for the incubation of the eggs of Reptiles. It is important to see that the atmosphere of whatever incubator used is not so dry as to shrivel the eggs, nor so moist as to encourage the growth of fungus. If an ordinary tin canister be employed for the hatching of Lizards' eggs, the bottom of it should be covered rather thickly with damp moss, above which the eggs ought to be packed interspersed with more moss. A few small holes for ventilation should be made in the lid of the tin. A good position for this rough-and-ready canister-incubator is to place it upon the top of the little boiler which is used to heat such a Vivarium as that illustrated at Fig. 6. Of course the temperature ought to be watched and tested from time to time.

The young Lizards will be ready to feed almost directly they have left the shell, and they can be reared without difficulty if the directions, which will be given in another place, are followed.

Perhaps the most popular of the *Lacertae*, as an inmate of the Vivarium, is the Green Lizard (*Lacerta viridis*, Fig. 39). It not only bears confinement exceedingly well, but it is also very beautiful in colour and graceful in form. I can well remember, though it is many years ago, my great delight when I first saw one of these Lizards. Up to that time I had been familiar with English Lizards only, and I did not even think of asking the price of the animal (for it was in a shop for sale), as I somewhat naturally jumped to the conclusion that to purchase so beautiful a Reptile would cost more than I could afford. The prices, however, of these Lizards are low. Fine healthy specimens can generally be bought for sums ranging from 9d. to 2s.

I have noticed that when strangers are looking at a collection of Lizards, they are almost certain to point out the *L. viridis* as being conspicuous for its beauty. Yet its chief colour, as its specific name implies, is green, the commonest colour in nature, but a very lovely emerald-green.

The illustration gives a good general idea of the shape of the reptile. The tail is usually about twice the length of the rest of the body. The rostral shield touches the nostril. The scales on the back are oval-hexagonal and keeled.

The colour of the young of this Lizard differs from that of the adult. The former are either a greenish-brown or green on the upper part of the body, sometimes with several horizontal streaks of yellow; similar markings may also be found upon the full-grown female. The adult is of a brilliant emerald-green colour on the back and sides, often spotted with black, the under-parts being of a greenish-yellow. The adult male has generally a blue throat, and frequently grows to a length of over 16in.

There are at least three varieties of the *L. viridis*, viz., *schreiberi*, *major*, and *strigata*. According to Mr. Boulenger, the variety *schreiberi* is a much smaller Lizard than the typical form, and the "young" are "olive or brownish above, with large yellow or bluish-white, black edged ocelli on the sides of the head and body. These ocelli often disappear in the adult, which are green or brown above, variously spotted or reticulated with black. Lower surfaces yellowish, spotless in the young, often with

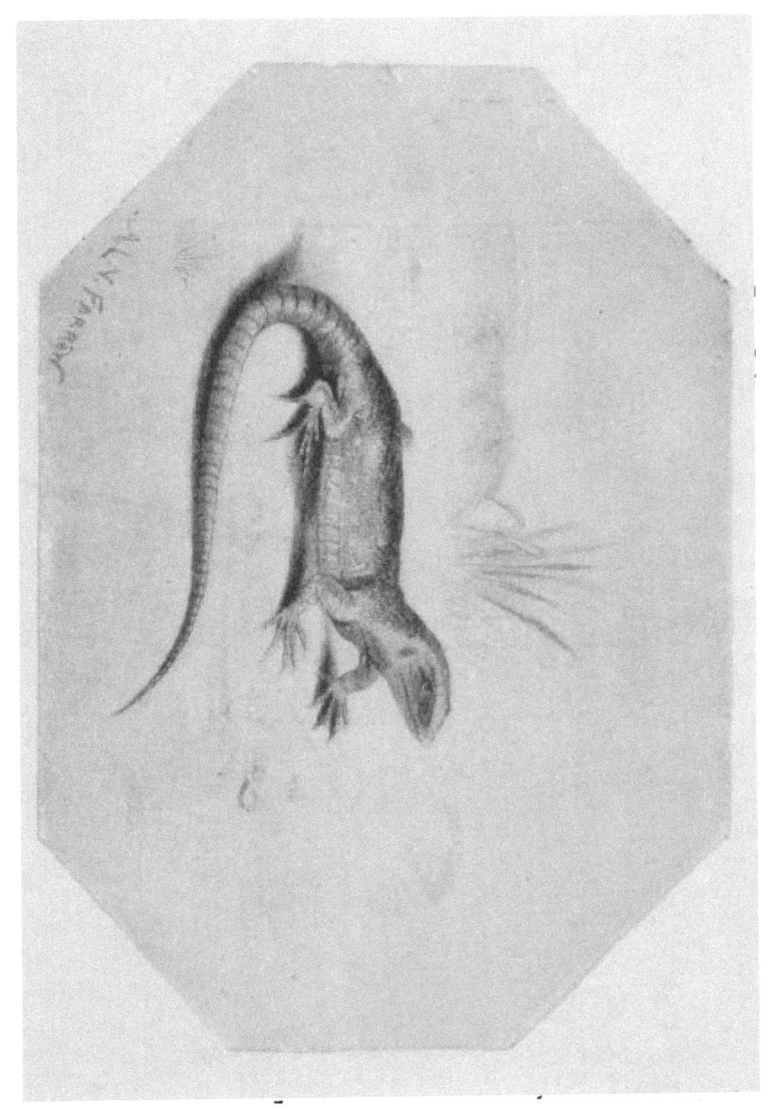

FIG. 39.—THE GREEN LIZARD (*Lacerta viridis*).

round black spots in the adult. Throat blue in the adult." The entire length is about 12in.

The var. *major*, as its name implies, is larger than the typical form, and the young are "olive above, usually with three or five yellowish longitudinal streaks, the lowermost of which, extending from axilla to groin, is often replaced by a series of round spots. These bands usually disappearing in the adult, which are green on the body or limbs, uniform or finely speckled with black; upper surface of head vermiculated with black; lower surfaces yellow, the outer ventrals often speckled with black; throat never blue." This variety is generally about 18in. long, and comes from Turkey, Greece, and Asia Minor.

The var. *strigata* is slightly smaller than the type, and the colour of the young is "greenish or olive spotted or marbled with black, and with three or five light dorsal streaks, which may disappear completely in the adult; these may be closely dotted with black, as certain specimens of the typical form and of var. *major*; belly yellowish, often dotted with black on the sides." Total length about 16in. This animal is met with in Persia, Asia Minor, and Syria. It is not at all uncommon in the Holy Land. The males of the Green Lizard and its varieties are generally of greater length than the females. I think it may safely be said that the head of a male is always larger than that of a female of the same age.

L. viridis very soon becomes perfectly tame, so much so that it will readily come and take food from the fingers; and it will, also, quietly submit to being handled, showing no nervousness.

It has been frequently asserted that the Green Lizard is a native of Britain, and in proof of this assertion, so-called specimens of the species have been exhibited from time to time as having been found in this country. Some years ago, there was not a little correspondence in the *Zoologist* on this point, many writers bringing forth evidence which seemed to show that this beautiful Reptile was a native of England at any rate. Nevertheless, I am sorry to say, that this Lizard cannot fairly be considered as a denizen of our banks and hedges. It may only be classed among the British fauna, inasmuch as it is a native of the Channel Islands. The specimens which have been found in

England have probably escaped from confinement, or green representatives of the Sand Lizard (*L. agilis*) may have been mistaken for the *L. viridis*.

In captivity, the Green Lizard will feed upon flies, mealworms, cockroaches, earwigs, nearly any insect, in fact, as well as spiders and garden worms, gentles, and their pupæ.

The general treatment of these Lizards in confinement may be the same as that described for the Eyed Lizard (*L. ocellata*). They, like the latter, live quite peacefully with their smaller relatives.

The Green Lizard will frequently deposit her eggs in the Vivarium, bury them in the sand, and show a little amount of care concerning them. But if there is reason to believe them fertile they should at once be removed for artificial incubation, and treated as was suggested for those of the Eyed Lizard. *L. viridis* is very fond of climbing and will remain for days in dull weather or in winter-time apparently fast asleep upon the branch of a tree.

The beautiful Sand Lizard (*Lacerta agilis*, Fig 40) is, without any doubt, a native of England. Of it, the late Dr. Bell in his "British Reptiles," says that "when in confinement it ceases to feed, conceals itself with extreme timidity when approached, and ultimately pines and dies." This great authority must, however, have been as unfortunate in his experience of keeping this Lizard in captivity as he was fortunate in regard to the Common Snake (*Tropidonotus natrix*). Many people, myself among them, have found that this Lizard will often become exceedingly tame, and, like the Green Lizard, can be taught to come and take food from the fingers and drink water from the hollow of the hand. Of course, naturally, their individual temperaments differ, and consequently some are much more easily tamed than others, but all I believe, without exception, will, sooner or later, lose their fear of man if consistently treated with gentleness and kindness.

The Sand Lizard is also very hardy, and is decidedly a long liver in confinement. I have from time to time kept a great many of this species, and think them to be among the healthiest of Lizards.

FIG. 41.—THE COMMON LIZARD (*Lacerta vivipara*)

FIG. 40.—THE SAND LIZARD (*Lacerta agilis*).

L. agilis occurs in various parts of England. It is, however, very local, *e.g.*, it is fairly common in the neighbourhoods of Poole, in Dorsetshire; of Bournemouth, in Hampshire; of Southport, in Lancashire, and elsewhere; but in most of the counties it is never found. It is also a native of various other countries of Europe, such as France, Belgium, Holland, Switzerland, Germany, Austria, Denmark, Sweden, Russia, and the western and central parts of Asia.

The female lays eggs to the number of about twelve, and buries them in sand, entrusting their incubation to the sun. Her fertile eggs, like those of other Lizards, may be hatched artificially. The Sand Lizard often sheds its skin in an almost entire condition. The slough is a curious and beautiful object, showing clearly the markings of the animal it has lately covered. *L. agilis* seems to cast its *exuviæ* more frequently, and in a more perfect condition, than do its relatives, the Eyed and Green Lizards.

The Sand Lizard has a shorter snout and is altogether more stoutly built than *L. viridis*. The rostral shield does not touch the nostril. The scales on the back are hexagonal and well-keeled; on the sides they are smaller in size, and either only slightly keeled or perfectly smooth. The tail is about as long again as the rest of the body. The entire length of an English specimen is about 8in. At present I have a continental Sand Lizard which is quite a foot in length. When first I obtained him, he was exceedingly wild and shy, and always ready to bite, but now he is quite tame.

These Lizards certainly deserve their specific name of *agilis*, for they are wonderfully fleet. I shall not easily forget the difficulty I had when I tried to catch the one just mentioned after I had let him loose upon a smooth lawn.

Unfortunately the Sand Lizard is sometimes a cannibal, and should not be kept in the same Vivarium with other Lizards smaller than himself, for he may eat them even when he has been well supplied with suitable and legitimate food. I have seen some devouring a relative nearly as large as themselves.

L. agilis is generally found on sandy soil, but it may occasionally be met with in marshy places. It is frequently associated, in thought at any rate, with the very beautiful and rare little

English Smooth Snake (*Coronella austriaca*), the latter preferring the former as its favourite food.

This Lizard varies somewhat as regards colour. Speaking roughly, that of the male is principally green, and that of the female grey, spotted with white. The following is Mr. Boulenger's description: "Young, greyish brown above, with longitudinal series of white, black-edged ocelli; no light vertebral streak; lower surfaces whitish, immaculate. Adult female, brown or greyish above, the vertebral zone darker than the sides of the back, with large dark brown spots with a central white shaft or round spot; usually the larger spots form three longitudinal series on the body; belly cream-coloured, with or without black spots. Male during the breeding-season, green on the sides and lower surfaces, rarely also on the back; sides dark spotted, usually with lighter ocelli; lower surfaces more or less abundantly spotted with black. A form (*L. rubra*) is distinguished by the unspotted reddish-brown or brick-red back."

The variety of this Lizard, known as *exigua*, has, when young, "three well-marked, light, longitudinal streaks along the back, and a series of whitish ocelli on the sides; some specimens uniform olive-green, lower surfaces whitish, unspotted. The dorsal streaks of the young constantly persist in the adult female. . . The adult male is frequently entirely green above, dotted or spotted with black, with or without white ocelli on the sides; lower surfaces greenish, black spotted."

L. agilis in confinement may be treated in the same way as *L. viridis*, and be fed upon similar food. It will, however, more readily eat the small garden worm than its larger relative.

The very interesting Lizard known as the Common or Viviparous Lizard (*Lacerta vivipara*, Fig. 41) is common nearly all over the rural parts of England, and yet people who have not learnt to see them or hear them do not notice them. I have read somewhere—I cannot now remember where—that a naturalist making a survey of England in regard to Reptiles, came to the conclusion that the common Lizards in number equalled at least the population of this country.

I have pointed these interesting creatures out to my friends, and have shown them the specimens I have caught during a walk, only to hear the oft-repeated remark or equivalent words, "It is very strange, I never see them. I did not know there were any in the neighbourhood."

My two small boys—the eldest nine years old—have frequently caught for me, when I wanted them, several in a morning. They soon learnt to find them, and to catch them without breaking their tails or hurting them in any way.

The Lizards may generally be found in summer-time, basking in the sun on the banks of our hedges or on our moors and heaths. The banks which face the south are the most frequented by these little creatures. They generally prefer a small bare spot among the herbage on which to lie. They then get as much heat as possible. It is by no means difficult to see them when one knows what to look for. Sometimes they may be heard rushing away through the grass towards their hole, and one is just able to catch a glimpse of a tail as it disappears. After waiting a minute or two, the animal will cautiously reappear, and continue its interrupted basking.

Lizards can be caught in several ways. For example, with the help of a hand-net, with a snare, and with the hand. The last is, I think, the best way: the first, perhaps the least satisfactory. The net may break the tail, if the Reptile has not already escaped between its edge and the ground through the intervention of some stick or stone. The snare, which is just simply a horse-hair noose fixed to the end of a long and slender stick, is very effective if the spot where the Lizard is lying be not too much surrounded with vegetation. To catch these most active little creatures with the hand one must be exceedingly quick and gentle. With a little practice this quickness and lightness of hand will come, and the Lizards may be picked up with comparative ease. A small, thin canvas bag is, I have found, the best receptacle for the captives, the mouth of which may be kept closed by means of a strong elastic band.

Strangely enough, well-frequented country roads are the best for a Lizard hunt, providing, of course, that the bank be suitable and exposed to the south or southward. The reason for this is, I imagine, that the Reptiles get more or less used to passers-by, and do not scurry off at the sound of footsteps, as they certainly do when looked for in the fields. It is wise to arrange that your shadow does not precede you, for if it should, your prey will be warned.

I do earnestly hope that the hints given here for the capture of these beautiful and useful little creatures will not lead to their being hunted by anybody just simply for what he may call sport. No one should catch them and place them in captivity unless it be with the intention of caring for them properly. I believe, for the reasons stated elsewhere, that when kindly and wisely treated in confinement, they are as happy as at liberty. On the other hand, I trust that these remarks of mine on the keeping of Reptiles in confinement will tend to the comfort of many rather than the reverse.

These animals are often treated very cruelly through ignorance. For example, some time ago I entered a very large birdshop in London and asked, "What Reptiles or Batrachians have you in stock?" "Nothing," was the reply, "but some Tree-frogs and Fire-bellied Toads." I was shown an oblong aquarium, the bottom of which was covered thickly with common red bird sand. On the sand and in it were many Frogs and Toads looking most miserable. "What do you feed the poor beasts on?" "Oh, nothing. They want nothing. These things live without eating." "Live without eating." I exclaimed, "does anything live without eating?" Only to hear the stupid and rather sullen reply, "Well, there's lots of insects in the sand which you can't see, and which is enough for them." I am glad that I persuaded the man to give them some fresh water and a few mealworms before I left.

Then again, one hears of people offering Fresh-water Tortoises vegetable food, and Land Tortoises animal food; of Salamanders kept constantly in water; of snakes exposed without any shelter to the hottest sun, and supplied with bread and milk as food; of a kind of "happy family," where Snakes, Frogs, Toads, Lizards, Newts, and Salamanders are expected to live peacefully and comfortably together.

The Common Lizard (*Lacerta vivipara*, Fig. 41), is a very pretty little Reptile, and readily adapts itself to confinement, and quickly becomes tame. It will eat small earth-worms, as well as flies, spiders, earwigs, smooth caterpillars, gentles and their pupæ, ants' eggs and ants, cockroaches, mealworms, and the like.

In feeding Reptiles and Batrachians on earthworms, care should be taken not to give the highly-coloured and strong-smelling worm known as the "Brandling," and chiefly found in manure-heaps, for to such animals this worm seems to act as a poison. I remember losing a fine young Axolotl through carelessly giving it such a worm. Dr. Stradling, in one of his interesting articles on Snakes, refers, if I remember rightly, to losses brought about by unconsciously providing young Snakes with this noxious Annelid as food.

The Common Lizard, as its specific name implies, is viviparous, *i.e.*, the egg on being deposited breaks, and the young one is free. The gravid female may often be seen during the months of June and July flattening herself as much as possible while basking in the sun, in order that, as Dr. Bell remarked, "The solar heat may be communicated to the embryo through the medium of the mother." A Lizard in this condition is lethargic, and may easily be caught. The young, from two to six, will then be produced in confinement. They come into the world perfectly formed (all Reptiles do), of a bronzy-black colour, and about an 1½in. long. They are very pretty, and may easily be reared. As soon as they are discovered, they should be removed (though I have never known their mother to eat them, her fellow Lizards might) to another and smaller vivarium, where they can be kept under observation and provided with as much sunshine as possible. At the same time, they must not be left without means of taking shelter from the sun. The water should be placed in a very shallow vessel, and their food may consist of tiny flies (which may be caught according to directions given in another place), ants' eggs or rather their pupæ, the young ants as soon as they leave their pupal envelope (they are then soft and tender), the little green-fly found on rose-leaves, those that congregate on the underside of the leaves of the sycamore-tree, and other flies of a similar kind. As the young Lizards grow, they will eat small cockroaches, tiny worms, gentles of small flies, mealworms of a suitable size, and other prey. These little Reptiles grow quickly and are very interesting. They may be kept in a warm case all the winter, or allowed to hibernate, if they are in good condition, in the usual way.

It has been said of *Lacerta vivipara* as of the Viper, and other viviparous Snakes—that it refuges its young. This is decidedly doubtful.

The Common and other Lizards seize their prey in rather a dog-like fashion, and lick their jaws after swallowing it.

The following, communicated to the *Zoologist* for June, 1889, by Mr. Boulenger (I believe), shows the vitality of the Common Lizard : "Mr. R. H. Ramsbotham, Waterside, Todmorden, has sent to the British Museum for examination a Viper and Lizard in spirits with the following remarks: 'The Adder was caught . . . . on April 24, 1889, about noon. It was kept in this bottle without spirit till the following morning, between nine and ten, when the bottle was filled. Immediately after this was done, the Lizard (which is still in the bottle, and has not been touched) crawled out of the snake's mouth, and was quite lively for a short time.' *Observations*: 1. Vipers sometimes swallow Lizards, though generally small Rodents. 2. That the Snake did not use its poison apparatus in seizing its prey. 3. That the Lizard lived for nearly twenty-four hours in the gullet of the Viper. The Lizard was an adult female (*Lacerta vivipara*)." I suppose that the general appearance of the Common Lizard is so well known that no description is necessary, beyond later on comparing it with the Wall Lizard (*Lacerta muralis*) for the sake of facilitating the identification of the latter.

According to Mr. Boulenger, the colours of this species are: "Brown, yellowish, or reddish above in the adult, with small darker and lighter spots; frequently a blackish vertebral streak and a dark lateral band edged with yellowish; lower surfaces orange or vermilion in the male, largely spotted with black; yellow or pale orange in the female, immaculate or scantily spotted with black. Newly-born young almost black, which colouration sometimes persists in the adult."

Common Lizards may be bought during the summer months in London and other large towns at from 4d. to 6d. each. These creatures quickly reproduce a lost tail, the reproduced part for a long time being of a colour similar to that of the Lizard when it was first born. *Lacerta vivipara* is found in England, Scotland, and even Ireland, and Northern and Central Europe and Northern Asia. The average length of the species is 6in.

The Wall Lizard (*Lacerta muralis*) is a very pretty and graceful Reptile, and exceedingly active. At first sight it seems much like the viviparous Lizard. There are, however, several important differences between the two species. The Wall Lizard has a longer head and tail than its near relative. The tail of the former, gradually tapering to a very fine point, is more elegant in shape, as that of the latter retains almost the same thickness for nearly the first half of its length. The Wall Lizard has a series of granules between the two scales immediately over each eye known as the supraocular and supraciliary scales; these granules are not found on the head of *L. vivipara*. The scales on the temple of the former Lizard are much smaller than those of the latter: and *L. muralis* has generally twice as many femoral pores as the Common Lizard, and is longer than its relative, sometimes reaching a length of 9in. There are a great many varieties of this Lizard. Mr. Boulenger describes the colours of the typical form in the following words: "Upper parts brown or greyish, variously spotted, marbled or streaked with black; lower surfaces white, yellow, pink, or red, uniform, or (in males) more or less largely spotted with black; outer ventrals frequently blue."

According to the same authority the variety *tiliguerta* has the "upper parts green or greenish, uniform, or spotted or marbled with black, or with blackish and whitish streaks along the back; usually a large black ocellus with blue centre above the axilla (armpit); lower surfaces usually immaculate."

The variety *filfolensis* is "black; back with round greenish spots; throat and sides of belly with blue spots." Found on the Filfola Rock, near Malta.

The variety *lilfordii* is "blackish-brown above, sapphire-blue inferiorly." In addition to the above varieties there are several more, but space will not admit of their description.

The Lizard has a very wide range, being found nearly all over Europe and Western Asia.

It may be bought in London from 4d. to 6d. In confinement it does very well, feeding readily upon garden worms. It should be treated in the same way as suggested for the Common and other Lizards. I have neither found this Reptile quarrelsome nor a cannibal.

The Taurian Lizard (*Lacerta taurica*) is more stoutly built than *L. muralis*, and the long, narrow scales of the back are much more keeled. According to Lord Clermont " the upper parts of the body are olive, parts beneath whitish, with a blue or green tinge; the inside of the limbs and the under part of the tail are reddish. In the male, on the sides of the neck and body are confluent black zigzag spots. In the females are two whitish or yellowish streaks on each side of the back, with a number of black specks between them; the lower eyelid is scaly." The tail is about half as long again as the head and body. This Lizard is said to be very common in the Crimea. It is also found in Turkey in Europe, the south of Greece, and in Sicily. The full length is about 9in.

The Sharp-headed Lizard (*Lacerta oxycephala*) differs from its near relative *L. muralis* chiefly by having a more depressed head and body, a much sharper snout and by the smaller size of the scales which form the collar, but like the Wall Lizard it has a series of granules between the supraocular and the supraciliary scales. The tail is about twice as long as the head and body. The back of the animal is greyish or tinged with red-brown, olive-green, or blue, covered with small black spots; a brown network enclosing light spots covers the neck and back; the under parts are a greenish-white. The network is hardly apparent in the young. This Lizard is found in Corsica and Dalmatia, among the rocks, never, it is said, on the plains. The entire length of the Reptile is about 7in.

The Smooth Lizard (*Lacerta lævis*) has a depressed head, longish snout, and the series of granules already spoken of. The ventral scales are very broad. The back is olive-grey, sometimes spotted with black. There is a band of black spots on the sides; there are also white spots on the sides; the lower parts are greenish-white. The entire length is a little over 9in. The Smooth Lizard is found in Syria and the Holy Land, where it is fairly common.

Gallot's Lizard (*Lacerta galloti*) is a most interesting and lively Reptile, and lives a long time in confinement. It is, however, rather quarrelsome. The snout is long, and the head is moderately depressed. The rostral shield does not enter the nostril, and there is a series of granules between the two shields immediately over the eye. The dorsal scales are very small, and the tail, upon which the scales are strongly keeled, is more than twice as long as the head and body. There are about twenty-five femoral pores. Mr. Boulenger, describing the colour of this Lizard, says that it is an " olive-grey or dark olive above, with black and pale greenish spots; females and young with two light, black-edged longitudinal streaks on each side. Lower surfaces olive or blackish in the adult, paler in the young; throat, in the young, with angular grey bands converging forwards. A more or less distinct black band and a few whitish spots on the hinder side of the thighs."

This Lizard's beauty, liveliness, hardiness, and willingness, as a rule, to feed on meat, make it a very suitable inmate of the Vivarium. When full-grown it is about a foot in length. It comes from Madeira and the Canary Islands.

The Black-spotted Lizard (*Algiroides nigropunctatus*). The Lizards of this genus have their dorsal scales much larger and more strongly keeled than those of the former genus. This Lizard, also known as *Lacerta nigropunctata*, Dum. and Bibr., is about 8in. long, and has, for its size, a large and depressed head. The rostral scale touches the nostril. The collar, which is well-marked, has a serrated edge. The scales of the back are very large, strongly keeled, and imbricate. The hind leg is about as long as the body, and the tail is about twice as long as the head and body. The upper part of the body is olive-green, generally spotted with black (hence the specific name): the lower surfaces are a greenish or bluish-white. This Lizard is a native of the Ionian Islands.

The Spanish Sand Lizard (*Psammodromus hispanicus*) is very common in Spain, and is about 6in. in length. The scales on the back are very large, strongly keeled, and tiled; the scales on the tail are also strongly keeled and tiled and arranged in rings. The tail is cylindrical and nearly twice as long as the head and body. The collar is only feebly marked; but in other species of this genus it is not seen at all. The upper parts are a reddish-grey, spotted with black and white. On each side there are two or three parallel streaks of yellowish-white; the lower surfaces are white. This Reptile is also found in the south of France and Portugal.

I cannot give the usual market prices of the last few Lizards which have been described. Their value in England, of course, depends upon the numbers imported. They may be treated in confinement as already suggested: and any of the *Lacerta* and their near relatives which have not been mentioned for want of space shall be cared for in the same way.

Lord Derby's or the Derbian Lizard (*Zonurus derbianus*, Gray; *Z. giganteus* Boulenger). — To an observer who is not versed in reptilian matters this strange-looking creature has a little resemblance to the well-known Horned Lizard (*Phrynosoma cornutum*), often called the "Californian Toad." The arrangement of its scales is ring-like, or belt-like, hence the generic name. This Reptile occasionally reaches a length of 15in. It, and the other members of its family, have a short and hairy tongue, slightly nicked at the tip and hardly protractile. The teeth are pleurodont and very small; there are none on the palate. The head-shields of *Z. derbianus* are very rough; the dorsal scales are large and strongly keeled, ending in a sharp point. The scales of the body are arranged in about twenty-four belts. The ventral scales are also large and tiled, and those of the neck, sides, and tail end in conical spines. The limbs possess large, tiled, keeled scales ending in a spines. Of this Lizard Mr. Boulenger says that the "upper and lateral caudal scales are very large, strongly spinose, the lateral spines largest and horizontal; lower caudal scales long, narrow, pentagonal, smooth. Yellowish, back clouded with brown; upper surface of head brown. The young light yellowish, marbled and cross-barred with blackish-brown; the spines not at all developed, and all the scales more strongly imbricate." The animal is a native of South Africa.

This Lizard should be kept in a large case according to the size of the animal. In winter and during early spring and late autumn, it must be supplied with artificial heat, the temperature varying between 70deg. and 85deg. Fahr. The food may consist of cockroaches, mealworms, tiny frogs, small mice, and raw meat. The price of this Reptile, according to supply, ranges from 7s. 6d. to £2.

The Rough-scaled Zonure (*Zonurus cordylus*).—This Lizard differs from the last in having almost smooth head-shields. This, however, by no means is the only difference between the two Reptiles. The scales of the back are large, arranged in belts, tiled, and narrowing to a point, often serrated. Those on the sides are more strongly keeled still, and there is a lateral fold. The ventral scales are smooth, broad, quadrangular, and slightly tiled. The limbs have large, keeled, spinose, and tiled sides. The tail has "whorls of large, strongly-keeled, spinose, serrated scales, the spines strongest on the sides." The upper parts of the body are a dark-brown, the lower, a greenish-white. The entire length of the animal is about 7in. It may be treated in the same way as suggested for the Derbian Zonure. It also is a native of South Africa.

According to Mr. Boulenger, the important family of *Anguidæ* contains seven genera, which, for the most part differ in outward appearance very much from each other. Some have well-developed limbs, some have limbs scarcely visible and useless, and others have no external limbs at all. But every member of the family has a tongue, which may be described as being formed of two parts, the posterior and larger part is thick and covered with hair-like eminences, called *papillæ*; the anterior portion is thinner, extensible, slightly forked, and covered with scale-like tiled *papillæ*—and a body which is protected by a kind of bony and imbricate plates, situated beneath the scales. There are also other points of resemblance or "family likenesses," which are of a more covert character.

The Glass Snake (*Pseudopus pallasii*, Gray, or — and which seems a more appropriate title, but not so common a one—*Ophisaurus apus*, Boulenger, Fig. 42, p. 109) is a very popular and an interesting inmate of a Vivarium. It is also intelligent for a Reptile, exceedingly hardy, living usually a great number of years in confinement; one was in the Zoological Gardens, London, I believe, for more than twenty years.

It is well called the Glass Snake, for when it is quite still its smooth shiny appearance makes it look as if it had been moulded out of coloured glass, and its brittleness also entitles it to the same epithet; while its snake-like form often causes it to be mistaken by the unknowing in ophidian matters for a snake. However, anyone who at all understood these things, though quite unfamiliar with this particular Lizard, could tell almost at a glance that it was not a snake. He would see that the animal possessed eyelids which do not belong to any of the Serpent order. He would also notice that when the Scheltopusik (Russian), as it is called sometimes, put out its tongue, it had to open its mouth in order to do so; while a snake, because of a nick provided for the purpose, can extend that member without separating the jaws. Then again, the Glass Snake has decidedly a Lizard-like head; besides this, if the observer watched the creature's manner of locomotion, he would immediately see that it did not move with the grace and pliancy of a snake, and that it could not shape its body into so many curves.

If a Glass Snake and a true Snake were dissected, further differences would be manifest between them. For example, the former would be found to have fixed jaws, certain ribs fastened to to a sternum or breast-bone, and what may be called hips and shoulder-bones; whereas, the latter would be proved to possess loose jaws, *i.e.*, jaws capable of separation or dislocation at will, so to speak, and no sternum, or hips, or shoulder-bones. For this and other reasons the serpent can swallow, without danger to itself, prey of a diameter considerably greater than that of its body, which the Lizard cannot do. Finally, the Glass Snake has the rudiments of hind-legs, one of which may be seen situated in and near the extremity of each lateral fold or deep furrow which runs along the side.

The Glass Snake, with gentle treatment soon becomes tame, and quickly learns to distinguish its fosterer from all other people. It can easily be bought, as a rule, in this country, at sums ranging from 4s. to 7s. 6d. I have purchased very fine specimens at both the prices mentioned.

It may be kept in the same Vivarium with snakes, but bigger than itself; for it might mistake a small snake for a large worm,

FIG. 42.—THE GLASS SNAKE (*Pseudopus pallasii*).

upon which it is generally quite ready to feed. It will eat, while in confinement, worms, dead or live mice, snails, slugs, dead or live frogs, raw meat, and, occasionally, hard-boiled eggs. The readiness to take dead food adds much to its suitability as a Vivarium inmate.

The Glass Snake, when first obtained, either by capture or by purchase, is likely to be wild and shy, and should therefore be handled with great care, or in its struggles to get free it is likely to injure itself. After a time it will generally submit to being caught without showing any nervousness, not even hissing. It does not often, even when wild, attempt to bite. The Glass Snake should be kept in a heated Vivarium during winter; or, if it be in good condition it may be allowed to hibernate according to the directions already given.

As Fig. 42 represents this Reptile so faithfully, no detailed description is necessary. The tail is sometimes twice as long as the head and body; the males have the longer tails. Occasionally this creature attains a length of about 4ft. I think both my specimens are more than 36in. long, and quite perfect, not even the tip of a tail broken off.

The colour of the Glass Snake is a reddish-chestnut or dark brown on the back, and a lighter brown underneath. The young are olive-grey, with transverse dark brown bands on the upper surface of the body, brown streaks on the head and neck, and a greyish white below.

The Scheltopusik has somewhat the appearance of a gigantic slow-worm (*Anguis fragilis*). It is found in South-Eastern Europe, South-Western Asia, and North Africa. Many of those which are imported into this country come, I believe, from Dalmatia and Greece. It is very common in the uncultivated parts of the Holy Land.

The American Glass Snake (*Ophisaurus ventralis*) is of much slenderer build than that last described (Fig. 42). It is very common in some parts of North America, and is frequently dug up with the potato. As it is a burrowing animal, it should be provided, in its case, with plenty of fine sand or mould. Its food may consist of earthworms, slugs, snails and insects.

Unfortunately, this interesting Lizard is not often brought into this country. It differs from the Old World Glass Snake, among other things, in possessing no external rudiments of limbs. It is green above marked with yellow and black; the lower parts are yellow. It is about 30in. in length; the tail being nearly twice as long as the head and body.

The Slow-worm (*Anguis fragilis*, Fig. 43). An intelligent village carpenter was one day repairing the greenhouse in which I keep many Reptiles, and seeing them, told me that a small boy in the neighbourhood had lately been bitten by a viper. "But he did not die," I remarked. "No," said the man, "he didn't. It's lucky he wasn't stung by one of those Slow-worms. They are far worse, I have heard tell, than any viper." This man had lived in the country all his life, with the exception of a year or two spent in London to "improve himself," and yet he was able, in all good faith, to speak so unjustly of so harmless and gentle a Reptile as the Slow-worm. He, however, entertained no uncommon ideas in regard to this useful little Lizard.

Most of the country people who live where these creatures abound in the hedges and on the moors believe them to be capable of much injury. They hardly ever miss an opportunity of killing one, imagining that by their deed they have conferred a benefit upon the community. I am sure many a farmer or labourer would rather risk handling a viper than a Slow-worm. A young friend of mine, who is fond of Reptiles, told me, lately, that she was allowed to keep her Snake in the house, but not her Slow-worm lest it should escape. One is at a loss to understand how this general fear of such an innocuous animal as the Slow worm could have arisen. It should be considered as a useful friend rather than as a vindictive foe. It has not the power to hurt anyone, even if it had the will. When it does, under the influence of fear or in self-defence attempt to bite, its little fang-like teeth are not able to pierce the skin of the hand. However, it very rarely tries to bite. I have kept, from time to time, a great many of these interesting creatures, and have frequently handled them, taking up sometimes half-a-dozen or more at once, when they have formed themselves into a tangled mass under some piece of bark in the fernery, but have never seen them venture to use their teeth, not even when I have caught them in the hedges. I have read of Slow-worms snapping savagely at the fingers, so I suppose the *Anguis fragilis* will occasionally defend itself by biting.

A great many people still look upon the Slow-worm as a kind of Snake. Only lately I noticed, while reading two popular modern writers on natural history, that they both classed the Slow-worm as a Snake. However, it is a Lizard without any doubt, for it answers in many respects to the description already given of the Glass Snake (*P. pallasii*, Fig. 42); but unlike the latter it has no external rudiments of limbs.

The Slow-worm has received its generic title from its outward resemblance to a Snake, and it owes its specific name to its extreme brittleness. Like most Lizards its tail is very readily severed from the body. It is a useful animal, for it lives chiefly upon slugs, not confining itself, as has been said, to one particular white kind. I asked a gardener one day, who was complaining to me of these molluscs, why he killed the Slow-worms. "Oh! them's nasty things," he exclaimed; "and I always kills them whenever I gets the chance." A prejudice is far harder to kill than any amount of Reptiles. Slow-worms, like the common Lizards, are much more numerous than is generally supposed. They are not easily seen at the bottom of the hedges and among the moss of the banks, and they do not, like *L. vivipara*, rush off on the slightest alarm, but remain instead, quite motionless, and therefore, are passed by unnoticed and unheard.

The Slow-worms make regular runs, or burrows, in the thick moss which often covers our country banks, and their basking-places may be easily recognised by those who know what to look for, as the soft vegetation retains for a considerable time the impression of their body. When such a "sunning spot" is found, its position may be marked in some way or other, and probably the little animal will be seen there when next the sun is shining brightly.

The creature is easily mistaken by a casual observer for a piece of polished stick or a portion of an exposed and smooth small root of a tree. When discovered, the Slow-worm can be picked up with ease. But as this Reptile is so brittle it requires careful handling when it is first caught, for, when frightened, it stiffens itself so that in its rigidity it may be fairly likened to a piece of wire, and if, in that state, it is roughly treated, it is almost certain to "break in halves." It will sometimes be noticed that when a Slow-worm is first captured, it has already lost a portion of its tail. Occasionally a sudden fright is sufficient to make this Lizard part with its tail, and while he who was the origin of the fear is looking at the wriggling discarded member, the Reptile escapes. I have seen fowls and pheasants attack it, and no doubt the birds often content themselves with the tail, while the body hurries off into a place of safety. The lost tail is reproduced very slowly.

Many illustrations of Slow-worms which one sees are apparently taken from specimens which have formerly lost the extremity of their tail, and have commenced the work of reproduction. The uninjured tail tapers off gradually until the latter portion of it is far slenderer than any other part of the animal's body. Fig. 43 represents a perfect Slow-worm. A very fine specimen of a male Slow-worm which I have owned for a long time has a beautiful tapering tail, 10in. long, while the body of the animal is 8in. in length.

The Slow-worm like the Snake is almost helpless when placed upon a smooth surface, such as a piece of glass or polished marble. The former is a very clever climber, considering that he is a legless Lizard. It can get, without difficulty, out of an uncovered box which is only 1in. or 2in. less deep than the creature's total length.

The Slow-worm has made itself famous by being the first to reveal to science the mysterious pineal, or median, eye, which has already been referred to in the description of the *Tuatera*. Sir John Lubbock, in his "The Senses of Animals," says "De Graaf has the merit of discovering that in the Slow-worm the pineal gland is actually modified into a structure resembling an invertebrate eye."

The Slow-worm soon becomes exceedingly tame, and will live, if properly treated, for a great number of years in confinement. For example, a writer in "Science Gossip" for April, 1878, page 94, speaking of the longevity of this Reptile, says: "A very fine specimen was captured by me, near Beacontree Heath, in the

year 1850, and was killed by an unfortunate mischance a few days ago. It had consequently been in my possession twenty-eight years; it was several years old when caught, and was in sound health up to the time of the misadventure which caused its death."

Slow-worms will live very well in a fernery such as that illustrated at Fig. 9, p. 18, or in some case in which there has been placed a rather deep layer of mould or sand, for these animals are fond of burrowing; and they may frequently be seen with only their head just above the surface of the earth. These Reptiles should always be provided with shelter of some kind, such as pieces of cork, or oak bark; a box filled with moss, having a side perforated with a few round holes of sufficient size for the Reptiles to pass through; or a board with similar holes may fence off a corner or end of the case in which the animals are confined, and in this fenced-off portion some moss should be placed.

As the Slow-worm is a Lizard, it delights in sunshine. It is not kind to keep this Reptile in the same Vivarium with snakes. The Lizard-eating Snakes would probably eat it, and the presence of Snakes of other kinds would certainly not tend to the little animal's comfort. Besides, a case properly arranged for Slow-worms or other Lizards would be unsuitable for Snakes, with only a few exceptions. The Blind-worm will eat small slugs, garden-worms, and insects. It will not touch dead food. It seizes and devours its prey in rather a dog-like fashion, showing considerable intelligence in manipulating it, if such a word may be used in this sense. It should never be left without water, as for a Reptile, it drinks very frequently.

The Slow-worm is ovoviviparous, and its young, from five to twelve, are often produced in confinement. The latter are reared without much difficulty. They are very pretty little things when they first come into the world, being of a silvery light cream colour on the upper parts with a black spot on the head and a thin black line running down the centre of the back; below they are black or nearly so. In length, at first, they are about 3in. The young should be placed in a separate case, and provided with sand and moss, and water in a very shallow vessel. Their food ought to consist of tiny garden-worms, and slugs. I find it a good plan to place a quantity of slugs' eggs with some mould and green food in a large covered bottle, and then a supply of small slugs will always be at hand. Slugs' eggs may be roughly compared to boiled sago. Small slugs can also be obtained by placing pieces of board about the garden, and when wanted the molluscs will be found clinging to the underside. Greased cabbage leaves have also a great attraction for slugs.

The Slow-worm seems to be able to bear more cold than most of our British Reptiles. It is sometimes tempted, when at liberty, to leave its winter quarters on any unusually fine warm day in winter or early spring. In autumn it buries itself deeply in soft ground, or under some heap of leaves and rubbish, or in some suitable hole in a bank. While in confinement it may be allowed to hibernate, if in good condition, according to directions already given; or it may be kept in an unheated case in some room in which there is a fire daily, or in a greenhouse. Under these latter circumstances, however, it must be provided with plenty of mould in which to bury itself when it desires so to do. The Slow-worm casts its skin periodically, sometimes leaving it entire, but more frequently in two or more pieces.

The general appearance of this animal is so well known that no detailed description is necessary. The scales are very smooth and small. The eyes are also small, very bright, and provided with eyelids; the fact of its having eyelids has no doubt given this Lizard the name of Blind-worm. For when it is discovered in a state of torpor, the eyelids will be closed, and to the uninformed in these matters the creature would, under such circumstances, appear blind; especially would this be the case if found in the company of hybernating snakes, with their unclosable eyes. The ears of the Slow-worm, as a rule, are not exposed; the tongue is broad, notched, and fairly extensile. The male has a tail longer in proportion to its body than the female. Sometimes this animal reaches a length of 18in., but this is unusual. I think I shall not be far wrong if I say that the average length is about 13in.

The general colour of *A. fragilis* on the upper surface is a brownish-grey having a silvery sheen, and longitudinal lines of black spots, or zigzag unbroken black lines or fairly straight black lines. These markings, however, vary considerably. The underparts are black, marked with white.

The Slow-worm may be bought for sums varying from 6d. to 2s., according to the size and condition of the animal and the season of the year. It is found in England, Scotland, and in almost every part of the Continent, as well as in Western Asia.

The Skink Lizards (*Scincidæ*) have a moderately long tongue, slightly notched, extensile, and covered with scale-like papillæ; their teeth are pleurodont. Their body is covered with rounded imbricate scales arranged in fives, and beneath the scales there is a kind of armour formed of bony plates. Some of the Skinks possess limbs, others are without them. The eyes of all have round pupils and well-developed eye-lids. Their head is covered with symmetrical shields. No Skink has femoral pores, and all are supposed to be ovoviviparous. The family has a very wide distribution, representatives being found in almost every part of the world. None of its members, as a rule, climb trees nor enter water, but prefer dry, sandy, and stony localities. There are about 25 genera and nearly 400 species of Skinks.

The Stump-tailed Lizard (*Trachysaurus rugosus*), also known as the Two-headed Lizard and the Sleeping Lizard, comes from Australia, and lives fairly well in confinement. It is a curious-looking Reptile with its stump-like tail, long stout body, and short weak legs. When asleep, the strangely-shaped caudal member is sometimes mistaken by the unobservant for a second head; hence one of the popular names. The upper part of the tail and body, and of the head in a less degree, is covered with broad, large, rough or wrinkled scales (as the specific name implies), having somewhat the appearance of a pine-cone. The scales on the lower surfaces are smaller and smooth. The back is of a brown colour, marked with yellowish spots or bands; the lower parts are yellowish, spotted or streaked with brown.

The stump-tailed Lizard is very common in Western Australia, and is found on sandy and stony plains. In this country it is rather expensive to buy, costing generally about 30s. It ought to be kept in a heated Vivarium, the bottom of which should be covered with sand or gravel; and for food it will eat snails, slugs, fruit, and raw meat. The water may be placed in a small vessel. This Reptile is ovoviviparous, and produces three or four at one time. The entire length of the creature is about 13in.

The Great Cyclodus (*Cyclodus gigas*, Gray, or *Tiliqua scincoides*, Boulenger) is a large handsome Skink, and one which lives very well in confinement. It also comes from Australia, a country particularly rich in this kind of Lizard. It has often bred in captivity, and several times at the Zoological Gardens, London. The young, which are produced fully formed, may be reared upon minced raw meat.

Fig. 44 will give anyone who has never seen the animal a very good idea of its shape. It is one of the largest of the Skinks, being, when full grown, about 20in. in length. The Reptile's legs are short and strong, the toes on each foot are five in number, and are short and thick. Its ear-opening is very distinct, being about as large as the eye, and its anterior edge, to a certain extent, is serrated. Its tail is cylindrical, and a little shorter than the body, which is covered with smooth scales. The upper parts of this animal are of a yellowish-brown colour marked with cross-bands of a darker brown; the under parts are yellowish, sometimes spotted with brown. This hardy and very interesting Skink can generally be bought, when in the market, for about 30s. Except during summer, the Great Cyclodus should be kept in a heated case, and its food ought to consist of snails, slugs, sometimes fruit, and raw meat.

There are other Skinks of this genus which may occasionally be met with in this country, and which will live fairly well in captivity, *e.g.*, the black-and-yellow Cyclodus (*C. nigroluteus*, Gray, or *T. nigrolutea*, Boulenger). This Lizard differs from its larger relative, among other things, in having an ear-opening smaller than its eye, a tail shorter in proportion to the length of its body, and in its colouring, for, as its specific name implies, it is of a black-brown spotted or banded with yellow or dark brown. Its entire length is 14½in. It may be treated in the same way as has been suggested for the Great Cyclodus.

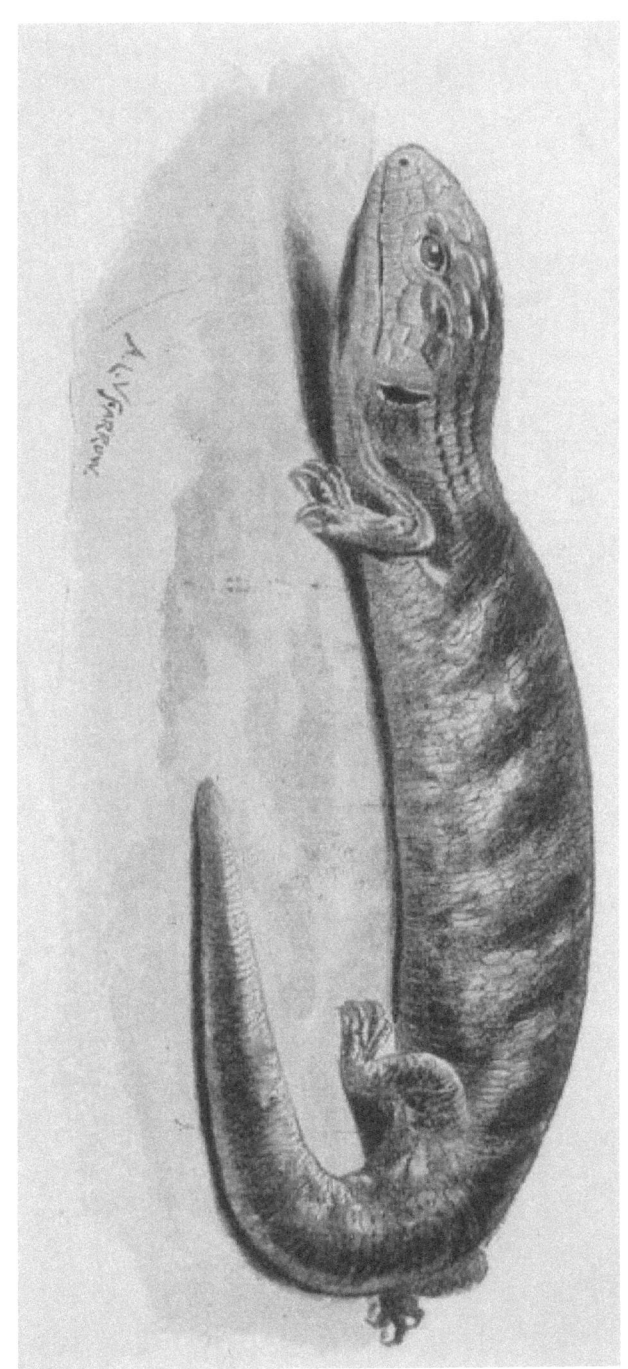

FIG. 44.—THE GREAT CYCLODUS (*Cyclodus gigas*).

Aldrovandi's Skink (*Plestiodon auratus*, Gray, or *Eumeces schneideri*, Boulenger), (Fig. 45, p. 125) is a very handsome Skink, and one that is, as a rule, easily procured in this country. It has been described as not being very hardy; however, personally I have found it to be anything but delicate while in confinement. If properly treated, it feeds very well, and soon becomes tame. It will eat cockroaches, meal-worms, snails, slugs, pieces of raw meat, but it prefers snails, I think, to any other food. It shows not a little skill and power of jaw in breaking the tough shell of some old mollusc. The Skink's method of devouring prey of this kind may be thus briefly described: First of all, by the help of its teeth, it breaks the shell in several places, in fact, all over, and then it seizes the body of the snail, and by vigorously shaking it frees it of every bit of shell. When this has been done, it begins, apparently with great deliberation, to swallow the tempting (to it) morsel.

Aldrovandi's Skink should be kept during the colder months of the year in a heated Vivarium, and allowed to have as much sunshine as possible. It is of a gentle disposition, and may be allowed to occupy the same case as smaller Lizards. This, however, cannot be said of many of the Skinks. Its body on the upper surface is brown and spotted, or striped with red or golden-orange (see specific name): the lower parts are of a yellowish-white. This Reptile may be frequently bought for sums ranging from 4s. to 7s. 6d. It is a native of the Holy Land, Egypt, Syria, and Persia.

The Common Skink (*Scincus officinalis*) is to a certain extent quite an historical character, having been mentioned as an important and useful animal by several of the writers of antiquity. For example, Pliny declares that if portions of its body, such as the scales of its nose and feet, are ground to powder and mixed with wine it will form a drink of great value as a tonic. Another speaks of parts of this Skink being used as an antidote against poisoned wounds. And many a physician among the ancient Greeks and Romans prescribed powders made from its dried body as a kind of universal remedy. As late as the fifteenth and sixteenth centuries this little creature was eagerly sought for by the chemist and apothecary. Since then it has been proved to possess no useful medicinal properties whatever.

The Common Skink is a curious-looking animal about, when full grown, 8in. long. It seems to have no neck, and its head is wedge-shape. Its tail, which is very thick at the base, is short in proportion to the body, conical, and pointed. The small ear-openings are placed near the corners of the mouth and are toothed in front; the digits, or toes, are also toothed laterally. The scales of the animal's body are quite smooth, and the rostral scale is very large. The limbs are short, and the body is long. The colour of the upper parts is yellowish-brown, sometimes silvery-grey, marked, as a rule, with darker cross-bands; the under-surfaces are whitish. This animal comes from the western and northern parts of Africa. In a wild state it lives on sandy plains, burrowing quickly into the sand on the approach of danger. It is very active, considering its build.

The Vivarium in which this and most other Skinks are confined should be provided with rather a deep layer of dry mould or fine sand. They need not be supplied with anything else for a shelter, as they will bury themselves quite out of sight in the sand or mould whenever they desire to hide. On bright sunny days they come from their places of retirement and bask upon the surface of that which covers the bottom of their case.

As the Skinks do not bathe, the water need only be supplied in a very small and shallow vessel. The Common Skink will eat, while in confinement, mealworms, cockroaches, gentles, and flies. Some individuals may be persuaded to partake of pieces of raw meat.

The price of this Reptile varies from 2s. 6d. to 10s., according to supply and demand. It should be kept during winter in a heated Vivarium.

The Ocellated Sand-Skink (*Gongylus ocellatus*, Gray, or *Chalcides ocellatus*, Boulenger, Fig. 46, p. 127), is a very handsome Reptile, whose scales are smooth and glossy, and whose colouration, though various, is in all cases pleasing. Its upper parts are tawny, brown, or olive, with a bronzed appearance, and marked with black spots, which sometimes run into each other, and which have an oblong white mark in their centre; hence the specific name. The markings, however, vary, not only in arrangement, but also in the proportions

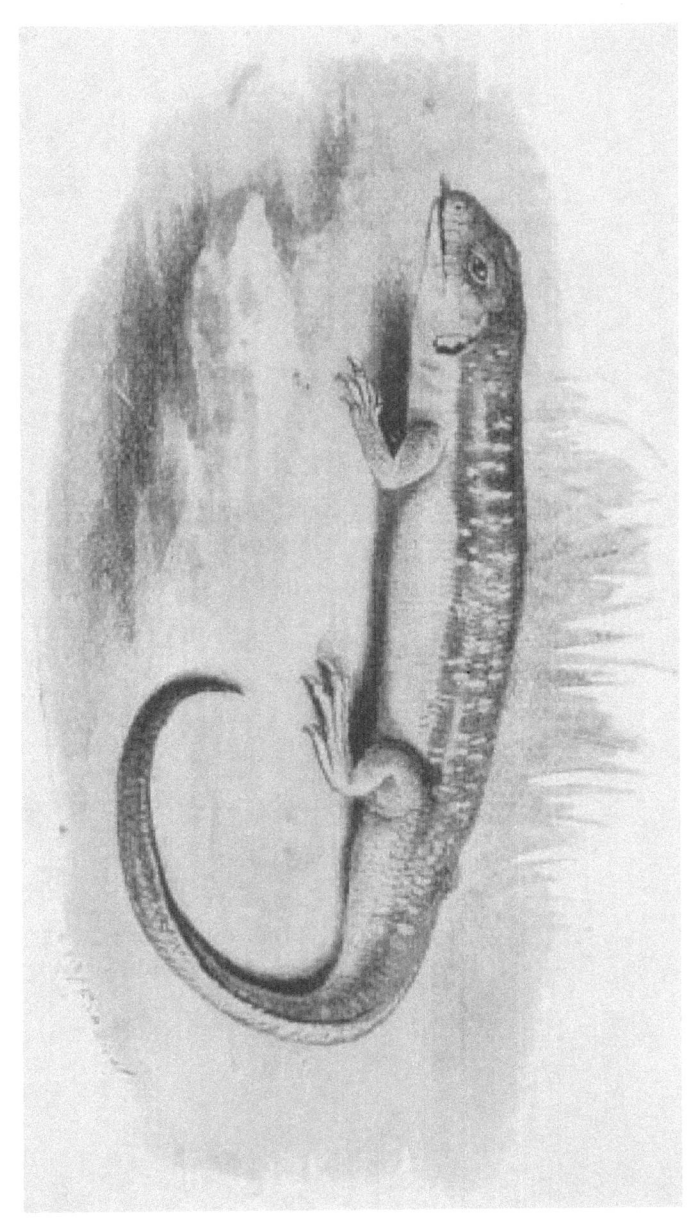

FIG. 45.—ALDROVANDI'S SKINK (*Plestiodon auratus*).

which the black and white bear to one another. Occasionally the spots are absent. The lower parts of the creature's body are of a yellowish-white.

This beautiful Skink lives very well in confinement, and is not difficult to procure in this country, costing, generally, about 7s. 6d. Except when the sun is shining, it lives under the sand with which the bottom of the Vivarium is covered. It will eat small snails, beetles, cockroaches, mealworms, and flies; and as

FIG. 46.—OCELLATED SAND-SKINK (*Gongylus ocellatus*).

it has more than a predisposition to cannibalism it must not be kept with other Reptiles smaller than itself. I have seen one of these Skinks swallow without much difficulty a full-grown Viviparous Lizard (*L. vivipara*). The total length of this animal is about 10in. It comes from Sicily, Sardinia, Malta, Greece, Cyprus, Palestine, Syria, Persia, Arabia, and Abyssinia.

The Greenish Sand-Skink (*Seps viridanus*, Gravenh., or *Chalcides viridanus*, Boulenger), which is closely related to the

Sand-Skink just described, is also a very handsome Lizard, and one which lives well and for long in captivity. Its habits are very like those of its near relative. It soon makes a home for itself in some particular part of the case in which it is confined, e.g., under a piece of cork-bark or beneath a stone, and should a fly, beetle, or cockroach stray near its den, the little creature, apparently generally alert, darts out, seizes its prey, and immediately withdraws into retirement to devour it. This conduct is characteristic of many Lizards, but it is very noticeable in this little Skink and the one next to be described.

S. Viridanus can sometimes be bought fairly cheaply in this country. I was once fortunate in procuring a perfect specimen for 3s. The colour of this Lizard on the upper parts is olive-green, marked with light black-edged spots. The sides of the head and body, the limbs, and lower parts are of a darker colour generally, sometimes almost quite black. The tail is about as long as the head and body. The four limbs are short, but strong, and are each furnished with five toes. The entire length of the little animal is about $5\frac{1}{2}$in. It comes from Madeira and the Canary Isles. I have one which came as a stowaway in a box of fruit from Teneriffe.

The Three-toed Sand-Skink (*Seps tridactylus*, Gray, or, *Chalcides tridactylus*, Boulenger), is a curious-looking and interesting animal (Fig. 47), not counting its short and almost, if not quite, useless legs, is somewhat like in its general shape to the Common Slow-worm (*Anguis fragilis*). The limbs of the Three-toed Skink, though they vary not a little in different specimens, are insignificant. But notwithstanding their weakness, the Reptile is by no means slow and inactive. I have had one which climbed up a small orange-tree, and escaped through a feeding-hole (see Fig. 12, p. 20) in the roof of its case.

We see in this Skink an animal very closely approaching the snake-like form, and yet possessing legs and toes. It lives well in confinement, and is not difficult to procure in this country, costing generally about 7s. Its food should consist of cockroaches, beetles, mealworms, gentles, flies, and other insects.

The Three-toed Skink comes from the South of France, Italy, Algeria, Morocco, and all the islands of the Mediterranean.

The colour of its upper parts is olive or bronzed-grey, frequently marked with darker and lighter longitudinal streaks. Lord Clermont says that some specimens exhibit as many as "sixteen or eighteen streaks on the back alternately black and dull white." Sometimes these streaks are very indistinct. The lower parts are whitish. The entire length of the full-grown animal is about 13in.

The Bipes (*Scelotes bipes*) is also a very curious and interesting Skink, and one which is occasionally brought into this country. It comes from South Africa. As its specific name implies, it has only two legs—the hind ones. On each leg there are two unequal-clawed toes. The scales are smooth; the body is cylindrical and elongate. The conical and pointed tail is shorter than the body; the eyes, which possess eyelids, the lower ones being transparent, and the ear-openings are very small indeed. The upper parts of this Skink's body are of a silvery-brown colour, each scale growing darker towards the centre. There is a longitudinal streak of dark brown on each side of the body, apparently passing through the eye. There are also, occasionally, several other longitudinal lines on the back which are more or less distinct. The lower parts of the body are whitish. The Bipes is about 6in. long, and should be treated in confinement as the other Skinks just described.

The Spotted Slow-worm (*Acontias meleagris*).—The general shape of this Lizard is not unlike that of the Common Slow-worm (*Anguis fragilis*), hence its English name. Its rostral and mental scales are unusually large; and its head is conical. The eyes are very small, the upper eyelids are wanting, and the lower ones are transparent. There are no visible limbs or ear-openings, and the cylindrical tail is very short, not a quarter so long as the body, and rounded at the end. The upper parts are coloured a pale or greenish-brown, and the dark spot in the centre of each dorsal scale helps to form a series of longitudinal dark streaks. The lower parts are yellowish-white. This Lizard should be treated in captivity in the same way as has been recommended for the Bipes.

Though several of the Skinks are very like in their outward appearance to some of the snakes, not one of them can be fairly said to be a connecting link between their order and that of the serpents.

The Agamidæ family is a very large one, containing some thirty genera and 202 species, and numbers among its members several very interesting and extraordinary Lizards. Some of them are arboreal in their habits; and others terrestrial. Most of them are carnivorous, and a few are herbivorous, but all, with the exception of the members of one genus, are oviparous.

The *Agamidæ* are closely related to the *Iguanidæ*, another large and important family. The former are confined to the Old World and Australia, while the latter, with an exception or two, are natives of the New. Unfortunately, only a comparative few of these Lizards are suitable, as a rule, for confinement in this country, as the greater portion of them come from the tropics and their neighbourhood.

The famous flying Lizards, called the Dragons, belong to the *Agamidæ*. Of these extraordinary Reptiles, Cantor says, who is quoted by Dr. Günther in the "Reptiles of British India," that "the transcendent beauty of their colours baffles description. As the Lizard lies in the shade along the trunk of a tree, its colours, at a distance, appear like a mixture of brown and grey, and render it scarcely distinguishable from the bark. Thus it remains, with no signs of life except its restless eyes, watching passing insects, which, suddenly expanding its wings, it seizes with a sometimes considerable unerring leap." The wings are more correctly described as parachutes, and are formed, according to Dr. Günther, "by the much-prolonged five or six hind ribs; these are connected by a broad, expansible fold of the skin, the whole forming a sub-semicircular wing on each side of the body. The Dragons are Tree Lizards, and jumping from branch to branch, they are supported in the air by their expanded parachutes, which are laid backwards at the sides of the animal while it is sitting or merely running." The tail is very long and slender, and does not easily break. I have never owned a live Dragon, nor have I ever seen one in confinement; but I do not know any reason why they should not do well in captivity if kept in a large, heated Vivarium, in which were placed some suitable branches or small trees.

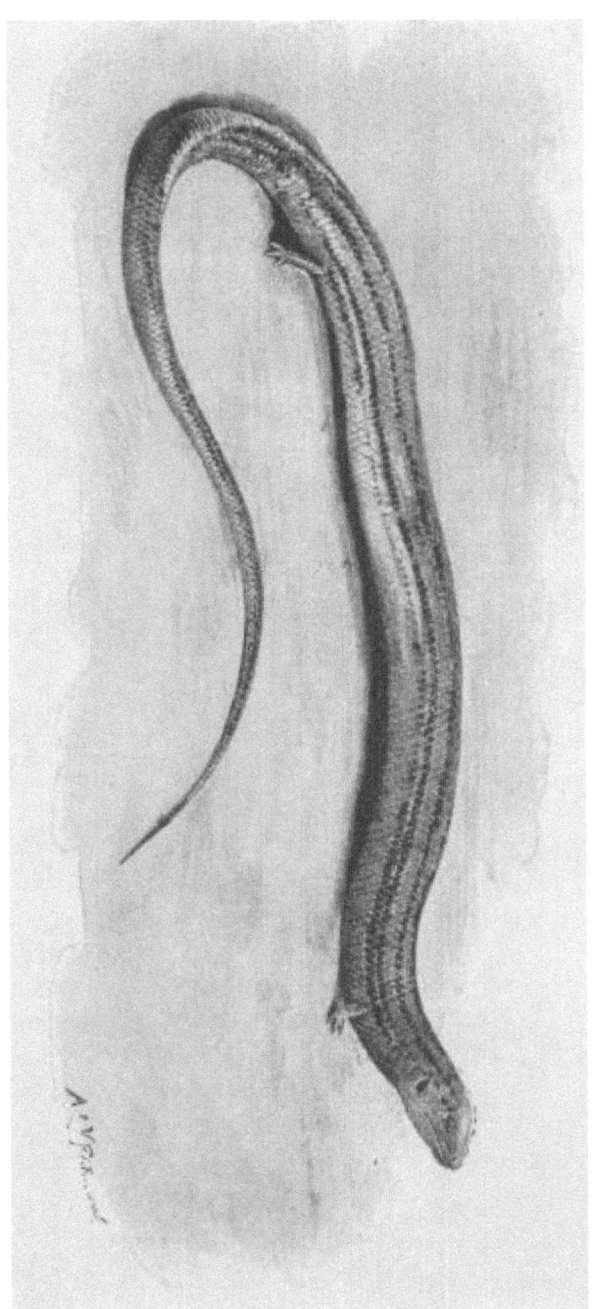

FIG. 47.—THE THREE-TOED SKINK (*Scelotes tridactylus*).

Both sexes have three dewlaps, one in the middle of the throat, and one on each side. The males possess the larger gular appendages, the centre dewlap sometimes being twice the length of the head in depth. These ornamental wattle-like possessions can be erected at will. The Dragons, which are confined to the East Indies, never attain a greater length than 7in. or 8in., of which the tail forms one-half at least.

The Frilled Lizard (*Chlamydosaurus kingi*) is another very extraordinary Reptile belonging to this family. It is a native of Queensland, and attains a length of about 2ft. It possesses round its neck a fold of skin which, when erected, reminds one of the huge lace collars formerly worn by the fashionable in Queen Elizabeth's reign. It spreads about 5in., somewhat in shape of an open umbrella. The edges of this frill are serrated. The animal has rather large and prominent eyes and a long tail, and is said to squat and jump in kangaroo fashion, "thus," as Dr. Günther says, "reminding us of the peculiar locomotion ascribed to certain gigantic extinct Reptiles." Some living specimens of this interesting Lizard were lately in the Reptile House of the Zoological Gardens, Regent's Park, London.

The *Agamidæ* are chiefly distinguished from the *Iguanidæ* by having acrodont teeth. Those *Agamidæ* which live generally in trees possess compressed bodies, while those which confine themselves for the most part to the ground, have depressed bodies. The former own the longer tail; the tails do not easily break. The head is covered with small flat or convex shields; and the thick tongue is more or less fixed to the bottom of the mouth, and is not nicked in front, or only feebly so. The eyes, which possess eyelids, have round pupils; and the limbs are well developed. Like the *Iguanidæ*, many of the *Agamidæ* are provided with crests and gular appendages.

The following are some of the *Agamidæ* which can be kept in confinement in this country.

The Knob-nosed Lizard (*Lyriocephalus scutatus*) has, as its name implies, a curious lump on the nose. Its head is lyre-shaped or lyrate (hence generic name), and its throat sac is fairly developed. There is a small toothed crest running along the animal's neck, back, and tail; the scales on the body are very small. The tail is about as long as the head and body. The upper parts are of an olive colour, the lower surfaces being of a lighter shade. The Lizard is a native of Ceylon, and grows to a length of 15in. It is both carnivorous and herbivorous. In confinement it should be provided with mealworms, cockroaches, beetles, lettuces, ripe fruit, and boiled rice. Except in the hottest weather, its case ought to be artificially heated.

The Bloodsucker (*Calotes versicolor*) is a beautiful and interesting Lizard, and common in India and Ceylon. It has two spines, or separate bunches of spines, one in front of the other, above each ear-opening. The adults of this species possess a crest running along the neck and back: in the young the crest only reaches to about the middle of the back. In describing the Bloodsucker's colour, Dr. Günther says that the " ground-colour is generally a light brownish-olive, but the Lizard can change it to bright red, to black, and to a mixture of both. This change is sometimes confined to the head, at other times diffused over the whole body and tail. A common state in which it may be seen (as stated by Mr. Jerdon) is seated on a hedge or bush, with the tail and limbs black, head and neck yellow, picked out with red, and the rest of the body red." The name " Bloodsucker " has been given probably because of the red colour which is sometimes seen on the animal's head and neck.

The female is said to lay about ten eggs, about the size of those of a sparrow, and which hatch, according to temperature, in from eight to ten weeks. In a state of nature this Lizard feeds upon insects, young leaves, and berries, and in captivity it may be provided, as food, with beetles, mealworms, cockroaches, other small animals of a similar nature, young lettuces, and ripe fruit. It must be kept, at any rate during the greater part of the year, in a heated Vivarium, and as its habits are arboreal, it should have access to an orange-tree or some other tree of a like kind, upon which to climb and sleep. The entire length of the Bloodsucker is about 15in., the tail being a little more than twice the length of the head and body.

The Bearded Lizard (*Amphibolurus barbatus*).—This very strange-looking animal is hardy and interesting. When it is in a state of irritation, and most of the members of this family are

FIG. 48.—HARDWICKE'S MASTIGURE.

excitable, it will make manifest why it has received the above name. It is a stoutly-built Reptile, and of a pale olive colour. The large triangular head has a cross ridge of spines behind it. Like most of the *Agamidæ*, it has a pair of canine teeth in each jaw. The throat is not pouched, but there is a kind of plait across the chest which it spreads or erects when angry. The long, conical tail is depressed at the base, and is covered with keeled, tiled, and unequal scales.

During the colder parts of the year, the Bearded Lizard should be kept in a heated Vivarium. It may be fed upon meat, snails, slugs, and occasionally fruit. When in the market it can generally be bought at sums ranging from 10s. to £1.

Hardwicke's Mastigure (*Uromastix Hardwickii*, Fig. 48).—This curious and interesting animal is easily kept in confinement, and can generally be procured without difficulty in England for about 7s. It is both herbivorous and carnivorous, though it is frequently described as being entirely a vegetable feeder. In captivity it may be provided with pieces of raw meat, cockroaches, mealworms, lettuces, and cabbages. It has a curious habit of rearing itself against the side of its case, and sleeping supported on its tail.

As this Mastigure is a native of India, it must be confined in a heated Vivarium. At night, or when the temperature of its cage has been allowed to sink too low, it will seem to be dead. It will then submit to being handled without showing any manifest signs of life. Of course this kind of thing is characteristic, more or less, of all Reptiles, but it is very noticeable in the Mastigures and the Horned Lizards (*Phrynosoma*) of Texas.

The Mastigure is an inhabitant of rocky plains, where it lives in holes in the rocks or in burrows in the sand. Its strong, massive, spiny tail is its weapon of defence. When hot this animal is very lively, and if then handled strikes frantic blows with that member. It does not bite, at least, such is my own experience, but Canon Tristram, speaking of its relative the Egyptian Mastigure (*U. spinipes*), says that when it does "bite nothing will induce it to relinquish its grasp."

One of the peculiarities of this and many other Lizards, e.g., the *Tuatera*, is that they will often remain quite motionless for a considerable time in the position in which they are placed. For instance, when it is necessary to clean their Vivarium they will frequently not move if taken gently from the case, and put on a table or the top of another case until their own home is ready for their reception. They have, however, to be retaken in the hand quickly and quietly, for if they notice the intention of touching them they will dart away with considerable celerity. The illustration is an exact drawing of a Hardwicke's Mastigure, in the position he assumed when taken out of his cage and placed on a board in front of the camera.

Canon Tristram in speaking of the Dhabb or Egyptian Mastigure (*U. spinipes*), says that he kept one tame for some months, and that it was very docile "and would come at his call." He further mentions that the Arabs told him that this Mastigure is a match for the "Horned Cerastes (*C. hasselquistii*), which often enters its holes but soon has its vertebræ dislocated by the vigorous blows of the Dhabb's tail. The Dhabb is eaten by the Bedouin."

Hardwicke's Mastigure has a naked tympanum and a tranverse fold of skin below the throat. The upper parts of its body are covered with exceedingly small granular scales of equal size. The animal's tail possesses incomplete rings of spinous tubercles which do not encircle the lower side. The ventral scales are smooth and small. There are both femoral and præ-anal pores. The toes are short, with keeled scales below; the fourth toe of each hind-foot is one-third longer than the third toe; the legs and claws are very strong. Dr. Günther describes the colour of the Reptile as "lighter or dark yellowish grey or greyish olive, uniform, or clouded or with waved, blackish, tranverse lines; sometimes a large black spot on the inner side of the femur."

This Lizard comes chiefly from the plains of Hindostan; it is said not to be found in Bengal. When fully grown, it sometimes attains a length of 16in. Every other species of Mastigure may be treated in confinement in the same way as suggested for the one just described.

The Moloch Lizard (*Moloch horridus*) is one of the most extraordinary-looking Reptiles in existence. In its native country, Australia, it is also known as the "Thorn Devil" and the "Mountain Devil." The head has two very large horn-like spines, above the eyes, and several other spines of smaller size.

The body is depressed, and covered above and below with curious scales, each containing in its centre a spine which varies a great deal in size. Many of the spines are very large and prominent, and are placed more or less in rows along the creature's body. There are rings of large and sharp spines around the tail. There are five toes on each foot, armed with long, sharp claws. The colour is a palish yellow, spotted with dark brown.

The Moloch is not often brought into this country, and I believe only one specimen has been kept at the Zoological Gardens, London; but as it is so strange and interesting an animal, there ought, I think, to be a brief mention of it in these articles. In captivity it has been fed upon mealworms, beetles, young and hairless mice, and raw meat. It grows to a length of about 6in. It is not very hardy.

Reference has already been made to one of the chief differences between the Iguanidæ family and that of the *Agamidæ*. The former is even a larger family than the latter, for it numbers nearly 300 species, and quite fifty genera. Some of the *Iguanidæ* are among the ugliest Reptiles in existence, while others are certainly very beautiful.

"The habits of the numerous members of this family are as varied as their physiognomy. All the forms which we have observed in the Agamoids are repeated here, save the parachute-bearing Dragons, which have no pleurodont analogues. On the other hand, such types as the Anoles, with their digital expansions, and the semi-marine algivorous *Amblyrhynchus*, are unrepresented in the acrodont series. However, this apparent parallelism between the Agamoid and Iguanoid series of genera is very superficial, and there is, it appears to me, not one form so exactly repeated in both as to deserve to be united into the same genus, were the character of the dentition, on which the family distinction is based, not to be considered."—(Catalogue of Lizards, Brit. Mus., N.H., 1885.)

Some of the *Iguanidæ* are nearly six feet in length, while others, when fully grown, are not as many inches. Several of the most beautiful and interesting of the family may be kept happily in captivity with moderate care. Most of these Lizards are insectivorous, the members of only seven genera being herbivorous, *e.g.*, *Iguana*, *Brachylophus*, *Amblyrhynchus*, *Conolophus*, *Phymaturus*, *Sauromalus*, and *Basiliscus*; the genus *Ctenosaura* is supposed to be both insectivorous and herbivorous. All the *Iguanidæ*, with one or two exceptions, are thought to be oviparous.

Many of these interesting Reptiles are able to change their colours in a wonderful manner, so much so indeed, that some of them for this reason have been called chameleons, by people who imagine that only the chameleon has this strange power. Other Reptiles, as well as certain of the Batrachians, have this capability in a more or less marked degree.

Some of the larger of the *Iguanidæ* readily take to water, and swim, by the help of their compressed and powerful tail, in a very Newt-like fashion. Travellers tell us that while ascending the rivers of Tropical America, they have been frequently startled by the sudden splash made by one of these creatures, as, frightened by the boat, it jumps clumsily into the water. The late Mr. Charles Darwin, in his "Voyage of H.M.S. Beagle," relates a curious fact concerning the sea-inhabiting *Amblyrhynchus*, a Lizard which is able to swim and to dive exceedingly well, and remain under water for at least an hour. He says that when it is frightened it is unwilling to take refuge in the sea, and will not even be driven into it. The great naturalist accounted for this strange conduct by "the circumstances that this Reptile has no enemy whatever on shore, whereas at sea it must often fall a prey to numerous sharks." This Lizard lives chiefly upon sea-weed.

The flesh of the larger of the *Iguanidæ* is considered a great delicacy by the people who live in the lands where the creatures are found. The eggs of the animals, which are covered with a yellow parchment-like envelope, and are buried, for incubation, in sand, are also eaten, and are more relished, as a rule, than even those of the Turtle.

These large Lizards are hunted for with dogs trained for the purpose, and their flesh and eggs, in former times, used to be regarded as articles of commerce. It is very difficult to find the Reptiles without the assistance of dogs, for their colouring, which is so like that of their surroundings, and their almost invariable habit, except perhaps when water is near, of remaining perfectly still while danger is at hand, combine to help them to escape the eye of man.

The tail of these Lizards is frequently of great length, sometimes longer than twice the head and body of the animal. It is also very flexible, and compressed. Some of these creatures are able to give a severe wound, especially in the face, by furiously lashing their tail. Certain species can reproduce a lost portion of tail. Some of the *Iguanidæ* have prehensile tails; but most of them possess tails which are not prehensile. The teeth of the herbivorous members of this family are wonderfully adapted for their duties: the lateral ones are denticulated, and so arranged that as the mouth closes upon a leaf they overlap each other and cut it through with the greatest ease.

One of the most remarkable of the *Iguanidæ* is the Basilisk, probably so called after the fabulous king of serpents, whose very look was said to be sudden death. Perhaps the name Basilisk, a corruption apparently of *basileus*, the Greek for a king, was given to this strange animal because of its crown-like head-crest. It "might be taken for an heraldic rather than a real and living active tree-lizard. If it were 12ft. in length instead of as many inches, it would not be unlike a mediæval dragon without wings, and even in its small development it looks very uncanny. Its broad and rather sharp-pointed scaly head has a tall, cap-like crest sticking up and back from the hinder part. A tall, thin, fin-like, movable crest, with spines on it, passes along the back, being highest over the loins, and there is a corresponding one on the top of the long tail. The body is scaly and marked in zigzag. There is a very marked fold of the skin on the throat, and the hind digits are fringed at their sides. It inhabits Central America." The above is so good a description of this extraordinary-looking beast that I have ventured to copy it from Cassell's "Natural History." Only the males have crests on the back and tail. The dorsal crest, which sometimes is as deep as the animal's body, bears, in certain respects, not a little resemblance to the erected dorsal fin of a perch.

The Basilisk occasionally reaches a length of over 30in., of which at least 22in. are owned by the tail. The species described is *Basilicus americanus*; there are three other species. These Lizards are herbivorous.

Anyone who is lucky enough to possess a living specimen of this curious and interesting Reptile, and should wish to keep it in confinement, ought to place it in a large and well-heated Vivarium in which there are some growing trees, and offer it as food young lettuces, young cabbages, watercress, fruit and berries. The case should be kept at a temperature of about 85deg. Fahr.

Among the most beautiful of the *Iguanidæ* are the Anoles. The males have gular appendages. All have their toes more or less dilated, and have, therefore, great powers of climbing. The tail is very long, compressed, or cylindrical, and sometimes extremely slender. It is not prehensile; but it is frequently reproduced when broken, the new part being at first of a black colour.

The genus *Anolis* is so large as to number about 106 species. Some of the Anoles make very charming pets. Personally, I think them to be the most beautiful of all Lizards. Those I have been fortunate enough to possess have proved themselves hardy while in confinement. They are extraordinarily active, and, for Reptiles, very intelligent: they soon become tame enough to take a fly from the fingers. Owing to their great activity and power of changing colour, mine have several times escaped from their case. For instance, when the case has been opened for cleaning purposes or for a change of water, the little creatures while clinging to the leaf of an orange tree, and having assumed the exact hue of the leaf, have been unnoticed until, like a flash of green light, if such an expression may be used here, they have gone. However, I have always been lucky enough to re-capture them. One lived, unobserved, for at least two months, on a vine in a greenhouse. As a rule, my Anoles sleep, hanging head downwards, on the outside of a large leaf of an orange-tree.

Speaking of these Lizards, Mr. Gosse, in his "A Naturalist's Sojourn in Jamaica," says, "The little Anoles are chasing each other in and out between the jalousies, now stopping to protrude from the throat a broad disc of brilliant colour, crimson or orange, like the petal of a flower, then withdrawing it, and again displaying it in coquettish sport. Then one leaps a yard or two through the air, and alights on the back of his playfellow, and both struggle and twist about in unimaginable contortions. Another is running up and down on the plastered wall, catching the ants as they roam in black lines over its whitened surface, and another leaps from some piece of furniture upon the back of the visitor's chair, and scampers nimbly along the collar of his coat. It jumps on the table—can it be the same? An instant ago it was of the most beautiful golden-green, except the base of the tail, which was of a soft, light purple hue; now, as if changed by an enchanter's wand, it is of a dull, sooty brown all over, and becomes momentarily darker and darker, or mottled with dark and pale patches of a most unpleasing aspect. Presently, however, the mental emotion, whatever it was—anger, or fear, or dislike—has passed away, and the lovely green hue sparkles in the glancing sunlight as before."

In captivity, the Anoles often have what may be called a romp among themselves, exhibiting as they do so their great activity and brilliant colours. They will eat small cockroaches, ants, beetles, and mealworms; but I believe they prefer the common bluebottle fly to anything else. The Reptiles jump upon their prey, which they are wonderfully quick to see, from a great distance, and seize it with their jaws without any assistance of the tongue.

As they can assume a hue so exactly like that of the leaf upon which they are resting, the insects seem to have no knowledge of the neighbourhood of their enemy. The wary little Lizards wait until their spoil is within the distance of a leap, and then, with a bound, they spring upon the luckless creature. They seldom fail to make a catch.

Mr. Gosse, in speaking of the great similarity between the colours of these Reptiles and the leaves among which they live, says that on one occasion he was trying to catch a butterfly, when he suddenly saw that it was fluttering as if unable to get away. His first impression was that an invisible spider's web was holding it, but on looking more closely he discovered that a little Anolis had the butterfly in its mouth. The Lizard's colour was so exactly like that of the green leaves of the bush that he had not perceived it before, though his eyes were fixed upon the spot.

The Anoles, at any rate the smaller kinds, seem most beautiful, strangely enough, when shedding their skins. The half-shed skin has the appearance of the finest muslin imaginable, which seems to envelope the little creatures like a shawl arranged in graceful folds. The sloughing does not appear to interfere in the least with either their activity or their appetite.

Some of the Anoles can be bought occasionally in this country for so low a sum as half-a-crown. They are known here as "Chameleon-Lizards." They will live in England during the winter, in either a moderately-heated Vivarium or in a heated green-house. In summer they need not be provided with artificial

FIG. 49.—GRAHAM'S ANOLIS (*Anolis grahami*).

warmth, but they must have access to as much sunshine as possible. The larger their Vivarium is, the better, and there should be within it at least two small orange-trees or other trees of a similar kind. The pots in which the trees are growing can be arranged as already suggested. A small glass funnel should be inserted in a hole in the lid of the case through which insects may be dropped, or through which flies will very often voluntarily crawl, especially if the lower part of it be lightly smeared with treacle or honey. The funnel will prevent the escape of the Anoles. This is a much safer arrangement than having the hole for the insertion of food simply covered with a lid; for sometime or other the closing of the hole will be forgotten, and the captives, being able to climb the glass sides of their case, will get free, a circumstance which is likely to lead to the annoyance of the owner and the death of the fugitives. Such an arrangement as that which I have just described may be adapted to almost any Vivarium in which Lizards are kept.

Fig. 49 is a very good illustration of the *Anolis grahami*, and it will give the novice in these matters an idea of what these creatures are like in shape. This species is very suitable for confinement. M. Boulenger, in describing its colouring, says that it is "green, purplish, or brownish above, usually with darker reticulation enclosing round light spots; females sometimes with a few angular cross-bars on the back, with or without a light vertebral band; throat with dark reticulation." The entire length is about 6½in. long, of which the tail measures 4in.

The members of the genus *Anolis* vary in length from 4in. to 18in. They come from Tropical and Subtropical America.

The Tuberculated Iguana (*Iguana tuberculata*) is a large Lizard whose habitat is Tropical America; while in this country it should always be kept in a heated Vivarium, except perhaps during the hottest part of the year. It is an interesting animal, but it is oftener seen in public zoological gardens than in a private collection of Reptiles. Since it occasionally grows to a length of more than 4½ft., it is wise for the amateur to procure a specimen when it is young and small.

It may be fed, while in confinement, upon bananas, grapes, lettuces, watercress, and the like. It should also be provided with a tree, or a portion of a tree, to climb on and a suitable bath to bathe in. This Iguana can be bought, when in the market, for about £1.

The animal has a rather large head, with a rounded snout; but perhaps the most noticeable parts of it are its large non-dilatable gular appendage, with a kind of crest in front, and its curious-looking toothed crest which runs along the neck, back, and tail. The crest is usually most developed in the full-grown males. The ear-opening is distinct. The scales are small, the ventral scales being the larger. The tail is long, powerful, and compressed. The upper parts of the animal are often of a beautiful green colour, but sometimes bluish and sometimes of a slate colour; the under-parts are yellowish-green. There is frequently a whitish band in front of the shoulders. The tail is generally rayed or ringed with green, yellow, and brown; on the sides there are zigzag, dark yellowish-edged markings. The Reptile is naturally gentle, but it is able to give, when frightened or when struggling, a nasty wound with its tail if it strikes an unprotected part of the human body.

The Naked-necked Iguana (*I. delicatissima*) and the Black Iguana (*Metopoceros cornutus*) should receive the same treatment in confinement as that recommended for the Tuberculated Iguana. The Naked-necked Iguana differs from *I. tuberculata*, among other things, in the size of some of its scales, in having a rather lower dorsal crest, and in possessing ventral scales which are more distinctly keeled. The black Iguana may be known from its tuberculated relative by its much smaller gular sac and gular fold, its longer tail, and black colour.

The Horned Lizard (*Phrynosoma cornutum*, Fig. 50) is a very extraordinary-looking Lizard; it is also known as the Horned Toad, the Californian Toad, the Stagyrite, and the Tapayaxin. My own children call it the Lizard which "dies every night and comes to life again every morning." This variety of names, at any rate, goes far to imply that the creature is at least remarkable and interesting. Though frequently called a Toad, it certainly is not one, but a true Lizard, belonging to the family of the *Iguanidæ*. I have already mentioned that this family contains some of the ugliest of Lizards as well as some of the most beautiful, and I think anyone would be willing to endorse this statement if, for example, an Anolis and a Phrynosoma were placed side by side. At first sight it would seem impossible that there could be any relationship between them. The one so active, smooth, slender, long-tailed, and gaily-coloured; the other inactive (certainly in captivity), rough to an extraordinary degree, broad, short-tailed, and soberly-tinted. Both, however, have considerable powers of changing colour, and both use this power as a means of defence against their common enemies—*e.g.*, the former assuming the exact green of the leaves of the tree in

LIZARDS. 145

which it is climbing, the latter becoming grey like the stones or sand upon which it is resting.

It is said that the remains of the Horned Lizard have not yet been found in the stomach of a snake. A glance at the illustration (Fig. 50) would incline most people to believe that no snake would be greatly tempted to try to swallow such an uncomfortable-looking mouthful.

This Reptile has another means of defence which is very extraordinary, viz., the ability to squirt blood, or what seems to be blood, from the eyes. Dr. Günther has said, however, that "nothing has been found, on anatomical examination, to establish the correctness of this assertion." Personally, I have never seen

FIG. 50.—THE HORNED LIZARD (*Phrynosoma cornutum*).

the animal discharge this blood-red fluid, but I have noticed signs on a specimen of my own which led me to believe that he had recently been throwing the liquid. There can be no doubt, I think, that the Horned Lizard has this capability in question. A dog would most likely drop a Phrynosoma for the same reason that he would let go a common Toad—namely, on account of a bitter, burning secretion the animal is capable of emitting into the dog's mouth.

Concerning this strange habit of "ejecting blood," Dr. O. P. Hay, in an interesting article in the Proc. U.S. Nat. Mus., XV., 1892, pp. 375-378, says that "about the 1st of August it (the

L

Phrynosoma blainvillii) was shedding its outer skin, and the process appeared a difficult one, since the skin was dried and adhered closely. One day it occurred to me that it might facilitate matters if I should give the animal a wetting; so, taking it up, I carried it to a wash-basin of water near by, and suddenly tossed the Lizard in the water. The first surprise was probably experienced by the Phrynosoma, but the next was my own, for on one side of the basin there suddenly appeared a number of spots of red fluid, which resembled blood. . . . . . . A microscope was soon procured, and an examination was made, which immediately showed that the matter ejected was really blood.

"The affair now became very interesting. Just where the blood came from I could not determine with certainty, the whole thing having happened so suddenly and unexpectedly; yet the appearance seemed to indicate that the blood came from the region about one of the eyes. There appeared to be a considerable quantity of the blood, since on the sides of the vessel and on the wall near it I counted ninety of the little splotches. A consultation was had with Mr. Stejneger the next day with regard to the propriety of dashing the animal into the water again, to discover, if possible, where the blood came from. It was thought, however, that such blood-lettings must be somewhat exhausting, and that it would be better to allow the animal a day to recuperate. While talking, I picked up the Lizard, and was holding it between my thumb and middle finger, and stroking its horns with my fore-finger. All at once a quantity of blood was thrown out against my fingers, and a portion of it ran down on the animal's neck; and this blood came directly out of the right eye."

The above interesting quotation is made by Mr. Stejneger, in his official report on the "Reptiles of the Death Valley Expedition," who also produces other testimony in support of the assertion that the Horned Lizard has the power of throwing, even to a distance of 15in., a blood-red fluid.

Dr. Stradling says that the Horned Lizard may be "commonly seen in Californian houses, not in a cage, but secured with a long, narrow, bright ribbon, catching flies and spiders through the day, and burrowing at night in a box of sand provided for the purpose." The animal is not very lively while in captivity, but it does show a little activity when placed in the hot rays of the sun. It will not even feed unless it has plenty of sun. At night, when the sun goes down and the temperature becomes cooler, the creature seems, at first sight, to have lost what little life it had during the day, appearing, to the unobservant, quite dead. For this reason children have called it "the Lizard which dies every night and comes to life again every morning." This nightly torpor is characteristic of many Reptiles, but it is very noticeable in the case of *P. cornutum*.

The Californian Toad is a native of some of the hottest and driest parts of America—California, Kansas, Texas, Mexico, etc.; it is even found in the Death Valley of Colorado. In certain places it is very common, and from time to time has been imported into this country in considerable numbers, its market price during the summer ranging from 5s. to 8s. 6d. It is generally under 6in. in length.

The Vivarium in which the Horned Lizard is confined should have a thick layer of fine and dry sand, in which it will bury itself at night. I have never seen the creature drink, and I am not sure that it does drink; but, still, I have always supplied mine with a small quantity of water. While at liberty, in its native land, it must at times be obliged to forego the slaking of its thirst, if it ever has one. It is, indeed, a curious creature. Its food in captivity may consist of spiders, cockroaches, beetles, mealworms, flies, gentles, earwigs and the like. It will not eat anything which is dead.

Fig. 50 obviates the necessity of any detailed description of the Lizard. It is greyish or brownish on the back, down the centre of which runs a lighter coloured streak. Dr. Stradling, in describing the colouring of the *P. cornutum*, says: "The usual colour of these Lizards is a dull brown, with indistinct markings, relieved by the white edges or red tips of the spines, but they become bright red or orange at times, and the pattern shows up much more plainly on the lighter ground. I have one which glows out in crimson patches suddenly when disturbed, as though red fire were lighted up inside him; another, a very fine one, displays pale grey marks along the sides, which turn sea-green now and then."

The Horned Lizards of the *Iguanidæ* correspond, to a certain extent, with the Moloch Lizards of the *Agamidæ*. The genus *Phrynosoma* contains at least twelve species.

The members of the Amphisbænidæ family are snake-like Lizards, without legs. The *Chirotes canaliculatus* has, however, two fore-legs, each with four clawed toes; but this is the only exception. The name is derived from Greek words, which mean an animal that can walk in both directions. These creatures live in burrows in the ground, and in the narrow galleries which they make there they are able to crawl in either direction. Their manner of progression is different from that of other legless Reptiles. Instead of moving their body laterally as snakes do, they move it in vertical undulation, just as serpents were often represented in old pictures to be doing.

Some of these creatures are occasionally brought into this country, where they may, with care, be kept in confinement. There is still much to be learnt concerning these curious Lizards, so that it would be quite worth one's while to tend them and study them if they should happen to fall into his possession. They ought to be kept in a rather narrow though long case, having four glass sides, the bottom of which should be rather thickly covered with earth. Through the glass some of their habits, while under ground, may be observed. They are hardy while in confinement.

The Amphisbænidæ have worm-like bodies well suited to their underground life. The eyes are small, and covered with skin; the ears are not exposed, and the tail is very short. There are about eleven genera and sixty-five species. Most of the species come from America.

The Grey Amphisbæna (*Blanus cinereus*) is the most easy of its family to be obtained in this country. It is a native of Spain, Portugal, Morocco, and Algiers. It is about as thick as one's finger, and reaches a length of about 8in. It is of a brownish flesh-colour, the segments of the body being of a darker shade. The lateral line is well marked, and there are generally six preanal pores.

The White Amphisbæna (*A. alba*), which comes from Brazil, sometimes is nearly 2ft. in length. In captivity these

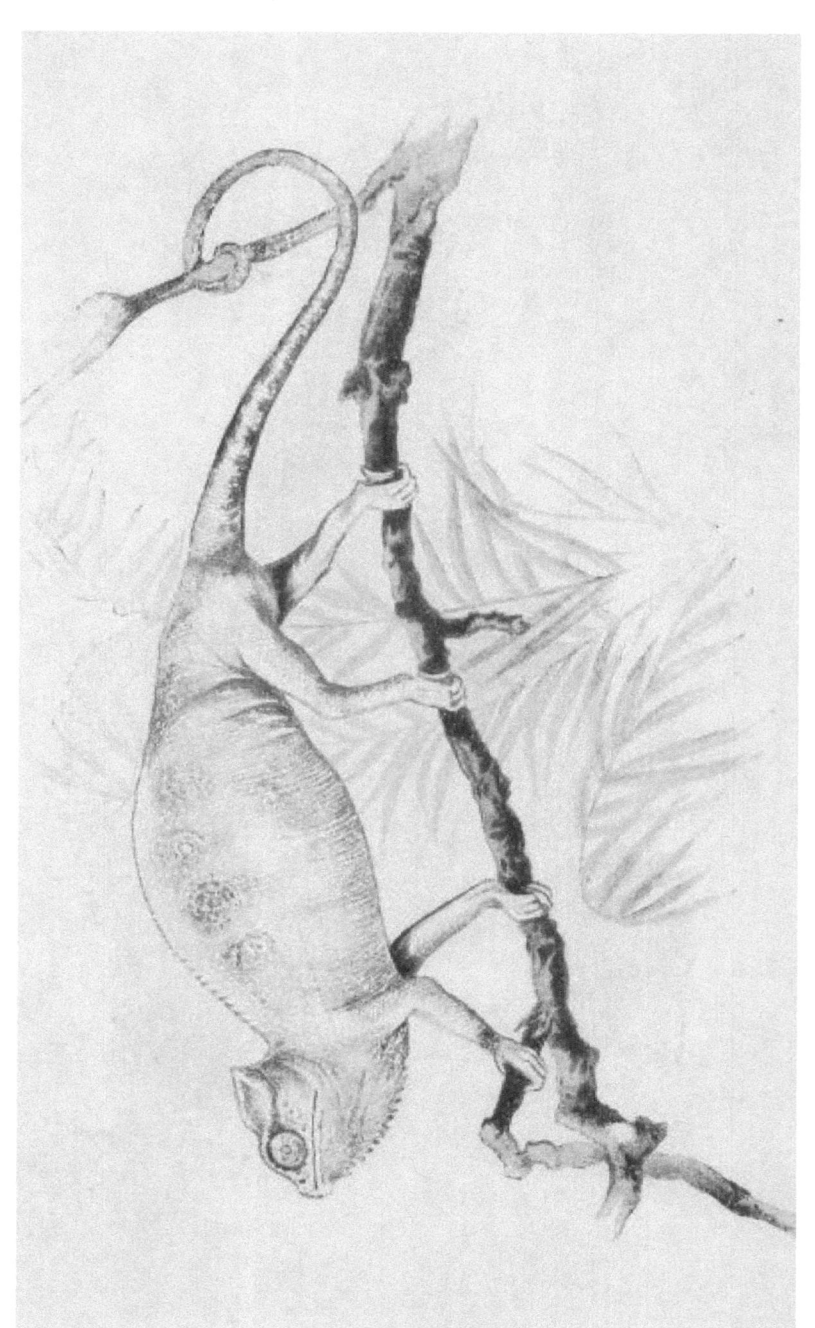

Fig. 51.—THE COMMON CHAMELEON (*Chamæleon vulgaris*.

Reptiles should be fed upon earth-worms, slugs, and raw meat. They should be handled carefully, for though they have very small mouths they are able to bite a tiny piece of flesh out of the hand or elsewhere.

The Common Chameleon (*Chamaeleon vulgaris*), Fig. 51, is so extraordinary a Lizard in many ways that it has been placed in the above sub-order. It is indeed a wonderful creature, but not nearly so wonderful as it is sometimes reported to be. There are perhaps more delusions in regard to the Chameleon than any other Reptile, except the snake. Old writers asserted that it lived upon air, and that it could not only change its shape, but also assume any colour it wished. There is, however, a foundation of truth for all these false statements. The Chameleon has considerable powers of fasting, and it can, by means of its very capacious lungs, greatly inflate its body with air; hence the assumption that it fed only upon air. And when the animal has exhaled the air which it contained, the lately-swollen body becomes very much compressed; there is, therefore, in this sense not a little change in the creature's shape.

Then, again, the Chameleon has great capability of changing colour, perhaps greater than any other Reptile, not even excepting the *Calotes* of India, of which mention has already been made. But it does not, as a rule, assume the colour of the object upon which it is resting; and yet one reads in a modern Natural History for Children that its colour is so exactly like that of the surrounding leaves or flowers that the animal cannot easily be detected, and should it change its post and quit a clump of bright green leaves in favour of a cluster of brilliant scarlet or blue blossoms its colour changes to the *same* tint. That the Chameleon becomes blue in colour when among blue flowers and brilliant scarlet in colour when surrounded by brilliant scarlet flowers, is certainly not the case.

The colouring of the Chameleon is chiefly controlled by its passions, such as fear, anger, and pleasure. People who have no individuality, so to speak, of their own, and who are ready to follow the lead and adopt the opinions of others, have often been likened to the Chameleon; but not justly, for this Reptile has a certain amount of character. It very seldom assumes the exact colour of the object upon which it is resting. It does so, indeed, sometimes; but more by accident than by intention. Nor can it conceal its feelings; for example, no sooner does it experience fear than it proclaims that emotion by a change in the colouring of its body.

Several explanations have been given in regard to the Chameleon's great power of changing colour; while some authorities have declared that this phenomenon is entirely inexplicable. It is, however, probably chiefly due to layers of pigment-cells placed deeply in the skin, and which are acted upon partly by the air which fills the lungs, and partly by two sets of "nerve-fibres," one set of which, the constrictors, withdraws the cells from near the surface of the skin; while the other set, the dilators, presses them forward towards the skin's surface. These nerves are more or less governed by the brain of the animal.

The eyes of the Chameleon are in their way as extraordinary as the animal's power of changing colour. "One eye is able to look north and the other to look south," as a friend one day quaintly put it while looking at my Reptiles; or as the French say, "it can look into Champagne and see Picardy in flames." The eye-ball is very large and prominent, and is covered with a single eyelid, which is pierced in the centre for the pupil. This opening is about as large as the head of a common pin. When the animal sleeps, it closes this aperture transversely.

The eyes give the Chameleon the power of looking in nearly every direction without bending its stiff neck or altering the position of its body in the slightest degree. One eye, for instance, may be looking at the observer, while the other is watching the movements of a fly in a different quarter. But both eyes are invariably fixed upon the insect which the Reptile is on the point of capturing. In pictures, one sometimes sees Chameleons represented as looking in one direction, while the tongue is being thrown forward at a fly in another. If the Chameleon ever does act so injudiciously as this, he will surely make a bad shot with his tongue.

When it is necessary to speak of the tongue of this strange creature, there is a temptation to say that it is even more extraordinary than its eyes. The Chameleon is the only Lizard which is placed in the sub-order *Rhiptoglossa*, an order whose members are able to shoot out their tongue in order to catch their prey. As the Chameleon is extremely slow and deliberate in its movements, the tongue may be well said to be the most agile part of the creature. The wonderful activity of the tongue makes up, in a sense, for the great sluggishness of the rest of the parts of the animal. The tongue is very long, longer often than the Reptile's body—worm-like in form, and provided with a club-shaped end. This end is covered with a viscous secretion. The tongue is also hollow to a great extent, and when not in use is folded in a telescopic manner and packed away in the capacious mouth of the Lizard.

The Chameleon's manner of taking food is very interesting and curious. After waiting until its prey is in a suitable position, it slightly moves its tongue, without hardly separating the jaws, as if to supply the tongue's end with a sufficient amount of adhesive matter. This latter action is followed by the opening of the mouth and the slow protrusion of the tongue to the distance of about 1in. and then the succeeding movement is so extremely rapid that the eye can scarcely follow it. The insect, however, has disappeared, and the Chameleon is seen slowly crushing something between its jaws. The Chameleon generally waits until the prey is within from 3in. to 6in. before it attempts a shot with its tongue. It does not often miss. It is prudent in this matter, for it appears to take every precaution to ensure success, such as rarely attacking an insect when it is moving rapidly, and pressing its body forward without unclasping the claws, and so lessening the distance between itself and its victim.

Occasionally, when the Chameleon strikes with its tongue, say, a very large cockroach, which is clinging to any object, the secretion at the end of the Reptile's tongue fails to be sufficiently adhesive, and the tongue's end returns to its owner without booty; but a second shot at the shaken and astonished animal generally effects a capture. The tongue of the Chameleon is so extraordinary that no other creature has one anything like it.

The five toes on each foot are arranged in two sets, three in one set and two in the other. The set containing two claws is placed on the outside on the fore-feet, and on the inside on the hind-feet. The feet are really grasping organs, or hands.

The tail of the Chameleon is long, with the exception of that of the members of the genera *Brookesia* and *Rhampholeon*, about the length of the head and body of the animal, conical, and prehensile. It is, therefore, a fifth hand. The limbs are long. The head and body are covered with granules instead of scales.

The name Chameleon is derived from two Greek words which mean "ground-lion." But why the ancients gave this unlion-like Reptile, which lives chiefly in trees, so strange a name is difficult to understand, except it be on the *lucus à non lucendo* principle.

The Chameleon, as most people know, lives chiefly in trees, and rarely comes to the ground, where its movements are exceedingly awkward. In the trees and smaller plants it apparently moves with the greatest deliberation and care, its prehensile tail much helping the animal to maintain its upright position upon the branches. It sleeps carefully extended upon some suitable bough, which is not only firmly grasped by the four hands, but also by the tail. It will assume an almost similar attitude for hours while basking in the sun and watching for insects.

The colouring of the Chameleon assists it greatly in escaping observation, not because its colour is identical with that of the object upon which it is resting, but because it harmonises so completely with its surroundings, just as a tiger, giraffe, or zebra, owing to the light and dark markings of its body, eludes notice among the lights and shades of the woods or jungles. I have sometimes given a Chameleon its liberty on a grape vine, and in an hour or two have had not a little difficulty in finding it again, owing to its colouring and attitude helping it so marvellously to escape detection. I have also taken part in a search in a comparatively small conservatory, with seven other people, for a Chameleon which had been allowed to climb in some creepers, and it was a very long time before the animal was found. No wonder, then, that unsuspecting insects are so likely to come within range of the keen eyes and the active tongue of this Lizard.

Many people who have tried to keep this very quaint and interesting creature, complain that it is impossible to get it to live through the winter of this country. I have had no difficulty in keeping this Reptile all the year round. For instance, one specimen which had been in my possession since the end of the summer of

1893, died on the 8th January, 1895, probably through misadventure. It was very lively and active on the morning of its death.

A Chameleon can be kept all through the year in a vivarium like either Fig. 3 or Fig. 12. If the former kind of case be adopted, the hot-water arrangement, already spoken of in connection with Fig. 3, could be dispensed with, and a piece of stout zinc or sheet iron, cut the size of the base of the case, should be fastened to the bottom on the outside. There will then be a distance of about an inch between the zinc or iron on the outside and the perforated zinc bottom on the inside. The case must be then raised, by means of four short wooden legs, so high that a small paraffin-lamp may be placed underneath. And then the temperature within the case can be kept at any reasonable degree of heat. The heat, according to this plan, is more easily applied than when hot water is used. But a case which is heated by means of a boiler, will retain its warmth for a considerable time, if by chance the lamp should go out. It is wise to keep a small thermometer in the vivarium.

During the summer a Chameleon need not be kept in a case which is artificially warmed, but it must be supplied with as much sunshine as possible. When the sun is very powerful the Reptile should always have access to shade, an absence of which will sometimes cause the animal's death.

The Chameleon will not, as a rule, drink from any vessel. If the interior of the case be periodically syringed with water, the Reptile will take a drop here and there; but the constant syringing has a tendency to make the vivarium very damp, and in an unsuitable condition for a Chameleon. As far as my own experience goes, the following is the best plan for supplying this creature with water. A small bottle of water is placed on the top of the case; a tiny stone is tied to the end of a piece of coarse string of a length three times that of the bottle. The stone is then dropped into the bottle, and thus, one part of the string being in the bottle and two-thirds out, a kind of slow-running siphon is formed. The bottle is in this way slowly emptied drop by drop. A drop of water will generally hang for some little time at the end of the string. The longer arm of the syphon is inserted through a little hole in the top of the case. A small vessel should be placed on the bottom of the vivarium into which the drops, which are unconsumed by the Chameleon, may fall. This will not only prevent a dampness, but will also supply water for any other animal which may be kept with the Chameleon. It will be found that the Chameleon will readily drink the water which hangs at the end of the siphon.

It is not wise to keep any other Lizard in the case which will be likely to cause fear in so timid and nervous an animal as the Chameleon. The Chameleon will show its terror by its restless movements and the colouring of its skin, such as dark green spots upon a ground of lighter green.

Mealworms, beetles, cockroaches, wasps, flies, and the like may be provided as food for the Chameleon while in confinement. It will take a mealworm if it be fastened at the end of a piece of thin wire and waved to and fro within 2in. or 3in. of its head. Cockroaches are a very suitable and easily obtained winter food; the Chameleon will frequently cast up the hard parts of their body in the form of pellets, or quids.

The Chameleon when handled does not bite. I once saw a Chameleon, amongst several others, running about with its mouth wide open and placed my finger within to test the power of its jaws, and found it to be by no means inconsiderable. This animal, with kindness and gentleness, will soon become so tame as to take flies from the window while being held in the hand. I have known a lady to carry her Chameleon in summer time, clinging to her hair or her hat, the animal during that experience showing no signs of nervousness.

These Reptiles are often brought into this country in considerable numbers, and can be bought during the season at sums ranging from 3s. 6d. to 7s. 6d.

A dealer was once showing me several Chameleons in his possession, and when I told him that I thought none of them looked very well, replied that he knew some of them would die, but he did not mind, as he could get as much for them when dead as alive. I asked what the dead animals could be used for, and learnt that their skins were sold to cover the handles of umbrellas and walking-sticks. However, I have never seen a Chameleon's skin so utilised.

In the family of the *Chamœleontidœ* there are three genera and about fifty species. In the genus *Chamœleon* there are about forty-four species. Most of the members of this family are oviparous, but a few are ovoviviparous. The eggs when laid are generally placed in the ground, and covered with earth and leaves. Sometimes as many as thirty are deposited at one time. A Chameleon of my own has produced nearly this number while in confinement. If eggs are laid while the animals are in captivity, and there is reason to believe that they may be fertile, they should be treated in the way already recommended for the incubation of the eggs of other Lizards.

When Chameleons are born alive, they almost immediately clasp something or other with their hands and tail, and commence to look out for prey.

In a collection of Reptiles the Chameleon seems generally to attract more notice than any other Lizard. Its eyes, affected gravity, claws, tail, tongue, and colouring are all so extraordinary, that the unlearned in these matters seem loath to cease looking at and asking questions about the strange beast.

Most of the Chameleons come from Madagascar and the neighbouring islands, and nearly all the rest are found in Africa. The Common Chameleon (*C. vulgaris*) has a very wide range, from Spain, Africa, Asia Minor, Arabia, to India. It is about a foot long when fully grown.

The Tuatera Lizard (*Hatteria punctata*).—" Both near Warwick," said the late Canon Kingsley in his lecture on " The Stones in the Wall," " and near Elgin in Scotland, in Central India, and in South Africa, fossil remains are found of a family of Lizards utterly unlike anything now living, save one, and that one is crawling about plentifully I believe—of all places in the world—in New Zealand. How it got there, how so strange a type of creature should have died out over the rest of the world and yet have lasted over that remote island for ages, ever since the days of the New Red Sandstone, is one of those questions—quite awful questions I consider them —with which I will not puzzle my readers. I only mention it to show them what serious questions the scientific man has to face, and to answer if he can; only the next time they go to the Zoological Gardens in London, let them go to the Reptile House, and ask the very clever and courteous attendant to show them the Sphenodons, or Hatterias as he will probably call them, and then look, I hope with kindly interest, at the oldest conservatives they ever saw, or are likely to see; gentlemen of most ancient pedigree who have remained all but unchanged, while the whole surface of the globe has changed around them more than once or twice."

Fig. 52 represents the very interesting Reptile of which the above quotation speaks. Dr. Gunther, after having dissected a specimen or two, placed the Tuateras in the order *Rhynchocephalia*, or Beak-headed Lizards, an order of which the Tuateras, or Hatterias, are the only living representatives. These Reptiles are said to have been first mentioned by Mr. Anderson, a companion of Captain Cook during his "Third Voyage." He erroneously described them as being more than 7ft. in length, and possessing a body equalling in circumference that of a man.

Dr. Dieffenbach, however, in 1843 was the first, I believe, to give anything like a trustworthy account of this strange creature. He said that the natives called it "Tuatera" or "Narara," and that they were afraid of it. Although he searched for the animal diligently, and even offered a large price for one, it was only just on his departure from the country that he was successful in obtaining a specimen, which ultimately found its way to the British Museum. Dr. Dieffenbach also procured the following information concerning the Tuatera Lizard, viz., that it used to be very plentiful in all the islands, especially on the sand-hills near the coast; that it was hunted by the natives for its flesh; and that, owing to this circumstance and to the importation of pigs, which also take pleasure in feeding upon it, it had become so scarce that some of the oldest inhabitants declared that they had never seen the animal.

In 1867, Dr. Günther expressed the fear that, within a very few years, this interesting creature would be numbered among the extinct Reptiles. Since then, however, from time to time, many specimens have been brought to this country, and recently, I

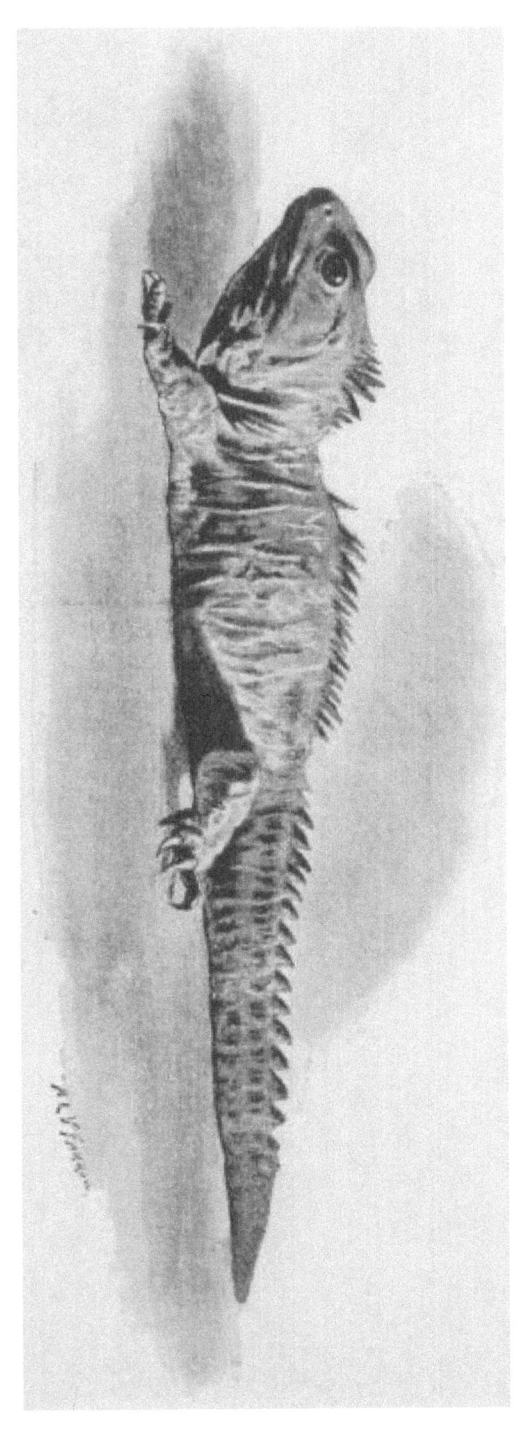

FIG. 52.—TUATERA LIZARD (*Hatteria punctata*).

believe, the authorities at the Zoological Gardens, Regent's Park, have been able to dispose of them for so low a sum as £2 a pair. Nevertheless, there is still the danger that before long they will become extinct. The climate of this country naturally suits these New Zealand Reptiles very well; so much so, indeed, that they are able to pass the winter out of doors, even when it is unusually cold, but of course in a state of hibernation.

The following is Dr. J. E. Gray's description of the Hatteria: "Head, quadrangular, covered with small scales; throat, lax, with a cross fold behind; nape and back, with a crest of compressed spines; body, covered with small and larger scales; belly and underside of tail with large, squarish, keelless, flat scales, placed in cross series; tail, compressed, triangular, covered with small scales, and with a ridge of large compressed spines; legs, strong; toes 5—5 short, strong, cylindrical, slightly webbed at the base, covered above and below with small scales; claws, short, blunt; femoral (inner part of thigh) pores, none; preanal scales, small, a few of them are pierced in the centre." I have often heard people, when looking at my own Tuateras, remark upon the rabbit-like appearance of their head. A glance at the illustration (Fig. 52), will show that is by no means a bad comparison.

The Tuatera Lizard, which is very stoutly-built and about 19in. in length when full grown, is extremely sluggish in the daytime, but by no means inactive during the night. In the day they will sometimes remain in exactly the same position for hours. I remember suddenly coming across a pair of these creatures in a glass case which contained no gravel, water or food, nothing but the Reptiles, and I think that my first impression—that they were stuffed—was quite a natural one. They were standing with their large eyes wide open, perfectly still and apparently taking no notice of anything at all. If lifted gently by the body, they may be handled quite safely, for they will not attempt to bite; but it is not wise to catch them by the tail, as they probably would resent such a liberty.

Some time ago, I was looking at the various animals in a very large dealer's establishment, when I made a remark about a fine pair of Tuateras which I saw in a big cage. The assistant who was with me immediately opened the door of the den and seized one of the reptiles by the tail, and I shall not readily forget the ominous sound made by the animal's closing jaws as he just missed the man's fingers, at which he had snapped. I at once mentally resolved never to catch a Tuatera by the tail. As I congratulated the man upon his escape, he said, "I am a bit lucky this time, for I have only just come out of 'orspital, where I have been laid up with blood-poisoning through the bite of one of them pythons."

The Tuateras, in common with many other Reptiles, have the power of reproducing a lost portion of their tail. These creatures are good burrowers, and if provided with the opportunity will soon make for themselves little caves, in which they will spend a great part of their time. They make these hiding-places generally at night.

The Hatterias are by no means active animals, and they can hardly climb at all. Their run has a very comical appearance, for they move their legs in a stiff and oar-like manner. Usually they are most deliberate in all their movements, especially when they are eating, their jaws moving so extremely slow, that it is quite a trial of one's patience to watch them complete a meal. When in confinement, these Reptiles will eat raw or cooked meat, live or dead mice, dead young birds, beetles, cockroaches, large earthworms, meal worms, and similar food. They have no little power of changing their colour, or perhaps it will be more correct to say that their colour is changeable to a certain degree. For example, sometimes their bodies will be of a light green tinge; at others, of either a dark or light cement colour; and occasionally, they will be partly of one colour, and partly of another.

Tuateras may be kept in a large case somewhat similar to that represented at Fig. 3, p. 11, or a run may be made for them of any reasonable size, the larger, of course, the better, either in a greenhouse or in a sheltered part of a garden. A fence of about 2½ft. high will be quite sufficient to keep them from escaping. If the run be made for them out of doors, they should be provided with a mound of light soil, surrounded by rockwork, into which they will burrow; and in the little caves they will then make, they can hibernate successfully. When the winter weather is exceptionally severe, the mound should be covered all round and over with some sacking or matting.

Tuateras ought to have access to plenty of water, which of course must not be allowed to get foul. If they are confined during the winter months in a heated green house or in a warm room, they will not hibernate. It goes without saying that the Reptiles should be kept quite clean, but those who have anything to do with them will soon see that it is a very easy matter. The Tuatera, like the Crocodile and some other animals, has nictitating eyelids, which it frequently uses; but this animal is particularly famous for its median, parietal, or pineal eye. It is called the "median" eye because of its position in regard to the other two eyes; the "parietal," from its connection with the parietal bone; and the "pineal," from its association with a gland, or small organ, situated on the brain, which resembles in shape the cone of the pine. This pineal gland of the human being was suggested by Descartes to be the seat of the soul, though I believe that suggestion was never seriously entertained. Other Lizards, such as Monitors, Slow-worms, Sand-Lizards and the like, have this strange third eye, but in none of them is it so highly developed as in the Hatteria, and even in this animal it is only rudimentary.

Though New Zealand possesses this famous Lizard, she is wonderfully devoid of other Reptiles, with the exception of a few Skinks and Geckos. I think that at the present time, because of the reasons given above, in only two islands of this country can these interesting creatures be found.

CHAPTER VII.

SNAKES.

OF all Reptiles, the Snake is the most interesting, either at liberty or in confinement. As a rule, people do not look upon the animal with indifference; they are either attracted to it or repelled by it. The Snake is one of the most remarkable of all creatures. It has always held an important place in the history of mankind. By some nations it has been worshipped as a god, by others reviled and dreaded as the embodiment of evil. Nor does this appear strange to those who are at all familiar with the Reptile. No wonder that the heathen reverenced an animal so beautiful in colouring, graceful in movement and swift in action; or feared one so strong, deadly and incomprehensible. The Snake has been closely connected with the religion of every pagan country wherever it was known. It is said that there are hardly any ancient sacred carvings of Egypt, India, China, Japan, or Mexico in which the Serpent is not represented. Probably, since ornaments were first used up to the present day, the Snake has been a favourite device. We see it constantly on rings, bracelets, vases, coats-of-arms, and the like. And yet, for all this, the Snake is so little understood. There are certainly more delusions concerning it than any other animal. A great authority on ophidian matters has said that "almost *every* popular notion about a Snake is an error."

It will be well here, I think, to briefly allude to some of the delusions in regard to the Snake. A parishioner of mine, a farmer's wife, was looking one day at my Snakes, and seeing them vibrate their tongues, exclaimed, "Arn't those their 'speers' that they sting with?" And when I explained that the animals were only putting out their tongues, being, no doubt, a little nervous at the presence of a stranger, and that no Snake could hurt anybody with its tongue, my companion remarked, "No, sir," the "No" being said very slowly indeed. That is, the two words were uttered politely, but not believingly. And as, to prove the truth of my assertion, I allowed a tongue or two to touch my hand, the woman started back with an expression of terror in her face, and apparently expected that I would immediately turn pale, fall down, and begin at once to leave off living.

The idea that Snakes sting with their tongue is so common that one can hardly ever stay long in the Reptile House, London, without hearing, for instance, a father saying to his son, "Do you see the thing that Snake is putting in and out? That's its sting." Or one friend may remark to another, "There! did you see the brute put out its sting? You would not think that one touch of that little thing could kill a man? But it would, you know, and quickly, too." The tongue, though very useful to the Snake, is perfectly harmless. Most Snakes will not survive any serious injury to their tongues, but some have been known to eat and drink after having been deprived of them. I have read, but never ventured to test the truth of the statement, that if nicotine be applied to a Snake's tongue the whole of the animal becomes at once perfectly stiff and straight like a stick. This assertion naturally calls to mind the tricks of the ancient Egyptians.

The tongue seems to be used by a Snake as insects use their antennæ, as an organ of touch or contact. Some authorities have thought that it is also employed as a decoy for prey, *e.g.*, a bird will occasionally be tempted to approach a snake, and peck at the quickly-vibrating tongue, probably mistaking it for a worm or something else of a similar nature.

The tongue when not in use is withdrawn into a sheath at the bottom of the Snake's mouth. It must be well protected when prey is being swallowed, for it is very delicate—so delicate that the touch of the tongue of a moderately-sized Snake is scarcely felt on the hand. It also seems so sensitive that its owner is able to obtain by its help some knowledge of an object without bringing the tongue quite in contact with it; just as a blinded bat is said to have the power, by means of its extremely sensitive wings, of detecting the presence of an object it cannot see.

In some books of natural history it is asserted that the Snake uses its tongue for licking its prey in order to cover it with saliva, and so facilitate the act of swallowing. This is, however, a mistake; the prey is indeed enveloped with saliva before it passes the throat, but not by means of the tongue, which could not possibly perform such an office. Occasionally one reads that the tongue of a Snake is used as an organ of sound, but this is another delusion. The lung produces the sound known as hissing, and which often is a cause of terror to both man and beast.

The Snake, therefore, does not use its long, slender, pliant, forked tongue for wounding its enemies, for lubricating its prey, or for making sound.

That a Snake is slimy or clammy to the touch, like a worm, slug, or eel, is also one of the common mistakes referred to in regard to these Reptiles. People, when I have prevailed upon them to place a hand on the body of a Snake, have exclaimed, "Why, it is not slimy after all!" or some similar expression. It seems quite a revelation to them that it is no more unpleasant to touch a Snake than a piece of ivory. Both are quite dry, and both are warm or cold according to their surroundings. If a Snake be taken from a well-heated vivarium its body will be warm and the converse.

A great deal has been written from time to time concerning the Snake's power of fascination. It may be safely said that the popular idea about this supposed power is an illusion. That some animals have this property to a certain extent there can be no doubt, e.g., a stoat can exert a strange influence over a rabbit, and a cat over a mouse. There is foundation for most delusions of this kind, and the one now referred to is no exception to the rule. An observer, for instance, has seen a mouse fleeing with great apparent difficulty from a pursuing Viper. Presently the quadruped ceases to run, staggers, becomes almost motionless, and in due time is seized and swallowed by the Reptile. The conclusion naturally arrived at, under these circumstances, is that the Snake has fascinated its prey; but the real state of affairs was that the Viper had previously struck, with its fangs, the mouse, which when first noticed was really dying from the effects of the poison. A bird bitten by a venomous Snake flies on to the bough of a neighbouring tree, and presently, overcome by the poison, drops down in a helpless condition near its enemy, and is eaten. Here we have another seeming proof of the Snake's powers of fascination. Fear, however, can so paralyse an animal's movements that it loses nearly all powers of action, and the Snake has no other capability of fascination than creating such terror.

Again, the curiosity aroused in a bird by the movements of a Snake's tongue has, according to Dr. Stradling and other authorities on these matters, helped to give rise to the Snake's powers of fascination.

Many people are under the impression that the Snake is ever ready to act on the offensive, and even to go out of its way to attack man; but this is certainly not the case. A Snake will frequently bite in self-defence, and not otherwise, as a rule. Some Snakes, indeed, cannot be induced to bite under any circumstances. It may be taken for granted that a Snake will not try to hurt man if man does not in any way interfere with it. Some Snakes, I know, are always spiteful and ready to bite when handled; but generally a Snake when treated with kindness and care soon becomes so tame as not to resent being handled. Even certain of the most poisonous Snakes — the Rattlesnake, for instance—can be so tamed by gentleness that it may be taken in the hand with impunity. However, I do not recommend any of my readers to test this latter assertion, but in support of it I venture to quote the following from *Health*: " A monarch among poisonous Snakes is the enormous Hamadryas, which grows to be as much as 14ft. in length, and is so fierce that it will sometimes attack and even chase anyone who ventures near its nest. . . . Curiously enough, it is not always aggressive. Indeed, it sometimes happens that it is quite unwilling to strike. Superficially it is not unlike a harmless Rock-snake, and not very long ago, in Burmah, a man brought one in from the jungle and kept it loose in his house for some days, under the impression that it was one of these creatures. During the whole of its captivity it never attempted to bite anyone, and its captor, who had been familiarly pulling it about by the tail, was only apprised of his mistake by a forest officer who happened to turn up, and who knew a good deal about snakes." The writer of the above has evidently lived in India, for he speaks of having occasionally seen a large specimen of the *Hamadryas* in the bags of snake-charmers.

There are many erroneous ideas in regard to the size of the largest Snakes. One reads, for instance, of a Snake 30ft. in length swallowing a cow, and sometimes of Snakes being more than 40ft. long. A few weeks ago there was some correspondence upon this subject in the *Field*. In one letter, Mr. Jamrach referred to his great experience with large Pythons, and said that he was prepared to give £1,000 for a Snake 30ft. long, and £10,000 for a Snake 40ft. in length. Therefore, I think it may be taken for granted that Snakes as long as 30ft. are not to be found.

Not only in old books, but also in some modern ones, illustrations may be seen in which Snakes are represented as progressing by means of vertical motions of their body. In a "Natural History of Reptiles," published not fifty years ago, and which is now before me, there are illustrations of Serpents so travelling. A Snake cannot advance in this fashion.

All the movements of a Snake are not only wonderful, but also exceedingly graceful. The wisest of men and one of the very earliest of naturalists said that one of the three things which were too wonderful for him was " the way of a serpent upon a rock ;" and I think it may be truly asserted that few things in nature are more astonishing than the movements of a Snake. It has no hands, and yet it is all hands ; it has no feet, and yet it is all feet. This is a strange statement to make, but it will not appear altogether inapt to anyone who carefully watches, say, a small constricting Snake capturing and devouring its prey, and one of the very active Snakes travelling over the ground and ascending a tree. Concerning these Reptiles, Professor Huxley has said that " except flying, there is no limit to their locomotion," and that " the most beautiful piece of anatomy he knew was the vertebra of a Snake." The late Sir Richard Owen in speaking of Snakes in his "Anatomy of the Vertebrates" asserted that "they can out-climb the monkey, out-swim the fish, out-leap the jerboa, . . . and out-wrestle the athlete." Another writer, Chateaubriand, quoted by Miss Hopley in her very interesting book on "Snakes," remarks concerning the Snake that "Everything is mysterious, secret, astonishing in this incomprehensible Reptile. His movements differ from those of all other animals. It is impossible to say where his locomotive principle lies, for he has neither fins, nor feet, nor wings; and yet he flits like a shadow, he vanishes as if by magic, he reappears, and is gone again like a light azure vapour on the gleams of a sabre in the dark."

Dr. Günther, in his "Reptiles of British India," and in his article on "Snakes" in the "Encyclopædia Britannica," describes the Snake's manner of locomotion in the following words: "Their organs of locomotion are the ribs (see Fig. 52), the number of which is very great, nearly corresponding to that of the vertebræ of the trunk. They can adapt their motions to every variation of the ground over which they move, yet all varieties of Snake locomotion are founded on the following simple process: When a part of the body has found some projection of the ground which affords it a point of support, the ribs are drawn more closely together, on alternate sides, thereby producing alternate bends of the body. The hinder portion of the body being drawn after some

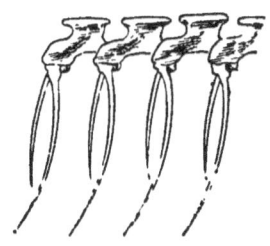

FIG. 52.—SOME OF THE RIBS AND VERTEBRÆ OF THE COMMON OR RINGED SNAKE (*Tropidonotus natrix*) much enlarged from nature.

part of it (Fig. 53, c) finds another support on the rough ground or a projection; and, the anterior bends being stretched in a straight line, the front part of the body is propelled (from Fig. 53, a to d) in consequence. During this peculiar locomotion, the numerous broad shields (Fig. 54) of the belly are of great advantage, as, by means of their free edges, the Snake is enabled to catch and use, as points of support, the slightest projection of the ground. A pair of ribs corresponds to each of these ventral shields (see Fig. 54). Snakes are not able to move over a perfectly smooth surface. Thus it is evident that they move

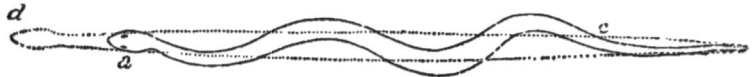

Fig. 53.—Diagram showing Natural Locomotion of a Snake, after Dr. Günther.

by dragging their body over the ground, or over some other firm base, such as the branch of a tree; hence the conventional representation of the progress of a Snake, in which its undulating body

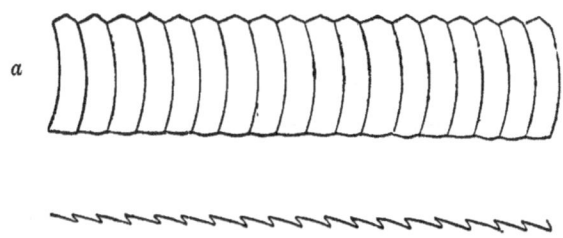

Fig. 54.—(a) Showing the Ventral Scales or Scutæ of a Snake, (Dice Snake *Coluber tessellatus*); (b) Section of a.

is depicted (Fig. 55) as resting, by a series of lower bends, on the ground, whilst the alternate bends are raised above it, is an impossible attitude." Much of the above statement can easily be

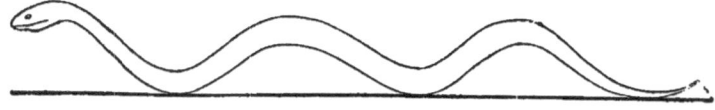

Fig. 55.—Diagram of Conventional Idea of a Snake's Locomotion, after Dr. Günther.

proved, to a certain extent, by placing a Snake on a large piece of well-polished glass. The Reptile is only then able to progress by what may be called a series of frantic wriggles. There is no purchase on such a smooth surface for the free edges of the scutæ.

If a Snake be taken in the hands and loosely held, its body will seem to flow through the fingers in a marvellous manner, apparently without any assistance of the ribs and ventral scales. A good way to feel the movements of the abdominal scutæ, is to allow a Snake to crawl round the neck just above the collar.

The late Sir Richard Owen says, in his "Anatomy of the Vertebrates," that "The vertebræ (Figs. 56 and 57) of Serpents articulate with each other by eight joints in addition to those of the cup and ball on the centrum; and interlock by parts reciprocally receiving and entering one another, like the joints called tenon and mortice in carpentry."

FIG. 56.—THE HIND ASPECT OF A VERTEBRA (much enlarged) OF A RINGED SNAKE (*Tropidonotus natrix*), SHOWING THE "BALL," FROM NATURE.

Some of the large Pythons have more than 400 vertebræ. Nearly every vertebra of the body is provided with a pair of ribs, on the tips of which the Reptile may be said to walk. In a sense, therefore, a Snake is almost all feet, as before remarked.

FIG. 57.—THE FRONT ASPECT OF A VERTEBRA (much enlarged) OF A RINGED SNAKE· (*Tropidonotus natrix*), SHOWING THE "CUP," FROM NATURE.

In Miss C. Hopley's book on the "Snakes," there are some interesting illustrations of three Four-rayed Snakes (*Elaphis quaterradiatus*). The first Snake is represented as holding one bird down with its body while it is preparing to eat another held in its coils. The second Snake is figured as holding one bird down on the ground, retaining another in its coils, and swallowing a third. The third Snake is shown in the act of devouring one bird, while it holds two others in different coils of its body. These illustrations are referred to as endorsing, in a degree, the assertion that though a Snake has no hands it seems to be all hands.

The idea that a Snake is able to leap or spring a long distance is rather common; but this is another fallacy concerning this Reptile. The most active Snake is not able to jump a distance greater than about two-thirds of its own length.

I have heard people say, and have also seen it gravely asserted in books, that a poisonous Snake can easily be distinguished from a non-poisonous one by the greater thickness of its tail, and the greater bluntness of its head. This is a dangerous delusion. There are no outward signs by which all Snakes may be known as either venomous or not. Indeed, some Snakes which have a most noxious aspect, are quite harmless, and the reverse. If one be in doubt in regard to the character of a Snake, it is wise to hold the Reptile quite close to its head, firmly and carefully with one hand, while the other hand opens its mouth by the help of a small ivory paper-knife or similar article, and a search is made in the upper jaws for the fangs. However, it is much wiser for the amateur to have nothing to do with a Snake concerning whose harmlessness there can be any doubt.

There has been a great deal said and written from time to time about ovo-viviparous Snakes opening their mouth when danger is threatening their young and allowing them to take refuge within the maternal body. I will not venture to class this statement among the popular delusions concerning Snakes, yet I fear it to be but a delusion after all. It cannot very well be proved untrue, but, on the other hand, it has never been, I believe, satisfactorily proved to be true.

The common English Viper (*Vipera berus*) is one of the Snakes which is said to receive its young within its mouth in times of danger. People, but not naturalists, have frequently told me that they have seen the Viper thus refuging her young. Living in a county in which Vipers are common, I meet with many of them during the spring and summer months of the year; but I have never, I am sorry to say, witnessed such an act of motherly devotion on the part of these handsome little Snakes. That this proves nothing, either one way or the other, goes without saying. Still, if the habit were really so common as it is reported to be, I should have had a good chance of seeing it.

A mistake, under the circumstances, can easily be made. In support of which assertion I venture to quote the following, taken from Mr. Arthur Nichols' very pleasingly written book on "Snakes, Marsupials, and Birds": "It has been most positively asserted and widely believed that young Snakes, when alarmed, take refuge in the stomach of the parent by going down her throat. Nature has made no provision for this, at all events, as far as anatomy can discover, and the notion is likely to have arisen in the mind of one who opened one of the viviparous Snakes, and found the unborn young within it, and jumped to the conclusion that they had gone there for safety. I witnessed an interesting performance of an Australian Snake, which at first struck me with considerable astonishment, and I might have gone away with a similar impression had I not inquired more closely into the phenomenon. The Snake was crossing a bare spot, followed by a number of young, and did not for a moment observe me. When she did, however, she coiled herself up, and the young disappeared like magic, while she raised her head and hissed continuously. There was no cover to hide a worm, yet, in an instant, every one of the young Reptiles had vanished. It floated across my mind at once that there was an opportunity of ascertaining whether they had gone down her throat, and I fired a charge of shot into the coiled-up mass. The parent was cut to pieces, together with some of the young, and I despatched several more which were still endeavouring to hide themselves among the shattered coils. This they did most persistently, for, whenever I turned the body over and rolled them from under it with a stick, they darted back to their place of concealment, no doubt made quite familiar to them by habit. Some squeezed themselves under the body, others lay close by the side of it, accommodating themselves to every bend in the coils. Not one was found in the throat or stomach either dead or alive, and it is impossible that some should not have been killed there had they been inside the parent at the moment she was shot."

Had this been a harmless Snake it would have been easy to have pinned it with a stick and made the examination at leisure; "but it was one of the most deadly . . ."

A great deal might be written for and against the statement that certain Snakes allow their young to enter their bodies in time of danger, did space permit.

Many people have an idea that most Snakes, if not all, are poisonous, whereas only a little more than a quarter of the 1800 or so species are able to give any poisonous wounds at all. And only a comparatively small proportion of these can give bites which are likely to prove fatal to man. There are no poisonous Snakes in the island of Madagascar. The Indian region is very rich in Snakes, and possesses at least 450 different species, and among which the poisonous Snake to the non-poisonous is as one to ten. Australia has more poisonous Ophidians than non-poisonous. All the Snakes of Tasmania are venomous. All the burrowing and freshwater Snakes are innocuous, while all the sea Snakes are poisonous. Though India possesses so many poisonous Snakes, yet it has been said that there is not a case on record of a European suffering death through the bite of a Snake. Thousands of the natives, as everybody knows, fall victims to the venomous Snakes every year, but much of this loss of life may be attributed to imprudence, carelessness, and superstition.

Of course, all Snakes which are non-venomous must not be considered as harmless. A large Python, for instance, though it has no poison-delivering fangs, can hurt severely with its teeth, and crush with its extremely powerful body. But I think it may be truly said that no Snake of this kind is likely to constrict anything unless it be with the intention of making a meal or in trying to escape when captured. An unhealthy man may suffer from blood-poisoning after having been bitten by an angry Python. I have known of one or two cases. However, it may, I believe, be taken for granted that only a few, comparatively, of the Ophidians are fatally noxious, and of these none, as a rule, go out of their way to attack man. Dr. E. Nicholson speaks of Snakes as "some of the most beautiful and harmless of God's creatures," and he wrote his book on "Indian Snakes" "in the hope of dispelling the lamentable ignorance regarding them."

That Snakes delight to bask in the hot sunshine is another of the delusions concerning them. Snakes, like all Reptiles, need warmth, and if they cannot get it otherwise, they will venture into the sunshine to obtain it there. The very hot rays of the sun are often fatal to Snakes. I have lost Snakes, which, owing to an oversight, had no shade provided for them during a hot day. A very intelligent dealer, from whom I have bought many Snakes from time to time, told me, that being away from his place of business one very warm summer's day, a case containing, I think, ten beautiful Leopard Snakes (*Coluber leopardinus*) was by inadvertence left exposed to the warm sunshine for some few hours, and that nine of the ten Snakes died that day in consequence. I keep in a conservatory, during the summer months, a large Vivarium containing Snakes of different kinds, and I have noticed that when the sun shines upon the case, all the Snakes, without exception, leave their favourite resting-places upon the branches of trees, and retire to the shade provided for them. All Reptiles, when in confinement, should be supplied with shade.

I think the general belief that Snakes can be charmed by music should be added to the list of fallacies about them. Snakes have no exposed ears, and, seemingly, their powers of hearing, like their powers of sight, are very limited. When a piccolo was played softly and shrilly before a case containing Snakes, neither the music nor the noise made any impression upon them as far as I could see.

Probably the so-called dancing to music of the Cobra, for instance, is due simply to excitement of some kind, such as anger or fear. The Indian and Egyptian Snake-charmers are very clever jugglers, and, no doubt, are able to deceive, without any difficulty, by far the greater proportion of their observers.

In those countries where Snakes are common, many a Snake story is told round the camp fire or in the tavern, and men may be heard gravely asserting that they have only escaped the fury of a certain Snake by being mounted on a good horse. The Snake in question may be the "Hoop Snake" or the *Hamadryas*. The former is said to put its tail in its mouth, so making itself into a hoop, and then to bowl itself along at great speed. This, of course, no Snake does, nor could do. Though Snakes can move with extreme rapidity, they can only maintain their celerity for a short distance. This can easily be proved by placing some active Snake in the centre of a smooth lawn, and after its course has been changed a few times by quietly heading it, the Reptile soon becomes exhausted, and ceases to move. Snakes may be readily tamed by taking them gently in the hand when they have been tired in this way. They seem quickly to learn that they cannot escape, and that they are not hurt when they are caught. That any Snake is able to pursue a man swiftly for a long distance is certainly a delusion, even if it had the desire to do so.

One reads occasionally that Snakes, particularly Rattle-snakes, will not cross a horsehair rope, and hunters are accustomed, so it is said, to surround their sleeping-places by the camp fire with such a rope in order that they may run no risk of a bite of a poisonous Serpent. This is also a delusion, I believe. I have found that Snakes will pass over horsehair bands without any hesitation. I must, however, confess that I have not tried the Rattle-snake. The idea is that the short bristly hairs get between the ventral scales (see Fig. 54), and this causes pain and inconvenience to the Snake.

A few other mistakes about these Reptiles are only worthy of a passing notice, viz., that Snakes make holes in the eggs of fowls and suck their contents; that they are accustomed to milk cows, and other animals; that they change their skins and eat only once a year. To anyone who has examined a Snake's mouth, the first two statements are absolutely absurd. Some Snakes, I know, do eat the eggs of birds, but they swallow them without breaking them. A healthy Snake sheds its slough, according to size and age, at intervals from three weeks to three months, or sometimes longer. All Snakes have great powers of fasting, but they would indeed fare very badly if they did not satisfy their appetite oftener than once a year.

Dr. Günther, in his "Reptiles of British India," defines a Snake in the following words: "Body exceedingly elongate, without limbs, or with merely rudiments of limbs, scarcely visible from without; the ribs are articulated movably with the vertebral column; no sternum; generally both jaws and palate toothed; the mandibles united in front by an elastic ligament, and generally very extensible. Eyelids none. Integuments with numerous scale-like folds, rarely tubercular."

There are some snake-like Lizards such as the Glass Snake (*Ophisaurus apus*, Fig. 42) and the Slowworm (*Anguis fragilis*, Fig. 43), and there are Lizard-like Snakes, for example, the Blind Snakes (*Typhlopidæ*) and the Short-Tails (*Tortricidæ*), these Snakes having many characteristics, which will be briefly referred to, of a Saurian type. But the former (the Snake-like Lizards) may be known from all Snakes—and the latter (the Lizard-like Snakes) from all Lizards by the formation of the jaws. The mouth of Ophidians, owing to this formation, is capable as a rule of very great extension. However, some Snakes can open the mouth, in proportion to their size, much wider than others; consequently there are the *Eurystomata*, or wide-mouthed Serpents, and the *Angiostomata*, or small-mouthed Serpents. Nevertheless, the looseness of the jaws, which is characteristic of all Snakes, is only rather less developed in some families than in others.

The jaws, therefore, of all Snakes are very loosely connected. The two halves of their lower jaw are united in front, at the chin, by an elastic ligament or string, instead of being joined together by a bony formation as in most other animals. The other jaws of these Reptiles are also connected very loosely by means of elastic ligaments, viz., the maxillaries or upper jaws, and the palatine jaws, the bones of the palate being generally provided with teeth. The bones called the pterygoid bones are movable, too, and can be pressed forwards and outwards. The lower jaws, or mandibles, are joined to, or suspended from, the skull by means of bones, which conduce to the expanding powers of the gullet. These bones from their position are called tympanic bones.

Most Snakes may be said to have, therefore, six jaws, viz., the two lower, the mandibles, four upper, *i.e.*, two maxillaries and two palatine jaws; but Pythons may be said to possess a seventh, for a bone, known as the intermaxillary, is in their case provided with from two to four teeth. This extra jaw, no doubt, is very useful in the seizing of prey.

For the reasons just mentioned a Snake is able not only to open its jaws exceedingly widely vertically, but also laterally. Each jaw is able to move independently of the other. All the jaws of a non-poisonous Snake are furnished with numerous fine teeth, arranged with their points slanting towards the throat. The teeth, therefore, can only be used for seizing, holding, and forcing the prey down the gullet, and not for division or mastication. Hence, Snakes are obliged to swallow their food undivided. And owing to the wonderful and unique arrangement of their jaws, the extreme dilatability of their throat or gullet, the absence of a sternum, or breast-bone, the looseness of their ribs and the great elasticity of their skin these strange creatures are able to swallow prey of a diameter far exceeding that of their own body.

Snakes in the matter of deglutition are able, in the estimation of the uninitiated, to do the impossible. For example, I was one day showing to a very near relative of mine a small Four-rayed Snake (*Elaphis quater-radiatus*), not much more than 3ft. in length, and I told him that the Snake could swallow, whole, a full-grown dead house-sparrow which I held in my hand. And I heard in reply, "Of course I believe what you say, but it seems to me that the Snake will have to perform an utter impossibility." The Snake, being very tame, readily took the dead bird, and in two or three minutes had swallowed it, claws, beak, and feathers altogether.

People have several times told me their inability to believe that, for instance, a Common English Grass Snake (*Tropidonotus natrix*) can swallow a full-grown frog (*Rana temporaria*). This, however, it generally is quite ready to do. Indeed, I have possessed for a very long time a beautiful variety of the Grass Snake, not 3ft. in length, which will occasionally take two large frogs, one after the other.

A full-sized Grass Snake will sometimes swallow even as many as three frogs at one feeding-time. When a Snake has partaken of a very large meal, the skin of the body, in places, is so stretched that the scales are quite separated one from another. This expansion of skin, especially about the neck of the Reptile, takes place in a greater or less degree whenever it swallows its prey.

We had an instance a little while ago, in the so-called "Tragedy at the Zoo," of the Snake's powers of deglutition. Two Boa Constrictors, one about 11ft. in length, the other about 9ft., were in the same case, when, one night, at feeding-time, the keeper gave them two pigeons, and before he left the Reptile House he noticed that each Snake had commenced to swallow a bird. Next morning the keeper was astonished to find that in the vivarium where he had left two Snakes and two pigeons the night before, there was only one Snake, and which was presenting a most unusual appearance. It was of about three times its normal diameter, and so stiff and uncomfortable that it could not coil itself properly. Its skin was stretched almost to breaking, and every scale in its body seemed separated from its neighbour. The fact, therefore, quickly dawned upon the observer that the larger Boa Constrictor had not only swallowed its own and its companion's supper, but its companion as well. This strange deed is said to have been the result of an accident. And most probably it was. No doubt the cannibal quickly ate its own prey, and being still hungry, and a little greedy also, seized and began to eat the portion of the pigeon which was then protruding from its friend's mouth; and as, under these circumstances, both Snakes were swallowing the same bird, their heads in course of time met, and, the deglutition being continued, the jaws of the larger Boa worked their way over those of the smaller, and thus, though slowly but surely and painfully, passed over the whole of the victim's body until it had disappeared entirely from view. Not only did this Reptile survive its unusual feast, but within a few weeks recommenced to feed.

I have several times nearly had the same kind of accident happen among my own Snakes. For instance, two Snakes have seized the same frog, and each Ophidian has continued swallowing until one Snake has been almost engulfed by the other. More than once or twice I have found a Snake half-way down another Snake's throat (having gone there, as my little son thought, after its own frog). But the stranger part of the matter is that, after I have made the bigger Snake disgorge its friend, the friend has been so little disconcerted by its late experience that it has eagerly taken another frog when it has been offered to him.

I think Dr. Stradling has said somewhere that he has known a frog, after having been swallowed by a Snake and disgorged at once, eat a mealworm within a minute or two of its return to light. One gathers from such circumstances as these, that being swallowed by a Snake need not be, after all, a very painful and terrifying operation to the victim : fear and appetite being, as a rule, incompatible.

Some forty years ago, a Python at the Zoological Gardens, London, swallowed another Python, and failing to digest its relative, died of blood-poisoning. Later than this, another Snake of the same species struck at a rabbit, but, making a bad shot, seized its blanket instead, and ultimately swallowed it; but this proving too much even for a Serpent's wonderful powers of digestion, it was, in course of time, disgorged. When the rug was washed and ironed out, it was found to be perforated by many small holes owing to the action of the animal's gastric juice.

The formation and position of the teeth of a Snake (Fig. 58), and the construction of its head, greatly conduce to such feats of deglutition as those just described. Owners of Snakes have taken advantage of these Reptiles' great persistence in swallowing, when once they have commenced the act, to force a shy feeder among Snakes to make a great meal if, haply, it has been tempted to begin to eat, by tying on other prey or pieces of meat to the body of a partially swallowed animal. The Snake will then, under these circumstances, continue to swallow until it has eaten all that is necessary.

FIG. 58.—LOWER JAW (from Nature) OF A FULL-GROWN RING SNAKE (*Tropidonotus natrix*). *a*, dentary; *b*, articular.

While the larger Boa Constrictor, mentioned above, was spending the greater portion of a night in swallowing its not much smaller relative, its mouth must have been so full of its prey for hours as to prevent all passage of air to its lungs during this time. How then did it breathe or why was it not suffocated? These are questions which are likely to be asked, and which may be answered by saying that Nature has provided Snakes with a means of respiration under such circumstances. If a Snake be watched during the time it is making a lengthened meal, a small, tube-like substance may sometimes be seen protruding between its lower jaw and its victim, and if this pipe-like affair be more closely examined, its orifice will be observed to be opening and closing.

Probably the first explanation of the phenomenon which the

uninitiated onlooker will feel inclined to give, is that it is something belonging to the victim. But, no doubt, on second thought this explanation will appear unsuitable if the prey is observed to be dead (as it would be, most likely, if in the jaws of a constricting or poisonous Snake), and this strange thing is noticed to be endowed with life. Then perhaps it will be supposed that the Snake in making the exertion which is necessary to swallow so large a mouthful, has injured itself.

The fact is, that this curious-looking substance does belong to the Snake, and the Reptile is not hurt. It is, indeed, the upper part of the windpipe, which has been brought forward by means of certain muscles provided for the purpose; and that which was observed to be opening and closing was the glottis, which is situated at the top of the windpipe. As this glottis can be brought forward beyond the limits of the jaws during the time the Snake is swallowing an unusually large mouthful, it will be plainly understood why the Reptile is not choked under such circumstances. While a large Python is performing a difficult act of deglutition, as much as an inch, or even more, of the upper part of the windpipe may be seen.

When a Snake's mouth is opened two tubes can be observed to be situated between the two lower jaws—the bottom one is the sheath of the tongue; and the top one, which is placed a little farther back, but above and parallel to the tongue-sheath, is the larynx or upper part of the wind-pipe. The glottis, under these circumstances, will probably be seen at work.

Reference has already been made to what is frequently called the "Snake's change of skin." This, however, is not a correct expression. The Reptile does not change its skin, but its epidermis, or cuticle. This is a thin membrane which covers the true skin. We have this possession, of course, in common with animals, and our attention is sometimes painfully drawn to it when we have blistered our hands through some unusual manual exercise, or our feet by ill-fitting boots. This epidermis is also known as scarf-skin. When a reptile, especially a Snake, casts its old epidermis that its place may be taken by new, it is said to slough. And that which is thrown off is called the slough, or cast, or exuviæ (there is no singular).

The act of sloughing is a very important one to the Snake, and always more or less affects its health. In fact, the preparation for sloughing is called "sickening" for the same, and the animal is really ill for the time. It becomes inactive and ceases to feed. The colouring of the animal grows dull, and gradually its eyes turn to a light bluish tint and assume an opaque appearance, and probably the creature is nearly, if not quite, blind. At this stage the Snake's disposition often changes for the time being. A quiet Snake sometimes becoming irritable and snappish, while a spiteful one not seldom grows phlegmatic. At from ten days to twenty from the commencement of the "sickening," a decided change takes place in the appearance of the Reptile; its colour gets brighter, and the animal appears to be no longer blind. The novice will at once conclude that the Snake has cast its slough, and will probably imagine, as the slough cannot be found, that the Snake, like the Toad and other Batrachians, is in the habit — at any rate sometimes — of swallowing its discarded garments. This, however, the Snake never does; but as the Reptile at this period will occasionally take food, the inexperienced Snake-owner has plenty of excuse for supposing that a "change of skin" has indeed taken place. The slough certainly has not been cast, but very soon will be. The clear eyes, the brighter colour, and the increased or regained activity of the animal are due to the dampness of the cuticle which is presently to be shed. This dampness seems to be necessary for the successful desquamation; and a slough which has very recently been shed is always moist and pliable.

The sloughing of a Snake is a very interesting operation to watch. When the Reptile has discarded its old cuticle, it is generally found to be, if the Snake be healthy and not very large or old, quite entire, from the covering of the eyes to the tip of the tail, and also turned inside out. A Snake usually gets rid of its slough as a football-player does of a tight jersey, by peeling it off.

If a tame Snake, which is about to "change," be watched, it will be noticed to be in a restless condition, and constantly moving to and fro, carrying its head as low as possible, sometimes rubbing its chin and then its snout against the ground, bottom of its cage, a piece of cork, the side of its bath, or a branch of a tree. It is trying to peel back the epidermis from the edges of its upper and lower jaws, prompted, no doubt, to make this attempt by some unpleasant irritation. Presently the creature's endeavours meet with success, and the delicate membrane may be seen turned back, both above and below, from the jaws. When such a start as this has been made, the rest of the operation is comparatively easy. By the help of the action of the ribs, by crawling among coarse herbage if the animal be at liberty, by climbing trees, by creeping under piles of cork bark, or by working its way under the body of a comrade, the Snake sheds its cuticle, leaving it reversed, and generally entire. A perfect slough is a very beautiful and interesting object and quite worthy of careful preservation. Sometimes a portion of the cuticle of the tail is left unreversed.

If a Snake be old, very large, or not in good health, the slough comes off in pieces, parts sometimes not being removed at all. In the latter case, the Snake should be bathed in warm water, and the remaining pieces of the old epidermis gently peeled off. I have noticed that even a tame Snake is likely to attempt to bite while this operation is being performed. This, of course, is only natural. Therefore, the creature should be properly held by an assistant, if there be any objection to a bite. The bite of a small innocuous Snake may be treated with indifference, but that of a larger animal is another matter.

When a Snake has shed its skin, it appears in all its beauty. Its colours are bright, its movements are quick and graceful, and its scales glisten with a lovely iridescence. Its first act, probably, will be to drink; its second, perhaps, to look for food. At any rate, it may be taken for granted that a healthy Snake will feed within three or four days of "change of skin." A tame Snake of my own has completed the shedding of its slough while I was holding a portion of the latter in my hand.

Young Snakes shed their "skin" for the first time when they are from about six to ten days old. Sometimes they do not feed at all until they have accomplished this operation. Snakes in their early life slough much more frequently than they do when mature.

A slough when perfect is an exact copy of the exterior of the Snake from which it came. The portions which covered the eyes are very curious and interesting. They may be likened, and have been so likened, to tiny watch glasses. In the inverted slough their edges stand up from the rest of the cuticle. They are also far more transparent than any other part of the slough.

A good plan to find out the exact length of a snake is to take the measurement of its unstretched slough. A snake, when alive, is a very difficult subject to gauge accurately. It is generally longer than it seems to be. It is never straight.

If a series of sloughs of any particular Snake be kept, a good idea of the rate of the animal's growth may be obtained.

Snakes are divided by Dr. Günther into the five following groups: (1) The Burrowing Snakes; (2) The Ground Snakes; (3) The Tree Snakes; (4) The Freshwater Snakes; (5) The Sea Snakes.

(1) The Burrowing Snakes live chiefly under the ground, and do not often come above its surface. They have a stiff, cylindrical body covered with smooth and polished scales well adapted for their habit of life. The scales are of the same character all over the body, with the exception, sometimes, of very narrow ventral scutes. The head is small and provided with a narrow mouth which contains comparatively only a few teeth. The eyes are either very small or rudimentary; the tail is short and strong. These Reptiles possess signs or traces of a pelvis; and they feed on worms and other invertebrate animals. None have any power of giving poisonous wounds.

(2) The Ground Snakes, as their name implies, live chiefly on the ground, seldom either climbing trees or entering water. However, when needful they can both climb and swim. Their cylindrical and very flexible body is covered, above, with smooth or keeled scales, and below, with broad scutes (Fig. 54). Of all Snakes, these are perhaps the most beautiful and typical in shape, being exceedingly well-proportioned in every part. The non-poisonous representatives of this group are more numerous than the poisonous. They all feed upon such animals as small mammals, birds, frogs, and the like. The greater proportion of all Snakes belong to this group.

(3) The Tree Snakes are extremely active, wonderful climbers, and spend the greater part of their time in trees. They are the most strikingly coloured of all the Ophidians, their colouring frequently closely resembling that of their surroundings. Their body, which is often very slender, is seldom cylindrical, but frequently compressed. Their eyes, with exceptions, are beautiful and large, and for their size these creatures generally possess an enormous gape of mouth. Their food, as a rule, consists of those animals which lead an arboreal life, such as tree-frogs and birds. The members of this group are both poisonous and non-poisonous ; the latter being more numerous than the former.

(4) The Freshwater Snakes are naturally good swimmers and divers. Their nostrils are arranged to suit their manner of life, being placed on the top of the nose, and possessing the power of closing at will, or when the animal is under water. Their cylindrical and rather long body is provided with a tapering tail and ventral scutes, which are narrow. Their head is short and rather flat, and the eyes are small. These Snakes, which do not often leave the water, are natives of the tropical and sub-tropical parts of the world. They are non-poisonous, and bring forth their young in the water.

(5) The Sea Snakes are beautifully adapted for their mode of life. Their valvular nostrils are placed on the top of the snout ; and their prehensile tail is so strongly compressed as to resemble a kind of vertical fin. As the creatures, with one exception, according to Dr. Günther, never leave the sea, they need no ventral scutes, and therefore possess none. The lower part of their body is shaped somewhat like the keel of a boat. Their eyes are very small, and their scales are not tiled or only slightly so. This arrangement of the scaling, of course, assists their movements in the water. All these snakes are poisonous, and cannot be kept in captivity. They belong to the tropical part of the world, and of that, the Eastern Hemisphere. They feed on marine animals and are viviparous.

Most Snakes lead a diurnal life ; those which are active during the night may generally be known by the pupils of their eyes being contracted into a vertical slit ; sometimes this slit is horizontal in position. Some snakes are ovoviviparous, others are oviparous. These Reptiles are most numerous in the hottest parts of the world; and there, both their size and variety is greatest. In the temperate latitudes they hibernate. Dr. Günther says that "the limits of their distribution seem to be the 70th parallel N. lat. in Europe, the 54th in British Columbia, and the 40th parallel S. lat. in the Southern Hemisphere." The same great authority on these matters also says that "Snakes are the most stationary of all Vertebrates; as long as a locality affords them a sufficiency of food and some shelter to which they can retreat, they have no inducement to change it. Their dispersal, therefore, must have been extremely slow and gradual." This seems to be one of the reasons why Snakes, when properly treated, do so well in captivity. As the shape and arrangement of the head-shields are of great use in distinguishing the various genera and species, and as these shields will be frequently referred to in describing the different Snakes, I have ventured to show, by means of Figs. 59, 60, and 61, their position and names.

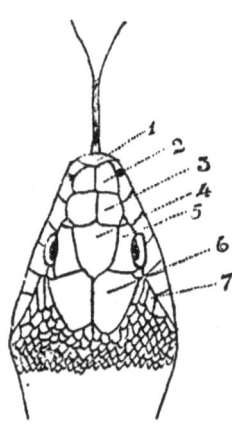

FIG. 59. — DIAGRAM showing the Position and Names of some of the Principal Shields on the Top of a Snake's Head (*Elaphis quaterradiatus*), from nature: 1, Rostral; 2, Anterior frontal; 3, Posterior frontal; 4, Vertical; 5, Supraocular; 6, Occipital or parietal; 7, Temporal.

The Blind Snakes (*Typhlopidæ*) are small burrowing Reptiles, which possess a cylindrical body of almost a uniform thickness throughout. They are covered with smooth tiled scales, all of about the same size and shape. Their stiff polished bodies are well adapted for burrowing purposes. Their eyes, as their name implies, are very small or only rudimentary, by means of which, at the most, some of them have only a perception of light. They are protected from damage while burrowing in the earth by the ocular and præ-ocular shields which cover them, and which are more or less transparent. The front part of their head is covered with large shields. Their blunt conical tail is short, strong, and slightly bent. There are a few teeth in the upper jaws, none on the palate or in the mandibles. The head is small and not distinct from the body; the gape of the narrow mouth is very limited.

These animals feed on earth-worms and insects. After rain, they sometimes appear above the surface of the ground, when they show a certain amount of activity. The family of the *Typhlopidæ* is divided into the following genera: *Helminthophis*, containing about five species; *Typhlops*, numbering about ninety-seven species; and *Typhlophis*, of one species. These creatures are sometimes brought to this country, and therefore, I think, a

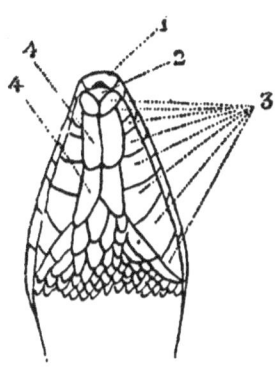

FIG. 60.—DIAGRAM showing the Position and Names of some of the Principal Shields, etc., on the Under Part of a Snake's Head (*Elaphis quaterradiatus*), from nature: 1, Chink through which the tongue is exserted: 2, Mental or middle lower lip shields; 3, Lower labials, or lip shields; 4, Chin shields.

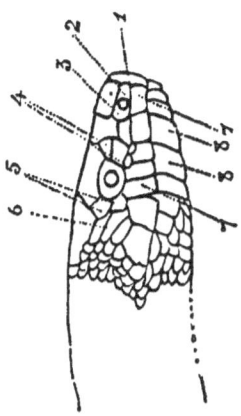

FIG. 61.—DIAGRAM showing the Position and Names of some of the Principal Shields on the Side of a Snake's Head (*Elaphis quaterradiatus*), from nature: 1, Rostral; 2 and 3, Nasal; 4, Præ-orbital or anterior ocular; 5, Post-orbital or Post-ocular; 6, Temporals; 7, Upper labials, lip shields; 8, Lower labials, or lip shields.

short reference to them should not be omitted. They are very far removed from the true Ophidian type, and might be classed as Lizards rather than as Snakes except for the reasons already given. When in captivity they should receive the same treatment as that recommended for the *Amphisbanidæ*. They are natives of Southern Europe, India, Africa, Australia, and Tropical America.

The Black-and-White Blind Snake (*Typhlops nigroalbus*) is about 12in. or 13in. long when full grown, the body being almost

½ in. in diameter. The upper part of the creature is black in colour, and the lower part of a yellowish-white; hence the specific name. The snout of the Reptile is round and very projecting; the nostrils are placed on the sides of the head, level with the eyes, which are visible under shields: the rostral shield is narrow and extends to between the eyes. The Blind Snake comes from Sumatra and the Malay Peninsula; and it has been sometimes seen at the Zoological Gardens, London.

The *Glauconiidæ* chiefly differ from the *Typhlopidæ* in having teeth in the mandibles instead of in the maxillaries, and in possessing a much more developed pelvis and relics of hind limbs in the shape of small cylindrical bones. They are natives of Southern Europe, India, Africa, Australia, and Tropical America. The family of the *Glauconiidæ* numbers the two genera *Anomalepis* and *Glauconia*, and about twenty-eight species, of which the former genus only claims one species.

All the Blind Snakes when in captivity should be kept under the influence of artificial heat.

The Boidæ.—This family is chiefly remarkable for the great size of some of its members, but their size is not nearly so great as is often supposed. In all times the magnitude of these Serpents has been much exaggerated. For example, as many readers will remember, Pliny the elder, the naturalist, quoting from Livy, that inaccurate historian, refers to the huge Snake 120ft. in length which is said to have kept a portion of the Roman army at bay, and that, after it had been killed by catapults and ballistæ, its skin and jaws were exhibited in one of the temples of Rome for considerably more than a hundred years. Aristotle also speaks of Sea-Snakes off the coast of Africa of such a size as to be able to upset the ships of war. Suetonius, the Roman historian, speaks of a Snake shown in Rome as being 75ft. in length. Even modern writers sometimes tell of Pythons as being more than 40ft. long, and that they are capable of killing and swallowing animals as large as cows, and even, in one case, a horse and its rider. In 1877, a captain, officer, and crew of a barque declared, upon oath before a Liverpool magistrate, that they had seen a huge Serpent encircle a whale with its coils, and, after a struggle of some fifteen minutes, take it to the bottom of the sea. "The head and tail appeared to have a length beyond the coils of about 30ft." I dare not venture to say that there is no such animal as that called the "Great Sea-Serpent," for there may be, somewhere in the ocean, a few representatives of those creatures which we know as "extinct gigantic Reptiles," and whose fossil remains are now occasionally found. If the animal were nocturnal in its habits, we should naturally expect it to be only very rarely seen. When people declare that they have met with such a beast, we have no right, I think, to take for granted that they have been mistaken in what they thought they saw. Apparently trustworthy men have affirmed repeatedly that a certain beast known as the "Sea-Serpent" has been observed by them. However, I believe that it may safely be considered very doubtful whether a Serpent possessing a length of 40ft. exists or whether it ever did.

Nearly every large constricting Snake is popularly known as a Boa Constrictor, whereas the true Boa Constrictor is a small animal compared with some of the larger Pythons, hardly ever exceeding a length of 12ft., and is confined to South America. The Python is not found in America at all, but is a native of the tropical and sub-tropical parts of the Old World and Australia. The largest, perhaps, of all the *Boidæ* is the Anaconda (*Eunectes murinus*), a native of the Guianas, Peru, and Brazil, especially in the neighbourhood of the River Amazon. It is said to attain a length of more than 30ft.

Not only are the representatives of this family the most intelligent of all Snakes, but some are also very beautifully marked. Many of them, when properly cared for, do exceedingly well in confinement, living thus for a great number of years.

Those who intend to keep in captivity one or more of these large Snakes ought, of course, to prepare a Vivarium suitable for Reptiles of their size and strength. The case may be made somewhat similar to those represented by Fig. 1 and Fig. 3 (see pages 9 and 11), but the framework must be very strong, and glazed with stout plate-glass. The Vivarium should be at least as long as the length of the Snake or Snakes it is intended to contain, and built according to the proportions already suggested. But if expense be no object, it will be wise to have a den or dens made on the same plan as those are constructed on in which the Pythons and Boas are kept in the Reptile House in the Zoological Gardens, London.

In preparing any kind of case for these Snakes, it should always be an aim to see that it is so arranged that the temperature within it shall be under complete control; that there is plenty of room within it, with the help of shelves and suitable branches of trees, for the inmates to obtain exercise; that the tank is large, large enough, if possible, to allow of the Snake or Snakes bathing without causing the water to overflow its sides (the tank should be square or oblong, so that it can be placed quite close to two sides of the case, or the Snakes will squeeze themselves between it and the walls of the den, and be constantly pushing it from its proper position); and that there are no narrow spaces inside the Vivarium—a shelf, for instance, must be quite close to the side of the case, or well away from it, or the Snakes will be sure to hurt themselves by trying to get through an opening which is far too small to receive their bodies (these Reptiles seem very stupid in this respect).

Of course, it is not wise to give any detailed directions for the construction of these larger and more expensive vivaria, which should be made, as far as possible, of plate glass, Portland cement, and brick or stone, for every amateur will be obliged to arrange for their building according to his surroundings and conveniences. But many of the *Boidæ* can be kept satisfactorily in confinement without going to the expense of making Vivaria as costly as those just referred to.

The Snakes under these circumstances should be young and small for their size. Personally, I prefer small Snakes to large ones, and I dare say there are many other amateurs who have similar tastes. Of course, these Snakes, when properly managed, soon increase in size, but by that time they will probably have become so tame that they may frequently be allowed out of their cases to enjoy a roam about some warm and suitable room or a climb about the person of their owner. To my mind one of the attractions of Snakes is that they may be handled, and that the handling does not hurt them, but conduces very much to their tameness. I cannot see how anybody can love his horse or dog unless it be a pleasure to him to stroke the one and pat the other. So Snakes (at any rate to me) are far more interesting when they will suffer themselves to be handled with impunity and show some affection for their owner, than when they can only be seen while confined in their cases.

To keep these Snakes, then, inexpensively, they should be procured when they are about 4ft. long, or, if possible, even shorter than this. As a rule, Pythons and Boas are priced according to their length, and the smaller they are the less they cost.

The following are brief and, I hope, clear descriptions of cheaply-constructed cases suitable for such Snakes as those just mentioned. As all these Reptiles, while in this country, must be kept under the influence of artificial heat throughout the year, it is therefore necessary that the cases should be so made that the required warmth can be easily supplied.

A large well-made packing-case can be transformed into a Vivarium suitable for a young Boa or Python or two. The box should not be less than 4ft. long, 3ft. deep, and 2½ft. wide. Take the lid off the box and place the latter on one of its sides. In the centre of that side which has been chosen to act as the bottom of the Vivarium, cut an oblong hole about 2ft. long and 18in. wide, the longer sides running lengthwise with the box. On the outside of the box, covering this hole by about 2in. on all sides, screw a piece of thin sheet-iron. Around the inside of the box, nail or screw strong strips of wood 4in. from the bottom. Then cut a piece of finely-perforated zinc the exact width and length of the interior of the case, and nail it very tightly on to the tops of the pieces of wood just referred to, thus forming a kind of false bottom. A small paraffin lamp placed under the centre of the sheet-iron will cause heat to arise through the perforated zinc, and so sufficiently warm the interior of the case. The case may be raised upon four legs of a convenient height, and between them can be hung a small platform upon which to stand the lamp. A sheet of stout plate-glass should be let into the front of the case, covering the whole of the front, and reaching down as far as the perforated zinc. Beneath the glass front a long strip of wood, 4in. wide and as long as the case, ought to be hinged to the front part of the frame which supports the zinc bottom. This will act as a door to close the opening between the zinc bottom and the bottom of the case upon which the sheet-iron has been fastened. The door, which may be fastened below by means of a couple of buttons, is useful for cleaning out the débris which from time to time must fall through the perforated zinc on to the floor of wood and sheet-iron below. The débris will chiefly consist of particles of dried fæces and bits of shed cuticle. A hinged door is made in one or both ends of the case, which will be very useful for cleansing purposes, and for the insertion of food and water. The bottom of the door or doors should be quite level with the perforated zinc floor. This latter arrangement is very convenient for sweeping out the interior of the Vivarium. The doors should be fastened by means of a small, strong spring-bolt—a bolt which always shoots into its socket when the door is closed. The particular bolt I am recommending is made with a small ring-handle which lies flush with its brass surroundings, and which withdraws the bolt from its socket when used to open the door. In addition to this bolt, each door should be fastened at the top and the bottom by a little button.

In the centre of the roof of the case there ought to be another door, not less than $1\frac{1}{2}$ft. square, formed of perforated zinc. The door may be made in the following way : A strong frame of wood is constructed to exactly fit the square or oblong opening made in the top of the case, and over the outside or upper part of this frame is nailed a stout piece of perforated zinc—the zinc extending beyond the outside of the frame by at least $1\frac{1}{2}$in. This overlapping of the zinc will prevent the door from falling through into the case. The door is fastened by means of at least four wooden or metal buttons. This is the door which should be chiefly used in attending to the wants of the inmates of the Vivarium. The interior of the case ought to be quite smooth, and coloured according to the taste of the owner. The outside of the Vivarium, in order to prevent the loss of heat, should be covered with some thick felt of a pleasing colour, the felt being fastened in its place by strong drawing-pins ; for if it be glued on to the wood, there will be a difficulty in removing it should occasion require.

Snakes, like cage-birds, sometimes suffer from troublesome insects, which especially attack the reptiles in the neighbourhood of their eyes. These pests could not be exterminated as far as this particular Vivarium is concerned if they once got under the felt when glued to the outside of the case. But if this covering be only fastened on by drawing-pins, it may at any time be removed and cleansed, and the woodwork painted with paraffin. Further remarks concerning this insect trouble will be made in another place.

Such a case as the one just described is not at all unsightly, and is very useful as a cheap Vivarium for young Pythons and Boas. It should be placed so that its front faces the light. A small paraffin lamp will keep the interior of the case at the desired degree of heat; an extra lamp being used, if necessary, for raising the temperature at feeding-times. In very cold weather, the whole of the perforated door may be covered with felt. A small thermometer, hung inside the case near the top, will help in keeping the temperature under complete control. The perforated zinc bottom may be covered with clean and fine gravel or with a piece of felt cut to such a size that it will cover the bottom of the case with the exception of a margin all round, of about 3in., which (the margin) will allow the heat from the lamp to rise into the case. Two pieces of felt should be made for each Vivarium, so that a clean piece may always be ready to take the place of the dirty one. The felt is easily cleaned when quite dry by means of a hard brush. If gravel be used, a quantity, dried and cleaned, should be ready at any time to take the place of the soiled. I think, however, that the felt is preferable to the stones. Branches of trees and a shelf or two will, in a sense, materially increase the roominess of the case. The bath, made according to the dimensions already suggested, must be placed in one corner of the case. It ought always to contain clean, soft water, which, when freshly introduced, should be warm or tepid: a hot Snake is very likely to get a dangerous chill if it should enter a tank of quite cold water.

Another useful and inexpensive Vivarium for the young members of the *Boidæ* family may be built in a suitable recess of a room. I have such a Vivarium, and have found it very useful and convenient. Such a recess as the one I am speaking of often contains a cupboard which fills the whole space, or two cupboards, one above the other, or one which only occupies the lower part of the recess.

I will suppose that the last arrangement suggested is the existing one, and will describe what should be done in order to construct a Vivarium under such circumstances. The top of the cupboard forms a very convenient resting-place on which to stand the lamp used for heating the case above. The two bottoms of the Vivarium should be made according to the directions given for the case just treated of; that is, the lower or real bottom should be made of strong wood and sheet iron, and the upper or false bottom of perforated zinc. There must be a space of at least 4in. between the two bottoms, or the perforated zinc may get so hot at times as to scorch the Snakes lying immediately above the lamp. The lowest part of the Vivarium—that is, the sheet of iron—ought to be so high above the existing cupboard as to allow the top of the chimney of the lamp it is decided to use, while standing on the cupboard, to reach within about 2in. of the sheet iron it is intended to heat. For convenience a lamp should be chosen for this purpose which will burn for rather more than twenty-four hours without attention. I prefer a small lamp in which a circular wick is used, as this seems to give a great quantity of heat in proportion to oil consumed. Gas, of course, can be utilised instead of a paraffin lamp.

This case should be made of the same proportions as the one last described. It may extend to the ceiling of the room or not: this naturally depends upon such circumstances as the loftiness of the room and the taste of the owner. If the case be not built up to the ceiling of the room, it should be provided with a roof and a perforated zinc door, as already suggested for the former Vivarium. The front of the Vivarium should be formed of two doors, meeting at the centre of the case. The framework ought to be made strongly of wood, and glazed with stout plate-glass. The bottom of these doors must be level with the false bottom of perforated zinc: cleaning purposes make this a necessity. One door, preferably the left, is fastened at the top and bottom by two small bolts, made for such purposes. To this door, that on the right hand is fastened by means of the spring bolt and the buttons already described. If the Vivarium is intended to reach to the ceiling of the room, the doors need not extend to quite the same height; but the space between their tops and the ceiling can be filled in with woodwork, in which ventilators have been made, capable of being closed or opened at will. The openings which go to form the ventilators must be covered, on the inside, with finely-perforated zinc.

This Vivarium of course will be built high or low in the recess according to the height of the cupboard underneath. If it be high, I will here venture to give the amateur Snake-keeper, who has not had much experience in these matters, a caution, viz., in going to this case he should see that his face be well above the floor of the Vivarium, for an angry or vindictive Snake might give him a bite in the face as he incautiously opens the door. He ought to stand on a stool or chair as he attends to his charges, especially when they have not been tamed.

If the recess spoken of be empty, the Vivarium can be built at the most convenient height. In the case of the two cupboards, the upper one may possibly be converted very easily into a suitable Vivarium; in that of the single cupboard, a wise division can probably be made which will leave the lower part still as a cupboard (the top shelf of which may be used as a stand for the lamp), the upper division being converted into a Vivarium. Of course many modifications of the cases just described can be made. The internal arrangements of these cupboard Vivaria should be the same as those already suggested.

These Snakes may be kept temporarily in large boxes (and very often are so confined), but they must under these circumstances be supplied with artificial heat. This necessary warmth can be obtained (1) by placing within the boxes, together with the Snakes, india-rubber bottles or bags containing hot water, but not so hot as to hurt the Reptiles; or (2) the boxes may be provided with two bottoms, as already described, and placed over a small lamp. The latter arrangement, as a rule, is the more convenient, for the hot water bottles need frequent periodical attention. Each of the boxes should be furnished with a thermometer, so that the heat may be properly regulated.

The temperature at which the *Boidæ* should be kept may vary from 60deg. to 85deg. Fahr. It is not wise to keep these Reptiles always at the same, or about the same temperature; for it is certainly not a condition in which they would live while in a state of nature.

As a rule, Pythons and Boas will not feed unless they are very warm. The heat, therefore, of their cases at feeding-time should be raised to from 75deg. to 85deg.; and when they have eaten, the temperature may be allowed to sink gradually to 65deg. or 60deg., but only for a time. The food of these Snakes consists of rats, mice, guinea-pigs, birds, rabbits, and other animals of a like kind, which, unfortunately, must often be given alive to the Reptiles.

The Ophidians' method of feeding is their one drawback as pets. However, comparatively speaking, they eat very seldom. They can fast, though not in a torpid condition, with impunity for six months at least, and some of these creatures have been known to go without food for more than two years, and then recommence to feed. It certainly does seem cruel to place a living animal in a hungry Snake's Vivarium; but it is not nearly so cruel as at first sight it seems to be. Nevertheless, I am always glad when any of my Snakes will take dead food.

A member of the *Boidæ* will kill an animal far more quickly than a man can slay a fowl for his master's dinner, and cause it far less terror. I have seen, for instance, a sparrow, with apparent unconcern, hopping about close to a small constricting Snake, when suddenly there was a movement on the Reptile's part, so rapid that the eye could not follow it, and the bird had been crushed to death in its captor's coils. It seems far more cruel for a fisherman to throw a fish he has just caught upon the bank of a river and allow it to die gradually there, or for a sportsman to shoot at an animal when he has small chance of killing it at once, and so running the risk of causing the creature, after having escaped for the time being, to die in solitude, a slow and painful death, than to place a white rat or pigeon (both used to confinement) in a Python's Vivarium, where it will move about quite at its ease until it is instantaneously crushed in the folds of the Reptile's body. Sometimes, unfortunately, these Snakes do not use their coils when attacking their prey; but I have given reasons for thinking that the act of being swallowed alive by a Snake is not so painful and terrifying a process to the lower animals as is generally supposed. Some people, I know, have condemned in the strongest terms the feeding of reptiles in confinement upon live animals; and yet, perhaps, they will look with complacency or unconcern upon a blackbird on their lawns pulling a large worm out of its hole in the grass, or at a thrush banging a snail upon a stone until the crustacean's shell is broken to pieces. Of course, all unnecessary cruelty should be most sternly censured; and I have often and often wished that Snakes and all other animals were vegetarians. But how then could the balance of Nature be maintained?

The prey should be introduced to the Snake at night, and if not eaten by the morning, should then be removed. Animals which have been born in captivity ought to be preferred for this purpose, as they will spend the night in the Vivarium without experiencing any fear, and will not be likely to hurt the Snakes or gnaw holes in the cases as wild rats or mice would do. I have had from time to time valued Snakes killed by the rats and mice which had been placed in the cases with the reptiles. Even a guinea-pig will sometimes annoy a large Snake by repeatedly nibbling at various parts of its body. A Snake under these circumstances generally shows wonderful forbearance. I have seen a small white rat tease a savage Boa Constrictor by running up to the Reptile's nose and bite or touch it, and yet the animal bore all this apparent irritation very patiently, only gently resenting the rodent's interference. The Boa, however, was by no means too lazy to bite, for he struck at me most fiercely with wide open mouth when I attempted to remove the rat.

Young rats, before their eyes are open, will lie quite comfortably in the Snake's warm den until they are eaten, or until they are removed next day.

A Boa or a Python may be persuaded, sometimes, to take a dead mouse, bird, or rat, by gently swinging the body near its mouth, and when the Reptile has fairly commenced to eat, other dead animals or even pieces of raw meat may be tied to the creature that has been seized, and in this way the Snake is induced to consume a meal which will last him for a considerable time.

The following arrangement I have found successful in tempting Snakes to swallow dead animals. A piece of thin cotton, about 2in. long, is tied to the tail of a dead rat, or other suitable animal, and to the cotton is fastened a piece of strong thread, of a length sufficient to allow the nose of the dead animal to swing just clear of the floor of the Vivarium when the free end of the thread is affixed to a ring or hook in the roof of the case. The dead body will keep moving for a long time after it has once been put in motion. Even the Snake itself, while crawling about its den, is very likely to set the animal swinging again when it has stopped doing so. I once thus suspended a dead mouse for a large Dark Green or Angry Snake (*Zamenis atrovirens*), thinking that as the Reptile seized the animal the cotton by which it was partly hung would break and allow the act of deglutition to be successfully accomplished; but next morning I saw a sight which I had not expected to see, viz., a Snake hanging with its head quite close to the roof of the Vivarium. The fact was, that a small Zamenis, which I did not think would feed during that night, had seized the suspended mouse, and not being strong enough to break the cotton, had continued swallowing its prey until its own head was brought into the position in which I found it. Some Snakes will even habitually take dead animals in preference to live ones.

There is a way by which Snakes may be fed, even from their birth, without ever giving them live food. This method of feeding will be fully described in another place. Snakes do very well under such treatment, and if it be properly carried out, their owner is saved a great deal of trouble by not being obliged to procure the live animals, which are usually necessary for the feeding of these Reptiles.

The *Boidæ* are divided into two sub-families, viz., the *Pythoninæ* and the *Boinæ*, the chief difference between them being a supra-orbital bone which is possessed by the former and not by the latter. The *Pythoninæ* comprises seven genera and about twenty-one species, and the *Boinæ* numbers thirteen genera and about forty-five species.

, The *Boidæ* have rudiments or vestiges of a pelvis and hind limbs, the latter having the appearance of hook-like claws, and can be seen one on either side of the vent. The mandible, maxillary, palatine, and pterygoid bones are all toothed and movable; but the members of the genera *Loxocemus*, *Nardoa*, *Liasis*, and *Python* have also teeth on the intermaxillary or præmaxillary bone. The pterygoid or wing-like bones are behind the palatine bones, and in the *Boidæ* sometimes extend as far back as the quadrate or tympanic bone.

Some of these large Snakes, such, for instance, as the Anaconda (*Eunectes murinus*), spend a great part of their time in water; while others, *e.g.*, the Boa Constrictor, hardly ever enter it.

The Diamond Snake (*Python spilotes*, Boulenger, or *Morelia spilotes*, Lacép., is a native of Australia and New Guinea, and it has the distinction of being the only harmless Snake in the colony of Victoria. The other Snakes which are found in this Colony are more or less poisonous, for Australia unfortunately possesses more venomous Ophidians than non-venomous. However, only four or five species of the former can be considered deadly.

Some of the venomous Snakes are not provided with poison sufficiently strong to seriously injure a healthy person, and they can only inflict a wound a little more painful than that caused by the sting of a wasp. Others of the poisonous Snakes (*e.g.*, *Brachysoma diadema*), like our own Grass Snake (*Tropodonotus natrix*), are most unwilling to bite, and may generally be handled with impunity. A variety of the Diamond Snake (*P. spilotes*), generally called the Carpet Snake (*Morelia variegata*, Gray), which, of course, also is perfectly harmless, must not be confounded with another Carpet Snake of Australia (*Hoplocephalus curtus*), or with the Carpet Viper (*Echis carinata*) of India, both of which are very deadly.

The Diamond Snake is a small and slender Python of about 6ft. in length. It is easily tamed, but unfortunately is not very hardy. It should be fed upon rats, mice, and birds, and be kept fairly warm. The Snake can sometimes be bought in this country at sums ranging from 10s. to £3.

The following is part of Mr. Boulenger's description, given in the "Catalogue of Snakes in the British Museum," of this Snake and its varieties: "Rostral as broad as deep, or a little deeper than broad, visible from above; internasals (or anterior frontals, see (2) Fig. 6) as broad as long, followed by a pair of somewhat larger shields, which may be broken up; the rest of the upper surface of the head covered with scales or small irregular shields, among which, however, an enlarged frontal (or vertical, see (4) Fig. 59) shield and two or three supra-oculars are sometimes conspicuous; 11 to 13 upper labials, the first two or three deeply pitted; scales in 45-51 rows; ventrals 251-304; anal entire or divided; sub-caudals 63-92. Coloration very variable." The tail equals about one-eighth of the length of the entire animal.

The colour of the Diamond Snake (*P. spilotes*) is "black above, each scale with a yellowish dot, with or without scattered yellow, black-edged spots; upper labials black-edged; lower parts yellow, posterior ventrals and the sub-caudals spotted or edged with black."

The colour of the variety of *P. spilotes* known as the Carpet Snake (*Morelia variegata*, Gray) is "pale brown with dark brown black-edged spots or cross-bands, or dark brown with lighter markings; head with symmetrical dark brown markings; upper lip uniform yellowish, or only the anterior labials black-edged; a light, dark-edged streak may be present along each side of the anterior part of the body; lower parts yellowish, more or less spotted with black."

The colour of another variety (*Morelia variegata*, Krefft) is pale olive-brown above, each scale edged with black, with yellowish black-edged spots and crossbars, or with three yellowish stripes, the middle one partly broken up in spots; upper labials black-edged; lower parts pale yellow, the posterior ventrals and the sub-caudals spotted or edged with black."

The Reticulated Python (*Python reticulatus*) is one of the most beautiful members of the family to which it belongs. It is, according to Dr. Günther, the *Ular Sawa* of the Malays. It is a native of Burmah, India, the Malay Peninsula, and Archipelago. Though a delicate Snake, it has been known to live for a long time in confinement. There is, or was, a very fine specimen at the Zoological Gardens, London, whose length has been estimated at about 26ft., and its weight at about 18st.

Another Indian Python (*Python molurus*) (see Fig. 62), the West African Python (*P. sebæ*), and the Anaconda of South America (*Eunectes murinus*) are the largest living Reptiles, but not the heaviest, for some of the *Crocodilia* would weigh more. These huge non-venomous Serpents have immense muscular power, which they use with wonderful rapidity. They are able to kill, by constriction, animals far larger than they can swallow ; though they can eat creatures of greater diameter than that of their own body. When encouraged by hunger, they occasionally make a meal of an animal of the size of a large spaniel ; but, as a rule, they seem greatly to prefer such prey as small rodents and birds. They seize the victim with their teeth, and then quickly encircling it with the coils of their body crush it instantaneously to death. They generally commence swallowing the creature they have killed at the head, discharging over the victim as they do so a quantity of saliva, which helps to overcome the resistance offered by the fur or feathers. This saliva also, no doubt, is an aid to digestion.

The Reticulated Python is very fond of water, and it should therefore be provided while in confinement with a tank sufficiently large to receive the whole of the Reptile's body without causing the water to overflow. In captivity it will eat rats, rabbits, pigeons, ducks, and guinea-pigs.

This Snake's rostral shield is as broad as it is deep, and visible from above; and it has a pair of anterior and posterior frontals. Four of its upper labials are deeply pitted, and five or six of the lower. It has small scales, which are arranged in about 75 rows at the thickest part of the body. It has from 297 to 330 ventrals, and from about 80 to 102 sub-caudals. The anal scale is entire.

The ground-colour of the Reticulated Python is a light yellowish-brown with, according to Mr. Boulenger, " large circular, rhomboidal, or X-shaped markings; the young with three longitudinal series of light, black-edged spots; a black line along the middle of the head, from the end of the snout to the nape, and another on each side from behind the eye to the angle of the mouth; lower parts yellowish, with small spots on the sides, or nearly entirely brown." This Snake is said to reach a length of 30ft. Its tail measures a little more than one-seventh of the creature's entire length. There are some often quoted stories concerning the great Reptile which cannot be relied upon as to their accuracy.

Of all the large Snakes, the West African Python (*Python sebæ*) is the hardiest, being able to endure a comparatively low temperature. It is generally, while in captivity, a good feeder and, with proper treatment, is easily tamed. No large Snake used to be imported into this country in such large numbers as this, but of recent years the Indian Python (*P. molurus*) seems to have taken its place. Still, however, a healthy specimen of *P. sebæ*, of about 4ft. in length, can sometimes be bought for about 25s. At any time, I think that a Snake of this species and of the above size may be purchased of our largest dealers in these Reptiles for from £2 5s. to £3.

In buying any snake, the amateur, if possible, should see it travel over the ground or a floor, so that he may be able to judge from its movements whether it has been injured or not. Its motion should be graceful, easy, and flowing. A Snake, while being captured, is sometimes injured in the backbone, and any serious hurt would be likely to be noticed while the creature was crawling. A careful examination should also be made of the animal's head and body for any swellings or symptoms of disease. These large Serpents not seldom suffer from tumours. A Snake which has lately shed its slough should be chosen in preference to one which is about to do so. The Reptile ought also to be handled to test its vigour and firmness : when limp, the animal should be rejected. If it seems savage and tries to bite, so much the better. The colour should be bright and iridescent, and not dull or dead. It is always wise to buy Snakes and other Reptiles as soon after capture as possible.

The Pythons and some other Snakes incubate their eggs. In 1862 a *Python sebæ* laid upwards of a hundred eggs, and for more than seven weeks patiently "sate" on them, guarding them most jealously all the time. Unfortunately she was disturbed several times by the cleaning of her den; the giving of food to her companion, the male; the overflowing of the tank, and the necessary consequent re-arrangement of the eggs; the "changing of her skin" on the fifty-third day; and the insertion of a thermometer between her coils from time to time, to take her temperature. All these things, more or less, militated against her chance of success. The eggs, however, for the most part were fertile, though none were hatched. The Python's temperature, during the incubation, rose higher than that of the den in which she was confined.

The following table shows the variation of the temperature (Fahr.) between the female Python, her mate, and her den :

Date.	Temperature on the surface of Body.		Temperature between the Coils.		Temperature in Den.
1862.	Male.	Female.	Male.	Female.	
February 12..	70·2	73·0	74·8	81·6	58·6
February 23..	71·8	75·0	74·0	83·2	65·4
March 2	71·6	84·0	76·0	96·0	60·0
March 9	72·8	79·5	Not taken.	86·5	61·0
March 16	72·4	77·6	77·6	86·0	66·0

Each Snake had moss under it and a rug or blanket over it. The male Python showed not the slightest interest in his wife's occupation. During her attempted incubation of her eggs the female Snake was exceedingly savage, and very impatient of all interference.

Python sebæ, because of its hardiness, docility, and cheapness, is very commonly exhibited in travelling menageries, and there are generally several specimens of this Snake in the various zoological gardens.

The arrangement of the head-shields of the West African Python is very like that of the head-shields of the Reticulated Python; but the scales of its body are smaller than are those of its near relative just mentioned, being placed in from eighty-one to ninety-three rows. There are from 269 to 286 ventral scales; the anal scale is either entire or divided; the sub-caudals number from sixty-three to seventy-seven.

The ground-colour of the body of the *Python sebæ* is pale brown above, with, according to Mr. Boulenger, "dark brown, black-edged, more or less sinuous cross-bars, which are usually connected by a continuous or interrupted sinuous dark stripe running along each side of the back; sides with large spots, and finely dotted with black; a large triangular dark brown blotch occupies the top of the head, bordered on each side by a light stripe beginning at the end of the snout, above the nostril, and passing above the eye; a dark stripe on each side of the head, and a dark sub-triangular blotch below the eye; upper surface of tail with a light stripe between two black ones; belly spotted and dotted with dark brown."

This Snake is said to reach sometimes a length of 23ft. Its tail equals about one-ninth of its entire length. The reptile is a native of Tropical and South Africa, and many stories are told of its strength, activity, and voracity. Many of the statements, however, concerning it are greatly exaggerated.

The Indian Rock Snake (*P. molurus*, see Fig. 62) is one of the hardiest members of its family, being able to endure a greater amount of cold than any of its relatives. It feeds very readily while in captivity; and there is no difficulty in obtaining specimens in England. Some of the larger dealers in animals always have this Snake in stock. One dealer has often as many as 300 of these Serpents on his premises at the same time. When one sees box after box literally full of Pythons of all sizes one naturally asks what can possibly become of them all. The greater number are, no doubt, exported again to the Continent. Some are disposed of to owners of menageries and to the authorities in charge of Zoological Gardens; and only comparatively few of them are purchased by private persons.

Python molurus does not seem to be so easily tamed as its near relative of West Africa, *P. sebæ*. The former species is famous because one of its female members was the first which proved in public, while an inmate of the Paris Zoological Gardens, that certain Snakes brood their own eggs. She naturally excited a great deal of interest among scientific and other people by her feat of successful incubation. On 6th May, 1841, this Snake, about three months after pairing, laid fifteen eggs, all separated one from another, and as large as those of an ordinary goose. They were covered with a white leathery envelope. She arranged them in a cone-shaped heap, and placed herself round and over them, hiding all from view, and rested her head on the top of the pile.

The Python remained in this position, with an exception or two, for fifty-six days, when her young ones began to appear. Her temperature was carefully taken from time to time, and was always found to be considerably higher than the surrounding air. Of the fifteen eggs, eight were successfully hatched, the others being probably crushed or injured by the weight of the mother. During the incubation of her eggs, the Snake ate no food at all; but immediately before and after her brooding she consumed some raw meat. Between these two meals she fasted for more than four months. She drank water, however, during this period, several times. The young Pythons after shedding their sloughs, when about ten days old, constricted and swallowed some sparrows.

The Indian Rock Snake is called the *Adjigar* by the Hindoos, and by other people it is often misnamed the Boa. Though known as the Rock Snake, it prefers, like our own Ringed Snake, the neighbourhood of water or marshy ground. There it finds in plenty the food upon which it lives. Dr. Günther, in describing the head-shields of *P. molurus*, says that it has "a pair of anterior and posterior frontals; several other small shields between the vertical and posterior frontals. The two anterior upper labials and four of the lower ones are pitted. Supra-orbital not divided; the sixth upper labial is below the orbit, entering it. Scales small, in about sixty-five series round the middle of the trunk; those of the outer series large, half the size of the ventrals. Ventrals, 242-262; anal, entire; sub-caudals, 60-72. The ground-colour is light greyish-brown. A brown spot, shaped like the head of a lance, occupies the crown of the head and the nape; its point rests on the frontals, but frequently it is truncated anteriorly, its extremity being on or behind the vertical, a light, medium streak divides its triangular portion into two. A dark brown streak runs from the nostril through the eye to behind the angle of the mouth, gradually becoming broader and confluent with another band running along the lower jaw. A sub-triangular brown spot below the eye. Back of the body and tail with a vertebral series of large quadrangular spots, the margins of which are sometimes serrated, sometimes straight; an oblong spot on each side of each of these quadrangular spots. Sides of the body with another series of rather irregular brown spots, which sometimes have a light centre. Lower parts yellowish, brownish, or blackish on the sides." This Snake is said to have attained a length of 30ft. The tail of the animal is a little more than one-eighth of its entire length.

The Royal Python (*P. regius*) is a most suitable inmate of the Vivarium. It is a very gentle and handsome Reptile, and not by any means large for a Python. Dealers generally call it the "Ball Snake," from its habit of lying rolled up. It comes from West Africa, especially from the neighbourhood of Gambia and Sierra Leone. Though a rarer animal than either *P. sebæ* or *P. molurus*, it can sometimes be bought almost as cheaply as they can, probably because, being of a smaller size, it is not so attractive as its larger relatives in the eyes of the ordinary showman.

The head-shields of this Python are arranged, to a considerable extent, like those of the Reptile just described. It has about ten upper labials, the first four being deeply pitted, three or four of the lower labials being only slightly pitted. The scales are arranged in from fifty-three to sixty-three rows. The ventrals number about 200, the anal being either divided or entire. There are from thirty to thirty-seven sub-caudals. Mr. Boulenger, in describing the colour of the Royal Python, says that the upper surface of the head is "dark brown, with a pale, black-edged streak on each side, beginning above the nostril and passing through the eye; a dark brown, black-edged band occupies the back, sending down triangular or Y-shaped processes on the sides, which are pale brown; this dorsal band encloses a light streak on the neck, another on the tail, and a series of from ten to eighteen light round or oval spots; belly yellowish with or without small brown spots on the sides." This Snake is not often more than 4ft. long. The tail equals about one-twelfth of the animal's entire length.

All the members of the genus *Python* have nostrils which point upwards; moderately sized eyes, with vertical pupils; a body which is more or less compressed, and covered with small smooth scales; and a prehensile tail more or less short.

The Pale-headed Tree Boa (*Epicrates angulifer*) lives very well in confinement, but unfortunately it is rather rare in this country. It may sometimes, however, be bought at a reasonable price from the dealers in this kind of animal. It has bred while in captivity, and has also produced hybrids between itself and the Yellow Jamaica Boa (*Chilabothrus inornatus*). The hybrids were born in the Zoological Gardens, London, on 30th August, 1876, and on 9th September, 1879. In the former case the parents were a female *E. angulifer* and male *C. inornatus*; and in the latter, a male *E. angulifer* and a female *C. inornatus*.

In speaking of these hybrids, Mr. Boulenger, in his "Catalogue of Snakes" (1893), says that "they do not differ from *Epicrates striatus*, and as I entertain doubts concerning the correct determination of the parents (which I have not been able to trace) I feel justified in referring them to this species."

These crosses are referred to in the "Proceedings of the Zoological Society" for 1878, page 789, to which, however, I have not at present access, but Miss Hopley, in her book on "Snakes," said that "in recording the event the Secretary to the Zoological Society, P. Lutley Sclater, Esq., Ph.D., F.R.S., etc., writes that there can be no question as to the pairing of these two Snakes, both in the same cage, as there was no male *Epicrates* in the collection. Three were alive, and six bad eggs were produced."

The Pale-headed Tree Boa does not grow to any great size, a length of 7ft. being probably its limit. As all Snakes of the genus *Epicrates* are distinguished by the great length of their teeth in the front parts of their jaws, a bite from this animal and all its near relatives should be avoided as far as possible.

The *Epicrates angulifer* possesses a head distinct from the neck, and covered with shields, "the largest," according to Mr. Boulenger, "being a pair of præ-frontals, a pair of frontals (which may be broken up), and, on each side, a supra-ocular; a large, elongate loreal (a shield immediately above the labials, and between the nasals and the anterior ocular), sometimes divided into two, separated from the labials by a series of small shields; a large præ-ocular, and a series of six small shields below and behind the eye, which is entirely separated from the labials; thirteen or fourteen upper labials, with very feeble pits. Scales in fifty-one to sixty-five rows; ventrals, 276 to 290; anal, entire; sub-caudals, fifty to seventy-nine. Pale brown above, with a dorsal series of rhomboidal dark spots, and dark brown reticulated lines on the sides; a lateral series of dark-brown ocelli with yellowish centres; yellowish beneath." This snake comes from Cuba. Its tail is short.

The Jamaica Yellow Boa (*Epicrates inornatus*, Boulenger, or *Chilabothrus inornatus*, Dum. and Bibr.) is a hardy snake, common in its own country, and by no means rare in the various zoological gardens. It feeds well while in captivity, but is generally more or less spiteful. As already mentioned, it has bred in confinement. This Snake's head is distinct from its neck, and covered with shields which are more or less regular. Its rostral is a little broader than it is deep. It has a pair of anterior and posterior frontals, the latter pair being sometimes broken up into small irregular shields. Its vertical shield, supra-ocular, præ-ocular, and loreal shields are large; the last are also elongated. It has from two to four post-oculars; its labials are not pitted. Its scales are arranged in about forty-two rows; its ventrals number from 260 to 286; and its sub-caudals from sixty to eighty. Mr. Boulenger's description of the colour of this snake is "Yellow or pale olive anteriorly, frequently blackish-brown posteriorly; more or less distinct spots or cross-bars on the body; sometimes a pair of dark streaks along the neck; an ill-defined dark streak may be present behind the eye." The tail equals about one-sixth of the length of the entire animal.

The Anaconda or Water Boa (*Eunectes murinus*) is supposed to be the largest of all Snakes. As its generic name implies, it is very fond of water, and while in captivity it generally spends the greater portion of its time in the tank. It has received many titles, such as the "Bull-Killer" (*Matatoro*) and the "Deer-Swallower" (*El Troga Venado*); but its specific name, *murinus*, should remind us that its natural food consists of rodents and other animals of about the same size. It could no doubt kill a bull, for it has immense strength, and it might swallow a very small deer, but it certainly is not its custom to perform either of these feats.

It was a Snake of this species which by simply expanding its coils (it had lately been removed from its confined travelling-case, a large tub, I believe), as it reposed between the tree or tank and the plate glass, pushed out the whole front of its den, which, no doubt, would have fallen and broken had it not been for the presence of mind of some interested spectators, among whom, I believe, was the late Mr. Frank Buckland, who caught the frame and held it in or near its place until, after not a little trouble, it was properly and securely refixed. The den contained besides this Anaconda two others, and a large Python as well. The Vivarium—for this happened in the old Reptile House at the Zoological Gardens, London—was weak from age and damp. As far as I can remember, this particular Anaconda was about 18ft. long. Subsequently it produced several fully-developed young ones, all, however, born dead. She had, no doubt, owing to her captivity and journey, retained her offspring too long; for Snakes have this strange power of postponing, at will, the laying of their eggs or the birth of their little ones. Ultimately the poor Serpent showed signs of disease, and had to be destroyed.

The Anaconda is expensive to buy, a good one, according to Dr. Stradling, being worth about £30. It is a very beautiful animal, and though generally rather savage when first caught, quickly under wise treatment becomes tame.

The rostral of this Snake is hardly visible from above. The posterior frontals, loreals, præ-oculars, and supra-oculars are large. There are three post-oculars and two sub-oculars, which are separated from the labials by some small shields. The upper labials number about sixteen. The scales are smooth, and are arranged in about sixty rows. The anal scale is entire; the ventrals are from 242 to 266, and the sub-caudals from fifty-six to seventy-three. Mr. Boulenger describes the colour " as greyish brown or olive above, with a single series or with two alternating series of large blackish transverse spots and one or two lateral series of blackish ocelli with white centres; top of the head dark, separated from the paler sides by a black streak forming a point on the snout; an oblique black streak on each side of the head behind the eye, lower parts whitish, spotted with black." This snake is said to sometimes attain a length of 33ft. It comes from the tropical parts of South America, especially the neighbourhood of the River Amazon.

The Common Boa (*Boa constrictor*) is one of the most beautiful as well as one of the most intelligent of all Snakes. Because of its colouring it has been called *Constrictor formosissimus* and *Constrictor rex-serpentum*. In this country it is sometimes known as the "King Snake" and also as the "Harlequin Snake." Unfortunately the Boa is not quite so hardy as some of its family; but with care it lives for a long time in captivity, and when kindly treated and frequently handled it becomes quite tame, and, sometimes, shows no little affection for its owner. In support of this statement I venture to make a rather long quotation from the late Professor Romanes' book on "Animal Intelligence."

"The following interesting observation on the intelligence of Snakes shows, not only that these animals are well able to distinguish persons, and that they remember their friends for a period of at least six weeks, but also that they possess an intensity of amiable emotion scarcely to be expected in this class. Clearly the Snakes in question were not only perfectly tame, but entertained a remarkable affection for those who tended and petted them. The facts were communicated to me by Mr. Walter Severn, the well-known artist, who was a friend of Mr. and Mrs. Mann, the gentleman and his wife to whom the Snakes belonged. Mr. and Mrs. Mann having got into trouble with their neighbours on account of the fear and dislike which their pets occasioned, legal proceedings were instituted, and so the matter came before the public. Mr. Severn then wrote a letter to the *Times*, in order to show that the animals were harmless. From this letter the following is an extract:

"'I happen to know the gentleman and lady against whom a complaint has been made because of the Snakes they keep, and I should like to give a short account of my first visit to them. Mr. M., after we had talked for a little time, asked if I had any fear of Snakes: and after a timid "No, not very," from me, he produced out of a cupboard a large *Boa constrictor*, a Python, and several small Snakes, which at once made themselves at home on the writing-table among pens, ink, and books. I was at first a good deal startled, especially when the two large Snakes coiled round and round my friend, and began to notice me with their bright eyes and forked tongues; but soon finding how tame they were, I ceased to feel frightened. After a short time Mr. M. expressed a wish to call Mrs. M., and left me with the Boa deposited on an armchair. I felt a little queer when the animal began gradually to come near, but the entrance of my host and hostess, followed by two charming little children, put me at my ease again. After the first interchange of civilities, she and the children went at once to the Boa, and calling it by the most endearing names, allowed it to twine itself most gracefully round about them. I sat talking for a long time, lost in wonder at the picture before me.

"'Two beautiful little girls with their charming mother sat before me with a *Boa constrictor* (as thick as a small tree) twining playfully round the lady's waist and neck, and forming a kind of turban round her head, expecting to be petted and made much of like a kitten. The children over and over again took its head in their hands and kissed its mouth, pushing aside its forked tongue in doing so. The animal seemed much pleased, but kept turning its head continually towards me with a curious gaze until I allowed it to nestle its head for a moment up my sleeve. Nothing could be prettier than to see this splendid serpent coiled all round Mrs. M. while she moved about the room, and when she stood to pour out our coffee. He seemed to adjust his weight so nicely, and every coil with its beautiful marking relieved by the black velvet dress of the lady. It was long before I could make up my mind to end the visit, and I returned soon after with Lord Arthur Russell to see my Snake-taming acquaintance again. . . . .

"'These (the Snakes) seemed very obedient, and remained in their cupboard when told to do so.

"'About a week ago Mr. and Mrs. M. were away for six weeks, and left the Boa in charge of a keeper at the Zoo. The poor Reptile moped, slept, and refused to be comforted, but when his master and mistress appeared, he sprang upon them with delight,

P

coiling himself round them, and showing every symptom of intense delight.'" †

The end of this Boa was remarkable and pathetic. Mr. Severn told Professor Romanes that some years after he had written the letter to the *Times* from which the above extract has been made, Mr. M. was seized with an apoplectic fit. Mrs. Mann, being alone in the house with her husband, ran out to call a doctor. She was absent for about ten minutes, and found on her return that the Snake had crawled upstairs to the room in which her husband was lying and was beside him dead.

The late Mr. Frank Buckland, among many others, visited Mr. and Mrs. M. and their Snakes at Chelsea, and also published an account of his experience in one of the leading newspapers. The small Snakes which Mr. M. kept with the Boas and Python, were some African Lacertine Snakes, and the Common Ring-Snake.

I have known of a Boa, more than 5ft. in length, which lived for a long time in a box 2ft. long, 1ft. wide, and 1ft. deep, and yet the Snake was apparently in perfect health and fed exceedingly freely all the while. The box was placed near a stove which was not lighted in warm weather. This fact is mentioned to show that though this Snake is not so hardy as some of its relatives it can nevertheless endure, seemingly without hurt, a certain amount of what may be called rough-and-ready treatment.

The Common Boa, though not generally a lover of water, will occasionally after eating enter and remain in its tank for some time. It should, therefore, like the Pythons and the other Snakes lately described, be always provided with the means of taking a bath. The *Boa constrictor* is viviparous and has from time to time produced young while in captivity. Small specimens of this Snake, about 4ft. long, can sometimes be bought for 25s.; frequently, however, the price is higher than this, ranging from £2 to £5. The Common Boa is a native of tropical South America, and is found from Venezuela to Buenos Ayres. It hardly ever reaches a greater length than 12ft.

Mr. Boulenger's description of the *Boa constrictor* in his

---

† *The Times*, July 25th, 1872.

"Catalogue of Snakes," 1893, is as follows: "Snout slightly prominent in the adult, obliquely truncate in the young; rostral a little broader than deep; symphysial at least as long as broad; head-scales small, slightly larger on the snout; no shields; one of the præ-oculars slightly enlarged; eighteen to twenty-four scales across the forehead, from eye to eye; sixteen to twenty scales round the eye, which is separated from the labials by two or three series of scales; twenty-one to twenty-five upper labials. Scales in eighty-one to ninety-five rows. Ventrals 234 to 243; anal entire; sub-caudals forty-nine to sixty. Pale brown above, with fifteen to twenty dark brown crossbars, widening on each side, and is connected by a dark dorsolateral streak, enclosing large elongate oval or elliptical spots of the pale ground-colour; a light longitudinal line in the outer widened portion of the dark crossbars; on each side a series of large dark brown spots with light centres, most of which alternate with the dorsal bars; on the tail the markings become much larger, brick-red, edged with black, and separated by narrow yellowish interspaces; head with a dark brown median line extending from between the nostrils to the nape, widening behind, sometimes loop-shaped; a crescentic blackish marking on the rostral; a dark brown streak on each side of the head, passing through the eye, and sending down a process between the end of the snout and the eye; a dark brown bar below the eye and two on each side of the lower lip; belly yellowish, dotted, or dotted and spotted with black."

The tail of the Reptile equals about one-tenth of its entire length. There are seven species in the genus *Boa*. Boas have rather small eyes with a vertical pupil. Their body is round or slightly compressed; the scales of which are very small and smooth, and generally exhibit a beautiful iridescence. Their head is distinct from the neck and their teeth are largest in front, gradually decreasing in size. The Boa is said to "contract habits so inoffensive, that in Surinam it holds the rank of one of the domestic animals, with which it frequently lives in perfect harmony."

This Snake, when at liberty in its own country, spends a great deal of time in trees, watching for prey, or reposing. It also hides in burrows over the openings of which the natives spread nets for the purpose of catching the Reptile, whose fat they are reported to use for medicinal purposes, and its skin for boots and saddle-cloths.

Representatives of the genus *Eryx*, sometimes called Sand Snakes, are occasionally brought to England. They live fairly well in confinement, and are perfectly harmless, hardly ever attempting to bite. However, they are not so interesting as most Snakes, for being burrowers, more or less, they are apt to hide themselves beneath the gravel or sand which ought to cover the bottom of their case. They frequent, when at liberty, dry, sandy, or stony localities. They are very common in some parts of the North and East of Africa and the South and Centre of Asia. Their natural prey consists of other burrowing Snakes, Lizards, and Mice. In captivity they will readily feed upon young Mice and Rats.

Roguish Snake-charmers frequently impose a mutilated Eryx, generally *E. johnii*, as the dreaded two-headed Snake. The tail of the unfortunate Reptile is cut and flattened to represent a head. These rascals not only declare that the bite of the creature is instantaneously fatal, but also that the animal eats for six months with one mouth and for six months with the other.

The Snakes of this genus have very short tails, which are not prehensile, or only slightly so. Their head is hardly distinct from the neck. Their eyes, which possess vertical pupils, are either small or very small, and in some species are placed entirely on the upper surface of the head. The scales are small or feebly keeled.

The Egyptian Eryx (*Eryx jaculus*) comes from the Ionian Islands, Greece, Central Asia, and North Africa. It is very common in the Holy Land. The colour of the Reptile, according to Mr. Boulenger, is "pale greyish, reddish, or yellowish brown above, with dark brown or blackish transverse blotches or alternating spots; or brown with paler spots; a dark streak from the eye to the angle of the mouth; belly white, uniform or with blackish dots; a more or less distinct dark streak along each side of the tail." The end of the snout is wedge-shaped, and is thus adapted for the animal's manner of life. The tail is very stout, about 1in long in a full-grown specimen, and blunt at its extremity. The Reptile's entire length is about 22in. It is viviparous.

Fraudulent Egyptian snake-charmers exhibit this Eryx, after having affixed a bird's claw over each of its eyes, as the deadly Horned Snake (*Cerastes hasselquistii*), the Viper which has been identified by some as the Asp with which Cleopatra killed herself. It is known, therefore, occasionally as *Eryx cerastes* (Daud.) and *Anguis cerastes* (Linn.).

The Indian Eryx (*Eryx johnii*) is a little more than twice as large as its near relative just described, occasionally reaching a length of 4ft. Its colour above is a reddish-olive, or pale brown, sometimes marked with dark brown or black bands: the lower parts are spotted with black or dark brown. The young are of a lighter colour, and the banding is much more distinct than in the adult. The tail, when the animal is full grown, is about 4in. long, and is very blunt at its end. The general shape of this Reptile is very like that of the *E. jaculus*.

The genus Eryx numbers about seven species; the tails of some have a claw-like ending. The *E. jaculus*, *E. johnii*, and *E. thebaicus*, the Shielded Eryx, may sometimes be bought in this country at sums ranging from 10s. to £1.

The Colubridæ.—The very large family of the *Colubridæ* comprises the most snake-like of all Snakes, if such an expression may be used; that is, its members correspond in appearance with the popular idea of a figure of a Snake. The *Colubridæ* may, therefore, be called typical Snakes. Their body is extremely graceful, wonderfully pliant, well-proportioned, and many of them are very beautifully coloured.

Mr. Boulenger, in his "Catalogue of Snakes," has divided the *Colubridæ* into three parallel series:

(*a*) *Aglypha* (from the Greek *a*, not, and *glypho*, I hollow out). The representatives of this series possess solid teeth only, none being grooved.

(*b*) *Opisthoglypha* (Greek *opisthen*, behind, and *glypho*). The Snakes of this series are provided with "one or more of the posterior maxillary teeth grooved."

(*c*) *Proteroglypha* (Greek, *proteros*, before, and *glypho*). These Reptiles have "anterior maxillary teeth, grooved or 'perforated.'"

All the Aglyphodont Colubrine Snakes are non-poisonous, and are arranged in more than 700 species. It will, therefore, be easily seen that this family comprises a very great proportion of all Ophidians. Representatives of this series are found in every part of the temperate, sub-tropical, and tropical regions of the earth. The Aglyphodont Colubrine Snakes are arranged by the great authority just quoted in three sub-families : 1. *Acrochordinæ* (the Wart Snakes) ; 2. The *Colubrinæ* (the typical Snakes) ; 3. The *Rhachiodontinæ* (The Egg-eaters).

In the first sub-family there are five genera, and in the last there is only one genus; but in the second there are as many as 122.

The Wart Snakes, which are natives of South Eastern Asia and Central America, are of moderate length, and generally have their head and body covered with small granular or spiry scales, which do not overlap each other, or only slightly so—hence their name. These Snakes are mostly rare, aquatic, and viviparous, and not suitable for confinement.

As so many of the members of the very large sub-family *Colubrinæ* may be kept without difficulty in captivity, only, comparatively, a few of them can be described in these articles.

Mr. Boulenger has divided the *Colubrinæ* into two series, according to the presence or absence of the hypapophyses or hæmal processes on the posterior dorsal vertebræ (see Figs. 57 and 58), and the crest or tubercle which projects below.

The first genus of the *Colubrinæ* to which reference will be made is the genus *Tropidonotus*. This is a very large genus, and comprises about seventy-six species. Most of its members have keeled scales, hence its name (from Greek *tropis*, gen. *tropidos*, a keel, and *notus*, a back). Representatives of the genus are found in Europe, Asia, Africa, North Australia, and North and Central America.

The Green Spotted Garter Snake (*Tropidonotus ordinatus*), Fig. 63, is a native of North America, and lives exceedingly well in confinement, where it has sometimes bred, the young being produced alive. Chiefly owing to its very variable coloration, there are many varieties of this Reptile. When full-grown, it is about

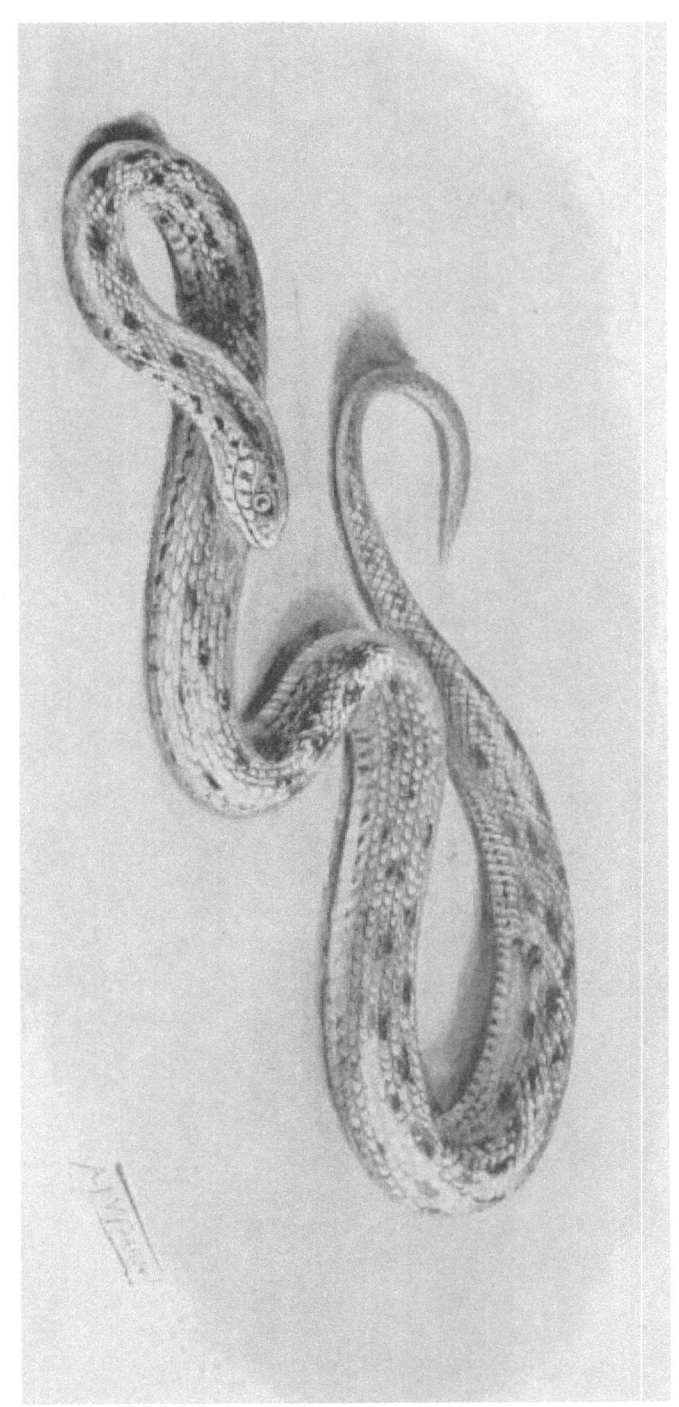

Fig. 63.—THE GREEN-SPOTTED GARTER SNAKE (*Tropidonotus ordinatus*).

3ft. long, the tail measuring nearly 8in. in length. The body and tail of the animal are moderately stout, the scales being arranged in from nineteen to twenty-one rows. The ventral scales are in number from 137 to 176, the anal being entire. There are seven upper labial shields, the third and fourth entering the eye. There is one anterior ocular shield, and there are three, rarely four, posterior ones. Whatever may be the variety of this Snake, there are nearly always two light yellow spots on the suture between the occipital shields.

The colouring of a typical specimen of the Garter Snake is, according to Mr. Boulenger, as follows: "Olive or green above, uniform or with black spots disposed quincuncially; stripes absent, or very indistinct; greenish white inferiorly, with a more or less distinct black spot at the outer end of the ventrals." It is found in the United States, east of the Mississippi.

The variety *sirtalis*, known as the Striped Snake (*T. sirtalis*), is coloured "brownish olive with black spots, or black above with three yellow, red, or pale green stripes." This specimen is a native of the eastern parts of the Rocky Mountains of North America, and also of North Mexico.

In captivity the Garter Snake need not be supplied with artificial heat, and if in good condition in the autumn, owing to regular feeding, it will spend our winter months successfully in a state of hibernation. Directions for preparing Snakes for this natural sleep will be given in another place.

While in confinement this Reptile may be fed upon frogs, small fish, and newts. Sometimes it may be tempted to take other food, such as half-grown toads, baby mice and rats. It, however, prefers frogs to any other form of food.

Occasionally a Garter Snake, which is easily tamed, may be bought in this country for so low a sum as 7s. 6d.; but generally the amateur is more likely to be asked as much as from £2 to £3 for a healthy specimen.

The Ringed or Common Snake (*Tropidonotus natrix*, Fig. 64) is one of the most beautiful as well as one of the most plentiful of all European non-poisonous Snakes. It lives very well in confinement, and with proper treatment soon becomes tame. The Grass Snake, as it is frequently called, very rarely bites those who handle it; indeed, so seldom does it attempt to use its teeth in self-defence that it would be almost correct to say that it never bites. After years of inquiry concerning and experience with this Reptile I have only known or heard of two instances in which it has bitten, viz., (1) a dealer, from whom I have obtained a great many Snakes, told me once, as something very extraordinary (as it undoubtedly was), that a Common Snake had lately seized one of his fingers with its teeth, making a tiny wound; (2) Dr. Stradling has recorded, in the *Zoologist* (I think), that a *T. natrix* of his, which was disturbed while incubating her eggs, had bitten him.

The Ringed Snake is a very nervous animal, and not only hisses loudly when frightened, but also emits an unpleasant smell. This latter capability is its chief means of defence. As soon as the creature becomes fairly tame, it ceases to make this disagreeable discharge. Notwithstanding that this Reptile is absolutely harmless, most men and boys consider it both a duty and a pleasure to kill it whenever they have the opportunity. It is rather a difficult matter to persuade such people, when they have been guilty of this unnecessary cruelty, that they have not at all performed a very meritorious action. For instance, I was riding one day to see a parishioner when I noticed, ahead of me, a man whom I knew very well, and who was walking by the side of his loaded cart. As he came to the foot of a steep hill I saw him suddenly leave his charge, run to the side of the hedge, strike violently with his whip, and then with its handle throw three objects into the road. I, supposing that the man had killed some Vipers, rode quickly forward, and as I did so found that he had been attacking three fine Ringed Snakes which had been basking in the sun. When I saw my dying favourites, I exclaimed: "Oh, M———, you should not have killed them, they are Grass Snakes and not Vipers; they do no one any harm." "Well, sir," he said, as he pointed with his whip to the quivering tongue of one of the poor half-dead Reptiles, "look at its 'spear'; that's what it stings with." Hereupon I dismounted, and taking the Snake up in my hand held it so that its moving tongue could just touch my cheek, while I watched the man's look of astonishment as he witnessed my action. He did not speak for the

FIG. 64.—COMMON RINGED SNAKE (*Tropidonotus natrix*).

moment, but as so many Devonshire people do, when expressing surprise, drew in his breath with a hissing noise through his closed teeth, and presently said, "Well, if I had not seen that I should never have believed it."

As I returned home in the evening, I put one of the dead Snakes in my pocket for the supper of a great pet of mine, a beautiful Indian mongoose.

The Ringed Snake, especially when young, has a great many other enemies besides men and boys, such as various birds, particularly the peacock and the barndoor fowl, hedgehogs, cats, pigs, and the like.

T. natrix inhabits every part of Europe, with the exception of Ireland and Northern Russia. It is also found in Algeria and West Central Asia. Its favourite place of resort during the warmer months of the year is the neighbourhood of ponds, streams, and damp, undrained land. Here it naturally finds its most suitable food.

This Snake is not so common a Reptile in England as the Viper (*Vipera berus*) and the Viviparous Lizard (*Lacerta vivipara*); however, it is by no means rare, though far rarer than formerly.

The Grass Snake can generally be bought, in this country, during the spring and summer months, for sums which range from 9d. to 2s. 6d., according to its size and condition. However, it is much more interesting for the amateur, if he should have the opportunity, to catch his specimens himself than to purchase them. Their capture is by no means a difficult matter if he goes to work wisely. First of all, before he makes any Snake-hunting excursions, he should learn to distinguish the Viper from the object of his search. Though the former is a very handsome and useful little Reptile, I think that it ought always to be killed when met with. For it not seldom injures dogs and cattle by biting them, and, of course, it is an extremely serious matter for any person to be wounded by this small Snake. The wound, however, very rarely indeed proves fatal to a healthy human being; but evil consequences are likely to be felt throughout the subsequent life of the unfortunate individual.

Luckily, Vipers are very nervous little creatures, and do their best to get out of the way of those who disturb them; still there is the danger of their being trodden upon and immediately resenting the accident. They are more numerous, as I have said, in this country than the Grass Snake, the chief reason for this being, I think, that while the latter deposits from fifteen to thirty eggs, rarely more, in some manure or leaf-heap, or similar situation, which are always running the risk of never being hatched, either through an insufficiency of heat or through the destruction by some enemy, the Viper produces, at one time, from thirty to fifty little Viperlings all ready and able to fight their way in the world. Besides this, the Adder, though it will not often live or feed in confinement, is the hardier of the two Reptiles.

Size, of course, is not a safe guide in distinguishing the Viper from the Common Snake, though the latter is far larger, when full-grown, than the former in a similar condition. There is in England a third Snake, which in size and colouring resembles the Adder far more closely than does *T. natrix*. Unfortunately, this beautiful, harmless, and interesting little creature, which will be described in another place, is not only rare here, but is confined to certain counties and districts.

Anyone who has once carefully compared, while seeing them together, the Viper and the Common Snake, will for the future have no difficulty in distinguishing the one from the other. The Common Snake (*T. natrix*) has nearly always a bright yellow collar, bordered behind by a second collar, which is never absent, of a deep black colour. The ground-colour of this Reptile's body is grey, olive, or brown, marked with rows of alternate black spots. The labial shields are bright yellow, and are divided, seemingly, from each other by black lines; the under-parts of the animal are generally of a dull bluish or lead colour, marbled with black, or the markings are yellowish-white and black, the former colour being most plentiful near the head and gradually decreasing in quantity towards the tail, where black predominates. In accordance with this Snake's generic name, most of its scales are strongly keeled. They are placed in nineteen rows. The ventral scales number from 160-190, and the sub-caudals are in from fifty to eighty-eight pairs. There is one præ-ocular shield and there are generally three post-oculars. There are also seven upper labials, of which the third and fourth enter the eye.

Though this Snake is generally found to be between 2½ft. and 3½ft. long, it is really one of the largest of the European Ophidians, having indeed attained a length of 6½ft. One was caught in the New Forest, in 1882, I think, which was 5½ft. long, and sent by Lord Londesborough to the Zoological Gardens, London. The tail of *T. natrix* is tapering, and equals about one-fifth of the animal's entire length.

The Viper (*V. berus*) hardly ever exceeds a length of 2ft. It has no yellow collar; and on its head, which is without the numerous large shields of the Common Snake, there is a dark marking, which bears some resemblance to the letter V. The ground-colour of the other part of the body of the Adder varies much, being sometimes red, olive, olive-brown, or black, and sometimes even nearly white; but it may be chiefly distinguished by a zigzag very dark or black marking running the whole length of the body and tail. The tail is short, only equalling about one-eighth of the reptile's entire length. The Viper, unlike the Common Snake, frequents dry, sandy localities, and is often seen on the dust at the road-side, or in tufts of dry grass, or on beds of dead leaves near some bush in an open part of a wood or plantation. The appearance of the two Reptiles is really so different, that even children quickly learn to readily recognise the one from the other.

I do not recommend anyone to keep a Viper in captivity. It will rarely feed, as just mentioned, and it might escape and injure somebody or something. Fig. 65 shows the great difference there is between the *T. natrix* and the *V. berus* in the arrangement of their teeth in their upper jaws. The most favourable time in England for catching Ringed Snakes is during some bright, sunny day, between the hours of ten and four, preferably after rain. They are then likely to be found basking near their haunts in the sun, such as the sides of a hedge, the banks of a pond or stream, or near bushes on marshy ground. The eye of the amateur will need a little training before he is able to see quickly what he is seeking, the colour of the Snakes is so like that of the ground upon which they lie coiled up. Frequently, the reptiles are only seen as they glide rapidly away towards a safe retreat. Had they remained stationary, they would, perhaps, have been entirely unnoticed. It is strange how often animals bring captivity, death, or loss upon themselves by moving, whereas, had they kept perfectly still, they would, in all probability, have run little or no risk of discovery. The bird reveals her nest by leaving it, and the Snake its presence by flight. Yet, on the other hand, we have the extraordinary bold, protective, and deceptive squatting of young plovers and other animals.

If he who is about to set out on a Grass-Snake (*Tropidonotus*

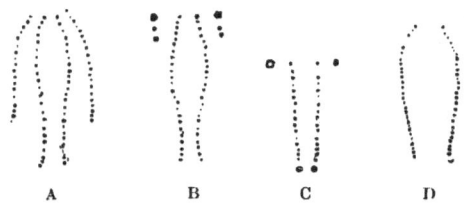

FIG. 65.—TEETH MARKS OF NON-POISONOUS AND POISONOUS SNAKES.

a, Diagram of tooth-marks of the four rows of teeth in the upper jaws of a non-venomous snake.
b, A diagram of tooth-marks of the palate teeth (the inner rows) and of the poison fangs, and four simple teeth of a Colubrine Venomous Snake, *e.g.*, Cobra di Capello.
c, Diagram of tooth-marks of the palate teeth and fangs of a Viperine (venomous) Snake, *e.g.*, a viper.
d, Diagram of tooth-marks of lower jaw of almost any Snake.

natrix, Fig. 65) hunting expedition knows so well the difference between the Viper and the Common Snake that he can recognise either at a glance, he needs no other equipment than a long or deep bag having a piece of string or tape sewn at its centre to the outside of the bag at a distance of about 4in. from the mouth, and a hooked stick. When a Snake is seen, if it cannot be caught at once, it should be hooked out into the open, if possible, seized with the hands, and placed in the bag, which is then tied up tightly by means of the string or tape round the neck. Care should be taken that all the mouth of the bag is gathered up and confined by the string, or an opening may be left which will give the Snake a chance of escape. After a little struggling the captured Reptile will generally lie so quietly at the bottom of its prison that it will not show any inclination to move when a fellow captive is introduced.

However, all chance of escape of the first caught Snake as a second is introduced may be prevented by tying a piece of string round the bag immediately above the spot where the former is lying coiled up at the bottom. The mouth of the bag may then be left open ready for the quick insertion of the next capture, which can be associated with the other Snakes or Snake by first tying up the mouth of the bag and then untying the string around the lower part of the bag, the mouth then being re-opened for the next victim, and the operation just described repeated. The bag thus used has not only the advantage of security against escape, but it is thus always ready for the next captive, and this is a great convenience. I know, from experience, that it is no easy matter to undo a bag with one hand while the other is holding a fiercely-struggling Snake. Of course, several small bags, already prepared with string and ready open, may be used instead of a single one.

If the amateur Snake-hunter has neither the nerve, knowledge, nor inclination to attempt

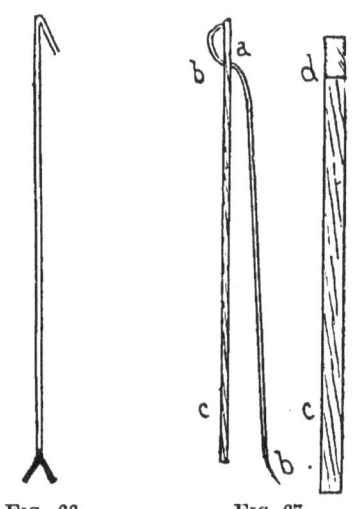

FIG. 66.
HOOKED AND FORKED STICK FOR CATCHING SNAKES.

FIG. 67.
SIDE AND FRONT VIEW OF NOOSE FOR CATCHING SNAKES.

to catch a Snake with his uncovered hands, he should provide himself with a suitable forked stick (Fig. 66) and a properly-contrived slip-noose (Fig. 67). The noose is composed of a piece of pliant strap (a, b) about ½in. wide, and a flat length of wood (c), having a width of 1in. and a thickness of ¼in. At a (Fig. 67) the strap is nailed to the wood and is passed through a hole in the wood at b, cut as shown at d. The hole (d) should be cut slanting slightly upwards from the back of the stick, to allow of the easy working of the strap. The hole ought to be made at about

Q

1in. from the end of the wood. The strap and lath may be from 2ft. to 3ft. long; a greater length than this will make the affair rather awkward for quick handling. With this apparatus almost any Snake may be rapidly noosed and unnoosed.

The following is a brief description of the manner of usage of these implements just described. The Snake (when found) is hooked into the open, if needful and possible, pinned down gently and firmly with the forked end of the stick, and held thus while the noose is slipped adroitly over the creature's head and tightened just sufficiently to keep the reptile a prisoner until it can be dropped into a bag by the loosening of the strap. When these contrivances are used, the assistance of a companion is a great convenience to the catcher, either to hold the bag open, or to apply the noose.

Tongs, something like long and very blunt scissors, are often used for catching Snakes, especially poisonous ones; but I do not recommend them, as unless they are very skilfully and gently used they are apt to injure the captives they make. I have at the present moment a beautiful yellow variety of the Æsculapian Snake (*Coluber æsculapii*) which has evidently been so hurt. The noose or lasso just described can do no injury to the reptiles if temperately applied.

As the Grass Snake is a lover of water it should always, while in captivity, be provided with a fairly large bath almost filled with clear soft water. The following is a short description of the most suitable Vivarium (as far as my own experience goes) for this and other Snakes of similar habits and size. The case may be made like that represented by Figs. 1, 3, 6, or 9; but it should be provided with a false bottom, made of thin wood, placed at a distance of 4in. from the true bottom. The false, or upper, bottom ought to be completely and exactly covered with a piece of thick felt. For a bath, two round "punched" or "blocked" tin saucers, about 9in. or 10in. in diameter, and 3½in. to 4in. deep, should be procured, one a size larger than the other. A round hole must then be carefully cut through the felt and the false bottom, so that it will just receive the body of the larger tin, whose rim prevents it from falling through the hole, and which overlaps the edge of the felt all round the hole. The felt will thus be kept in its place, and the Snakes cannot burrow under it. Two tins are used, so that when the smaller, whose place is within that of the larger, is removed daily for cleansing purposes and for fresh water, the Snakes will be prevented by the larger from getting between the two bottoms of the Vivarium. The false bottom is constructed in order that the Snakes, when on the floor of their case, may have no difficulty in finding the water. The felt I have found more suitable for such a Vivarium as this than gravel, for the gravel, when used, is constantly being swept by the Snakes into their bath. The felt is very easily cleaned. Two pieces should be provided for each Vivarium, so that a clean and dry piece may always be ready to take the place of that which is dirty and damp. When the dirty felt has been well dried, it can be quickly cleaned by being rubbed with a hard brush. The tins may be protected from rust by a coat or two of Brunswick black, or some similar preparation.

The branches of trees, as already described, should not be omitted from the case, nor pieces of cork or oak-bark under which the Snake can hide. Snakes not only like, but need places of retirement. A box, half full of dry moss, may be prepared as a substitute for the cork or bark. The length of the box should equal the width of the case (inside measurement). A little door, which will open and close easily, must be made in one side of the box. The box, which should also be provided with a lid capable of being very securely fastened, may be placed at one end of the case inside, or hung to the outside of an end of the case (if the side be of wood) through which a hole has been cut to correspond to the door in the side of the box. Of course, the box should be fastened so firmly to the outside of the Vivarium that there can be no chance of a Snake's escape. This box arrangement is very convenient, for the Snakes can be shut in when the Vivarium is being cleaned; besides, the box, when placed inside the Vivarium, can be removed anywhere with the Snakes it contains.

The Snakes will lie often with their heads outside the box, watching seemingly for the introduction of food into their tank. The box retreat, however, does not interfere with their becoming tame, or with their climbing into the branches of trees, or with their reclining in full view upon the felt.

In a Vivarium arranged in the manner just described, I keep some varieties of the Common Snake (*T. Natrix*), and also of the Dice Snake (*T. tessellatus*). Both kinds of Snakes are non-biters and good feeders. They will eat readily, not only frogs, alive or dead, but also dead minnows and other little fish. I have often placed five or six dead minnows in their water, and within five minutes all the fish have disappeared. These Snakes will swallow the fish in the presence of strangers.

It is very interesting to watch the Snakes' graceful movements in the water as they dive after minnows either alive or dead. A Grass Snake can easily catch an active minnow under water. It generally seizes the fish by the middle, and then swims with it, holding it high in the air, out of the water, and at the water's edge swallows the prey. Sometimes a Snake will carry the fish to its retreat in the box or under a piece of cork, and eats it in the privacy which it finds there.

By the skilful use of its jaws, the Snake turns the fish round until the head is in a suitable position for swallowing. Anyone who had never seen the sight would think it impossible that a small Snake could hold and turn with its jaws a large and struggling minnow or frog.

I have timed a small Snake, not 2ft. in length, while it caught and swallowed two very large minnows. The first fish was seized round the body and had disappeared in a minute and a half, then, after yawning, as Snakes do immediately after feeding, the reptile again entered the bath and caught the second minnow by the head and disposed of it in twenty-five seconds.

One of the reasons why these Snakes will eat readily dead minnows is, I think, that the movement of the reptile in the water gives motion, and probably to the Snake, the appearance of life to the fish. However, I have known a hungry Snake to take a dead minnow when not in water. Generally, when one Snake begins to feed, the others, its companions, quickly follow its example.

The Grass Snake is also very fond of frogs, which it frequently seizes by the hind leg; this it proceeds slowly to swallow, until it has doubled forward the other hind leg, and ultimately the unfortunate batrachian disappears from view. If a Snake happens to take a frog by the middle of the body, it will probably turn its prey round until the head is in its mouth, and thus the batrachian is swallowed head foremost. I find that Common Snakes, when they have been accustomed to feed upon minnows, prefer them to frogs. The fish are certainly the easier to swallow. One must conclude, I think, after having witnessed a feat of deglutition on the part of the Snake, that the act was not conducive to pleasure of any sort; but, probably, instead, to something like pain, or at any rate, discomfort. And I believe, therefore, that most Snakes, as a rule, prefer a small mouthful to a large.

One often reads that Ringed Snakes eat the eggs of small birds. This I very much doubt, for I have never, by any means, been able to persuade one of these reptiles to swallow an egg. The chief food of these Ophidians consists, undoubtedly, of frogs, newts, and small fish. They will eat, if they cannot get anything they prefer better, young and half-grown toads. Old toads disagree with them. The Ringed Snake does not care much for young mice or rats, and will only very rarely eat them. I have never known it to swallow a young bird, or to drink milk when it could get water.

Sometimes this Snake (*Tropidonotus natrix*, Fig. 64, p. 219) will swallow while under water a minnow, roach, or other small fish; and sometimes it will take prey of this kind tail foremost. Under the latter circumstances the act of deglutition is a difficult one because the fins of the fish hook over the jaws of the Snake and serve as an impediment. In this case there is a good opportunity of witnessing the protrusion of the glottis.

Minnows (*Leuciscus phoxinus*) can generally be bought in towns very cheaply, and as they are very hardy little fish, they may easily be kept alive for a long time. They can also be caught by those who live in the country, by means of the net, to which the fish may be attracted by a piece of red braid tied to or near the centre. These lively little creatures are to be taken, too, with a rod and line. The hook, of course, must be very small, and baited with worm, paste, or artificial fly. Minnows may also be procured by means of glass traps sold for the purpose, and by snaring them. Care must be taken not to give the Snakes either the Bullhead, or Miller's Thumb (*Cottus gobio*), or any species of stickleback, because of the spines with which these fish are armed.

The eggs of the Ringed Snake are of the size of those of a blackbird, and are stuck together by means of some glutinous secretion; they may be found in the situations already indicated, and can be hatched without difficulty by artificial means. The most convenient way of doing this is by placing them in an incubator. They can also be hatched in the simple contrivance which was suggested in a former article for incubating Lizards' eggs. I have found a temperature of about 96deg. Fahr. is suitable for the incubation of Snakes' eggs. It is not easy to say how long such eggs are in hatching, for much, of course, depends upon their condition when first placed in the incubator. If found as soon as deposited by the Snake, they should take from sixty to eighty days to hatch at the heat just mentioned. The eggs must not be kept too dry, or they will shrivel, nor so moist that they run the risk of being destroyed by fungus. I have bought eggs nearly all of which produced young Snakes within forty-eight hours after they were placed in the incubator.

The female Ringed Snake, which is larger than the male, has been known to incubate her own eggs, forming them, like the Python already spoken of, into a pyramid and covering them with her body. A keeper at the Zoological Gardens, Paris, showed the late Mr. Frank Buckland a Ringed Snake which had hatched her own eggs for three successive years. The Snake possessed by Dr. Stradling has already been alluded to.

The young Snakes when just out of the eggs are very beautiful creatures, about 7in. and 8in. long, and much darker than their adult relatives. Their yellow collar is very bright and distinct. Sometimes a pretty variety is found among a batch of freshly hatched Snakes of this kind. These young Reptiles will feed upon frogs, garden worms, slugs, and occasionally even upon pieces of meat. They may also be reared by being fed artificially. They change their skins when from four to ten days old. As they are very active and small, their case must be carefully and well made or they will escape. I once lost, to my annoyance, a great many young Snakes through not closing a hole which I thought was far too small to receive their bodies. However, they got away, and I learnt a lesson.

Care should be taken not to give them the gaily-coloured worms alluded to in a former article, as they seem to act as a poison to all reptiles and batrachians which happen to eat them. Young Snakes slough more frequently than their older relatives do, and the process does not seem to try them so much as it certainly will do should they reach maturity.

The Grass Snake when gently and regularly handled soon becomes quite tame. It is, however, even for a Snake, a nervous animal, and should be treated accordingly. The late Mr. Thomas Bell, in his "British Reptiles," says that this creature "may be made to distinguish those who caress and feed it. I had one many years since, which knew me from all other persons; and, when let out of his box, would immediately come to me and crawl under the sleeve of my coat, where he was fond of lying perfectly still, and enjoying the warmth. He was accustomed to come to my hand for a draught of milk every morning at breakfast, which he always did of his own accord; but he would fly from strangers, and hiss if they meddled with him." In the ninth volume of "Chambers's Miscellany," the writer of an article on "Anecdotes of Serpents" says that "We have ourselves known the Common Ringed Snake of our heaths so tamed by a herd-boy as to coil and uncoil itself at his desire, to follow even in the fields for a short distance, and to retreat to the box in which it was usually kept on his giving a peculiar signal. The specimen was the largest of its size we have ever seen, being more than 2½ft. in length; it lived for several summers, and died, we believe, from being over-fed, and not being allowed the necessary duration of torpidity during winter."

I once possessed a large Grass Snake which was so unusually tame (he was also a great eater) as to leave his fellows, and to come to me when the door of his case was opened. Some friends seeing him do this one day exclaimed: "Why, how fond that Snake is of you." I think, however, that his affection for me was doubtful, but I believe he appreciated the warmth of my hands.

T. natrix does not require much heat during winter when not hibernating. The temperature of a greenhouse, or that of an ordinary room in which a fire is burning during the day and evening, is generally sufficient to prevent it from becoming torpid. If the creature be in good condition, when autumn arrives it may be packed away, as already directed, for its natural winter sleep. Labourers sometimes when at work find great numbers of Snakes of this species hibernating together. For example, Miss Hopley, in her book on Snakes, records that " at the end of September . . . a farmer in Wales, who, with his labourers, was removing a heap of manure, came upon an extraordinary bed of Snakes and Slow-worms, and no less than 352 were killed, together with an enormous quantity of eggs; thousands in clusters were destroyed. Three Snakes were of immense size, and one hundred of them nine to twelve inches long . . . . . One feels curious to know whether judgment for this act of wanton cruelty visited that farmer in a destruction of his crops next year by the mice and insects from which these harmless reptiles would have saved them!"

A collection of the different varieties of the Ringed Snake would be a very interesting one. Many beautiful varieties are imported into this country from the Continent, especially from Italy. I believe that foreign specimens are rather hardier than our own, or perhaps it may be that they are more suited to a life in confinement. The Snake which I have had longest in my possession is such an one. It is a very beautiful striped variety. Mr. Boulenger speaks of the following varieties of *T. natrix*, viz. :—

(A) The typical form. A white, yellow, or orange collar, usually divided in the middle, sometimes absent, bordered behind by a broad, deep black collar, which is constant.

(B) Collar altogether absent, or reduced to a small black blotch on each side of the nape (var. *astreptophorus*, Seoane).

(C) Collar well marked, though widely interrupted in the middle; a yellowish streak along each side of the back. (*C. Persa*, Pall.; *C. bilineatus*, Bibr.; var. *murorum*, Bp.)

(D) Black above, checkered black and white inferiorly. (*C. scutatus*, Pall.; var., *nigra*, Nordm.)

(E) Uniform black above and below. (*T. ater*, Eichw.)

The above list does not exhaust the different varieties of this Snake, e.g., I have owned a specimen, the ground-colour of whose body was of a lovely orange colour. This beautiful reptile, unfortunately, escaped through the accidental breaking of the glass of the case in which it was confined. I had another variety which possessed a body of a light bluish-slate colour, marked with the usual black spots.

The Snake just mentioned, for it was one of the sufferers, reminds me of a mistake I once made in regard to the cleansing of a Snake-case, and I venture to record the circumstance, as my experience may be of use to others who keep these creatures. When cleaning out a Vivarium that contained several young Ringed Snakes, which I had hatched artificially, and which were thriving very well, I sprinkled the freshly-brushed felt covering the bottom of the case with some diluted "Jeyes' Perfect Purifier Disinfectant." This Vivarium was heated by a small lamp, for it was winter time, and I was not allowing the young Snakes to hibernate during their first year, which, I think, is a good plan. The high temperature may have increased the power of the disinfectant. When I looked at the Snakes within an hour after having cleaned their case, I was surprised to find many of them stretched quite straight and motionless upon the felt. Some of them were quite dead and others nearly so. A few of them when placed immediately in another Vivarium revived for a time, but never wholly recovered their health. The felt was placed out of doors at once, and left in the rain all night, and was restored to its place in the morning, after being thoroughly dried; but when the remaining or surviving Snakes were returned to their home, they were again strongly affected by the disinfectant. Since then in cleaning Vivaria I have been careful to use nothing but a hard brush, and, when necessary, soap, water, and soda.

The Ribbon Snake (*Tropidonotus saurita*) is beautiful and fairly hardy, and, with ordinary care, a long liver in confinement, where it will occasionally breed. Anyone who possesses a healthy specimen of this Snake will be sure to make it a great favourite. It is a native of N. America.

The body and tail of *T. saurita* are slender and elongate, and the eye is large. The upper labials are generally eight in number, and the lower ones always seven. The scales are arranged in nineteen rows; the ventrals number from 144 to 178; the sub-caudals are placed in from 86 to 127 pairs, and the anal scute is entire. The colour above is dark olive or dark brown, marked with three yellow, orange, or light green longitudinal stripes; and the lower parts are greenish-white. Its slender and graceful form, large eye, and pleasing colouring altogether make it a very beautiful reptile.

The Ribbon Snake attains a length of at least 2ft. 6in., of which the tail measures 9in. It will feed upon frogs, newts, and small fish.

This and all other Snakes of the genus *Tropidonotus* may (and should, I think) be kept in Vivaria arranged similarly to that suggested for *T. natrix*; the larger they are, of course, the better.

The Dice Snake (*Tropidonotus tessellatus*, Fig. 68) is so like a Viper in appearance that most people would hesitate a long while before they touched it, even though they have been told of its perfect harmlessness. Not only is it quite innocuous, but, like its near relative *T. natrix*, it is most unwilling to use its teeth in self-defence. This Snake is a very suitable inmate of a Vivarium, as it is easily tamed and a good feeder. I have known it to take food readily on the day following its purchase and a long journey; indeed, it seems incapable of fasting nearly so long as most Ophidians. The Dice Snake should be kept in a case arranged as already suggested, and fed upon small fish, frogs, newts, and tadpoles, after which animals it will dive very cleverly and gracefully. Like *T. natrix*, it is quite ready to eat dead minnows when they are placed in its bath.

This reptile while at liberty is generally found in or near either running or stagnant water. It is able to swim very quickly and easily. It is a native of France, Spain, Hungary, Germany, Switzerland, and South Western and Central Asia. As *T. tessellatus* is often imported into England during spring and summer, it may generally be bought at prices which range from 2s. to 4s., according to size and condition. It sometimes exceeds a length of 3ft., of which its tail equals one-fifth.

The eye of the Dice Snake, which is rather small, has a dark yellow iris. The muzzle is thick. The præ-ocular shields are

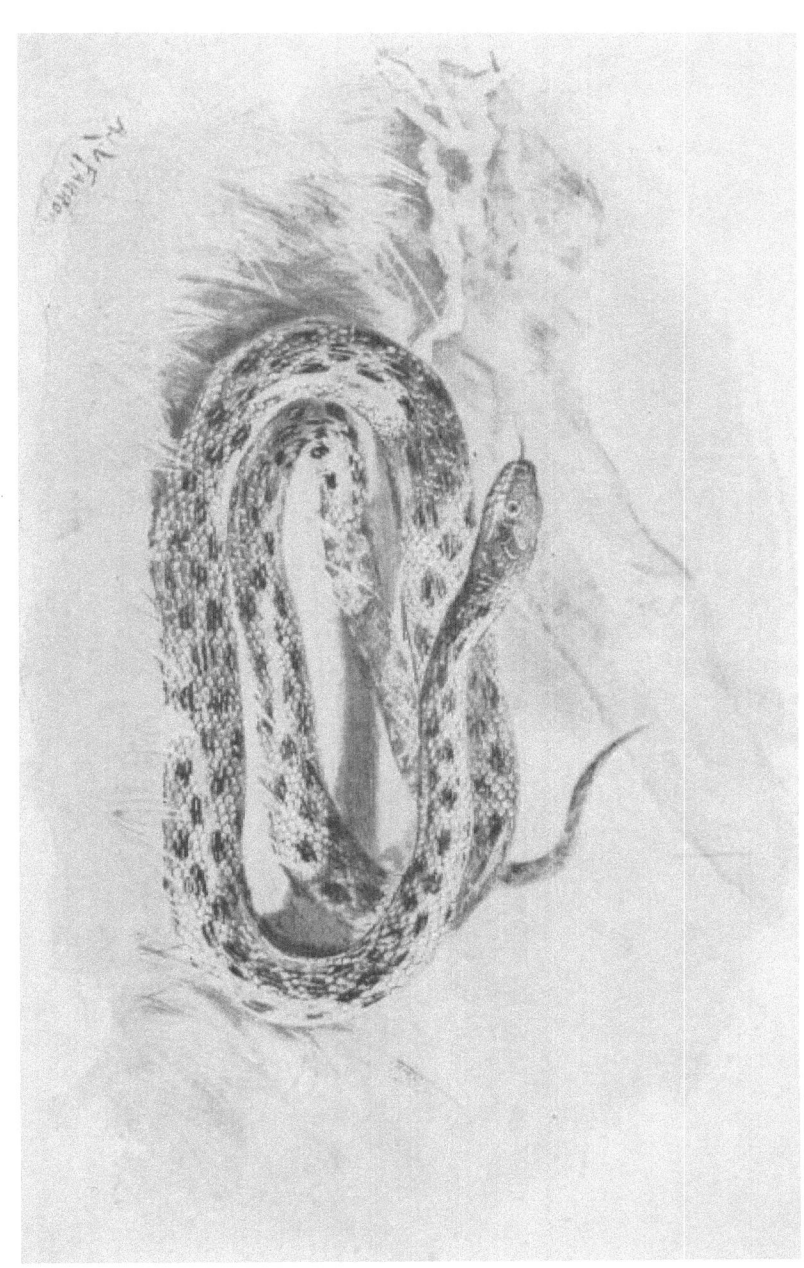

FIG. 68.—THE DICE SNAKE (*Tropidonotus tessellatus*).

generally two in number, and the post-oculars three. There are eight upper labials, as a rule, and five lower ones. The scales, which are strongly keeled, are placed in nineteen rows; the ventrals number 160 to 197; the sub-caudals, 48 to 86; the anal plate is double. This Snake is olive, bluish-grey, or yellow (rarely) above, sometimes uniform, but more often marked with dark spots arranged quincuncially, or in a series of inverted V's. There is generally an inverted V-like marking on the back of the neck. The labials are of a dusky orange colour, apparently divided by darker markings. The lower parts of this creature's body are variously coloured, such as with yellow or red marbled with black, or nearly black; or slaty-blue edged with salmon-pink, finely speckled with black or brown; or black broadly bordered with orange, sprinkled with black spots.

The Viperine Snake (*Tropidonotus viperinus*), though perfectly harmless, is even more like a viper in appearance than the Dice Snake—hence its specific name; but a glance at the size and arrangement of the head-shields would show it to be no Viper. Like its near relative *T. tessellatus*, it is very suitable for confinement, for it is also a good feeder and a non-biter. This Snake often has back-markings almost identical with those of the Common Viper (*Vipera berus*), and, no doubt, has been frequently mistaken for a viper. I remember how very cautiously I used to handle the first Snake of this species which I possessed, for though I had been told by a great authority that it was quite harmless, I could scarcely believe it to be so, for its appearance was so against it. However, the creature's habits were much in its favour, and it quickly became much liked.

In some parts of the Continent this reptile is very common. It is a native of France, Switzerland, Spain, Portugal, Italy, and Barbary. When imported into this country it may generally be bought, according to size, for from 2s. to 4s. It is slightly cheaper than the Dice Snake.

For a long time this Snake was confounded with that just mentioned. Perhaps the chief difference between the two reptiles, not considering their coloration, is that the Viperine Snake's scales are placed in from twenty-one to twenty-three rows, whereas those of the Dice Snake are arranged in nineteen and the former has seven upper labials and two post-ocular shields, while the latter possesses generally eight (hardly ever seven) upper labials and three post-oculars. The colour of the *T. viperinus* above is brownish-grey, or reddish, marked down the back with a dark brown or black zigzag stripe; along the sides there is a series of black or dark-brown spots, each having a yellowish or greenish centre. There is generally a V-like dark marking on the back of the head and neck, which tends to increase the animal's likeness to the viper. *T. viperinus* sometimes reaches a length of 3ft.; it is therefore a much larger reptile than that for which it is frequently mistaken. It should be fed and treated exactly as has been suggested for the Dice Snake. These two Snakes and the Ringed Snake (*T. natrix*) live very well together in the same Vivarium. All these Snakes, when young, will feed upon earthworms.

Mr. Boulenger describes a variety of *T. viperinus—N. ocellata*, Wagl., *C. aurolineatus* Gerv.,—having "two yellow or reddish longitudinal dorsal lines in addition to the usual markings."

The Seven-Banded Snake (*Tropidonotus septemvittatus*) is an exceedingly hardy reptile, and very well fitted for confinement, where it will live, under good treatment, for a considerable time. It is a handsome Snake, and easily tamed. Its head is small and hardly distinct from the neck, its eye is also small, and possesses two præ-ocular shields and two post-ocular ones. This Snake has the same number of labials as *T. natrix*, and its scales are also arranged in nineteen rows; but the ventrals of the former animal number from 140 to 151, and the sub-caudals are placed in from sixty-four to eighty-six pairs.

T. septemvittatus is dusky olive-brown above, with a lateral yellow band, and, generally, three dark dorsal lines; the belly of the creature is yellowish, with four dusky or brown stripes; the middle stripes, however, are sometimes broken up into spots.

The Seven-Banded Snake is a native of North America, east of the Mississippi. It is also found in Texas. This reptile has frequently been bred in captivity, where the young have been produced alive, and reared on tiny frogs. It reaches a length of more than 2ft., of which the tail measures 6in. It may be sometimes bought in England for 10s., but it is generally much dearer than this. Of course, the price of this and other Snakes depends upon the supply and demand, and the season during which they are imported. *T. septemvittatus* will feed on frogs, small toads, newts, and tiny fish.

The Mocassin Snake (*Tropidonotus fasciatus*) is an exceedingly hardy North American Snake, which has often been confounded, owing to its English name, with the Water Viper or Water Mocassin (*Cenchris piscivora*). *T. fasciatus* is quite innocuous, and altogether a very suitable inmate of a Vivarium. It is generally a most ready feeder. I think I have read that Dr. Stradling possesses, or possessed a specimen which was so tame, that while being held in the hand it would swallow a frog. The Mocassin Snake will not only take as food frogs, newts, and small fish, but also, sometimes, pieces of raw meat. Occasionally, however, a representative of this species may be found to be a shy feeder.

T. fasciatus in a state of freedom lives in the neighbourhood of water, or in water; and it was probably owing to this habit, and also, perhaps, because it is viviparous, that Catesby, the author of "The Natural History of Carolina," was induced to call it the "Brown Water Viper;" hence, possibly, its frequent confusion with the poisonous reptile, *C. piscivora*. Unlike its near relative *T. natrix*, the Mocassin Snake is often quite ready to bite, the bite of course being harmless. This readiness to attack, and the animal's stout, heavy-looking build and rather sinister expression, tend to make people look upon it with suspicion. It is not seldom pointed out by visitors to the Reptile House, Regent's Park, as an exceedingly dangerous reptile; the name and appearance both conducing to this mistake.

Several specimens of the Snake have been born from time to time in the Zoological Gardens, London, and were reared upon small frogs. The Mocassin Snake has sometimes produced live young ones and eggs at the same time.

The head of *T. fasciatus* has a close resemblance to that of *T. natrix*. The former, however, has rather smaller eyes, internasals narrower in front, and one more upper labial than the latter. The Mocassin Snake possesses also strongly keeled scales, which are placed in from twenty-three to twenty-seven rows; the ventrals number 128 to 154, and the sub-caudals are arranged in from fifty-eight to eighty-two pairs, and the anal scute is divided.

This reptile grows to a length of about 3ft. 6in., of which the tail measures about 9½in. It is found in North America, east of the Rocky Mountains, and in Central America. Its colours are liable to great variations, of which the following are given by Mr. Boulenger, viz. :

- (A) (*forma typica*). Brown above, with a dorsal row of large transverse blackish spots, and an alternating series of smaller spots on each side, or with dark-brown cross bands; belly spotted with black or brown. Scales in twenty-three to twenty-five rows.
- (B) (var. *sipedon*). The dorsal spots as in the preceding, but much paler, the interspaces between them appearing as narrow transverse light bands margined with black; belly with pale brown blotches. Scales in twenty-three rows.
- (C) (var. *erythrogaster*). Brick-red or dark-brown above, uniform red or copper colour beneath. Scales in twenty three or twenty-five rows.
- (D) (var. *rhombifer*). Pale brown above, with three alternating series of transverse dark brown spots, the median not larger than the lateral; these spots may be connected by dark-brown meshes; belly with brown spots.
- (E) Like the preceding, but spots paler and smaller; belly immaculate.

The Mocassin Snake can sometimes be bought in this country for so low a sum as 7s. 6d., but generally it is much more expensive.

The Tigrine Snake (*Tropidonotus tigrinus*) is the representative of the English Ringed Snake (*T. natrix*) in Japan, China, and Siam. It is very hardy, and should be kept under the same conditions as those recommended for its near relative just mentioned. Some of the slight differences between this Snake and *T. natrix* are that the former reptile has a larger eye, one more anterior ocular (*T. natrix* has nearly always only one), a squarer loreal (*i.e.*, the shield between the nasal and the anterior ocular), and longer anterior frontals, or internasals, than the latter. According to Dr. Günther, the usual colouring of the Tigrine Snake is as follows:—Greenish, or brownish-olive, with three series of sub-quadrangular black spots; a series of reddish spots on the anterior part of the side, these spots alternating with the black ones. Belly with a series of rounded small black spots anteriorly, nearly entirely black posteriorly; neck with an oblique black spot on each side. A black spot below the eye, on the suture between the fourth and fifth labials; a black blotch on the temple descending obliquely to the angle of the mouth.

The Stoled Snake (*Tropidonotus stolatus*), very common in India, is not a large reptile, hardly ever exceeding a length of 2ft., and very easily tamed. Of this Snake, the head is rather narrow and the eye is of moderate size; the anterior frontals are pointed before, and the parietals are rounded behind; one præ-ocular, and three post-oculars; eight upper labials, the third, fourth, and fifth entering the eye. The scales are placed in nineteen rows, and are strongly keeled, except the outer rows, which are smooth. The ventrals number from 120 to 160, the subcaudals are in pairs from 50 to 80, and the anal scute is divided. The colour is olive-brown above, marked with two white or yellow longitudinal bands (hence specific name), between which there is a series of serrated or reticulated crossbands. The lower surfaces are white, with (generally) a black dot on each side of every scute. The Stoled Snake should be kept under the same conditions as those recommended for its relatives of this genus, except that it will require more artificial heat.

There are many other Snakes of the genus *Tropidonotus*, which may at times be procured in this country, and which also can be kept without difficulty in confinement. Those, however, which have been described, are, perhaps, either the more hardy, the more easily obtained in England, or the more interesting.

The Infernal Snake (*Boodon infernalis*) is a native of East and South Africa, is fairly hardy, and easily tamed. It may be kept in a case like that represented by either Fig. 3 or Fig. 6, but which should be heated except during the hottest parts of the year. This snake will feed readily upon mice and young birds. It is, however, somewhat of a cannibal. I have seen it even trying to swallow a Striped Snake (*Tropidonotus sirtalis*) of quite its own size, and not by accident (which might be caused by two snakes taking the same prey), but by design, if such a term may be used. The Snakes of this genus possess five or six enlarged anterior maxillary teeth slightly separated from the rest, hence the generic name, which means "ox-toothed."

The following is a brief description of the Infernal Snake. The eye, which possesses a vertical elliptical pupil, is small; the rostral shield is twice as broad as deep; the upper labials are eight in number, of which the third, fourth, and fifth touch the eye; the loreal is elongated, and the parietal shields are longer than the vertical, which is five-sided and pointed. The scales are in twenty-three or twenty-five rows, and are smooth and pitted; the ventral scales, which are rounded, number from 175 to 195, the sub-caudals from 48 to 70, and the anal is entire. The colour above is either a uniform dark green or black; the under parts are yellowish. The entire length is about 27in., of which the tail measures 5in. Occasionally this Snake may be bought for about 10s.

The Lineated Boodon (*Boodon lineatus*) is very like, except in colouring, its near relative just described. The scales, however, are placed in from twenty-five to thirty-one rows, and the ventrals number from 192 to 237. The colour above is either a uniform dark brown or the brown is marked by a yellow streak running along each side; the sides of the head are of a light colour, causing, as it were, the darker colour of the upper part of the body to end in a point at the rostral; the under-parts are yellowish. This snake is slightly longer when full grown than the one last mentioned. The treatment in confinement of the two reptiles should be the same. *Boodon lineatus* is a native of the tropical and southern parts of Africa.

As the Aulic Lycodon (*Lycodon aulicus*) is one of the commonest Snakes of India, a short description of it should not be omitted here. The members of the genus *Lycodon* (wolf-toothed), which numbers about fifteen species, are remarkable for the character of their anterior teeth, which are much enlarged and fang-like, and separated from the rest by a considerable space. These teeth gradually increase in size until they reach that portion of the jaw which is toothless. The Lycodons of Southern

Asia feed chiefly on skinks, whose closely-scaled bodies they are able to pierce by means of their fang-like teeth; and those of Africa live principally upon small rodents, such as mice. They are all ground Snakes, and mostly of an earth-brown colour. Their bodies are generally slender, and the entire length of the longest of them does not often exceed 3ft.

The Aulic Lycodon has a small eye, with a vertically elongated pupil, a depressed snout and swollen lips, one præ-ocular, and, generally, two post-oculars, nine upper labials, of which the third, fourth, and fifth touch the eye. Its scales are smooth, and placed in seventeen rows. The upper parts are chiefly of an earth-brown colour, uniform, or marked with white. The coloration of the species, however, is very varied. The Aulic Lycodon should be kept in a heated Vivarium, and fed upon lizards or slow-worms, or, if it can be induced to take them, on young mice. This Snake is not easily tamed, and is generally ready to bite, making, when it succeeds in doing so, owing to its long front teeth, a larger wound than most Snakes of its size could do.

The Hoary Snake (*Pseudaspis cana*, Boulenger; or *Coronella cana*, Dum. and Bibr.) is not infrequently imported into this country, where it lives fairly well in confinement. It is the only representative of its genus, according to Mr. Boulenger. By some other authorities it is classed among the *Coronellæ*. This Snake's head is short, pointed in front and broad behind. The scales are placed in from twenty-seven to thirty-one rows, and are smooth and pitted; the ventrals number from 175 to 212; and the sub-caudals 50 to 70 pairs; and the anal scute is divided. The adult members of this species vary much in colour, and are pale brown, dark brown, reddish-brown, and blackish-ash. Sometimes these colours are uniform, and sometimes spotted more or less distinctly. The younger specimens are pale brown above, marked with dark brown white-edged spots. The underparts are yellowish-brown, either uniform or spotted with black.

The Hoary Snake, except during the warmest months of the year, should be kept in a heated case. As food, it ought to be provided with mice and small rats. It is a native of South Africa, and occasionally grows to a length of more than 5ft., of which its tail measures about 10in. *P. cana* may sometimes be bought here for 15s.

The Angry or Dark Green Snake (*Zamenis atrovirens*, Gunther, or *Zamenis gemonensis*, Boulenger, Fig. 69) is a hardy and beautiful Snake. The members of its genus, which numbers about thirty-one species, are chiefly distinguished by their dentition. The maxillary teeth increase in size posteriorly, the last two being sometimes separated from the rest by a short portion of toothless jaw. Representatives of this genus are found in both the Old and New World—namely in Europe, Asia, Northern Africa, and Northern and Central America. The Dark Green Snake is a native of France, Switzerland, Italy, Dalmatia, Greece, Malta, Cyprus, Egypt, the Holy Land, and Persia. It may often be bought in this country, for from 4s. to 6s. Its food consists of lizards, slow-worms, and mice. *Z. atrovirens* can be kept here without artificial heat, and may be allowed, if in good condition, to pass the winter in a state of hibernation. This Snake I have found generally ready to bite, but its bite is nothing serious, sometimes the teeth do not even pierce the skin of the hand. A scratch, or scratches, however, are likely to be caused by tearing the hand or fingers out of the Snake's mouth. These remarks apply to most of the small, non-poisonous Snakes.

The Dark Green Snake possesses one (occasionally two) præ-ocular, two (occasionally three) post-oculars, eight upper labials, of which the fourth and fifth touch the eye, long, smooth scales, which are arranged in seventeen or nineteen rows, ventral scales numbering from 190 to 250, sub-caudals in from 90 to 130 pairs, and a divided anal scale.

This Snake, which is very common in Southern Europe, varies a great deal in its colouring. The following colours and markings are given by Mr. Boulenger in his "Catalogue of Snakes" (1893).

> (A) *Forma Typica.*—Young, pale olive above, the head black, with yellow markings. Some adults preserve the pale coloration of the young, whilst others are dark green or black, with yellow spots or longitudinal streaks, etc.; the tail is usually striated, black or yellow; belly yellow or greenish-white, uniform, or with small black dots.

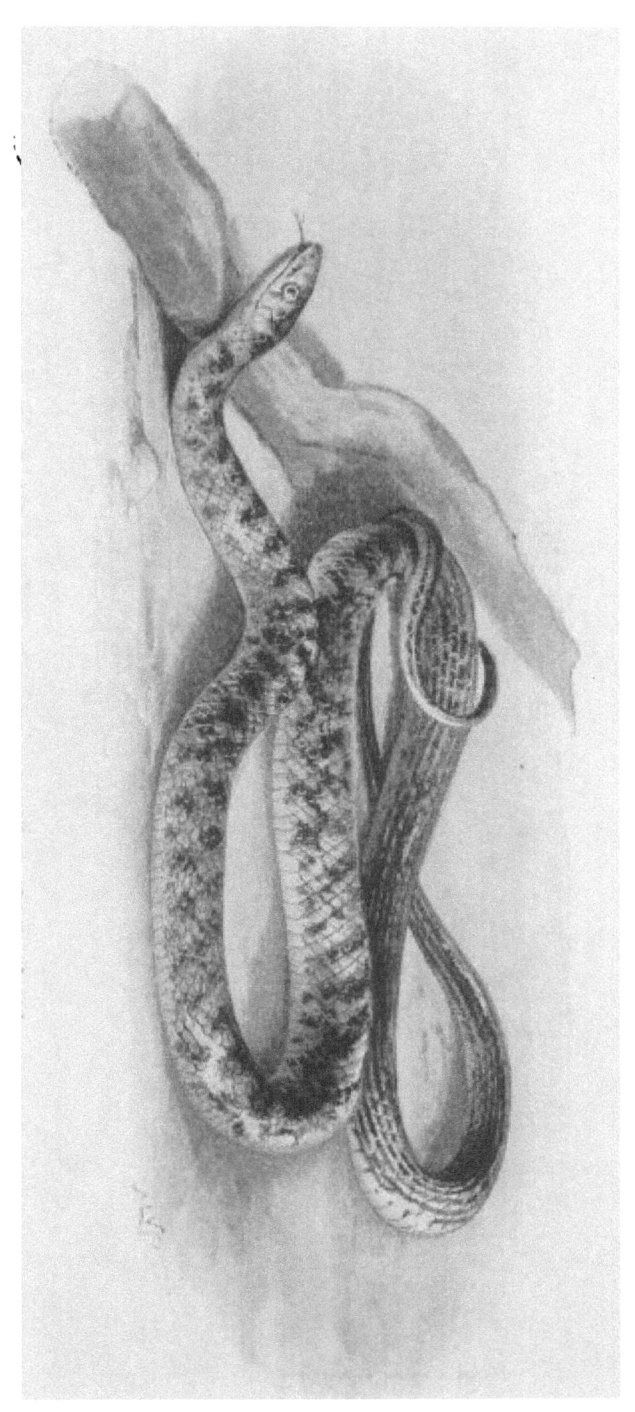

FIG. 69.—THE DARK GREEN SNAKE (*Zamenis atrovirens*).

(B) Var. *Caspius*, Iwan (*trabalis*, Pall. ; *erythrogasten*, Fisch.).—Grey or pale olive above, each scale with a yellowish or pale brown longitudinal streak, with or without black spots ; belly, uniform orange or red.

(C) Var. *Asianus*, Boettg.—Brown or olive above, each scale with a longitudinal light streak, and usually with large black spots relieved by yellowish shafts ; belly, red, spotted or dotted with black. Melanotic specimens entirely black, with the chin and throat yellow, variegated with red, are frequent.

The Dark Green Snake is a very handsome reptile when it retains the full coloration of its earliest days. It will occasionally take a dead mouse or lizard when the body of the creature is gently put in motion near its head. This reptile sometimes reaches a length of more than 5ft. (I have owned one 4ft. 4in.), of which its tapering tail measures about 18in.

The Indian Rat Snake (*Zamenis mucosus*, Boulenger, or *Ptyas mucosus*, Günth.) is a very useful and powerful creature, and common in its own country. It is said to have the peculiar capability of uttering a strange *diminuendo* sound, something like that produced by a tuning fork when gently struck. It is sometimes encouraged, owing to its usefulness in destroying mice and rats, to take up its abode in the walls and over the ceilings of houses in India and Ceylon. However, it occasionally balances the good it does by entering poultry-yards and swallowing the chickens it finds there.

The Indian Rat Snake is wonderfully active, and generally ready to bite. When procured before it is fully grown, and then properly managed, it will frequently become exceedingly tame. One of the nicest and tamest snakes I ever knew was of this species. An old specimen, if wild, is not likely to be amenable at all to judicious treatment, but will probably remain persistently savage and untrustworthy to the end.

Zamenis mucosus may be easily recognised by its very large eye and the possession of three loreal shields, one above two. It has one large præ-ocular and two post-oculars ; eight upper labials, of which the fourth and fifth enter the eye, and five lower labials ; strongly keeled scales arranged in seventeen rows, ventrals numbering from 187 to 208, from 95 to 140 pairs of sub-caudals, and an anal scute which is divided. It is brown, olive, or silvery above, the scales having darker margins. There are often black crossbands on the tail and latter half of the body. The young frequently possess transverse, light streaks on the fore part of their body. The under-surfaces are yellow. This reptile sometimes exceeds a length of 7ft., of which the tail measures nearly one-third. It is common in India and Ceylon, and is also found in Afghanistan, Burmah, South China, Java, and the Malay Peninsula. It can be bought, as a rule, here for sums ranging between 15s. and £3. It requires artificial heat constantly, and it should be fed upon rats, mice, and frogs.

There is a species, *Z. korros*, very closely allied to *Z. mucosus*, which may be kept under the same conditions as its near relative. It chiefly differs from *Z. mucosus* in the possession of smoother scales, two loreals in the place of three (generally), in being of a smaller size, and in the scales being placed in fifteen rows instead of seventeen. It is a native of the East Indian Archipelago, Siam and Southern China.

The Black Snake (*Zamenis constrictor*, Boulenger, or *Coryphodon constrictor*, Dum. and Bibr.) is not only a very beautiful reptile, but also one of the most active animals in existence. For the latter reason it is sometimes called the "Racer"; this name, however, is assigned as well to other Snakes. *Z. constrictor* is very useful to man as a destroyer of rats and mice, yet man, as a rule, does not recognise his obligation, but slays the poor beast at the first opportunity. It is said that this creature is a determined enemy of the Rattlesnake. One observer and naturalist, Dr. Elliot Coues, records that he saw a "Racer" (*Z. constrictor*) throw with extraordinary quickness two coils round the body of a Rattlesnake, one coil near the victim's head, the other near the tail, and then, by forcibly stretching its own body, literally tear its adversary in halves. This Snake should certainly be preserved instead of being killed whenever met with. It is generally a quiet reptile while in captivity, though now and then a specimen may be met with which is persistently spiteful. The "Racer" will eat mice, rats, small birds, and sometimes eggs, which it swallows whole. It may occasionally be bought here for 15s.

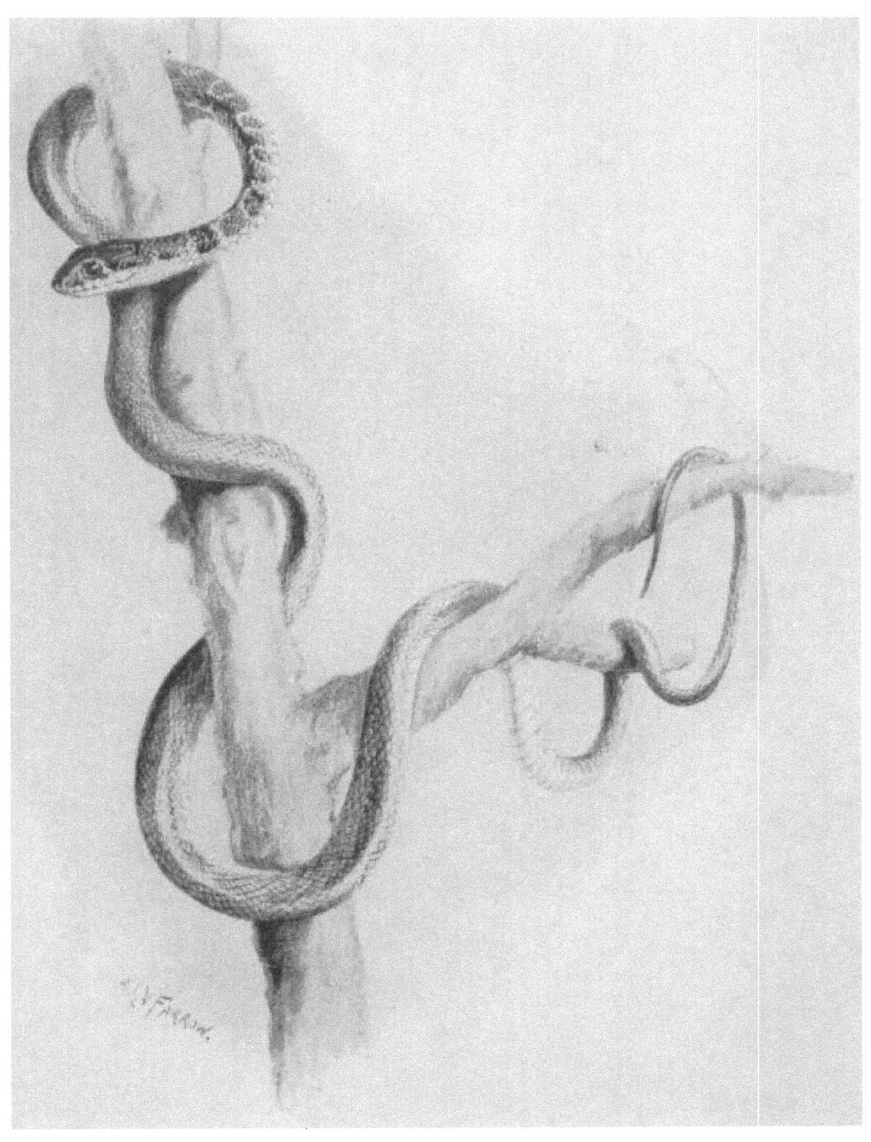

Fig. 70.—Dahl's Snake (*Zamenis dahlii*).

Z. constrictor has one præ-ocular, under which there is a small sub-ocular, two post-oculars, seven upper labials (of which the third and fourth usually touch the eye), four lower labials, smooth lustrous scales, placed in nineteen rows, ventrals numbering 160 to 180, sub-caudals in from 74 to 104 pairs, and an anal scale, which is divided.

As its common name implies, it is often of a black colour, both above and below, with lips and throat which are whitish or yellowish. The young are olive, marked with oval spots of a darker colour. A variety (*C. flaviventris*) is olive or brown above, and yellow below.

This Snake reaches a length of 5ft., of which the tail measures about a quarter. It is a native of North America, and may be kept in this country without artificial heat, and allowed, if in good condition, to hibernate at the proper season.

Dahl's Snake (*Zamenis dahlii*, Fig. 70) is one of the most beautiful and graceful of European Snakes. Unfortunately it is rather rare, but I have been able to buy it sometimes in this country for so low a sum as 8s. It is generally ready to bite; its teeth, however, hardly pierce the skin. In captivity it will feed upon small lizards and young mice. Z. dahlii has a very slender body and tail, one præ-ocular (under which there is a sub-ocular), two post-oculars, eight or nine upper labials, four or five lower ones, smooth, narrow, pitted scales, arranged in nineteen rows, and an anal scale, which is divided. The upper parts of this reptile's body are generally of a pale uniform green. On each side of the neck there are some large brown spots, with white or yellow edges; the lower parts are a yellowish white. The eye is large.

Dahl's Snake is a native of Southern Europe, Asia Minor, West Persia, Syria, and Egypt. As it is fairly hardy it needs very little, if any, artificial heat during the summer, and may be allowed, if fat, to hibernate.

. The Horseshoe Snake (*Zamenis hippocrepis*) has received its name from a mark very like a horse's shoe on the back of its neck. This marking, however, is not constant.

The following is a short description of the reptile: The head is fairly distinct from the neck, and rather broad behind; there are one or two præ-oculars and three post-oculars; the labials, which are eight or nine in number, do not touch the eye, owing to the interposition of several smaller shields; the scales are smooth, and arranged, generally, in twenty-seven rows, the ventrals number from 222 to 258; the sub-caudals are in from 77 to 107 pairs, and the anal scute is divided as a rule, though occasionally entire. The ground-colour of the upper part of the Snake, which varies, is generally reddish- or yellowish-brown, marked by a series of large, dark spots along the back, and a series of smaller spots on the sides, alternating with the dorsal ones. Sometimes these spots are so large as nearly to obscure the ground-colour, and those on the tail join and form three longitudinal bands. The head, especially of young specimens, is marked with transverse lines. The under parts are yellowish or reddish, either uniform or thickly dotted with black.

The Horseshoe Snake may be bought in this country for from 6s. to 9s. It should be kept in captivity, under the conditions recommended for the Dark Green Snake (*Z. atrovirens*, Fig. 70). It will feed upon young mice, and sometimes upon lizards.

Z. hippocrepis is a native of Spain, Portugal, Sardinia, Morocco, Egypt, and Palestine. It grows to a length of about 4ft.; of this the stoutish tail measures nearly 10in.

The South American Rat Snake (*Spilotes pullatus* or *variabilis*) is a beautiful, active, and curious-looking reptile. In its native country it is known as the *Crebo*; here it is sometimes called the Wasp-snake, owing to its colouring. It is not so easily tamed as the Indian Rat Snake (*Z. mucosus*), but, like that Ophidian, it is occasionally domesticated (so called) in its own country because of its usefulness in the destruction of rats and mice, and even of venomous Snakes. It has the habit of making, when excited, a curious rattling noise with its tail; hence its rather common name of "rat-tail."

S. pullatus possesses pointed scales, which are both strongly keeled and imbricated. Its moderately-sized eye has a round pupil. It has either a very small loreal or none at all; one præ-ocular and two post-oculars; scales arranged in sixteen rows (an even number is unusual); ventrals numbering from 198 to 232; sub-caudals in from 90 to 120 pairs, and an anal scale which is

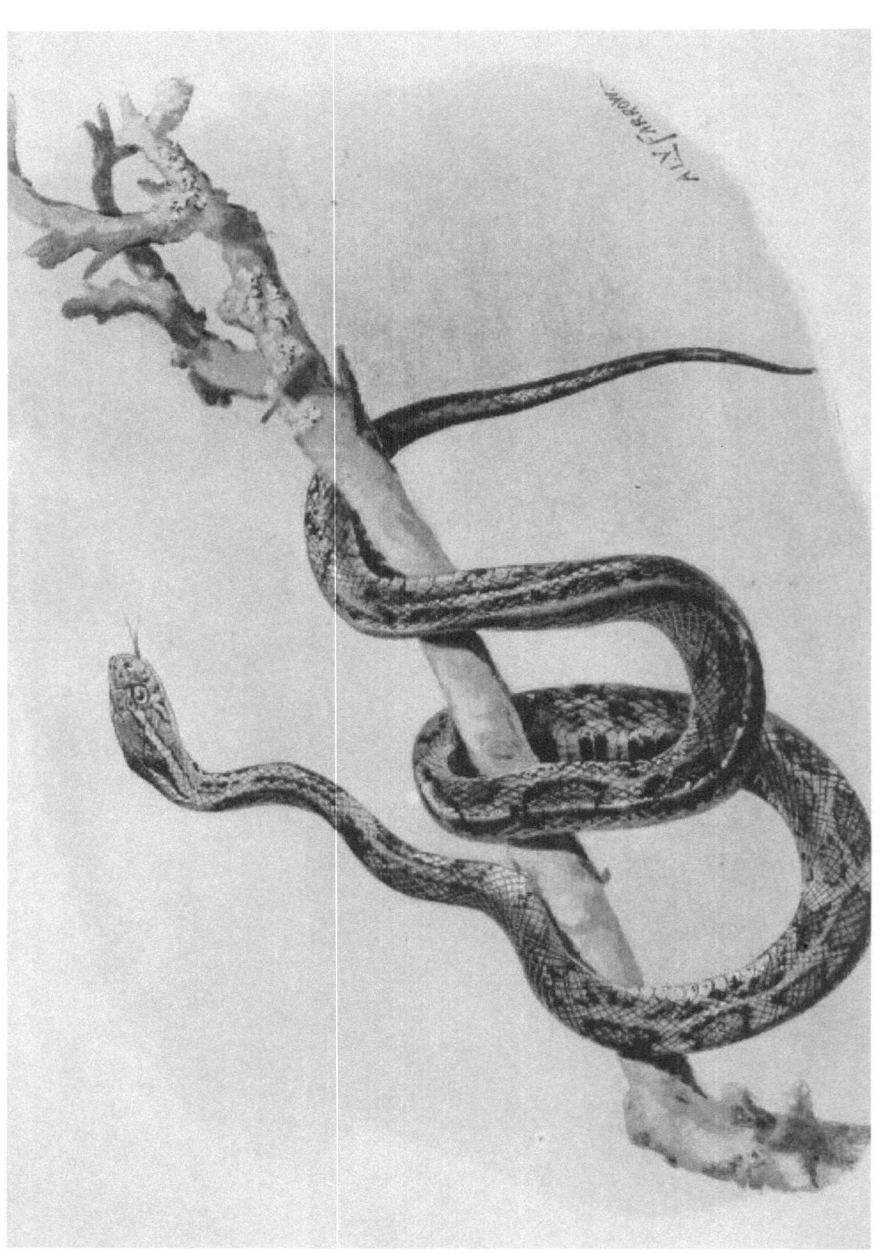

entire. The colouring according to the proportion of the black to the yellow varies very much. It may, indeed, be of a uniform black above, with the exception of a little yellow on the snout and sides of the head. Sometimes its marking fairly closely resembles that of a wasp; hence one of its common names. Occasionally the black of the upper parts is simply spotted with yellow. The under parts are nearly invariably yellow with black tranverse streakings.

S. pullatus is a native of South America, East of the Andes, and is a somewhat rarer importation into this country than the Indian Rat Snake (*Z. mucosus*). It requires here artificial heat; and its food should consist of frogs, mice, and small rats. There are only two species, very closely allied, in the genus *Spilotes*.

The Corn Snake (*Coluber guttatus*, Fig. 71), is sometimes called the American Black Snake; but I do not know why, for the reptile is certainly not black. The names of Snakes, particularly their English ones, are extremely puzzling. For example, even Devonshire peasants do not agree which Snake it is they call the "long cripple." Some of them have told me that it is the Viper (*Vipera berus*), while others have just as positively asserted that it is the Ringed Snake (*Tropidonotus natrix*) which bears this most curious title. However, I incline to the belief that the latter reptile is really the "long cripple," for I cannot understand why the comparatively short Viper should ever be qualified as "long." The reason of the use of the word "cripple," is, of course, plain enough, as it comes naturally from "creep." Again, in the North of England, the Common Snake is, or was, frequently spoken of as the Adder; for example, the late Mr. Waterton, in his essay on Snakes, speaks of the Adder and the Viper as being two different Reptiles.

C. guttatus is an elegant and hardy Snake, very suitable for confinement in this country. It requires no artificial heat during the summer; and if in good condition in the early autumn, it may be safely allowed to pass the winter in a state of hibernation.

This Snake possesses a long loreal; one præ-ocular, two or three post-oculars, eight upper labials, of which the fourth and fifth touch the eye, and four or five lower labials; scales, which on the back of the animal are very slightly keeled, placed in from twenty-five to twenty-nine rows; ventrals numbering from 200 to 239; sub-caudals in from sixty to eighty-eight pairs, and an anal scute which is divided. The following is Mr. Boulenger's description of the colouring of the *C. guttatus*: "Yellowish or pale brown above, with a dorsal series of large brown or red black-edged spots, and an alternating lateral series of smaller spots; a curved dark band from eye to eye across the præ-frontals, continued behind the eye to the angle of the mouth; a ⋂- or O- shaped marking from the frontal-shield to the nape; labials usually with black sutures or spots, belly yellow, with large squarish black blotches."

This Snake's entire length is about 3½ft., of which the tail measures some 6in. The animal is a native of the United States, east of the Rocky mountains; it is also found in North Mexico. Its food should consist of mice, rats, and small birds. I do not think it can be bought in England for much less than 30s.

The Leopard Snake (*Coluber leopardinus*, Fig. 72) is an exceedingly beautiful Ophidian, and a general favourite with those who care for Reptiles. Of late years, though this creature is comparatively rare, it has been imported into this country in considerable numbers, and it may now be bought from dealers in London at prices ranging from 7s. to 12s. If properly treated, the Leopard Snake will live for a long time in confinement. It is, however, a shy feeder; but it may generally be persuaded to take young and hairless mice and rats. If it will not eat such (to Snakes) tempting morsels, it should be fed artificially. Full-grown mice should not be placed in the same Vivarium with the Leopard Snake, for they are likely, unless eaten at once, to kill the reptile. I lost a *C. leopardinus* which I had had for a very long time, and which was a great favourite, through its being bitten in the head by a mouse, the latter, owing to an oversight, having been left in the case with it and its fellows. The Leopard Snake is generally very ready to bite the hands which hold it: the bite, however, as the teeth hardly pierce the skin, is insignificant.

The arrangement of the shields on the head of *C. leopardinus* is very like that of *C. guttatus*. The scales of the former are smooth and are placed in from twenty-five to twenty-seven rows;

FIG. 72.—THE LEOPARD SNAKE (*Coluber leopardinus*).

the ventrals, which are rounded, number from 222 to 260; the sub-caudals are in pairs, from sixty-eight to eighty-nine, and the anal scale is divided. The colouring of the Leopard Snake is so difficult to describe that I again venture to quote Mr. Boulenger, who says that *C. leopardinus* is "greyish or pale brown above, with a dorsal series of dark brown or reddish black-edged transverse spots and a lateral alternating series of smaller black spots, or with two dark brown black-edged stripes, bordering a yellowish vertebral stripe, usually a ∩- shaped dark marking on the occiput and the nape, a crescentric black band from eye to eye, an oblique black band from the post-oculars to the angle of the mouth, and a black spot below the eye; lower parts white, checkered with black or nearly entirely black." •The striped specimen is known as *C. quadrilineatus*, Pallas.

The Leopard Snake grows to nearly 4ft. in length. It is a native of Southern Italy, Malta, Dalmatia, the Crimea, and Asia Minor.

The Four-rayed Snake (*Coluber quatuor-lineatus*, (Fig. 73) is the largest and the most easily tamed of all the European Snakes. It is, indeed, a very beautiful and gentle reptile, and most suitable for confinement, where it is sure to make itself a great favourite. It is a constrictor, and the facility with which it is able to use its coils has been referred to in a former article.

The first Snake of this species I ever possessed astonished me greatly by its wonderful quickness of movement. I had not had it many days, when, to see if it would feed, I placed a live sparrow in its Vivarium; and before I quite realised what had happened, I saw that the bird was crushed to death in the reptile's coils. This most active Snake had seized and constricted its prey so rapidly that my eyes quite failed to follow its movements. It held the bird quite tightly in its embraces for a minute or two, and then proceeded to slowly swallow its victim. After this I found that this particular Snake was so ready a feeder that it would, without hesitation, take a dead bird or mouse from my fingers. This Snake once escaped, and was lost for four or five days. A parishioner of mine, a farmer, found it by the side of a hedge more than a mile away from its home, and brought it back. I remember how astonished I was to see my neighbour with it in his hands and allowing the reptile to crawl over his arms and round his neck, for I knew the antipathy of most people in his position to Snakes. When I expressed my surprise, he replied that he had felt no nervousness about handling the Snake, as he had not forgotten I had told him that no English Snake was poisonous except the Viper, and he knew this Reptile was no Viper, and thought it most probably belonged to me. I was, of course, gratified, not only at the recovery of my favourite, but also at the man's confidence in me. The escape and recapture had, however, a curious effect upon the Snake. After I returned it to its case, it refused to eat anything at all for nearly, if not quite, a year. During this time I fed it occasionally, artificially, to prevent it from becoming very thin and weak. It made its escape one July, and in the following July it recommenced to feed. Why it fasted thus strangely I do not know. Its little adventure did not seem to make it wild or nervous, for it was just as gentle as it had ever been; nor was it hurt in any way when recaught, as far as I could ascertain.

I can most strongly recommend the Four-rayed Snake as an inmate of the Vivarium. It is gentle, hardy, beautiful, and interesting. It can generally be bought, according to size and condition, for from 15s. to 25s. Its food may consist of small birds, mice, rats, and eggs. It will sometimes swallow an egg as large as that of a barndoor hen. As already mentioned, a good feeder is quite ready to accept dead animals. It needs no artificial heat during the summer, and, if in good condition, may safely be allowed to hibernate.

The following is a description of the *Coluber quatuor-lineatus* : One præ-ocular over one sub-ocular, two post-oculars (rarely three); the large eye is overshadowed by the supra-ocular shield, which projects; the vertical is shorter than the parietals, which are slightly pointed posteriorly; eight upper labials, of which the fourth and fifth enter the eye, four or five lower labials; the head is distinct from the neck; the lanceolate scales, except the outer rows, which are smooth, are distinctly though feebly keeled, and are arranged, nearly always, in twenty-five rows; the rounded ventrals number from 195 to 234, the sub-caudals, in pairs, from sixty-three to ninety, and the anal scute is divided ; the scales on the sides of the body are larger than those on the back. The general colour of the animal is yellowish brown, marked by a pair of nearly black lines running along each side of the body from the head to the tail, hence the various specific names which have been given to this reptile from time to time by different authorities, e.g., *quatuor-lineatus* (Lacép.), *quadristriatus* (Donnd.), *quaterradiatus* (Dum. and Bibr.), and *quadrilineatus* (Daud) ; a black, broad streak runs from the eye to the corner of the mouth ; the under parts are yellow marbled with a yellowish-brown. The young of this species is spotted on the upper parts of the body with dark-brown, black-edged spots, which gradually, as the reptile grows, disappear, and are replaced by the nearly black lines just described. Those specimens which retain the spots throughout life were called by Pallas *Coluber sauromates*.

As the Four-rayed Snake sometimes exceeds 7ft. in length, it is certainly the largest as well as the gentlest and most easily tamed of all European Ophidians. It is said to prefer the hilly parts of those countries of which it is a native. The tail equals about one-fifth of the animal's entire length. This Snake is frequently known as *Elaphis quaterradiatus* (Dum. and Bibr.). As a pet, with the exception of the Royal Python (*Python regius*), there is no Snake which I can recommend more highly than *C. quatuor-lineatus*.

In Fig. 73 the eye is not represented as being sufficiently full and black.

The Chicken Snake (*Coluber quadrivittatus*, Günther, or *Coluber obsoletus*, Boulenger) is a fairly hardy reptile, and easily tamed. It may be bought, when in the market in this country, for sums which range from 15s. to £3. It is a strong, active Snake, and sometimes grows to a length of more than 5ft., of which the tail measures nearly one-fourth. The following is a short description of this Snake : The loreal is long ; there are one præ-ocular and two post-oculars, eight upper labials, of which the fourth and fifth touch the eye, and four or five lower labials. The scales, which are very strongly keeled, are arranged in from twenty-five to twenty-nine rows; the ventrals number from 217 to 245 ; the sub-caudals are in from seventy-two to ninety-three pairs; and the anal scute is divided. The colour above is brown or black. The young of the species are marked with large dark spots which, when they disappear with age, are replaced by four dark lines (hence specific name). There are several varieties of this Snake, of which the descriptions below are given by Mr. Boulenger in his "Catalogue of Snakes."

> (A.) Nearly uniform black above and on the posterior two-thirds of the lower parts. (*C. obsoletus*, Say).
> (B.) Dark brown above, but with distinct traces of the large spots; belly largely blotched with blackish (*C. alleghaniensis* Holbr., *C. lindheimeri*, B. and G.).
> (C.) Pale brown above, with large dark brown spots; yellowish inferiorly. (*C. spiloides*, D. and B.).
> (D.) Spots, as in C, combined with stripes, as in E; belly with large spots.
> (E.) Pale brown above, with four dark brown or blackish stripes; belly yellowish, without or with a few brown spots. (*C. quadrivittatus*, Holbr.).

The Chicken Snake comes from the United States, east of the Rocky Mountains. It is hardy enough to be kept in this country without artificial heat, and may be allowed, if it has fed well during the summer, to hibernate. Its food while in captivity should consist of young rats, small birds, and eggs. It will swallow, whole, eggs as large as those of an ordinary barn-door fowl. From this it may be readily seen why it has received its English name.

The Æsculapian Snake (*Coluber æsculapii*, Sturm; or *C. longissimus*, Boulenger). Æsculapius, the mythological god of Health, had a temple at Epidaurus, where he was worshipped under the figure of a serpent. The priests attached to the temple tamed a Snake of the above species, which they taught, it is said, to follow any person where they pleased. The greater proportion of the people of that neighbourhood honoured the reptile as much as they did the god himself. The animal's usual hole was under the beautiful statue of Æsculapius, which the great sculptor Thrasymedes of Paros had made, and whenever the creature came forth from this retreat his appearance was understood to foretell the cure of some sick person. About 280 years B.C. the

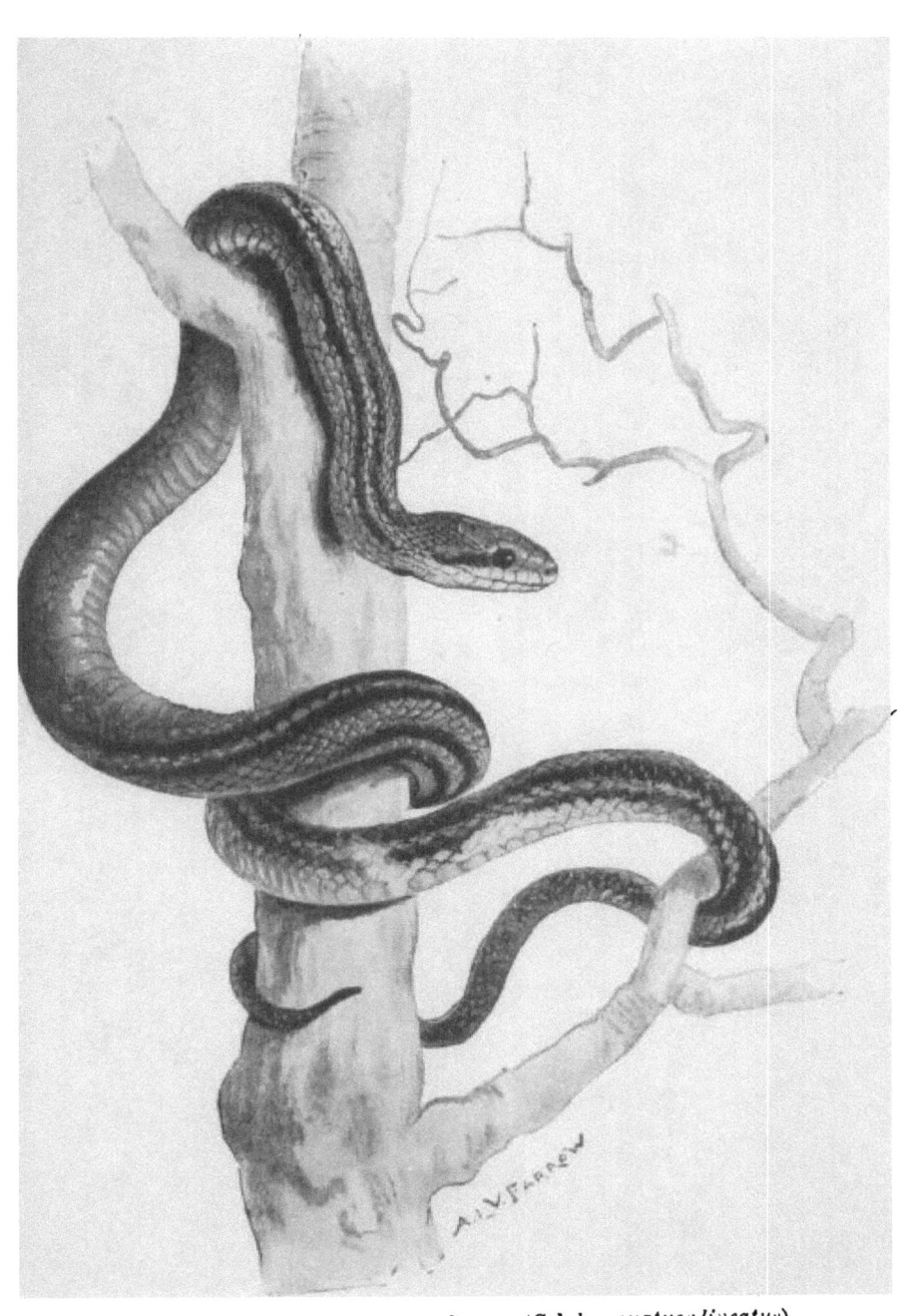

FIG. 73.—THE FOUR-RAYED SNAKE (*Coluber quatuor-lineatus*).

citizens of Rome were suffering from a plague so troublesome that they were induced to consult the Sibylline books, and in them they read that their only hope of a remedy lay in bringing the god Æsculapius from Epidaurus to Rome (see Livy, Book X., chap. 47). An embassy was, therefore, appointed for the purpose, which, after certain arrangements, persuaded the Epidaurians to part with their god, or rather, his representative. He was brought to Rome, and the joy and gratitude of the people at his arrival were so great that they built altars all along the banks of the Tiber, and offered on them many sacrifices. The Romans intended to receive him within their city, and build him a temple there. But the god, it is said, decreed otherwise, and chose for his abode a small island on the River Tiber, to which he gracefully swam. From that time the spot was called the Island of Æsculapius, and on it a temple was built and dedicated to the god, and enriched by many presents. The sick of the great city close by often visited and passed the night in the temple: and if by chance or imagination cures were wrought they were gratefully ascribed to the power and mercy of their god. The healed, as a thank-offering, were expected to sacrifice a cock, the fowl which was not only sacred to Æsculapius, but which was also a symbol of that vigilance which is so necessary for the cure of disease. The plague is recorded to have ceased soon after the arrival of the Snake (See Cicero, "Concerning the Nature of the Gods." Book III.).

The Romans so venerated this species of Snake that, it is said, they carried specimens with them during their expeditions, and gave the creatures liberty in those countries over which they (the Romans) had control. To this custom it is supposed to owe its wide distribution. This, however, appears a doubtful conclusion, as at the present time the reptile seems to be still extending its range.

The Æsculapian Snake is not only interesting because of the circumstances referred to above, but also because of its beauty, hardiness, and docility. It is imported into this country in considerable numbers, and often may be bought for so low a sum as 4s. Its food consists of birds, mice, and lizards. In captivity it will frequently take dead food, such as the bodies of dead hairless young mice and rats, and those of sparrows and other small birds when they have been deprived of their feathers.

C. æsculapii is unusually narrow across the temples: its head is fairly distinct from the body; it has one præ-ocular, two post-oculars, eight or nine upper labials, of which the fourth and fifth, or fifth and sixth, touch the eye. The scales, which are smooth, or feebly keeled on the posterior part of the body, are arranged in twenty-one or twenty-three rows; the ventral scales, which terminate at the sides angulately, number from 212 to 248; the sub-caudals are in pairs, from sixty to ninety-one. The colour above is grey, olive-brown, or a very beautiful light yellowish-green. The scales are sometimes finely edged with white, or bluish-white; thus the beauty of the animal is much added to. There is a dark mark from the eye to the angle of the mouth; the under parts are a pale yellow or a yellowish-green. When young, the animal is generally of a greyish-brown above, marked with four or five rows of spots of a darker shade; there is a ∧-shaped black marking on the nape of the neck.

This species sometimes reaches a length of more than 4ft., of which the tail measures about 10in. It is a native of most of the warmer countries of Europe. It need not be supplied with artificial heat while in captivity in this country, and as winter approaches, if in good condition, it may be allowed to hibernate.

When first caught it is generally ready to bite; but the teeth, however, are hardly able to pierce the skin. It soon becomes quite tame after being gently and properly handled. As a rule, an untamed Snake of any kind which tries to bite while being caught or released, ceases to attack when held securely in the hand. In other words, there is less danger of a bite while holding a Snake than in catching it or letting it go.

The Back-marked Snake (*Coluber scalaris*, Boulenger, or *Rhinechis scalaris*, Dum. and Bibr.) is a native of Europe, and is chiefly found in the South of France and Spain. It feeds on lizards and mice, and, as it is fairly hardy, it may be kept in captivity without artificial heat, and if in good condition, allowed to pass the winter in a state of hibernation. It is a curiously marked Snake; hence its specific name. The head of the animal is distinct from the body, and wide at its base: the rostral shield, which is pointed behind, projects considerably, and the snout is pointed; the loreal is longer than deep; there is one præ-ocular, and there are two or three post-oculars, seven or eight upper labials, and four or five lower ones. The smooth scales are nearly always arranged in twenty-seven rows; the ventral shields number from 201 to 220, and the sub-caudals, in pairs, from forty-eight to sixty-eight, and the anal scute is generally divided. The colour of the Snake above is reddish, yellowish, or pale brown, marked by two black lines running down the whole length of the body; these two lines are joined at almost equal distances by broader black lines, and thus a series of H-shaped markings is formed. There are small black spots on the sides. The above markings often disappear with age—especially, it is said, in the case of males—and are then replaced by two brown stripes which run down the back. The underparts are yellowish white, rarely marked with blackish spots. The animal when full grown is about 3ft. long, and the tail is short and conical. *C. scalaris* may be bought, when on the market, for from 4s. to 7s.

The Bull Snake (*Coluber melanoleucus* Daud., or *Pituophis Sayi*, Baird) is one of the largest and most active of the North American Colubers. It has received its English name from a supposed power of being able to roar like a bull. Some writers have gone so far as to say that it can make a noise like that of thunder. The Snake, before it makes the sound which has given it the above title, is said to inflate itself slowly with air, until it is double its usual girth, and then by expiring makes its strange noise. Of course, a large and angry Snake can make considerable noise by expelling air forcibly from its lung, but I doubt very much whether any Snake could make a sound like that of thunder or the roaring of a bull. I have heard friends remark that the hissing of a savage Boa Constrictor of my own reminded them of a railway engine blowing off steam, and such a remark I can understand; but I do not understand how the sibilant sound made by a hissing Snake can ever fairly be likened either to the roaring of a bull or to a clap of thunder. I should be glad to possess a *C. melanoleucus* which could, and would, roar like a bull. I cannot, however, say that the Bull Snake does not deserve its name, for some writers affirm that they have repeatedly heard it make the strange un-snake-like sound; while others, who are very well acquainted with the animal, declare that they have never known it roar or make a noise which bears any resemblance to thunder. As there is an unusually large covering, so called, at the end of its glottis, probably the animal is capable of making more noise than most Ophidians of its size. However, the more I learn of Snakes, the more I am convinced of the necessity of exercising great caution in obtaining information concerning these strange and very interesting creatures.

The Bull Snake is a native of North America and Mexico. It will eat small rats, mice, and sometimes eggs. Care must be taken in associating other Snakes with *C. melanoleucus*, for it is somewhat of a cannibal. It is very hardy and easily tamed, and may sometimes be bought for about £1. The Bull Snake can be kept in captivity under the same conditions which have been suggested for the care of the other hardy Colubers.

The following is a brief description of this Snake: The snout slightly projects; the nostril is much deeper than it is broad; the frontals are broken up into four shields and sometimes more; and the parietals or occipitals are also broken up posteriorly; the loreal is longer than it is broad; there is one præ-ocular, with occasionally a small sub-ocular beneath, and there are two or three post-oculars; there are eight or nine upper labials, of which the fourth or fifth touch the eye; and five or six lower labials. The scales, which are strongly keeled on the back of the animal, are arranged in from twenty-nine to thirty-five rows, the ventrals number from 209 to 239, the sub-caudals are placed in pairs from forty-five to sixty-five, and the anal scute is entire. The colour above is a lightish brown marked with a series of large, dark-brown, black-edged spots. There are smaller spots on the sides.

The young have a dark band running across the head from eye to eye and another dark band running from each eye to the corner of the mouth. The labials have generally black divisions. The under parts are whitish, frequently spotted with brown.

This Snake is said to sometimes exceed a length of 7ft., of which the tail measures about one-seventh. *C. melanoleucus* is also known as the Pine Snake, the Pilot Snake, and the Black and White Snake.

The Painted Tree-Snake (*Dendrophis pictus*). The members of this genus and of some other genera have received the common title of Tree-Snakes. These are chiefly remarkable for their slender and elongated bodies, and generally for the great beauty of their colours. Their movements are exceedingly graceful and wonderfully rapid. Dr. Wurcherer, on writing of these very interesting ophidians, says: " I am always delighted when I find that another Tree-Snake has settled in my garden. You look for a birds' nest; the young ones have gone, but you find their bed occupied by one of these beautiful creatures, which will coil up its body, of 2ft. in length, within a space not larger than the hollow of your hand. They appear to be always watchful; for at the instant you discover one, the quick playing of the long, black, forked tongue will show you that you too are observed. On perceiving the slightest sign of your intention to disturb it, the snake will dart upwards through the branches and over the leaves, which scarcely seem to bend beneath the weight. A moment more, and you have lost sight of it."

The Painted Tree-Snake is one of the commonest Snakes in South-eastern Asia. It is subject to considerable variation in not only its colouring, but also in the arrangement of the shields of its head. It sometimes grows to a length of nearly 4ft., of which the tail measures more than one-third.

This Snake has a large and beautiful eye, with round pupil, an elongated loreal, one præ-ocular and two post-oculars, nine upper labials, and five, generally, lower ones. Its pitted scales are placed in fifteen rows, its ventrals—which are keeled and notched—number from 165 to 190, and its sub-caudals are arranged in from 122 to 164 pairs, and the anal scute is divided. *D. pictus* is olive or bronze-brown above; there is a black stripe on either side of the head, which appears to pass through the eye; there is also a yellow stripe, edged below with black, which runs along each side of the body, and sometimes there is another, which runs along the front part of the back. The under-parts are white or yellowish-white.

The Painted Tree-Snake feeds upon lizards and frogs. While in captivity in this country it should be provided with artificial heat. The cases in which all Tree-Snakes are kept ought to be furnished with some plant upon which they can climb and in which they can chiefly live. Under most circumstances an orange or lemon-tree will answer the purpose very well. Even in such trees, small as they necessarily must be, it is wonderful how these Snakes, owing to the colouring of their bodies and the manner of their coiling, are able to hide themselves. I have occasionally looked for some little time at a small tree, in the branches of which I knew there was one of these creatures, before I was able to discover the Reptile.

The Punctulated Tree-Snake (*Dendrophis punctulatus*) is a native of Australia. It is hardy and easily tamed. The following is a short description of the reptile : A long loreal, one præ-ocular and two post-oculars, seven or eight upper labials, and five lower ones. . The scales are placed in thirteen rows ; the ventrals, which are keeled and notched, number from 191 to 220 ; the sub-caudals are arranged in from 120 to 144 pairs, and the anal scute is divided. The colour above is olive or brown, the scales sometimes being edged with black ; the lower parts and the upper lip are yellowish.

The Punctulated Tree-Snake may, occasionally, be bought in this country for about £1. It reaches a length of more than 5ft. of which the tail measures one-quarter.

The Variegated Bush-Snake (*Philothamnus semivariegatus*). The members of this genus possess twenty-five teeth in each maxillary jaw, the longest of which are the posterior. They are natives of Tropical and South Africa. *P. semivariegatus* has a long head, which is distinct from the neck, a large eye, with round pupil, a narrow loreal, one præ-ocular, two post-oculars, nine upper labials, five lower labials, pitted scales placed in fifteen rows, notched and keeled, ventrals, which number from 169 to 207, sub-caudals, also notched and keeled, arranged in from 112 to 155 pairs, and an anal scute which is divided. The upper parts of this Snake are of a green or olive colour, which is either uniform or marked with spots or cross-bars. The under parts are a greenish-yellow. The reptile grows to a length of 4ft., of which the tail measures nearly one third.

The Variegated Bush-Snake should be provided with artificial heat during the whole time of its captivity in this country, and a bushy tree in which it may hide and climb. Its food ought to consist of frogs and lizards. The frogs supplied to these slender Snakes must not be more than half-grown. Some of the Tree- and Bush-Snakes will eat hairless mice.

The Banded-tail Tree-Snake (*Leptophis liocercus*, Bouleng., or *Ahætulla liocercus*, Günth.) It is a most beautiful and elegant creature. For so slender an animal it has an enormous gape of mouth. This Snake and the other members of the same genus are natives of Central and South America. *L. liocercus*, in captivity, should be provided with artificial heat, and fed upon rather small frogs. It has an elongated head, a large eye, with a round pupil, no loreal, one præ-ocular, and two post-oculars ; the posterior frontals in contact with the upper labials, which number eight or nine, and five or six lower labials ; its scales, which are strongly keeled, with the exception of the outer rows and those on the neck and tail, are arranged in fifteen rows. Its angulated ventrals number from 151 to 167, its sub-caudals are in from 140 to 173 pairs, and the anal scute is divided. The following description of its colouring is given by Mr. Boulenger : "Bronzy or golden above, head, neck, and usually vertebral region bright green ; or a bright green above and on the sides ; the keels on the scales dark brown or black ; a black streak on each side of the head, passing through the eye ; scales and head-shields some- times black-edged, upper lip and lower parts white or yellow." This Snake, which is occasionally called the "Parrot Snake," sometimes grows to a length of 5ft., of which the tail measures nearly one third.

Merrem's Snake (*Liophis pœcilogyrus*, Boulenger ; or *Liophis merremii*, Dum. and Bibr.) is a very nice little Reptile indeed, and hardy. It is easily tamed. Its food should consist of frogs. Merrem's Snake has a most extended range, being found nearly all over South America. It needs no artificial heat while in captivity in this country, except during the colder months, if it be not allowed to hibernate. It might be naturalised in England. *L. merremii* has a nearly square loreal, one præ-ocular, two post-oculars, eight upper labials, and four or five lower ones. Its smooth, pitted scales are arranged in nineteen rows; the ventrals number from 143 to 179, the sub-caudals are in from forty to sixty-three pairs, and the anal scute is divided. It is brownish, greenish, or reddish above, spotted or reticulated with black. Sometimes there are black cross-bands. The lower parts are yellowish or reddish, frequently spotted with black. This Snake grows to a length of a little over 2ft., of which the tail measures a little more than one-fifth. It may sometimes be bought for about 15s.

The Royal Snake (*Liophis reginæ*) is a pretty Snake, and fairly hardy while in captivity. It is a native of tropical South America, and therefore should be kept under the influence of artificial heat. It may be fed upon frogs. The following is a short description of the Snake. The eye is large, and the snout short; the loreal is deeper than it is long; there are one præ-ocular and two post-oculars; there are eight upper labials and five lower ones; the smooth, pitted scales are arranged in seventeen rows; the ventrals number from 136 to 150; the sub-caudals are in from fifty-eight to eighty-one pairs, and the anal scute is divided. The colour of the upper parts of the body is greenish or olive, the scales being frequently edged with black. There is a black stripe on each side of the tail; the upper lip is yellow; the under parts are yellowish, and often spotted with black. The Royal Snake does not often exceed a length of 2ft., of which the tail measures about one quarter. The last two teeth in each maxillary jaw of *L. reginæ* and the other members of the same genus are very large, and are separated from the rest by a considerable interspace. The genus *Liophis* numbers about twenty-one species, all of which are natives of America and the West Indies.

The Colubrine Xenodon (*Xenodon colubrinus*) belongs to a genus the members of which are remarkable for the curious formation of their teeth. They are, therefore, well-called "Xenodons" the "strange-toothed." They are natives of Tropical America. These Snakes, though perfectly harmless and inoffensive in every way, have often been regarded, and are now too, I believe, by the natives of the countries in which they are found, as being exceedingly poisonous. They do certainly possess two large fang-like and movable teeth in each maxillary jaw, but they are ungrooved, and not connected with any poisonous glands. Besides, these movable teeth have not the position in the mouth of the ordinary poison-delivering fang. These movable teeth are separated from the rest of the comparatively few teeth in the maxillary jaws by a considerable interspace.

X. colubrinus, which is also known as the Long-headed Snake (*X. rhabdocephalus*, Dum. and Bibr.), has a large and beautiful eye, a head which is slightly compressed and distinct from the neck, a square loreal, one præ-ocular, two post-oculars, eight upper labials, four or five lower labials, smooth and pitted scales arranged in nineteen rows, ventrals which number from 131 to 153, sub-caudals in from thirty-six to fifty pairs, and an anal scute which is undivided. The colour of the upper parts of this Snake's body is lightish brown marked with darker brown black-edged cross-bands, which are interrupted in the middle. There is a dark marking on the crown of the head and on the nape of the neck, and there is also another dark band which runs from the eye to the angle of the mouth. The underparts are yellowish, covered thickly with small brown spots. The Long-headed Snake sometimes reaches a length of more than 3ft. 6in., of which the tail measures less than one-seventh. This Reptile, while in captivity in England, should be kept under the influence of artificial heat, and fed upon frogs.

The Hog-Nosed Snake (*Heterodon platyrhinus*), notwithstanding its numerous terror-inspiring names, its movable fangs, and its viperish appearance, is a perfectly harmless and very gentle little Reptile. It is known as the "Chequered Adder," the "Spreading Adder," the "Blowing Viper," the "Spread Head," and the "Hissing Snake." These are some of its local titles, and there is, naturally, a reason for each of them. For example, the epithet "chequered" is given because of the markings on the creature's back, and the names of "Adder" and "Viper" because of its appearance. The adjective "spreading" is deserved by reason of the animal's capacity of spreading or widening its neck. In this, to a certain extent, it resembles the Cobra and other Snakes. When frightened, *H. platyrhinus* flattens its head, and thus it earns the appellation of "Spread Head."

The Snake is supposed to have the power of hissing unusually loudly, hence it is known as the "Blowing Viper"; and it is of this Ophidian that Chateaubriand writes: "When approached it becomes flat, appears of different colours, and opens its mouth hissing. Great caution is necessary not to enter the atmosphere which surrounds it. It decomposes the air, which, imprudently inhaled, induces languor. The person wastes away, the lungs are affected, and in the course of four months he dies of consumption." Much of this quotation is, of course, nonsense.

The generic name *Heterodon* (abnormal toothed) is given to the members of this genus because they possess a very short maxillary jaw, furnished with from six to eleven teeth, which, after an interspace, are followed by a pair of large, movable fangs. These fangs, however, are not connected with any poison gland, nor are they grooved. The Heterodons are natives of North America, and are confined to the three species—*platyrhinus*, *simus*, and *nasicus*. *H. platyrhinus* has a stout body and a short tail; a head which is hardly distinct from the body; a snout which is very short and projecting; an eye of moderate size, which possesses a round pupil; its anterior frontals separated from each other by a small shield; a deep loreal, and its eyes surrounded by several small shields; seven or eight upper labials, and three lower ones. Its scales, with the exception of the outer rows, are keeled and pitted, and arranged in from twenty-three to twenty-seven rows. The ventrals number from 120 to 150, the sub-caudals are placed in from thirty-seven to sixty pairs, and the anal scute is divided.

Mr. Boulenger describes the colouring of *H. platyrhinus* in the following words: "Brown or red above, with a dorsal series of large square or transverse dark brown or black spots, separated from each other by light interspaces, and a lateral alternating series of smaller spots; an elongate black blotch or band on each side of the head, sometimes extending forwards to the frontal, a transverse dark band between the eyes, and an oblique one from the eye to the angle of the mouth; belly yellowish or reddish, clouded with brown." There is a variety which is black or blackish above.

The Hog-nosed Snake is found in the United States east of the Rocky Mountains. It is a very inoffensive little creature, hardly ever attempting to bite, even when much provoked to do so. It grows to a length of about 30in. Its food should consist of frogs. It need not be supplied with artificial heat while in captivity in this country, if it be allowed, provided that it is in good condition, to hibernate during the colder months of the year.

The Smooth Snake (*Coronella austriaca*, Laur., or *Coronella lævis*, Lacep., Fig. 74) is by far the most interesting of our three English Snakes. Less than half a century ago it was not recognised as a British reptile at all. "Many years since," writes the late Mr. Bell in his *British Reptiles*, "a small Snake, having the characters of one of the *Colubridæ*, was taken by Mr. J. W. Simmons near Dumfries. It was published as a new species of Mr. Sowerby in his *British Miscellany*, and figured in the third plate of that work. It was there named *Coluber dumfrisiensis*. The specimen remained until within the last few years in the possession of Mr. Sowerby's family, but having come into my hands, it was unfortunately lost or mislaid, and I have never since been able to recover it. There is, I think, great reason to believe that it was a very young *Natrix torquata*, but differing certainly in many respects from the usual appearance and characteristics of that species. The most remarkable peculiarity mentioned, however, is, that the scales are simple, *not* carinated." There is no doubt now that the Smooth Snake (*Coronella lævis*) and the *Coluber Dumfrisiensis* of Sowerby, are one and the same species.

Numerous specimens of this harmless and beautiful little Snake (*C. lævis*) have been killed in mistake for the Common Viper (*Pelias berus*), which it not a little resembles in marking. It was owing, probably, to this likeness between the two Reptiles that the Smooth Snake has only, comparatively, very lately been classed as a native of Great Britain. It is fairly common on the Continent.

Mr. Frederick Bond caught a male Smooth Snake at Ringwood, in Hampshire, in 1854, which was preserved in spirits, and ultimately sent to the British Museum. This is one of the

T

earliest recorded captures of the reptile in England. Five years later another specimen was taken at Bournemouth, and forwarded by Lord Arthur Russell to the British Museum. This was also a male.

Mr. Bartlett, the well-known Superintendent of the Zoological Gardens, London, once wrote in the *Intellectual Observer* that, "It was on the morning of the 24th August, 1862, I saw for the first time one of these animals, Mr. Fenton having stopped me as I was driving along the road in the Regent's Park, and taking from his pocket what I then thought was a Viper, asked me if I would accept it for the Zoological Gardens." About this time, the late Mr. Frank Buckland claimed, in the *Field*, the Smooth Snake as a native of Great Britain. Now there is no doubt whatever concerning the creature's right to be classed among the British fauna. Several specimens are taken every summer in Hampshire and the neighbouring counties. I have had no difficulty for some years past in procuring English Smooth Snakes from a naturalist living in Bournemouth. The price is 5s. each. European representatives of this species can generally, during summer, be bought in London of a certain dealer, for even a lower sum than that just quoted.

Like the common viper (*Pelias berus*) the *C. lævis* brings forth its young alive. One Smooth Snake, I believe, produced six little ones at the *Field* office, then at 346, Strand. Of these, Mr. Frank Buckland wrote the following very interesting account (see the *Field*, October, 1862): "The old mother Snake is coiled up in a graceful combination of circles, her little family are nestled together on her back; they have twisted their tiny bodies together into a shape somewhat resembling a double figure of eight, and there they lie basking at their ease in the mid-day sun. The old mother is vibrating her forked tongue at me; the little ones are imitating their mother's action, and are vibrating their tiny tongues also. The mamma's head is most beautifully iridescent in the sun, and her babies are in this respect nearly as pretty as their mother. They are about 5in. long, about as thick as a small goose-quill, and smoother than the finest velvet. Their skins are of a brownish black colour, and marked like their mother's, only that these markings are not yet well developed. The scales on

FIG. 74.—THE SMOOTH SNAKE (*Coronella austriaca*).

the under parts of their bodies are of a beautiful, pale, glittering blue. Altogether, they are real little beauties."

Since the above was written these Snakes have been frequently born in captivity. The young, when produced in confinement, should be fed on very small lizards. This is their natural food. Unlike the Common Snake (*T. natrix*), *C. lævis* prefers dry and rather hilly ground, such as moors and commons. In such situations as these, its prey (the lizard) abounds. Though lizards form the principal food of the Smooth Snake, it will occasionally take young and hairless mice, and now and then a slow-worm. This Reptile, if properly treated, soon becomes very tame, and will sometimes accept food from the fingers. I have possessed a specimen which would readily take at one meal several small lizards, either alive or dead, from the hand; and I have known of others which would eat young mice in the same way.

One naturalist, Dr. Opel, has given in the *Zoologist* a very interesting account of a Smooth Snake of his own attacking and eating a Slow-worm (*Anguis fragilis*) nearly as large as its captor and devourer.

The Smooth Snakes, to a certain extent, constrict their prey. This may readily be seen when *C. lævis* seizes a victim. The lizard is generally swallowed head-foremost; and the small Snake shows not a little skill in the way he manages to turn the lizard with its jaws, until it is in a position suitable for being swallowed.

Dr. Günther has recorded that a certain Smooth Snake of his own got into the habit of eating only the tails of lizards. This particular Snake showed a great readiness to profit by experience. It had been fed for some time upon viviparous lizards and others of similar size. One day, however, the naturalist thought he would test the strength of his captive by giving it a large Sand Lizard (*Lacerta agilis*). " The lizard was immediately seized; but after a long fight, during which the lizard several times appeared to be entangled in the writhings of the Snake, always managing, however, to free its head, which had been seized by the Snake, the latter changed the point of attack, and got hold of the tail of the lizard. This, of course, broke off, and was devoured by the Snake. From this time the Snake always seized the tails of the lizards given him for food, without further attacking them; nor, if tailless lizards were put to him, would he attempt to devour them."

It is said that when the Smooth Snake is handled it generally shows a readiness to bite, especially when first caught. I must confess, however, that this does not agree with my own experience. Though I have owned from time to time many of these interesting little Snakes, I have never possessed one which showed any inclination to resent being touched. I was mentioning this fact one day to a keeper of a Reptile-house, when he at once said: "We have one here that will bite you quickly enough." And I asked if I might try it. It was accordingly taken from its case, and soon was persuaded to seize, with its teeth, the keeper's finger. I then took the Reptile in my hands, and attempted to make it bite me, but it steadily refused to do so. "That's queer," said the keeper, as he regained possession of the animal, and once more was successful in obtaining a bite, this time so sharp a one that the blood flowed fairly freely from the small wounds. I therefore made a second endeavour to get bitten, and though I tried with considerable perseverance, could not prevail upon the little creature to even open its mouth. There were many interested witnesses of my fruitless essays. Why I was unsuccessful, I do not know. My failures, however, endorsed my assertion that the Smooth Snake is not nearly so fierce a reptile as it is generally reported to be. It cannot be with Snakes as it is with gnats, midges, and the well-known insects of the genus *Pulex*, which will with pertinacity and appetite attack some people and leave others entirely alone. But, however, it is surprising that when one shows an indifference to bites, as he handles Snakes, how very seldom indeed he is bitten.

The Smooth Snake is a hardy little animal, and has the power, when in good condition, of fasting for at least a year. The case in which it is confined must be carefully made, for the Reptile is very clever in squeezing itself through a hole apparently too small to receive its body, and so effecting its escape. *C. lævis*, for a Snake, can endure a considerable amount of cold. It is supposed not to spend so long a time in hibernation as either the Common Snake (*Tropidonotus natrix*) or the Viper (*Pelias berus*).

The following is a brief description of *C. lævis*: The head is slightly distinct from the neck; the eye is small, and has a round pupil; the rostral, broad as deep, is produced posteriorily between the internasals; the loreal is long; there is one præ-ocular and there are two post-oculars, seven upper labials and four lower ones. The scales are smooth, having apical pits, and are arranged in nineteen rows; the ventrals number from 153 to 199, the sub-caudals are placed in from forty-two to seventy pairs, and the anal scute is, as a rule, divided. The upper parts are brown, greenish-brown, or reddish, marked along the back with two parallel rows of dark brown or brick-red spots. Sometimes these spots are confluent, and then these dorsal markings somewhat resemble those of the Viper (*P. berus*). There are generally on the top of the head, two broad dark brown or brick-red streaks which form a scape like that of an inverted V. There is a dark thinnish stripe on each side of the head, which runs from the nostril and apparently through the eye to the angle of the mouth. The colours of the lower parts are various, such as red, pinkish, orange, brown, grey, and almost black, uniform or spotted with black and white.

This Snake hardly ever exceeds a length of 2ft., of which the tail measures about one-fifth. It is found in Hampshire, Dorsetshire, and Surrey, and on the Continent as far north as 62½deg. It is also a native of Syria.

The genus *Coronella* numbers about eighteen species, and has representatives not only in Europe, but also in Asia (South-west), India, and in America, north of the Equator.

The Bordeaux Snake (*Coronella girondica*) is a nice little animal and very easily tamed. In appearance it is much like the Smooth Snake (*C. lævis*). The following are the chief differences between the two reptiles: *C. girondica* has eight upper labials instead of, as a rule, seven; a broader rostral than its near relative, hardly visible from above, and ending very obtusely; scales generally in twenty-one rows, and not always in nineteen. While the Smooth Snake has the markings on its back usually disposed in pairs, the Bordeaux Snake possesses them placed in one row. And the lower parts of the latter animal, instead of being usually uniform in colour or finely speckled, are often marked with four-sided black spots or two black longitudinal lines.

The entire length of the Bordeaux Snake is about 2ft., of which the tail measures one-sixth. This Snake is found in the south of France, Italy, Morocco, and Algeria. In captivity it may be treated and fed in the same way as suggested for *C. lævis*. It will more frequently than its near relative take young mice. It is sometimes sold for the Smooth Snake, but it is not so hardy as that reptile.

The King Snake (*Coronella getula*) is very beautiful, hardy, and easily tamed. It is a native of North America, and may be kept in this country during the summer without the help of artificial heat. It is usually a very ready feeder on rats, mice, birds, and small eggs. Without much difficulty it can be persuaded to take the animals when they are dead, and even dead Snakes. The dead creatures should be moved gently in front of the Reptile's head, and generally it will at once seize and swallow them, that is to say if it be hungry. Smaller Snakes should not be kept with the King Snake, or it will very likely adopt the habits of the cannibal. The King Snake is said to do a great deal of good by killing Rattlesnakes. Of this Snake, the rostral is broad; the vertical much longer than broad, but shorter than the parietals; the loreal is sometimes absent; there is one præ-ocular and there are two post-oculars, seven upper labials, of which the third and fourth touch the eye, and four lower ones. The scales are arranged in twenty-one or twenty-three rows, very rarely in nineteen; the ventrals number from 198 to 240; the sub-caudals are in from forty-one to sixty-five pairs, and the anal scute is undivided.

This Snake is coloured very variously. The following is the description given by Mr. Boulenger in "The Catalogue of Snakes": "Dark brown or black above, with yellow or white markings; labials and lower parts black and white or black and yellow.

- A. Above with small yellow spots, or narrow yellow transverse bands restricted to the back. (*C. Sayi.*)
- B. Above with yellow transverse bands connected with their fellows on the sides. (*C. getula.*)
- C. More or less complete whitish annuli round the body, widening on the belly. (*C. californiæ, C. Boylii.*)"

The King Snake is almost sure to become a great favourite of all those who care for it properly. It grows to a length of about 6ft., of which the tail measures nearly one-seventh. It may sometimes be bought in England for £1 to £2.

The Milk Snake (*Coronella triangulum*, Daud., or *Coluber eximius*, Holbr.) is also a native of North America, but not found, I think, on the west of the Mississippi. As it is fairly hardy it need not be provided with artificial heat during the summer months while in captivity in this country. If in good condition as winter draws on it may be allowed to hibernate. The Milk Snake will eat mice and birds. I have never known it to take milk or heard of its doing so. When in the market it may be bought for about 10s.

The following is a short description of *C. triangulum*: A broad rostral and a long loreal, one præ-ocular and two post-oculars, seven upper labials (of which the third and fourth touch the eye), and four lower labials. The smooth scales are generally placed in twenty-one rows, very rarely nineteen; ventrals number from 184 to 214; the sub-caudals are in from forty-three to fifty-five pairs; and the anal scute is entire. This Snake is yellowish-grey above, marked with brownish or reddish black-edged spots, placed in three rows, the largest spots running along the centre of the back. From the eye to the angle to the mouth there is a black line. The lower parts are white, chequered with black.

The Milk Snake grows to a length of about 30in., of which the tail measures one seventh. Its body and tail are fairly stout.

The Egg-eating Snake (*Dasypeltis scabra*), though by no means striking in appearance, is one of the most interesting and curious of all Snakes. It is also known as *Deirodon scaber* (Owen), or "the rough-scaled neck-toothed" animal (*deiré*, a neck; and *odous*, *odontos*, a tooth; *scaber*, rough). The name *Deirodon* is well given, since there are several projections (each projection is called an *hypopophysis*, *i.e.*, an offshoot from below) from the anterior thoracic part of the backbone, which (the projections), tipped with enamel or dentine, pass through small holes into the gullet. These "gular teeth" form a kind of saw.

The food of *D. scaber* consists of eggs of birds, which it swallows whole. If anyone who is ignorant of this creature's extraordinary powers were shown the small reptile, less, perhaps, than 2ft. long, and not thicker in any part of its body than a man's little finger, and an egg of a common barn-door fowl, and then told that the snake could swallow the egg without losing any of its contents or even breaking the shell, they would be justified in doubting either the veracity or intelligence of the speaker and exhibitor. The Snake, however, owing to the marvellous distensibility of both its mouth and œsophagus (the canal through which the food passes to the stomach), is able to perform the apparently impossible feat of swallowing the egg.

D. scabra has such small and so few teeth in its jaws, that it once received the generic name of *anodon* (toothless). Yet this want of tooth-power ministers to the animal's well-being. For were the teeth long and strong the egg would run the risk of being cracked or pierced before it could pass into the Snake's gullet, and some of its contents would be lost. The teeth of the jaws, however, are just large enough to hold the egg firmly during the first stages of deglutition. When the egg has passed into the gullet, the mouth of the reptile is closed, and by the contraction of the muscles of the gullet the egg is pressed against those enamel-capped processes, already referred to, until the shell is cut and broken, and its contents are passed on to the stomach, while the crushed and folded shell is disgorged as a pellet. The egg is held stationary, while being thus pierced and crushed, at a distance of about 2in. from the angle of the mouth. Dr. Andrew Smith, in 1829, was one of the first, if not the first, to notice the capabilities and habits of this curious and interesting Snake. Other Snakes which swallow eggs whole do not eject the shell, but digest it.

D. scabra belongs to the sub-family *Rhachiodontinæ* (the Spine-toothed). This sub-family contains the single genus *Dasypeltis*, of which genus, I believe, *D. scabra* is the only species. This Snake has a small head, hardly distinct from the neck; a small eye, having a vertical pupil; a snout which is rounded, short, and convex; a rostral which is broader than deep, and scarcely visible from above; generally a groove running down the middle of the vertical shield; as a rule, one præ-ocular, two post-oculars, no loreal, generally seven upper labials, and a pair of large chin-shields, which are followed by two smaller ones. The scales of the

Reptile, which are very strongly keeled and pitted in the middle, are arranged in from twenty-three to twenty-seven rows ; the ventrals number from 185 to 263 ; the sub-caudals are in from forty-one to ninety-four pairs, and the anal scute is entire.

The following is a description of the colouring (which varies a great deal) of *D. scabra*, as given by Mr. Boulenger in his " Catalogue of Snakes " : "Pale olive or pale brown above, uniform or with dark brown spots, usually disposed in three longitudinal series ; a V-shaped dark marking on the nape, preceded by one or two on the head ; the latter may be broken up into spots ; upper labials with brown vertical bars ; belly yellowish, uniform or dotted or spotted with brown or blackish.

   A. Vertebral spots elongate, and more or less confluent into a zig-zag vertebral band ; a black stripe along upper surface of tail ; belly spotted with blackish.

   B. A dorsal series of large squarish or rhomboidal dark spots, separated by light intervals, alternating with a lateral series of spots or crossbars ; belly spotted or dotted only at the sides (*C. scaber*).

   C. Pale reddish-brown above, with the markings very much effaced. Intermediate between B. and F.

   D. Dorsal markings as in B., but ventrals edged with black.

   E. Dorsal spots confluent with lateral ones, forming cross-bands; belly unspotted (*D. medici*, Biarc. ; *D. fasciolata*, Peters).

   F. No spots or markings of any kind (*C. palmarum*, Leach ; *D. inornata*, Smith)."

The Egg-eating Snake or Eyervreter (a local name) is hardy when in confinement. As food, it should be provided with the eggs of pigeons, bantams, and small barn-door fowls. It must always be kept, while in this country, under the influence of artificial heat. Anyone who is lucky enough to own one of these Snakes will be sure, if he cares for these creatures at all, to acknowledge that he has a most interesting possession. It is such an ordinary-looking little creature that a dealer, ignorant of its habits, might be willing to part with it for a few shillings. Its real value I do not know.

D. scabra, which is a native of Tropical and South Africa, grows to a length of about 30in., of which the tail measures nearly one-seventh.

The following Snakes, which possess some grooved or furrowed teeth, but which nevertheless may be considered as innocuous, will be only briefly described.

The Cat or Vivacious Snake (*Tachymenis vivax*), one of the most beautiful and curious of European Snakes, has a small head with a flat crown, broad behind and distinct from the neck; a small eye, having a sub-elliptical pupil (owing to the great expansion of this pupil the appearance of the eye changes considerably, *e.g.*, in the daytime it seems at first sight to be yellowish, and at night a sparkling black, hence the name "Cat Snake"); a dark mark running from the eye to the angle of the mouth; a small rostral, scarcely visible from above; a vertical almost in the shape of an isosceles triangle, having a small notch at its base; large parietals; one præ-ocular, two post-oculars, eight upper labials, and an elongated loreal touching the eye; and the temple covered with a great number of very small scales. The smooth, lozenge-shaped scales are placed in nineteen rows; the ventrals number from 190 to 250, the sub-caudals are in from forty to sixty pairs, and the anal scute is divided.

The colour above is a dull olive, light or dark grey sprinkled thickly with very small black spots, hardly visible to the naked eye. There is a large dark spot on the nape of the neck joined to the parietals by a black thin streak, and there is a row of large very dark chestnut spots running down the middle of the back, with a similar row on each side of the body, but rather lighter in colour and smaller in size. The under-parts are a yellowish or greenish-white sprinkled finely with black.

The Cat Snake grows to a length of about 30in., of which the tail, which is finely pointed, measures one-seventh. It is said to be viviparous. It is a native of Southern Europe and Egypt. In England, this reptile needs no artificial heat during the summer months, and, if in good condition, it will pass the winter safely in a state of hibernation. The food of *T. vivax* should consist of small lizards and young mice. This Snake may be bought, when in the market, for from 4s. to 8s. It is a great favourite of mine, and I have always found it to be very gentle. I have never known it to attempt to bite, though I have heard of its doing so.

The Rhomb-marked Snake (*Psammophylax rhombeatus*) is a native of South Africa, and should be kept while in this country, except during the hottest months of the year, under the influence of artificial heat. Its food ought to consist of mice and rats. It is hardy and easily tamed. It may sometimes be bought for about 10s.

P. rhombeatus has a head with a flat crown, and distinct from the neck; an eye of moderate size, having a round pupil; a rostral which is carried backwards between the anterior frontals; one præ-ocular, two post-oculars, one loreal, and narrow ovate scales, arranged in seventeen or nineteen rows. The upper parts of the body are a greyish or yellowish-brown, marked with three or four rows of rhomboidal dark black-edged spots.

The All-green Tree Snake (*Philodryas viridissimus*), a most beautiful and active creature, is a native of South America. Its food should consist of small frogs (it prefers tree-frogs) and young, hairless mice. Its artificially-heated case ought to be provided with some retreat, such as an orange-tree or a fuchsia, in which, owing to its clever coiling and the colouring of its body, it will be able to hide itself, or, at any rate, to escape the notice of the unobservant.

P. viridissimus has a very slender body and tail, which are coloured uniformly green, a conical head and a moderately-sized eye, a rather elongated loreal, and smooth scales placed in nineteen rows.

The Cross-marked Snake (*Psammophis crucifer*) is an interesting and fairly hardy little animal. It is a member of a family of Bush Snakes (*Psammophidæ*), and a native of South Africa. Its food should consist of frogs, and it ought to be kept in an artificially-heated Vivarium.

P. crucifer has a slender body and tail, a groove before the eye, the pupil of which is round, a pointed snout, a long loreal, one præ-ocular, and two post-oculars. The scales are long and smooth. The upper parts are olive, and there is a black-edged streak running from the snout to the end of the tail. A transverse band forms a cross on the nape of the neck.

The Hissing Sand Snake (*Psammophis sibilans*) is also a native of South Africa. It may be fed upon birds and mice. Like its near relative just mentioned, it should be provided with artificial heat while in captivity in this country. This Snake is generally rather spiteful, and it consequently does not very readily become tame. It is fairly hardy.

P. sibilans is variable as to its colouring, *e.g.*:

(1.) The back is brown, with a very narrow band running down the middle: the sides are olive, and bounded below by a broadish yellow streak.

(2.) Like No. 1, but wanting the thin yellow dorsal line.

(3.) Back and sides uniform brown, with the exception of a yellow line on each side, just above the ventral scales.

(4.) Brown above, and yellowish below.

In other respects *P. sibilans* is very similar to *P. crucifer*.

The Hissing Sand Snake may sometimes be bought in London for about 10s.

The Lacertine Snake (*Cœlopeltis lacertina*) is a native of most of the countries bordering upon the Mediterranean Sea. It may be easily recognised by the concavity or grooving of the crown of its head, by a groove before the eye, by its very long and narrow vertical shield, and by its lanceolate scales, which are grooved longitudinally. The upper parts of this Snake's body are greenish-brown, either uniform or marked with rows of dark or black spots; the under parts are yellowish.

The Lacertine Snake is a very handsome reptile, and hardy enough to be kept in this country during the summer months without artificial heat. Its food should consist of lizards. I have found it to be very gentle. It may be bought in London, when in the market, for from 5s. to 9s.

The Cape Bucephalus (*Bucephalus capensis*) is a very beautiful Tree Snake, and a native of the Cape of Good Hope. One of its chief attractions consists in an exceedingly large eye, possessing a round pupil. It has a short, very thick head, distinct from the neck. Hence, of course, its generic name. It also possesses one loreal, one præ-ocular, three post-oculars, and seven upper labials.

The coloration of this Reptile is rather variable. For example, it may be (1.) green above, and very pale green below; (2.) a dark olive above, and greenish-yellow beneath;

(3.) a greenish-brown, having many of the scales on the sides marked with yellow at their centres. The scales, which are placed in twenty-one rows, are very strongly keeled. The Cape Bucephalus feeds upon frogs. It should be kept under the influence of artificial heat except during the hottest months of the year. It attains a length of more than 4ft.

The Ornamented Tree-Snake (*Chrysopelea ornata*) is very common in the Indian Archipelago, and in some parts of Asia, and is perhaps one of the most beautiful of all Snakes. Its coloration is variable. The following descriptions are given by Dr. Günther in his "Reptiles of British India."

"Head, black above, with yellow cross-bands; body beautifully ornamented with regular yellow or black markings, the arrangement of which is subject to great variation.

A. The black colour is predominant, each scale having a yellow central spot. The yellow bands on the head are numerous, and frequently broken up into spots.

B. The yellow colour is predominant, each scale being yellow, with a narrow black edge, and with a medium black streak, the streaks forming longitudinal lines.

C. The black colour is predominant, each scale having a yellow central spot. These spots are larger on the back, forming a series of tetrapetalous flowers. Five or six yellow cross-bands on the head, some of which are broken up into spots.

D. Much like B, but back with pairs of black cross-bars. Abdomen yellow; each ventral shield with a black lateral spot.

E. Back red, with pairs of black cross-bars, the bands of each pair being separated from each other by a narrow yellowish interval. Sides brown, with irregularly-scattered black dots. Belly dark green, the outer portion of each ventral shield being yellow, with a blackish spot."

The body and tail of *C. ornata* is very elongated, slender, and compressed. The eye is large and has a round pupil. The scales, which are smooth and grooved, are arranged in nineteen rows; the ventrals, which number from 180 to 236, are keeled laterally.

This Snake should be kept in an artificially-heated Vivarium which is furnished with some suitable plant. Its food ought to consist of lizards and frogs. It sometimes reaches a length of more than 4ft., of which the tail measures one-quarter. Though so long, it may be coiled up in the hollows of the hands. *C. ornata* is wonderfully quick in its movements.

The Long-snouted Whip Snake (*Passerita mycterizans*) belongs to the family of Whip Snakes (*Dryophidæ*), thus named because the bodies are so exceedingly slender that they may be fairly likened to the cord of a whip. Some of them are very common in certain parts of the intertropical regions of Asia, and of North and South America. They are generally of a brightish green colour, with two yellow stripes on the abdomen. As they are thoroughly Tree Snakes, their movements are far more active and graceful in the branches of trees than they are on the ground. They feed upon birds and lizards. The manner of taking their prey is rather interesting. Frequently, when they wish to seize a victim at some little distance, they coil their tail round a suitable bough and launch their body quickly forward, seizing as they do so the unfortunate bird or lizard in their widely-gaping jaws, the cleft of the mouth being enormous for such slender creatures. They have a tapering snout, which in some species is produced into a long, flexible appendage. The transversely-elongated pupil of the eye shows that they are animals of nocturnal habits. Some of the Whip Snakes attain a length of more than 7ft., of which the tail measures about one-third.

P. mycterizans is famous for the length of its flexible snout. It has no loreal, but a large concavity in the region before the eye; smooth scales, which are long, narrow, and considerably imbricated, and placed in fifteen rows. It possesses a long tooth, located in the middle of the maxillary jaw, which is supposed to be useful in seizing birds by piercing the feathers.

The Long-snouted Whip Snake should be kept in such a Vivarium as has been suggested for other Tree Snakes, and fed upon birds, lizards, and frogs. As it does not bathe, the receptacle for its water need not be large. This Snake is found in Southern India and in Ceylon. It sometimes grows to a length of more than .6ft.; of which the tail measures one-third. Old specimens are generally very ready to bite. It is interesting to see them open their wonderful mouths as they attempt to do so. Dr. Günther, in speaking of this Snake, says: "Examples sometimes occur which are brownish-olive instead of green, but they retain the yellow abdominal bands ; they are of small size, and have been named *Dryinus fuscus* (Dum. and Bibr., vii., p. 812)."

There are, of course, many other Snakes besides those already mentioned which are suitable for confinement in this country ; but I hope sufficient has been said to enable a novice at Snake-keeping to care for properly almost any Snake which is likely to come into his hands.

No animals, in their manner of taking food, are more capricious than Snakes. Sometimes their desire to feed is so great that they will eat a meal out of all proportion to their size ; and, sometimes, without any apparent cause, they will refuse food, even the most suitable, until they die of starvation. As a rule, these creatures cannot be persuaded to seize any prey but that which is natural to them. For example, a Snake which lives upon frogs will not on any account, as a general thing, take lizards, though the latter might be just as nourishing to the Ophidian as the former, and possibly even more so ; nor will a lizard-eating Snake be tempted to swallow a newt.

Even if Snakes did never refuse their natural food, the supplying of it is not always convenient, nor is it, to most people, pleasant. Young mice and rats, frogs and lizards are not continually at hand, and it is not, by any means, an attractive sight to see a Snake, at evident discomfort to itself, swallowing a live animal or one recently constricted or poisoned.

One of the drawbacks therefore, perhaps the only important one, to the keeping in confinement of these interesting reptiles is the feeding of them. This drawback, however, in a great measure, may be overcome by supplying the Snakes with their food artificially. Generally this means of feeding is very successful and satisfactory. The Snakes thus get sufficient food regularly ; and, if properly administered, the discomfort to the reptile, I believe, is not nearly so great as it is when it takes its food in a natural way. I think that most people, after they have watched the two operations, will be disposed to agree with me in this respect.

As far as I can see, no Snake is deprived of any pleasure by being fed artificially. For many reasons it is fairly safe to conclude that Snakes have little or no sense of taste whatever. Many of my own Snakes would have been dead long ago, had I not fed them forcibly, and so prevented them from starving themselves to death. Almost invariably when a Snake has been so treated it has recovered its appetite, and when given the opportunity, taken food of its own accord.

I believe many keepers of reptiles in Zoological Gardens adopt, to a greater or lesser extent, the artificial system of feeding their charges. The largest Snake in the Reptile House, Regent's Park, London, and which is also perhaps the largest Snake in captivity anywhere, has been fed by hand for the last three years at least, and is in splendid condition, weighing probably something like 18st. This Snake, the Reticulated Python (*Python reticulatus*), receives its food regularly once a week.

The forcible giving of food does not seem to interfere in the slightest degree with a Snake's becoming tame. Indeed, I think that this extra handling tends towards that desired end.

There are several methods of administering food to Snakes. For example (1) Some Snakes will swallow a dead animal, or even a piece of meat, when it has been simply placed between their jaws. (2) The Snake's mouth is forcibly opened, and a dead small animal, dipped in milk, is pushed down the throat, and then worked down the gullet by the manipulation of the fingers outside the Snake's body. (3) Pieces of meat, or portions of animals, dipped in milk, are pushed sufficiently far down the opened mouth of a Snake by means of a smooth stick. (4) A tube is filled with suitable food, and passed down the gullet of the reptile, and then the contents of the tube are discharged by means of a piece of cane used as a ramrod.

This last method I have generally adopted. I was told, a few months ago, by the keeper of a Reptile-house, that tubes were used for the purpose of artificially feeding Snakes in the Zoological Gardens of America. Until I received this information I was under the impression that I was the only one who employed tubes in the forcible administration of food to these Reptiles.

The tubes, which should be of glass for small Snakes, and of india-rubber for the larger Reptiles, may be filled with dead animals, portions of dead animals, or butchers' meat cut into pieces, minced or scraped.

Anyone who has a taste for anatomy may like to fill the tules with parts of dead animals. This, of course, is most suitable, but those who do not care for this kind of work should use butchers' meat instead, together with a few feathers, bits of fur, and the like. The butchers' meat which may be employed is the liver of bullocks, calves, sheep, and pigs for the larger Snakes, and beef-steak (which can be scraped) for the smaller reptiles. If the employment of raw meat be found to be unpleasant to some people, cooked meat may be substituted.

The tubes can be filled easily and quickly in the following ways: (1) Raw meat when cut up into pieces, just small enough to go down the tube chosen, should be inserted in the tube by means of a pair of forceps, such as those used for dissecting purposes. Each piece of meat, as it is taken up by the forceps, ought to be dipped into milk and then placed into the tube, and being thus lubricated slips in easily and pushes forward its predecessors, if any, also lubricated, and so the tube is filled with meat from end to end, if necessary. (2) When raw meat, such as beef steak, is scraped into very tiny parts by means of a sharp knife, a dry tube may be filled very rapidly with it, by placing the scraped meat in a mass on a board, and by dabbing quickly and repeatedly one end of the tube into the mass of meat. Under these circumstances, if the interior of the tube be quite dry, the meat is readily gathered up, and the tube soon becomes full from end to end. (3) When cooked meat is used, it may be prepared for the tubes by being passed two or three times through a mincing machine. When thus prepared, it should be treated as already suggested for the scraped meat. In both cases care ought to be taken that the meat does not become too closely packed, or it will not slip out of the tube sufficiently easily, and consequently it will enter the Snake in so compact a mass that the reptile will very likely get rid of it by disgorging. A Snake will seldom disgorge—I think less seldom than when it has swallowed prey naturally—if the food has been gently and loosely deposited within it. (4) A common metal squirt, having the aperture of its nozzle slightly enlarged, is a very convenient instrument for quickly filling the tubes with minced meat.

The tube should be of such a diameter that it will easily pass down the throat of the Snake for which it is used. For example, for a Snake 4ft. long and of stoutish build, glass tubes having a diameter of about ½in. and about 1ft. long should be used, the tube as a rule being filled full of meat.

For Snakes of less than 2ft. in length, tubes, such as those sold by chemists at ½d. each for babies' feeding-bottles, may be employed. These tubes are strong, and have, for their size, a large interior. They are, also, perfectly smooth at the ends. According to the needs of the Snakes, one or more tubesful of meat can be inserted into the gullet of each Reptile.

For Snakes less than a foot in length, a specially prepared tube (Fig. 76) should be used. The tube receives its desired shape by being heated in a hot flame, and then drawn out to the necessary length and slenderness. This tube is easily filled with scraped raw meat, according to the directions already given, the larger end (A) of the tube being dabbed down into the meat. This larger part (Fig. 76) should hold just about sufficient meat for a meal for one small Snake. A small ramrod, which exactly fits the broad part, is used to push the meat out of the lower part (B) into the gullet of the Snake. Of course, the narrow portion of the tube always remains full of meat until, when all the feeding is done, it is emptied by means of a piece of wire. Young Snakes may be reared from the egg or from their birth by such a contrivance as this tube.

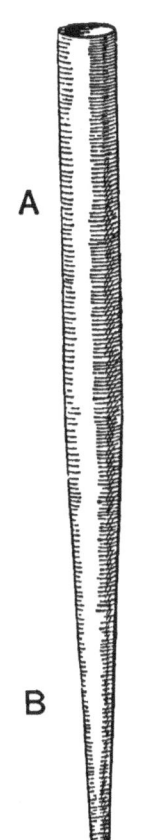

FIG. 76.—TUBE FOR FEEDING VERY SMALL SNAKES.

A Snake can be fed with the help of a tube in the following way: The reptile is taken gently, just behind the head, with the left hand, and its mouth is opened very carefully with a small paper-knife or some similar article. When this has been done the end of a filled tube, having been dipped in milk, is inserted into the opened mouth by an assistant. The tube is then, by the holder of the Snake, gently passed into its gullet, and as soon as it is there, the assistant, by means of a ramrod, discharges the contents of the tube into the interior of the Reptile. The animal is now fed, and should be returned to its Vivarium, where it will lie and quietly digest its food. After a very little practice the whole operation may be performed quickly and with hardly any trouble. The very small Snakes should have their mouths opened with a smooth piece of wire, such as the end of a hairpin. The tubes ought to possess no sharp edges, and be kept very clean. When a Snake is so large and strong as to be likely to break a glass tube, an india-rubber tube must be substituted.

Snakes, when fed artificially, should be so fed regularly once a week. These Reptiles, when fed by hand for the first time or two, sometimes disgorge.

CHAPTER VIII.

GENERAL CHARACTERISTICS OF BATRACHIANS.

THE Batrachians are exceedingly interesting creatures, and most of them will live for a very long time in a properly-arranged Vivarium. As a rule, they are more easily provided with food than are many of the Reptiles, and they do not require so much artificial heat, when any, as the latter animals.

Formerly, as already mentioned, Batrachians were included among the Reptiles; now they are placed in a class by themselves, which is divided into the following four orders:

(1) *Ecaudata*, or *Anoura*.—The Batrachians which absorb the tail of tadpolehood before they reach maturity, and may, therefore, be described as tailless Batrachians, such as are frogs and toads.

(2) *Caudata*, or *Urodela*.—The Batrachians which retain the tail throughout life, *e.g.*, Newts and Salamanders.

(3) *Apoda*, or *Ophiomorpha*.—The limbless or Snake-like Batrachians, for example, the Cœcilians.

(4) *Stegocephala*, or *Labyrinthodonta*.—The Batrachians of this order are extinct; but their remains are found from time to time. They generally possessed a long tail and four limbs. Some of them reached an enormous size, and the beautiful and curious structure of their teeth has given them the name of Labyrinthodonts.

Batrachians may be briefly defined as cold-blooded vertebrate animals, which, as a rule, commence their life in fresh water, which generally possess a naked skin, and which always pass through a *metamorphosis*. Some of the Batrachians have a very complete metamorphosis, *e.g.*, Frogs and Toads; others, such as Newts and Salamanders, not so complete. Certain of the Batrachians, for example the Surinam Toad (*Pipa americana*) and the Black Salamander (*Salamandra atra*), undergo their metamorphosis while still within the egg.

Batrachians are oviparous, like the Common Frog (*Rana temporaria*), or ovoviviparous, like the Spotted Salamander (*Salamandra maculosa*). By far the greater number are, however, oviparous.

The eggs of these creatures are deposited in fresh water either in masses, or strings, or singly, *e.g.*, the Common Frog (*Rana temporaria*), the Common Toad (*Bufo vulgaris*), and the Smooth Newt (*Molge vulgaris*), respectively; or in damp places, *e.g.*, the Black Salamander (*Salamandra atra*); or in the axils of the leaves of trees, *e.g.*, certain species of the genus *Hylodes*; or they are twisted in strings round the thighs of the males, *e.g.*, the Midwife Frog (*Alytes obstetricans*); or they are placed in a pouch upon the back of the female, *e.g.*, the American Pouched Tree Frog (*Nototrema marsupiatum*); or in cells formed in the thickened and loose skin of the female's back, *e.g.*, the Surinam Toad (*Pipa americana*); or in the throat-sac of the animal, *e.g.*, *Rhinoderma darwinii*; or buried in a hole in damp earth and protected by the female, *e.g.*, certain of the Cœcilians.

Tailless Batrachians are found in nearly every part of the world except New Zealand and the Arctic regions: the tailed Batrachians are natives of Europe, Asia, and North and South America. Though the *Batrachia* are closely allied to fishes, none of them are dwellers in salt water. In the colder parts of the world the Batrachians hibernate; and in the hotter parts many of them estivate.

Certain of the males of the *Ecaudata* are remarkable for their powers of making sound, often out of all proportion to their size.

The *Ecaudata* are divided into the two sub-orders—(1) *Phaneroglossa* (possessors of a tongue), and (2) *Aglossa* (lacking a tongue) —and fourteen families, twelve belonging to the former sub-order and two to the latter. The *Caudata* are arranged in four families ; and the *Apoda* consist of only one family. All the Batrachians, when they have completed their metamorphosis, partake of animal food, which they seize alive, such as insects, worms, slugs, and sometimes (in the case of the largest Batrachians) mice, birds, fish, and the like. Many of the Batrachians, during a portion of their tadpolehood, are vegetable feeders.

Before I describe any particular species of the Batrachia, perhaps it will be wise for me to sketch briefly the life of the Common Frog (which is very similar to that of the greater number of these creatures) from the time it leaves the egg until the completion of its metamorphosis.

In early spring, in England, sometimes during the latter part of January and in February, but oftener in March, frogs congregate in fresh water, such as in the stiller parts of rivers and streams, in lakes, ponds, and small pools, for the purpose of depositing their eggs. The eggs are fertilised by the male as they are ejected by the female.

At first they are little, almost black, bodies (Fig. 77*a*), enclosed in a glutinous envelope, into which a quantity of water is presently absorbed. When this absorption has taken place (Fig. 77*b*), the eggs may be likened to a kind of jelly, in which small shot have been imbedded. These shot-like bodies are the yolks of the eggs.

Frogs' spawn, as the eggs are commonly called, is found in masses, while that of Toads is regularly arranged in strings of two rows each. The eggs hatch in from four days to a month, or even more, according to the temperature of the water in which they are.

In all probability few things in Natural History are more interesting than the development of a tailless Batrachian from the egg. Some of the eggs of Frogs (and Toads), a short time after they have been deposited, assume a bluish-white colour, which shows that they are unfertile, and therefore of course that they will not hatch. The other eggs, sooner or later, according to the temperature of the water, exhibit signs of life by first undergoing what is known as "segmentation," or sub-division, and by the appearance of the "primitive groove," which may be seen by the help of a microscope. The margins of this groove fold upwards until they meet above; thus a kind of tube is formed, the interior of which becomes in time the spinal cord. Below the "primitive groove" is developed a "gelatinous rod," which gradually becomes the backbone. The process just described is common to every kind of egg which produces a vertebrate animal.

The Frog's (and Toad's) egg now, even by the unassisted eye, is seen to lose its roundness of shape and to become elongated, and then, sometimes in turn and sometimes concurrently with each other, the following changes take place: (1) a head, tail, and organs of adhesion appear; (2) branchiæ are developed on each side of what may be called the neck; (3) slight movements may be noticed; (4) nostrils or olfactory organs come into existence; (5) the branchiæ have so grown that the circulation of the blood may be seen in them by the help of a microscope; (6) frequent movement of the embryo from a curved to a straight position, and *vice versâ* (Fig. 77, c and d); (7) these movements or jerkings become so vigorous that the envelope is broken and the tadpole is free (Fig. 77, e and f); (8) soon after the tadpoles are hatched, they may be seen in rows and bunches adhering, by means of the organs provided for the purpose, to some substance, such as a weed, a stick, or a stone; (9) the head of the young animal is large, the body round, and the tail long and strongly compressed laterally (Fig. 77, g); (10) the creature's life is now very like that of a fish, and its food is chiefly vegetable matter; (11) the branchiæ grow in size, and are very plumose (Fig. 77, h); (12) the branchiæ are gradually absorbed, and are replaced by "gill-filaments" along each of the "branchial arches," *i.e.*, the spaces between the six openings on each side of the neck; (13) the animal, which is provided with horny and slightly protruding jaws, now begins to feed upon animal food, such as small aquatic creatures, dead worms, and the like; (14) the eyes become noticeable; (15) the tadpole, if provided with plenty of food, fresh water, and warmth, grows very quickly; (16) the hind legs bud and are produced (Fig. 77, i and

298   THE VIVARIUM.

k); (17) the forelegs bud and are produced (Fig. 77, *l*); (18) the tail is gradually absorbed, particle by particle; (19) the branchial openings are closed by the *opercula :* (20) lungs develop as the branchiæ are absorbed; (21) the animal comes frequently to the surface of the water for air; (22) the tadpole often before the tail is fully absorbed leaves the water, at any rate for a time, and will take any suitable food it may find on land, and will reject,

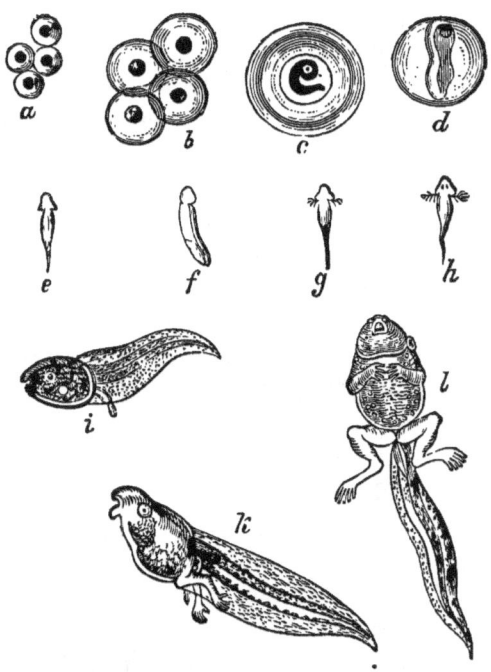

FIG. 77.—METAMORPHOSES OF THE FROG, showing the growth of the Embryo, from the egg to the Four-legged Tadpole.

now, all food without life; (23) as soon as the tail is completely absorbed, the young creature adopts the habits of the mature Frog.

As a rule, Reptiles and Batrachians should not be kept together in the same Vivarium. The latter animals naturally require a moister atmosphere than do the former. I was reminded of this fact very forcibly some time ago, when I thoughtlessly put a few Tree-Frogs, for less than an hour, in a Chameleon-case, the air of which was hot and dry, and the consequence was that all the little Batrachians, except one, died.

Batrachians require plenty of water, hiding-places, and shade. Cases like those shown in Figs. 1, 3, 6 (the lower case), 9, 10, 13, 14, and 23 may be used for these creatures, of which Figs. 1 and 9 are the most suitable.

The bottom of a case when prepared for Batrachians should be covered thickly with garden mould, over which may be spread clean fresh pieces of moss. The mould should come up nearly level with the receptacle which contains the water. If possible this receptacle ought to be provided with a hole at the bottom, to which is attached a piece of metal tubing of suitable length for the purpose of drawing off the water. The hole may be stopped by means of a small wooden plug. The water should be soft, and changed as often as it becomes dirty.

The bath should not be made so deep that the animals have difficulty in leaving it. A piece of cork-bark fastened to one side (inside) of the vessel will enable the creatures to leave the water with ease.

Small earthenware saucers, glazed on the inside, make very useful baths, but it is generally necessary to remove them when refilling them with water, which is not a little inconvenient, as the earth and moss fall into the cavity in which they have stood, and which must be cleared out before the saucers can be returned.

If possible, Batrachian cases should be furnished with some growing plants such as those already suggested for the fern-case (Fig. 9) and other cases, or lemon and orange-trees, and plants of a similar nature. Besides the plants, it is well to have some bare and rather stout branches of trees cut and fixed in such a way that they shall be an ornament to the case rather than the reverse. On these branches and the leaves of the various plants the Tree-Frogs will generally sit. Frequently a frog will choose a particular site for the purpose of rest and observation, to which it will always return after any venture for prey, either successful or not, and which it seems to claim as its own property. Sometimes when two of these Frogs have set their hearts upon the same position, there will be no giving up the one to the other, nor will there be any struggle; but the second to reach the coveted spot will calmly settle down upon the back of his more fortunate rival. If there be no suitable resting-places on branches of trees or leaves of plants, the Tree-Frogs will not seldom affix themselves to the corners of their case, and be constantly dirtying its glass sides by climbing about them; and then neither the Batrachians nor their abode will look comfortable or attractive.

A well-built and tastefully arranged Vivarium, wisely stocked with different kinds of Batrachia, is a very interesting possession, and is not out of place in either the conservatory, drawing-room, dining-room, or study. The animals differ much from each other in colour, habits, and shape, and altogether harmonise well with the plants and surroundings. To the observant owner there is always something new to learn concerning his charges, which give very little trouble, and if well managed are, as a rule, very hardy, and cause no untidiness in the room in which they are placed.

In the winter time, if the Vivarium be put just out of the reach of frost, its occupants will bury themselves under the mould, moss, and cork, and spend the cold months safely in a state of hibernation. Should there, however, be a desire to keep the Batrachians active and in feeding condition throughout the winter, the Vivarium must be supplied with artificial heat. The heat, under these circumstances, owing to the thick covering of mould at the bottom of the case and the requirements of the Batrachians, must be supplied from the top of the Vivarium, which may be done according to the directions already given. Of course, if the Vivarium should stand in a well-warmed conservatory or some such building, no additional heat need be provided.

As already said, Batrachians are easily supplied with food, which may consist of the following creatures, which should be placed alive in the Vivarium; garden-worms, cockroaches, flies, earwigs, slugs, mealworms, and any kind of insect. The worms may be emptied upon some spot in the Vivarium, kept clear of moss or cork for such a purpose. The Batrachians will readily see the Annelids before they can crawl away, and many of the frogs and toads will generally take up their abode near such a good hunting ground. The cockroaches, if turned out of the beetle-trap into the Vivarium, will hide under the moss until night, when, leaving their places of security, they fall a prey to their natural enemies. Cockroaches are not only most useful animals as kitchen scavengers, but also as a very suitable source of food supply to the keeper of a Vivarium. A little sugar should be placed in the case for those which are not eaten by the Batrachians. Flies, during the day, can be quickly and easily caught in a trap prepared for the purpose, and which is represented by Fig. 78. In the lower vessel (an ordinary glass fly-catcher) there is placed some dry sugar, a piece of meat, or a

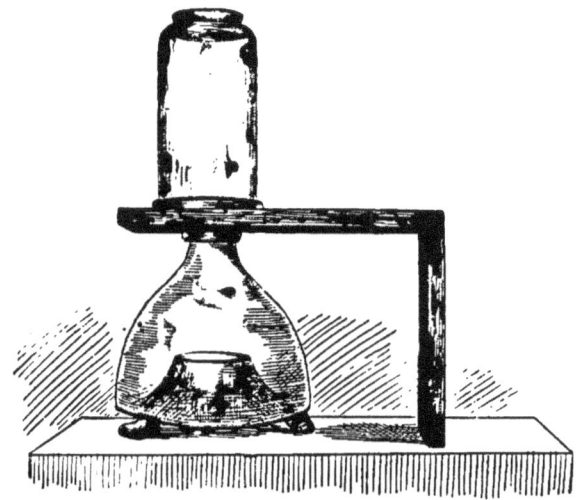

FIG. 78.—FLY-CATCHER.

dead mouse or bird. The flies enter from below, and gradually, in considerable numbers, find their way into the inverted bottle placed over the hole in the small wooden platform above. When one wide-mouthed bottle containing flies is removed, another should be immediately put in its place. Of course, this fly-catching arrangement ought to be placed out of doors when flesh of any kind is used as a bait.

Maggots, which can generally, in summer, be obtained without difficulty, may be thrown down upon the spot prepared for the worms. Those which are not eaten at once will work their way into the mould, to re-appear in course of time as flies. Earwigs form very favourite food with some Batrachians, such as Tree-frogs, and can often be secured in the autumn months by placing hiding-places, *e.g.*, inverted flower pots on sticks, in the different parts of the garden which are generally haunted by these creatures. Slugs are likewise secured without much trouble by laying down in the garden, upon those beds which are infested by these molluscs, pieces of flat board. In the morning the boards can be carried to the Vivarium, and the slugs, which will be found clinging to the under side of the wood, given to those animals which feed upon them. Slugs' eggs, found while digging, may be placed in the Vivarium, and so in time add to its food supply. Mealworms should be placed in a small glass dish, out of which they cannot climb. If they are not eaten after a reasonable time has elapsed, they should be returned to the crock from which they have been taken.

CHAPTER IX.

FROGS.

THERE are about a thousand different kinds of Frogs and Toads, of which by far the greater number, namely, the *Phaneroglossa*, are divided, owing to the formation of the pectoral arch (the construction of which need not be described here), into the two series, (1) *Firmisternia* and (2) *Arcifera*. Toads belong to the latter series. The *Firmisternia* are arranged in four and the *Arcifera* in eight families.

Of the *Firmisternia*, the *Ranidæ* is the first and by far the largest and most important family, numbering eighteen genera, and something like 245 species. The *Ranidæ* may be described as true Frogs. "It is probable," says Mr. St. George Mivart, "that no other existing animal is more replete with scientific interest of the highest kind than is the Frog." Owing to the sufferings it has endured in the cause of science, it is well called the "Martyr of Science."

A few matters of interest in regard to the Frog may be referred to here in the following brief fashion :

(1) The legs (the hind limbs) of a Frog have each four segments, instead of three, as in man and in most mammals, birds, and limb-bearing Reptiles.

(2) Behind the eye there is a rounded surface of "smooth, tightly-stretched skin" called the "tympanum," which covers the drum of the ear.

(3) There are small teeth on the inner margins of the upper jaws, but none at all on the lower ones. There are also some little teeth towards the front of the palate known as vomerine teeth.

(4) The skin of the Frog is naked and moist.

(5) The tongue of this animal is a very curious contrivance, being, unlike most other tongues, fixed in front and free behind. The Frog captures its prey by throwing forward, beyond the extremity of the mouth, the free hinder portion of tongue, which being covered with sticky secretion attaches itself to the victim and withdraws it into the mouth.

(6) The Frog, possessing no ribs to help in respiration, depends, in this matter, upon the assistance of its tongue, which it uses in the following manner, as described by Mr. St. George Mivart: " The mouth is filled with air through the nostrils and kept shut, while the internal openings of the nostrils are stopped by the tongue, and the entrance to the gullet is closed. Then by the contraction of the muscles attached to it, the os-hyoides is elevated, and every other exit from the mouth being closed, except that leading to the larynx, air is thus driven down the glottis into the lungs." Thus for pulmonary respiration it is necessary to the Frog to keep the mouth shut; and in this way, but for the action of the skin, the animal might be choked by keeping the mouth open. The external movements which the Frog makes as it thus pumps the air into the lungs are very manifest and frequent.

(7) Owing to the fact that all Reptiles and Batrachians, except the Crocodilia (and their blood, too, is mixed just outside the heart), have only three complete chambers in the heart (two auricles and one ventricle), and not four, as in warm-blooded animals, the oxygenated, or fresh blood, and the unoxygenated, or effete blood, become mingled in the one ventricle. But in the case of the Frog, because of an extraordinary arrangement by which the skin is made to assist in the work of respiration, " the unoxygenated fluid from the body is sent to the purifying respiratory surfaces (lungs and skin), and the pure, oxygenated blood alone goes to the head and the brain."

One of the experiments which tended to prove the existence of cutaneous respiration in the Frog was the tying of a piece of bladder so tightly over the animal's head that it could not obtain any air by way of the nostrils. The creature was then sunk under some water placed in a vessel, and when, after the lapse of an hour or two, this water was carefully examined, it was found to contain a considerable portion of carbonic acid gas. Frogs, with their heads enveloped as described, have been known to live under stagnant water, which was periodically changed, for at least ten weeks, and to die as soon as the water was allowed to remain unrenewed. A Frog, so bandaged, lived for twenty days in a damp atmosphere, and other Frogs existed for from thirty to forty days when deprived of their lungs by excision. On the other hand, experiments have tended to prove that Frogs cannot exist for any lengthened period when deprived, in the matter of respiration, of the assistance of the skin. For example, they cannot live in a perfectly dry atmosphere, nor when their skin is coated with some non-porous substance.

In order that the cutaneous respiration may be effectively carried on, the very sensitive skin of the Frog must be kept moist. Most people who have caught Frogs at any time will have noticed that they are apt to discharge from their body a clear, colourless fluid. They may do this under the influence of fear, or that, being relieved of the weight of the liquid, they may be the better able to escape. This fluid, the late Mr. Thomas Bell said, in his book on "British Reptiles," comes from a portable reservoir, which is provided for the purpose of supplying the necessary moisture to the skin of the Frog whenever it happens to be at some distance from water or dampness. The reservoir, which, he says, has been mistaken for the urinary bladder, is filled, according to him, by the absorption of water by the skin, and which can again be absorbed by the skin when it needs moisture.

(8) In many species of Frogs the males possess one sac or a pair, situated near the throat or on each side of the head. By means of these sacs the animal is able to make the noise which is commonly called croaking or roaring. These sounds are generally heard in spring-time.

(9) The leg of a Frog has in its thigh and calf a great resemblance to those parts of man.

(10) Some Frogs nearly equal the Chameleon in their powers of changing colour.

(11) Certain Frogs, in comparison to their size, are able to make marvellous leaps, and thus they are enabled to get over the ground with considerable rapidity, and also to capture their prey.

The Indian Bull Frog (*Rana tigrina*), the largest Frog of India, is very common nearly all over that country and in the southern parts of China. It may be to this Batrachian that the following native proverb has especial reference : " The crow steals the grain, and the string is round the leg of the Frog." The custom to which this quaint saying alludes is the tying of a Frog by a string to a peg driven into the ground near the spot where grain has been spread to dry in the sun, so that the animal, by his constant struggles to get free, shall deter the crows and other birds from stealing the seed.

This Frog, like its relative of America, has received its English name from its powers of making a noise which bears not a little resemblance to the bellowing of a bull.

The body of *R. tigrina* sometimes attains a length of 6in. or 7in. The lower jaw of the animal has two fairly distinct prominences in front. The tympanum is plainly visible. The skin on the back has some short longitudinal folds ; there is also such a fold above the tympanum. The hind limbs are comparatively short and thick. The toes are webbed, and the outer edge of the fifth toe is adorned with a fringe of skin. The male has two vocal sacs under the throat.

The coloration of the animal, like that of so many Frogs, is variable ; the following description is given by Mr. Boulenger : " Brown or olive above, with dark spots ; often a light vertebral line."

The Indian Bull Frog must not be kept in the same Vivarium with smaller Batrachians, or it would be very likely tempted to eat its companions. It should be provided with a large tank, in which it will spend a great part of its time, and some suitable hiding-places, such as cork bark or large pieces of damp moss. If it is not allowed to hibernate, a small lamp should be placed during the cold weather under the vessel containing the water.

The Bull Frog's food may consist of large worms, common frogs, small birds, such as sparrows, and mice. It is able to take wonderful leaps, and when it is frightened while in the water, will jump even there, leaping clumsily over the surface.

The Occipital Bull Frog (*Rana occipitalis*) is very like the last animal mentioned, and while in confinement should be treated in the same manner. The chief differences between this Batrachian and its near relative *R. tigrina*, consist in a fold of skin which unites the posterior angles of the eyelids, and in more developed vocal sacs. *R. occipitalis* is a native of West Africa.

The Graceful Frog (*R. gracilis*) is also closely related to the Indian Bull Frog. It is of smaller size and possesses half-webbed toes. It is a native of the East Indies and Southern China.

The American Bull Frog (*R. catesbiana*, Fig. 79), is nowadays frequently imported into this country, both as an object of interest and as a suitable inmate of the Vivarium. I remember quite well the first animal of this species I ever possessed and how quickly I concluded that it fully deserved its English epithet. I put it in a case placed in a shady spot in a conservatory. A few days after its arrival, as I was talking to the gardener, I suddenly heard the Frog begin to bellow; my companion heard it too, and listened, while his face betokened the greatest astonishment. Presently he looked up and said: "I am thinking, sir, that there's a calf in the green-house," and away he went to turn out the intruder. The garden is surrounded with a high wall, so a trespasser of the bovine kind is not to be expected; hence the man's manifest surprise.

The Bull Frog is eaten in America, and one would think, if there be no difference in the flavour, that it is a more suitable animal for this purpose, owing to its size, than the Edible Frog of the Old World. Some years ago Mr. Seth Green, an eminent American pisciculturist, suggested that a Frog Farm would be a successful undertaking. He calculated that if the spawn were carefully selected and put in a place suitable for its hatching and the growth of the tadpoles and young frogs, the animals would be easily reared, and be likely to realise a large profit. He planned that the stock might be fed by placing meat at the water's edge, some of which would be eaten by the tadpoles, and the remainder would attract flies, and supply maggots for the older Batrachians.

In America *R. catesbiana* has a very wide range, being found as far north as Quebec and as far south as Mexico. It spends, as a rule, the greater portion of its time in water, and frequents

FIG. 79.—THE AMERICAN BULL-FROG (*Rana catesbiana*).

slow-running rivers, ponds, and even small pools. It is rather a solitary animal, and only about the time of the breeding season does it join its fellows. Like the Indian Bull Frog, this creature, when frightened, jumps or skims over the water. *R. catesbiana* has wonderful leaping powers, and I believe that it was a Frog of this species which was the hero of Mark Twain's well-known story. I have heard, though I do not believe it, that an active man by jumping, or, as school-boys say, "clubbing," cannot overtake the creature when it has got a short start. The late Rev. J. G. Wood says, in the "Boy's Own Book of Natural History," that "an Indian was not able to overtake an irritated Bull Frog after it had sprung three leaps in advance." This summer I was forcibly reminded of this heavy-looking animal's activity. I placed a fine specimen in a run made for Tuatera Lizards (*Sphenodon punctatus*), and unwisely imagined that he would be in safe confinement. The run has a fence about 2ft. high, and a ledge fixed inside to prevent any escape by climbing. The Frog, however, jumped out and gained his freedom for some time. For four months he was at liberty in a walled garden, telling us occasionally of his whereabouts by bellowing during heavy showers. Anyone who went to the spot to recapture him would surely be disappointed, for, with a few bounds, the animal would quickly travel to some other part of the garden. However, when autumn had arrived he returned of his own accord to the conservatory from which he had escaped, all the better, I think, for his little adventure. I was glad to have him back, for he is a great favourite.

He is very useful for entertaining visitors. For example, if a friend expresses a wish to hear the Frog make the strange noise by which he has obtained his English name, he has not long to wait before his wish is gratified. "But," I imagine a reader saying, "how can this be managed. I can't believe that a Frog will croak by word of command. A dog, I know, can be made to bark by exciting him, a cock to crow by imitating him, a donkey to stop braying by tying a weight to its tail, but how a Frog is to be made to bellow I do not know." However, this particular Frog of mine will nearly always be persuaded to roar, and very loudly too, if water be slowly poured from one can to another. I have often thus used water, while I watched with amusement the look upon my guests' faces as they heard for the first time the curious sound.

The Bull Frog has, like the Ceratophrys, an enormous mouth, which he certainly knows quite well how to use. A full-grown common Frog swimming near him is sure to be engulfed without much difficulty ; and if a mouse be dropped out of a trap within comfortable reach, it will be almost certain to follow the unfortunate Batrachian ; the tail of the rodent may be left for a moment or two outside the huge jaws, only to be presently pushed out of sight by the skilful use of the gourmand's fore-feet, or rather hands, as they should be called.

Besides frogs and mice, *R. catesbiana* will eat lob-worms, sparrows, fish, tadpoles, and newts. Worms I find to be the most convenient to provide.

Though the Bull Frog, when full grown, is so large, its tadpole is extremely small by comparison. According to Cassell's "Natural History," "the mature animal measures from 13in. to 21in. in length, limbs included. The prices of American Bull Frogs in this country range from 5s. 6d. to 15s.

Of *R. catesbiana* the tympanum is generally much larger than the eye, particularly in the case of the male ; the eye, having a golden iris, is large and very beautiful ; the fingers are pointed, and the toes are fully webbed. The colour above is generally lightish green or dusky olive marbled with similar colours, but of a darker shade. The lower parts are yellowish-white, sometimes slightly marbled. The male has two internal vocal sacs. The late Mr. Frank Buckland, speaking of this Frog's power of making a noise, says, in his "Curiosities of Natural History," "In the Bull Frog we find a very peculiar piece of mechanism, by means of which the animal is enabled to produce the well-known bellowing sound described by travellers ; hence his name — Bull Frog. Certain portions of the larynx (the arytenoid cartilages) are convex externally, and concave internally, so that when the entrance to the larynx is closed, they form a dome over the windpipe,—which Cuvier has compared to a drum."

The American Bull Frog may be kept in the same manner as has been suggested for his Indian relative (*R. tigrina*). The two Batrachians will live very well in the same Vivarium, if both be of about the like size.

The Noisy Frog (*R. clamata*) is well named. It is now fairly frequently imported into this country, and may be purchased at about the same prices as those quoted for the sale of *R. cates-*

biana. In appearance the Noisy Frog is very like his relative, the Edible Frog (*R. esculenta*).

R. clamata has vomerine teeth, a moderately-sized head, a round snout, a tympanum generally much larger than the eye (sometimes nearly twice as large, particularly in the males), fingers with blunt tips, and toes not completely webbed, and a glandular fold on the side. The colour of the animal above is lightish-green, more or less spotted or marked with black or very dark-brown. The lower parts are yellowish-white, sometimes marbled with grey. The males, like *R. catesbiana*, have two internal vocal sacs. This

FIG. 80.—THE EDIBLE FROG (*Rana esculenta*).

Frog may be placed in the same Vivarium as the Common Frog (*R. temporaria*), and treated exactly in the same way. It is a handsome Batrachian.

The Edible Frog (*Rana esculenta*, Fig. 80) is an animal concerning which a great deal has been written from time to time. It has therefore some title to a certain kind of fame. People when they see this Batrachian for the first time and are told its name, frequently exclaim, "Oh! that is *the* Frog then which the French eat?" I used to assent to this remark; but now I do not do so, for I have seen that Mr. Boulenger, who is one of the greatest authorities on things concerning Batrachians, has said that "the current notion that the flesh of this Frog (*Rana esculenta*) is more valued than that of its European congeners, is entirely erroneous. The Frogs sold in the markets of Paris, Brussels, and Geneva are almost invariably *Rana temporaria*, which are commoner and more easily caught."

Anyone who has tried to catch Edible Frogs will certainly endorse what Mr. Boulenger says about their not being so readily procured as the more plentiful kind. The activity of *R. esculenta* is certainly very great indeed. Though *R. temporaria* is more easily found and captured than its more agile and aquatic relative, its flesh, according to the late Mr. Frank Buckland, is not so white and tender as that of the latter animal, which, when "cooked, as a Frenchman only knows how to cook, is a very good imitation of whitebait." He who wishes to test what Mr. Buckland has said can procure, I believe, in London tins of portions of the Edible Frog already prepared for being cooked and compare it as to the colour and tenderness of its flesh with that of the common Batrachian. Some people have described the flavour of Frog's cooked flesh as being like that of a rabbit, while others say it resembles very young boiled chickens.

In the First Series of the "Curiosities of Natural History," Mr. Buckland says that the woman of whom he bought Edible Frogs told him that she employed a man to catch them for her. "He went out every evening at dusk to the ponds in the neighbourhood of Paris, with a lantern and a long stick, to the end of which was attached a piece of red cloth. The Frogs were attracted by the light to the place where the fisherman stood. He then lightly dropped his cloth on the surface of the water. The Frogs, imagining that some dainty morsel was placed before them, eagerly snapped at it; and their teeth being entangled, they become an easy prey, destined for to-morrow's market, and the tender mercies of the fish or rather Frog-woman."

The same writer also tells us that this Frog "is brought from the country in quantities of from thirty to forty thousand at a time to Vienna, and sold to great dealers, who have conservatories for them. These conservatories are large holes, four or five feet deep, dug in the ground, the mouth covered with a board, and in severe weather with straw. In these conservatories, even during a hard frost, the Frogs never become quite torpid: they get together in heaps one upon another instinctively, and thereby prevent the evaporation of their humidity, for no water is ever put to them."

Lord Clermont, in his "Guide to the Quadrupeds and Reptiles of Europe," says that "this Frog is found all over Europe, except in the British Islands; throughout the North of Asia to Japan, and in Egypt." At the time these words were written this Batrachian was certainly an inhabitant of England, though in all probability it must not be considered as indigenous to this country, but as an importation. When the first attempt to naturalise the Edible Frog here was made, it is very difficult to say. The late Mr. Thomas Bell, in his "British Reptiles," published in 1849, said that his father, when a boy, eighty years before that date, had discovered, in Norfolk, the distinction of this species of Frog. Mr. George Berney has given in the *Zoologist*, p. 6539, an interesting account of his introduction into this country of the *R. esculenta*. He records that in the year 1837 he brought home from Paris 200 of these Frogs, and a quantity of their spawn. These he placed in certain ditches, ponds, and meadows in Norfolk. Those animals which he had turned in the meadows left them for the ponds. In the years 1841 and 1842 he imported considerably over a thousand more.

Those Frogs of which Mr. Bell's father spoke, and which were known in the neighbourhood in which he lived as a boy as "Cambridgeshire nightingales" and "Whaddon Organs" may, like Mr. Berney's Frogs, have been importations or descendants of importations.

I believe that English-bred Edible Frogs are now difficult to procure. I have tried to obtain them occasionally, but have failed.

Mr. S. H. Miller, writing from Wisbech, in *Nature*, in 1874, referring to the Edible Frogs which, from time to time, had been brought into England, asks if they are dying out, for he cannot find any in his neighbourhood (portions of Norfolk and Cambridgeshire).

I venture to think that Mr. Miller's question may be answered in the affirmative, for it seems that these creatures, after being imported, gradually disappear. Lord Arthur Russell suggests, also in *Nature* for 1874, a reason for this gradual disappearance; for he says: "About ten years ago I imported a basketful (of Edible Frogs) from the Parisian market, where they can easily be obtained, and turned them into a pond at Woburn Abbey, in Bedfordshire. They thrived and multiplied there; but our summers are seldom hot enough to enable the tadpole to attain his full development before the cold autumnal nights set in."

It is probable that the gradual decrease in the numbers of these Frogs is owing to their inability to withstand, as a rule, while in an immature condition, the severity of our winters. It may, however, be said by some that they do not really slowly die out, but being far more aquatic in their habits than are the members of the commoner species, they are not so readily observed. Such argument can only have weight with those who forget, or who are ignorant of, the remarkable vocal powers of the males of these particular Batrachians. No one, I think, could live in the neighbourhood during spring of any fairly great number of Edible Frogs without being aware of their presence. Their croak is so sonorous that they have been called, as already mentioned, "Cambridgeshire nightingales" and the "Whaddon Organs."

The male Frog, when making his peculiar cry, inflates two large bladder-like sacs, one on each side of its head, which then attain a size much larger than that of an ordinary pea. These vocal sacs are not possessed by the common Frog. The Edible Frog uses its voice by both day and night.

R. esculenta is a very handsome animal, and an interesting inmate of a Vivarium where, with care and proper treatment, it will live for many years. Owing to its great fondness for water, it must be provided with a fairly large tank, where, however, it will not by any means spend all its time.

It is an animal with a large appetite, and sometimes, indeed, it brings shame upon its species by stooping to the low habits of a cannibal, and devouring a small brother Batrachian in the shape of a half-grown Frog or an immature Newt. Nevertheless, I think if it be given the choice, it will invariably prefer a large worm, instead of a tiny relative.

The Edible Frogs in their native country inhabit rivers, lakes, ponds, running streams, marshes, and even small pools of water. They are not only most active animals, but also exceedingly timid and wary. He who has been attracted to the water's edge by the sound of their strange voices, will be surprised, if he be ignorant of the habits of these creatures, to see on his arrival there little or no signs of Batrachian life, for on the very suspicion of danger they will have dived into the water, not to reappear until all signs of an enemy have gone. The wise observer, however, will conceal himself and remain perfectly still for a fairly long time, and he will be rewarded for his patience and caution by seeing these beautiful Batrachians gradually one by one emerge from their hiding places. Then, if he wishes to make any captures, he must summon all his activity and adroitness.

The spawn of *R. esculenta* is generally attached to the weeds and stones under the water, and is not often seen upon its surface, like that of the Common Frog.

The Edible Frog may be readily known from *R. temporaria* by the absence of the dark-coloured patch on the temples, which has given to the latter animal the specific name of *temporaria*.

Of *R. esculenta* the tympanum is distinct and nearly as large as the eye. The toes are entirely webbed. There is a prominent glandular lateral fold. The upper parts of the animal's body are generally of a rich bright green colour, spotted irregularly with dark brown or black. On the back, as a rule, there are three light-coloured streaks. The hinder parts of the thighs are striped and marbled with black. The head and body of the Edible Frog measure more than 3in. in length. It is rather a longer and narrower animal than *R. temporaria*. The fore limbs measure about 1½in., and the hind ones about 4½in. These Frogs, which have generally been imported, may be bought for 6d. each during the spring and summer months.

The American Green Frog (*Rana halecina*) is more than a little like the last-mentioned Batrachian, *R. esculenta*, which is not a native of the New World. *R. halecina* is occasionally brought into this country, where it lives well while in confinement. It is an inhabitant of North and Central America.

The American Green Frog has a moderately-sized head and a pointed snout. Its tympanum is distinct, and almost as large as its eye. Its toes are webbed nearly to their extremities. It has a narrow and prominent glandular fold. The upper parts of the animal are violet-green, marked with dark brown, light-edged spots. Its legs, like those of so many Frogs, are cross-barred. The lower parts are yellowish-white. The male possesses internal vocal sacs. This Frog may be treated in the same way as has been suggested for the Edible Frog (*R. esculenta*).

The Common Frog (*R. temporaria*, Fig. 81) is probably the most plentiful and the best known of all the Batrachians. It has

FIG. 81.—THE COMMON FROG (*Rana temporaria*).

a very extensive range, being found nearly all over Europe, and North and Temperate Asia.

The Common Frog spends the winter in a state of hibernation, huddled up with great numbers of its own species in the mud at the bottom of ponds, where the temperature, though low, is fairly even. The Batrachians in such a position are not only safe from the effects of frost, but are also out of the reach of their many natural enemies.

The spawn of the Common Frog is deposited at the bottom of ponds and pools, and in a little while, owing to a certain amount of gas, which has been generated because of some decomposition, it floats upon the surface of the water.

The hatching and life of the tadpole have already been described. During the latter part of spring portions of many of our ponds, pools, the sides of slow-running rivers and streams are literally black with the crowding together of thousands of tadpoles. And indeed, if it were not for their numerous foes these Batrachians would become a veritable plague. The word "plague" in this connection reminds me of the following, which I venture to relate: Some time ago I was examining my young son and his cousin as to their knowledge of Old Testament history. I was asking questions about the plagues of Egypt, and wanted the boys to mention them in their proper order. As they could not tell me what plague came before that of Frogs, I turned to my little daughter, five years of age, who was listening, but not being examined, and asked her the question, when she immediately replied, to both my astonishment and amusement, "Why, the plague of tadpoles, of course, daddy." The small maiden had certainly been using her powers of observation and reasoning.

Snakes, fish, ducks, other birds, stoats, cats, dogs, boys, and men are among the enemies of the useful and harmless Frog. Thousands of these Batrachians are caught annually for fishing purposes. Many dealers in London, for instance, always keep large quantities of these Batrachians. I find that I can, even in mid-winter, obtain almost any number of them from such people. Of course a great many Frogs are consumed every year at the London and other Zoological Gardens. And from what one reads, it may be fairly concluded that a great consumption of such Batrachians takes place in America as well as in Europe. For example, I quote the following (I do not know the species of Frog referred to, but of course it cannot be *R. temporaria*, as that animal is not found at all in America): "The quantity (of Frogs) disposed of in Buffalo is surprisingly large. The principal dealers sell easily 1,200 per day, and the consumption of four hotels which have the delicacy in their bills of fare will probably add 500 to that amount. As there are several smaller grocery stores which sell daily from twenty-five to fifty pairs, it will be safe to say that not less than 2,000 are being eaten in Buffalo every day. Already over 100,000 have been sold, and the remaining two months of the season will increase that amount to nearly 300,000, which is but a moderate quantity, considering the already large and yearly increasing numbers which inhabit the river islands, and all along the shore of Canada. The article retails at from one 1dol. to 50c. per 100."—*Buffalo Express* (quoted by *Science Gossip*, 1st Sepember, 1867.)

The Common Frog is a very useful animal, as it lives frequently upon such creatures as slugs, beetles, and wireworms. It is surprising how many of these (the last-mentioned) root-destroying larvæ one Frog will consume in twenty-four hours.

The vitality of the common and other ground Frogs is amazing. This vitality has helped to give rise to the fables which we from time to time hear and read of, concerning their living buried in stone for thousands of years. "It inspires us," says an extract which Mr. Frank Buckland quoted in the first series of his "Curiosities of Natural History," "with a kind of fear to be brought into contact with a living being that has, in all possibility, breathed the same air as Noah, or disported in the same limpid stream in which Adam bathed his sturdy limbs." The above, which was written concerning a Frog found in a coal-pit, is an example of the kind of matter which is penned occasionally concerning the discovery of Frogs and Toads in out-of-the-way places.

In speaking of the vitality of these creatures, a writer, in the *Zoologist*, I think, has stated that during some severe weather he found a Frog embedded in ice, and while breaking the ice he broke, by accident, a leg off the Frog. He thought no more of the circumstance, until, in the spring, he happened to see a Frog, minus a leg, swimming about in the water where the ice had been. He concluded, therefore, that this was the same Batrachian which he had mutilated in the winter.

It has been reported that in Australia, when a drought has been of so long a duration that horses, cattle, and even the marsupials have died for want of water, an hour or two's steady rain has been sufficient to revive the Frogs, which have often been for more than a year torpid in the sun-baked mud.

The Frog has no little power to assume various shades of colour. These Chameleon-like properties are very manifest when Frogs taken from different situations are placed together. For example, if a Batrachian be taken from, say, among heather on a moor, a hay-field, a fish-pond, and some cavity under a stone, and put in the same Vivarium, there would be an assemblage of animals exhibiting a considerable variety of really beautiful colouring.

Frogs, like Snakes, Lizards, and Toads, shed their cuticle periodically. A Frog, when about to "change its skin," often presents, as does the Snake under similar circumstances, a bluish-white appearance of the eye. It also spends a great portion of its time in water. It sometimes, as does the Toad, swallows its cast-off covering.

It is not a difficult matter to rear young Frogs from spawn. The spawn, in a small quantity, should be placed in a shallow vessel filled with water. The hatching of the eggs depends very greatly upon the temperature of the water in which they are kept. Spawn will hatch in a few days in a sunny greenhouse. For the first portion of their existence the young tadpoles are vegetable-feeders, but gradually they become carnivorous, and if flesh be not supplied to them in some form they will devour each other. A piece of raw meat or a dead garden-worm will provide many tadpoles with food for a long time. These little creatures must be furnished with some means of getting out of the rays of the sun when it becomes too hot for them, or they will die. The most trying time of a tadpole's existence is when it is about to complete the absorption of its tail, and to leave the water to seek food upon land. As the captive tadpoles arrive at this period of their lives they should be provided with some means of escaping for a time from the water. A piece of floating board will answer the purpose very well. Tadpoles of this age are wonderful climbers, and therefore the vessel in which they are confined must be covered, or they will be lost. The little Frogs, which are beautiful creatures, as soon as they have finally left the tadpole-state, should be put in some such place as a fernery, where they will thrive on tiny flies and worms, ants, and the like. They soon become tame.

The Frog's manner of taking food has already been described. It does not invariably obtain its victim by the help of its curiously-constructed tongue, but very often jumps forward and seizes it with the mouth.

A Frog is several years in reaching maturity; it may be said, therefore, to be a fairly long-lived animal. The Common Frog is a very skilful climber. It has been frequently found high up the trunks of trees, or squatting among their branches. It can scale walls of several feet in height, and even, sometimes, perpendicular glass. I have often turned quantities of Frogs in a kitchen garden, which is surrounded by a cob wall of more than 6ft. high, and as I seldom find these creatures there, I conclude they have escaped by climbing. Frogs, of course, should be encouraged in a garden, for they do a great deal of good.

The Common Frog may be kept in the same Vivarium as *R. esculenta*, and other relatives of a similar size.

R. temporaria has a moderately-sized head, and a short, blunt snout. The toes are webbed for at least two-thirds of their length. It has a glandular lateral fold, fairly prominent. The colour of the upper parts of this creature's body is very variable, and is spotted with dark brown or black. There is always a dark temporal mark, which has given to the Batrachian its specific name. The sides of the animal's body are also spotted, and its limbs are cross-barred. The male has two internal vocal sacs. The body and head of a Frog of an average size attain the length of 2¾in.

The *Cystignathidæ* (the Arch-jawed) has been placed as the first family of the *Arcifera*, to which allusion has already been made. This family, of which the genus *Ceratophrys* is one of the most interesting and curious, is very large, for it numbers as many as twenty-four genera, and about 156 species.

The genus *Ceratophrys* contains ten species, all of which are natives of South America. One of the chief characteristics of these strange Batrachians is the development of the upper eyelids into horn-like protuberances, which give the animals a very extraordinary appearance. These appendages can be raised or depressed at will. For instance, when these creatures are touched, frightened, threatened, or when they are swallowing a victim, the so-called horns seem to sink, more or less, into the head.

The *Ceratophrys* is ungainly in shape, and, as a rule, gaudy in colour. It is, however, a most interesting Frog and a long liver in confinement.

C. cornuta is a large Batrachian, being about six inches long, four inches across the back, and possesses a mouth of three inches in width. It is able to swallow with comparative ease a full-grown Common Frog (*Rana temporaria*). In captivity it may be fed upon Frogs, Toads, young rats, full-grown mice, and small birds, such as sparrows. Owing to the *Ceratophrys*' habit of almost completely burying itself, it should be provided, while in confinement, with plenty of garden mould, in which, with the help of its powerful metatarsal shovel, it will hide, leaving only its back and its eyes above the surface. It is then likely to escape detection. In such a position as this, while in a state of nature, it waits for the approach of those creatures upon which it is accustomed to prey. The *Ceratophrys* is not an active animal by any means. Its legs seem hardly long enough to carry forward its large body.

These Horned Frogs are plucky animals and not easily frightened. They are generally quite ready to attack anyone who is unkind enough to tease them, often, as they do so, barking like a small dog. They are, therefore, sometimes known as "Barking Frogs." The power of their jaws is immense. They will readily seize with their mouth a piece of stick which has been presented to them, leaving the marks of their teeth upon its surface. I have known one of these creatures cling so tenaciously to a hat it had caught with its mouth that it was quite a difficult matter, without hurting the Batrachian, to make it give up its hold.

The *Ceratophrys* is very bulldog-like in the tenacity with which it will usually cling to any substance it has taken in its jaws, sometimes suffering death in consequence. Mr. W. H. Hudson, in an article published in the *Field* for 31st March, 1883, and also in his very interesting book, "The Naturalist in the La Plata," speaking of *C. ornata*, says: "In disposition they are most truculent, savagely biting at anything which comes near them; and when they bite they hang on with the tenacity of a bulldog, poisoning the blood with their glandular secretions. When teased, the creature swells itself out to such an extent one

Y

almost expects to see him burst. He follows his tormentors about with slow awkward leaps, his vast mouth wide open, and uttering an incessant, harsh, croaking sound. A gaucho I knew was once bitten by one. He sat down on the grass, and dropping his hand at his side, had it seized, and only freed himself by using his hunting-knife to force the creature's mouth open. He washed and bandaged the wound, and no bad result followed; but when the Toad cannot be shaken off, then the result is different. One summer two horses were found dead on the plain near my home. One, while lying down, had been seized by a fold in the skin near the belly; the other had been grasped by the nose while cropping grass. In both instances the vicious Toad was found dead, with jaws tightly closed, still hanging to the dead horse. Perhaps they are sometimes incapable of letting go at will, and, like honey bees, destroy themselves in these savage attacks."

Mr. W. H. Hudson also says that the *Ceratophrys'* powerful voice may be heard distinctly, on still evenings, a mile off. Their cry he likens to the notes of some wind instrument, and the sound, he considers, not unmelodious.

The *Ceratophrys*, when in captivity, should not be kept in a temperature lower than 65deg. Fahr. Like other Frogs they congregate in pools during the breeding seasons; but I am sorry to say that I believe little or nothing is known concerning their mode of propagation, and the life and metamorphosis of their larvæ. I am hoping to persuade them some day to breed while in captivity.

Fine healthy specimens of these interesting Frogs may occasionally be bought for about £1 or £1 10s. each.

The Horned *Ceratophrys* (*C. cornuta*) has, like all its genus, a heart-shaped tongue free behind. It possesses two small groups of vomerine teeth, an exceedingly large and elevated head, a broad ridge running from the eye to above the tympanum (which is distinct), a nostril which is nearer to the small eye than the end of the nose, and a large horn-like protuberance above the eye. The upper surfaces of this creature's body are covered with small tubercles; the lower parts are granular. The following is Mr. Boulenger's description of the colour of this animal: "Greyish above, the median part of the back lighter; head with symmetrical markings; back with angular dark brown spots; sides marbled with dark brown; limbs with regular dark cross-bars. Male with subgular vocal sac, and the throat black." It is a native of Surinam and North Brazil.

The Adorned *Ceratophrys* or Esquerzo (*C. ornata*) has not nearly so large a horn-like appendage as the last-mentioned Batrachian. It possesses vomerine teeth, a very large head, which is rough and bony: the nostril is nearer to the eye, which is fairly large, than the end of the snout; a bony dorsal shield; stout fingers and toes, the latter being only half-webbed. The upper surfaces of the Frog's body are covered with small tubercles, and the lower surfaces with granules. The upper parts of the body are bright green in colour, marked with large, light-edged olive spots; the edge of the lower jaw is bright yellow; a yellow line runs from eye to eye; the upper surface of the hands and feet is yellowish; there are sometimes red lines between the spots on the back; the tongue is flesh-coloured. It is a native of Buenos Ayres and other parts of South America.

Mr. Hudson also says, in the article referred to above, that "The country people in South America believe that the milky secretion exuded by the Toad (the *Ceratophrys*, I suppose) possesses wonderful curative properties. It is their invariable specific for shingles, a painful and dangerous malady common amongst them; and to cure it living Toads are applied to the inflamed part."

The Slender-fingered Frog (*Leptodactylus pentadactylus*). The members of this genus are known as "Piping" Frogs because of their peculiar pipe-like croak, which differs in power and pitch according to the species. They are natives of Tropical America, and in general appearance much resemble the Common Frog. As they are occasionally imported into this country, it is wise, I think, to give a brief description of one or two species.

The manner of depositing the eggs by certain of these Frogs is peculiar and interesting. A hole is dug in the ground near to the water's edge. The little cave is then lined with a kind of frothy secretion, to which the eggs are attached until they are hatched. It is said that these caves or holes are so situated that at some period or other during the process of hatching they are sure to be flooded with water. In general appearance, there is not much difference between the tadpoles of this genus and those of the ordinary water Frogs of Europe.

The Slender-fingered Frog possesses an oval tongue, which is slightly nicked behind; vomerine teeth, which are placed in two arched series beyond the apertures of the inner nostrils; and a tympanum nearly as large as the eye (the pupil of which is horizontal). The hind toes are not webbed. The skin is smooth above, and there are generally large flat glands upon the flanks. The following is the description of the colouring of this Frog as given by Mr. Boulenger in his "Catalogue of Batrachia Salientia": "Brownish above, with dark spots generally arranged in transverse bars on the back; a black stripe along the canthus rostralis and the temporal fold; limbs cross-barred; hinder side of thighs black and yellowish marbled."

This Frog is a native of South America, and it may be kept, during the warmer parts of the year, in the same case as the Common and other Frogs of like size and similar habits.

The Ocellated Piping Frog (*Leptodactylus ocellatus*), sometimes known as the Bladder Frog, is also a native of South America. One of the chief differences between this Batrachian and that last described is the fringing of the toes on both sides. The colour of the animal is olive or brownish above, which is marked with roundish dark spots. There is a large spot between the eyes. The Frog should be treated in confinement in this country in the same way as has been suggested for the Slender-fingered Piping Frog.

The Australian Frog (*Pseudophryne australis*) is from time to time brought to this country, where it lives fairly well in captivity. It may sometimes be purchased for so low a sum as 5s.

This Frog has a rounded snout, an eye with a horizontal pupil, an elliptical tongue (free behind), and short fingers and toes, which are free, and not dilated, at the tips. The skin of the creature is either smooth or covered with small, round, flat warts on the back. Its colour above is blackish-brown, with a streak along the lower part of the back; there is one spot on the upper arm, and another on the thigh. The lower parts are blackish, and covered with large yellowish spots. It may be placed, while in captivity, with other Batrachians of its own size.

CHAPTER X.

TOADS.

THE *Bufonidæ*, or true Toads, are either terrestrial, burrowing, aquatic, or arboreal in habits. They form a fairly large family, numbering about ninety-five species. Their chief characteristic is the absence of teeth in both jaws. Representatives of this family are found almost everywhere except Australia.

The Natterjack Toad (*Bufo calamita*, Fig. 82) is a beautiful little Batrachian, and is usually a favourite with those who know it. It is a member of a large genus, which numbers more than eighty species, and which has representatives almost everywhere, except in Australia. This Toad is found in some parts of Great Britain, but not in others; but when seen, it may be easily distinguished from its near relative, the Common Toad (*B. vulgaris*), by its smaller size, more active movements, its curious gait, its brighter colouring, and by the golden or yellow stripe down its back.

The Natterjack is a very hardy little creature, sometimes living for more than ten or twelve years in confinement. It soon becomes tame, and quickly learns to accept food from its owner's fingers. Indeed, it will sometimes while held in the hand catch flies as they crawl over the window-panes. It appears to be much more intelligent than the Common Toad, and also more alert in discovering and seizing its prey. From its strange manner of progression it is known as the "walking" Toad, the action being compared to the slow running of a mouse. Like the Common Frog, *B. calamita* is a very clever climber, being occasionally found in apparently (for it) inaccessible places.

When irritated or excited in any way this Toad has the habit of sometimes producing a smell which may be compared to that

FIG. 82.—NATTERJACK TOAD (*Bufo calamita*).

of sulphur. The perfume, however, is not altogether unpleasant, notwithstanding that it has been described as "intolerable." I have kept these Toads for several years, often handling them, and yet I have only very rarely detected any scent at all. I mention this because I know that people have refrained from procuring these very interesting little creatures for pets just simply because they dread their "intolerable odour."

Though the Natterjack is chiefly nocturnal in its habits, it does not avoid or dread the rays of the sun; sometimes, it even basks in them. It is also a burrowing animal, making holes in either sand or soft mould. The holes are usually from 1ft. to 18in. deep, and the Toad generally rests in a small recess at the bottom of the hole. The Natterjacks are frequently found in pairs in these burrows, which they generally, if not always, enter by retreating backwards. When they are dug out of their holes they are invariably found, I believe, with their heads facing the opening to their domicile. Sometimes as many as three of these Toads are found in the same retreat, the entrance to which is, as a rule, sheltered by some piece of turf or mound of sand. These holes are, naturally, from time to time more or less filled with drifted sand, but the active little creatures seem to have no difficulty in escaping from their place of temporary entombment.

One of the easiest ways of obtaining these Batrachians is to dig them out of their burrows, which may be readily recognised after a little experience. Natterjacks also hide under stones, logs, and pieces of bark.

The croak of these creatures is harsher and more prolonged than that of the Common Toad, and sometimes may be heard, on still evenings, at a distance of at least 500 yards. They wisely, however, unlike their near relative just mentioned, cease to make any noise when they have reason to suspect the presence of an enemy.

From the beginning of April, or earlier, to the end of June, and sometimes later, these Toads may be found in considerable numbers in their own neighbourhood, near or in water. They prefer shallow water, especially where there are reeds or the like, and there they sit with their noses and eyes just above its surface. This habit of hiding among reeds has perhaps given them their specific name.

Natterjacks, like many other members of their order, have the power of assuming different shades of colour. For example, when they are squatting on the dry and light-coloured sand their hue may become so like that of their surroundings that there is no little difficulty in distinguishing the animals; and under these circumstances the yellow dorsal stripe is nearly sure to be mistaken for a blade of dead and bleached grass, or a split portion of the leaf of a reed.

The Natterjacks, like the Common Toads, deposit their eggs in water in strings, and which are, of course, fertilised in the same way as are those of other tailless Batrachians. Their eggs hatch, and their tadpoles attain the form of the adult animal much more quickly than do the spawn and larvæ of *B. vulgaris*. The absorbent nature of the soil which the Natterjacks inhabit makes this unusually rapid development a necessity. As the tadpoles cannot live without water they must arrive at that state in which they are to a great extent independent of water before the pool in which they have been born is sucked dry by the thirsty sand. I have gone to the spot at which there had been, a few weeks before, a small pond containing Natterjacks and their spawn, only to find that a slight hollow in the soil represented the position of the late pool which I was seeking, toads, spawn, tadpoles, and water having alike disappeared.

Probably, the larvæ of Natterjacks, on an average, leave their tadpolehood within six or seven weeks after they have been hatched. The tadpole of *B. calamita* is smaller and blacker than that of *B. vulgaris*; the process of development, however, of the larvæ of the two species is identical.

Natterjacks feed on worms, insects, slugs, and grubs. In captivity, they may be provided with insects, mealworms, earthworms, cockroaches, and "gentles." These Toads when very tame may sometimes be persuaded to take a worm-like piece of meat, waved before them at the end of a wire. Natterjacks capture their prey in the same way as do their relatives.

B. calamita may be or has been found in the following parts of Great Britain: On or near the coasts of Norfolk, Suffolk, Lincolnshire, Lancashire, in Cheshire, near London, such as on Barnes Common, Wisley Heath, etc., near Guildford, near Poole, Dorsetshire, near Eversley, Hampshire, on Gamlingay Heath, Cambridgeshire, on the shores of Solway Firth, and at Ross Bay, and in Kerry in Ireland, etc.

There are in different parts of the country several superstitions concerning the Natterjack. For instance, its dried body is thought to be a useful medicine for the horse. And if any person wishes to possess the powers which will fit him or her to play the part of a wizard or a witch, one of these Batrachians must be obtained, killed, and its body placed in an ant's hill, until nothing of the creature but the skeleton is left. The skeleton should then be divided and thrown into a running stream, and that bone which *floats against* the current is supposed to give its owner the coveted endowment.

The general form of the Natterjack is like that of the Common Toad, except that the body is much less clumsy-looking. The eyes are also more projecting, and their eyelids are more raised above the surface of the crown of the head. The upper parts are more or less thickly covered with irregular depressed and porous warts. There is a large gland on each hind leg. The male is provided with a subgular vocal sac. The upper parts of the animal are of a yellowish-brown or olive-like colour, marked with darker shades, especially on the back. The warts are often red or very dark red. The legs are marked with transverse black bands. There is generally, particularly with British specimens, a yellow or golden vertebral line. The lower parts are bluish-white, spotted with black, except towards the hind legs, where they are dusky and finely sprinkled with small white spots or pimples. The colouring of the underneath part of the body, like that of the back, however, is very various. *B. calamita*, when full grown, is nearly 3in. in length.

These very interesting and pretty little Batrachians can be bought in London and other large towns at from 4d. to 6d. each.

The Green Toad (*Bufo viridis*) is much handsomer than its commoner relative, *B. vulgaris*. It has a wide range, being found in Europe, Asia, and North Africa. It may be readily distinguished from the Common Toad by a fold on the ankle, a vocal sac beneath the throat of the male, a more distinct and larger tympanum, and by a narrower space between the eyes. The Green Toad is olive or greenish above, spotted or marbled with a darker shade of the same colour. Sometimes, however, the upper parts are nearly immaculate. Below it is of a yellowish-white colour, either uniform or spotted with black. *B. viridis* may occasionally be bought in England for a small sum. It will live, under proper treatment, for a long while in confinement. It may be kept in the same Vivarium as the Natterjack and other Toads of like size and habits.

The Moorish Toad (*Bufo mauritanicus*) is a large Batrachian. It has a concave space between the eyes, the first finger much longer than the second, and a very distinct tympanum. It is marked on the back with brown or olive spots, having darker edges. The lower parts are yellowish-white. The male has a subgular vocal sac. This Toad is a native of North-West Africa. Besides insects and the like, it will eat white mice and small rats. It should not be kept with other Batrachians much smaller than itself.

The Square-marked Toad (*Bufo regularis*) is also a large Batrachian, measuring sometimes as much as 5½in. or 6in. from snout to vent. It readily adapts itself to the circumstances of confinement, and may be fed and kept in the same way as has been suggested for the Moorish Toad. *B. regularis* is a native of Africa and Arabia. The snout of this Batrachian is short and rather blunt. Its tympanum is as large as the eye, or nearly so, and very distinct. Its first finger is much longer than the second, and its toes are webbed for one-third of their length. There is a fold on the ankle. On the upper parts of this creature's body there are large and flattish warts, which sometimes bear a kind of spine. The colour is darkish olive, either uniform or spotted: the lower parts are sometimes covered with large blotches. The male of *B. regularis* has a subgular vocal sac.

The Common Toad (*Bufo vulgaris*, Fig. 83). "Oh, you toad! what are you a doin' of?" exclaimed an ostler, with a certain amount of temper, one day, as he was getting my cob ready for me. And when asked why he had called the mare a "Toad," replied that "she had got the bit out of her mouth." It was through the man's own carelessness that he buckled the bridle leaving the bit under the animal's chin; and he blamed her unjustly, calling her, in his annoyance, one of the worst names he could think of—a "Toad." But why should he, and many others also, use the word "Toad" as a term of reproach and contempt? The Toad ought rather to excite one's admiration because of its usefulness, because of its equanimity of temper, and because of its retiring disposition.

Perhaps no animal has been more unjustly abused than the Common Toad. It has been reviled for its ugliness, feared for its supposed venomous properties, and hated for its imagined vindictiveness. Even Mr. Pennant speaks of it "as the most deformed and hideous of all animals." So ugly, indeed, that it required, so he said, a certain amount of resolution to view it with attention.

Though certain other Toads seem to possess poisonous properties, it has never been proved, I believe, that *B. vulgaris* has any venomous powers whatever.

Dogs do not care to seize with their mouth a Toad a second time because of a milky-looking acrid secretion, which comes from

FIG. 83.—THE COMMON TOAD (*Bufo vulgaris*).

a large gland on each side of the neck (the parotoids) and from other smaller glands which cover the animal's body. Dr. John Davy considered that the chief use of this secretion was as a means of defence against the attacks of carnivorous animals.

The Common Snake (*Tropidonotus natrix*) and many other species will readily eat Toads. A great authority on these Reptiles says that when a *T. natrix*, or other Snake of the same genus, swallows a large Toad it nearly always dies in consequence. This, however, has not been my experience. My Snakes have often taken Toads (not very large ones, indeed), and as far as I know have never suffered any ill effects therefrom.

Mr. St. George Mivart says that the tadpoles of both Frogs and Salamanders are very much affected by being kept in the same water with Toads.

The Common Toad soon becomes very tame, and, like the Natterjack, will learn to take flies from the window-panes while being held in its owner's hands. It will also sit in one of his hands and seize its prey when placed in the other. The late Professor Romanes, in his "Animal Intelligence," says that a case is "recorded by Mr. Pennant of a Toad which was domesticated for thirty-six years, and knew all his friends."

A Toad is not only nicer to touch, but it can also bear much more heat, than the Frog. It has, however, like the latter Batrachian, a portable reservoir for the storage and conveyance of water. When a Toad is frightened it will generally inflate itself, exude its cutaneous secretion, and discharge what water it has stored up in its reservoir. This water is regarded by those who are ignorant of the animal and its ways as highly poisonous, though it is really perfectly harmless and tasteless.

The Toad's powers of endurance are wonderful, but they are not nearly so wonderful as is generally supposed. From time to time we hear of Toads being found in blocks of stone and in lumps of coal. And it is not difficult to find people who will readily believe that these strange creatures have been cooped up in these small prisons for centuries. The following, quoted by the *Zoologist* (p. 9630) from the *Leeds Mercury* for 8th April, 1865, is an example of this belief: "During the excavations which are being carried out under the superintendence of Mr. James Yeal, of Dyke House Quay, in connection with the Hartlepool Waterworks, the workmen on Friday morning found a Toad embedded in a block of magnesian limestone, at a depth of 25ft. from the surface of the earth, and 8ft. from any springwater vein. The block of stone had been cut by a wedge, and was reduced by the workmen, when a pick split open the cavity in which the Toad had been incarcerated. The cavity was no larger than its body, and presented the appearance of being a cast of it. The Toad's eyes shone with unusual brilliancy, and it was full of vivacity on its liberation. It appeared, when first discovered, desirous to perform the process of respiration, but evidently experienced some difficulty, and the only sign of success consisted of a barking noise, which it continues invariably to make at present on being touched. The Toad is in the possession of Mr. S. Horner, the president of the Natural History Society, and continues in as lively a state as when found. On a minute examination, its mouth is found to be completely closed, and the barking noise it makes proceeds from its nostrils. The claws of its fore-feet are turned inwards, and its hind ones are of extraordinary length, and unlike the present English Toad. The Rev. R. Taylor, incumbent of St. Hilda's Church, Hartlepool, who is an eminent local geologist, gives it as his opinion that the animal must be at least 6,000 years old. This wonderful Toad is to be placed in its primary habitation, and will be added to the collection in the Hartlepool Museum." The following note was appended to the above extract: "It is stated in the *Sunderland Herald* that the Toad lately found by some quarrymen at Hartlepool, and announced to be 6,000 (six thousand) years old, is not a myth."

The late Dean Buckland in 1825 commenced some experiments which proved that no Toad could exist, even for one year, embedded in stone which is impervious to either water or air; and that this Batrachian could not live for two years in a comparatively large cavity made in a stone of such a nature that it was permeable for water and possibly for air. It was found, however, that the Toads in those cells which, by chance, contained such small openings (owing to the cracked glass which covered the cell —or to the broken luting round the glass) that minute insects could enter, had at the end of the first year increased slightly in weight. Thus one Toad which when immured weighed 1,185 grains was found to have increased to 1,265 grains. Another had increased from 988 grains to 1,116 grains. But all the other Toads had either died or decreased considerably in weight. These facts show the wonderful endurance of the Common Toad.

A Toad, when young, may fall into a pit and take up its abode in some hole or cavity in a piece of rock, which it enters by means of a narrow opening or crevice. This is just the kind of retreat to suit the taste of such a Batrachian, and he spends his days and nights, when not sleeping, with his face towards the opening of his den, watching, with all the gravity of his genus, for prey. Many insects are attracted by a hiding-place similar to that chosen by the Toad, and as they enter, the occupant of the abode bends slightly forward, its bright eye flashes, and its tongue is shot out and withdrawn with wonderful rapidity, and the unfortunate creatures find a retreat from which there is no escape. In course of time the Toad, as he grows, discovers that the opening to the den has become too narrow to admit its body without considerable inconvenience. And as the den is comfortable, and the passage out tedious, it remains within until it becomes too big to leave at all. Perhaps it lives thus, a prisoner, for a year or two, eating and growing, until it is freed by a chance stroke of a workman's pick. As the man has not noticed the narrow opening to the little den, he concludes, or others do to whom he relates the incident, that the Toad has been embedded in the stone for ages. Some such explanation as this will account, no doubt, for many an embedded Batrachian.

Toads are not very particular as to their food so long as it is small enough to enter their mouths, and is alive and moving. They will eat worms, maggots, flies, bees, wasps, slugs (but not readily); and occasionally tiny snakes, newts, young hairless mice, and the like. Sometimes they will attack any small thing that is moving, such as a twig waved before them. In this way they can be persuaded to take raw meat, or dead insects, or even burning cinders, as the following interesting quotation taken from the *Field* of 27th May, 1893, will show :—" *Los sapos comen fuego* (the Toads eat fire) is a common saying among the natives of the northern provinces of the Argentine Confederation, and that it is a fact, this fire-eating, or rather red-hot cinder-eating, the following will prove. When employed by a large firm of S. American contractors at a junction of the Central Cordoba Railway—Frias by name, I lived in a house which had a long verandah at the back, which looked on to an enclosed yard. At night we were in the habit of dining on the verandah by the light of a kerosene lamp affixed to the wall. This lamp attracted innumerable beetles and insects of all sorts, which, flying against the glass, fell to the ground, to be instantly snapped up by an expectant crowd of Toads. One night one of the party suggested throwing them a red-hot cinder, remarking that they might mistake it for a firefly. What was our surprise on seeing a Toad jump towards it, snap it up, and swallow it. We repeated the experiment, to see in every instance the cinder instantly swallowed. The Toads did not eject the cinders. On the contrary, they apparently liked them, as one ostrich-stomached and bloated individual took five or six consecutively. This new method of Toad-feeding soon became a regular evening diversion, and we never had a friend to dine without going through the performance for his benefit. I may mention that a man who was in the habit of imbibing large quantities of *cana*, or *aguardiente de uvas* (the native spirits), is nicknamed in many cases by his comrades *garganta de sapo* (toad-throat)."

The Toad's power of eating is nearly as remarkable as its powers of fasting. A large Toad of my own has swallowed, one after the other, a dozen full-grown cockroaches. A Toad will seize a lob-worm by the middle of its body and gradually force the two struggling ends into its mouth by the help of its hands. Frequently this feat is not accomplished without considerable exertion on the part of the Toad. Not seldom one portion of the worm wriggles out of the Batrachian's mouth, while the other portion is being pushed in. And if this in-and-out business be continued for any length of time, the Toad probably comes as near to losing its temper as it is possible for an animal of such a placid disposition to arrive at.

Toads are frequently regarded by entomologists as beetle-traps, and are robbed in the morning of their prey which they have captured during the night before. In this way many rare insects have been obtained.

The water to which Toads, while in confinement, have access should be changed regularly. The reason for this will soon become apparent to those who begin to keep these creatures.

The Toad, while watching some animal which it expects to capture, sometimes exhibits a curious nervous twitching of its toes, and as it swallows the victim its eyes seem to sink for a moment into its head.

When the time arrives for a Toad to shed its cuticle, it draws it off, somewhat in the same way as a football-player removes his jersey, and then swallows it. This change of skin takes place at irregular intervals. It seems that whenever the animal feels that it has become inconveniently dirty, it cleanses itself by sloughing.

Toads, like Frogs, considering their build, have extraordinary powers of climbing. They will frequently, by means of this ability, escape from a garden which is surrounded by a high wall. Sometimes they will even climb to and fro. And after months of hibernation, they will give proof of their memory by going to that part of the wall they had been accustomed to scale the summer before. They will not only remember the places where they fed, but also the appearance of those whom they had learned to regard as friends. Toads generally hibernate under large stones and logs, and in holes in banks and in hollows in trees.

Toads spawn a few weeks later in the spring than do Frogs, arranging their eggs, not in masses, but in double rows, or strings. The tadpoles of Toads pass through their metamorphoses exactly in the same manner as do those of their relatives mentioned above. The larvæ of the former, however, are rather smaller and blacker than that of the latter.

The Common Toad, which comes from Southern Europe, is often of a very great size, and is altogether a most interesting animal, and can be bought in this country, when in the market, for about half-a-crown.

Toads, while in confinement, should be provided with plenty of garden-mould, into which they can burrow whenever they feel inclined.

Bufo vulgaris is a native of Europe, Asia, and N.W. Africa. Its snout is short and blunt; its tympanum is small, round, and frequently indistinct. Its first and second fingers are almost of the same length, and its toes are webbed to about half their length. There is no fold on the ankle. This Toad is of a brownish colour above, spotted or marbled with a darker shade. The parotoids have black margins on their outer side. The male has no vocal sac. British specimens are generally about 3½ in. long from snout to vent.

The Dusky Toad (*Bufo lentiginosus*), a North American Batrachian, is now and then imported into this country, where it will live very well in confinement. It is rather a timid animal, but it may be kept with other Toads of a similar size and of like habits. *B. lentiginosus* is, when full grown, nearly 3in. in length from the nose to the vent. It has a smaller head in proportion to its size than the Common Toad; and its body is thickly covered with irregularly-shaped warts. On this Toad the tympanum is very distinct, and nearly as large as the eye; the first finger is longer than the second, and the toes are half-webbed. There is no fold on the ankle, but there are two metatarsal tubercles. The parotoids are rather large and kidney-shaped. The upper parts of the body are of a darkish-olive colour, marked with darker spots, and there is a V-shaped marking between the eyes. There is also, generally, a light streak running down the back. The under parts are either of a uniform light colour, or sprinkled with dark spots. This Toad has a very wide range in North America, where it is fairly common. It is frequently known as the "American Toad." There are several varieties.

The Giant Toad (*Bufo marinus*) is probably the largest of all Toads. It measures sometimes more than 8in. from the snout to the vent. With proper care it will live for a very long time in confinement. It is recognised also as the Agua Toad.

A very well-known specimen of the Giant Toad, the property of Dr. Stradling, was deposited for some years at the Reptile House, Zoological Gardens, London. "Ambrose," as he was called, died, I think, in 1891, when his owner wrote a "brief memorial notice of his life." This very interesting article was published in the *Boy's Own Paper* for January, 1892, and from which I venture to make one or two quotations. Concerning this famous Toad's size, Dr. Stradling says, "that those. . . . who never saw him in the flesh may be surprised to hear that he almost overlapped the margin when he settled down, flat, squat, and nearly circular in outline, on the crown of a man's 'box' hat." And in writing of the means of defence against carnivorous animals, which the toads of this species possess, the doctor remarks that "these Giant Toads have a very poisonous perspiration. All Toads excrete this acrid fluid, but in those of the family to which Ambrose belonged it is, as you might expect, considerable in quantity and exceedingly virulent. Not that it would do you any harm, unless it got into a cut or accidentally touched your eyes. This constitutes the creature's protection against enemies . . . This poisonous fluid retains its venomous property for many years if stored up and kept from air, longer even than snake poison; and it is remarkable that it seems to increase in virulence the longer it is kept. If an angry Giant Toad is plunged into water in which its own tadpoles are swimming, the latter will most likely be all killed by the contact of this powerful excretion. I lost a valuable West Indian serpent in this way. Having no cage at hand for it, I put it inadvertently into a box which contained three of these Giant Toads. The movements of the Snake (which was a large one) irritated them so much during the night that in the morning I found the floor of their box all awash with their swelter and the poor *cribo* lying on his back, absolutely blistered by it; and in spite of the most assiduous nursing he died a fortnight afterwards. This perspiration is acid in its reaction—it turns blue litmus paper red."

The Giant Toad will feed upon slugs, lob-worms, insects of almost any kind, mice, rats, and young birds. It should not be kept in a Vivarium with other Batrachians smaller than itself. Two or three of these large Toads will live very well together. Owing to their size the bottom of their case ought to be covered with garden mould to a considerable depth.

The following is a short description of *B. marinus:* The crown of the head has prominent long ridges; the snout is short and blunt; the eyes are wide apart; the tympanum is distinct and large; the first finger is longer than the second, and the toes are half-webbed; there is a fold on the ankle. The upper parts of the body are covered with many irregular warts, which sometime bear spines. The parotoids are very large indeed. The colour above is brownish, sometimes marked with darker spots. The male has a subgular vocal sac.

This large and interesting Toad is a native of South and Central America, and of the West Indies.

CHAPTER XI.

TREE-FROGS.

THE family of the *Hylidæ* is rather a large one, numbering about ten genera, and something like 170 species. The structure of their skeleton shows that these beautiful Frogs are closely related to the Toads, but are chiefly distinguished from them by the possession of teeth in their upper jaws.

Tree-frogs are very plentiful in Australia and America. They are also found in more or less abundance in Europe, Asia, chiefly north of the Himalayas, and in the northern parts of Africa. Many of them are very beautiful and wonderfully active.

The cases in which Tree-frogs are confined should be provided with some kind of growing plants, such as orange and lemon trees, geraniums, broad-fronded ferns, tradescantia, and the like. The larger the Vivarium is, of course, the better. There should also be within it hiding-places for its inmates, *e.g.*, pieces of cork, bark, or small hollow logs. The water may be contained in a large shallow clay saucer, or in a zinc tank made for the purpose. Tree-frogs *will* live in a small case about a foot square, but naturally they are far happier in one of greater dimensions.

Several different kinds of Tree-frogs may be kept in the same large Vivarium, where their beauty and activity will be seen to great advantage. Sometimes Tree-frogs, such as the common Green Tree-frog (*Hyla arborea*), are confined in a wide-mouthed bottle, which contains only a wooden ladder and a little water. Imprisoning such active animals as Tree-frogs in so small a space is, I think, little short of cruelty. Perhaps the most suitable place for Tree-frogs while in this country is a greenhouse, where they can have liberty. The window-frames of the greenhouse should be provided with perforated zinc in such a way that the Frogs cannot escape when the windows are open. If the Frogs have access to a large tank of rain-water in which some broad-leaved aquatic plants are growing, such as Villarsia (*Villarsia nymphæoides*), the Cape Fragrant Water Lily (*Aponogeton distachyon*), or the broad-leaved pond-weed (*Potamogeton natans*), some of them would be tempted to breed there, especially the beautiful European Tree-frog (*H. arborea*). Their tadpoles should be treated in the same way as has been suggested for those of the Common Frog, particular attention being given to regular feeding and change of water. The Vivarium in which Tree-frogs are confined should be so situated that its inmates may have access to both sunshine and shade.

The Grasshopper Frog (*Acris gryllus*) has received its English name from its voice, which resembles that of its insect namesake. It is a native of North America, being commonest in the Eastern and Central parts of that country. It is a dweller among plants, particularly aquatic, rather than a frequenter of trees. It is often found in stagnant waters.

The Grasshopper Frog has an eye with a horizontal pupil, a heart-shaped tongue, which is free behind, vomerine teeth, free fingers, and toes fully webbed and slightly dilated into small disks at the tips, a slender body, narrow head, and sharp snout. The skin of the upper part of the animal is either smooth or slightly tuberculous, while the under parts are granulated. The coloration is very variable, being reddish-brown, brown, or different shades of green, and mottled on the back and sides, and striped on the legs. There is, however, generally, a three-cornered brown spot between the eyes, and sometimes a light vertebral line. The male possesses a subgular vocal sac. *A. gryllus* when full grown is about 1½in. from the snout to the vent.

The Changeable Tree-frog (*Hyla versicolor*, Fig. 84) is sure to become a favourite of those who keep it in their Vivarium, as it

TREE-FROGS. 341

is very beautiful, active, and hardy. The Versicolor Frog is a native of North America, and ranges from Canada to perhaps as far south as Mexico. It is now frequently brought to England, where it can be bought, when in the market, for about 5s. It feeds at night, and is particularly fond of worms and cockroaches.

This Frog has a circular tongue, slightly nicked, and free

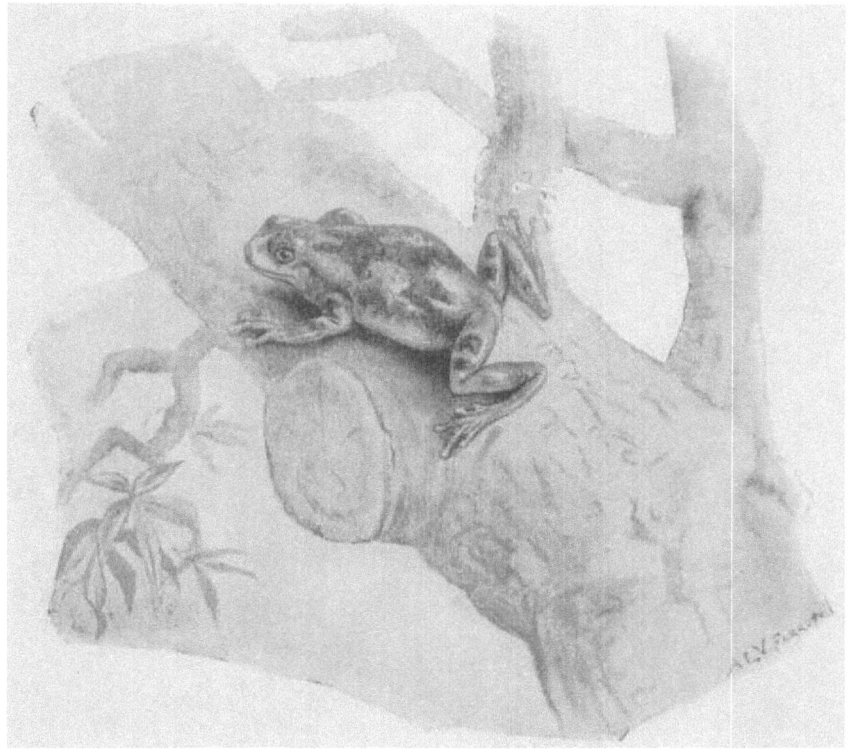

FIG. 84.—THE CHANGEABLE TREE-FROG (*Hyla versicolor*).

behind; a broad head and a round snout; and a very distinct tympanum, almost as large as the eye. Its fingers are webbed for nearly half their length, and its toes for nearly all. The disks of its toes are less than the size of its tympanum. It has an ankle fold.

The upper surfaces of its body are covered with small warts, and its lower parts are granulated. Its colour above is greyish, marked with fairly regular large spots, and dark cross-bars on the thighs. The sides of the thighs are yellow, edged with red. The under parts are of a uniform whitish colour. The male may be known by a dark-coloured external subgular vocal sac.

The general shape of this Tree-frog is somewhat like that of its

FIG. 85.—THE EUROPEAN GREEN TREE-FROG (*Hyla arborea*).

near relative, the Toad. It makes a good deal of noise during damp weather.

The European Green Tree-frog (*Hyla arborea*, Fig. 85), though so common and easily obtained, is one of the most charming species of all its family. It soon becomes so tame as to take food from its owner's fingers. By the help of the disks with which the extremities of the fingers and toes are furnished it is able to cling for hours to the glass sides of its Vivarium.

The Green Frog becomes particularly lively towards evening, sometimes making so loud a croaking that it may be heard a very long distance. Lord Clermont says that when "there are many together, they may be heard for two miles or more around." The "Royal Natural History" remarks that "when croaking, the sac on the throat of the males becomes so inflated as to make this appendage nearly as large as the body."

The European Tree-frog, owing to the colouring of its body, is very difficult to distinguish when at rest upon some green leaf. For this reason it is called in Germany *Laubfrosch*, or Leaf Frog. Flies and other insects, therefore, often come into the close neighbourhood of their enemy without any suspicion of danger. The Batrachian's active tongue shoots out and is as rapidly withdrawn, and the victims disappear, perhaps without having had time to experience any fear or pain.

This Tree-frog is very fond of flies and earwigs; but it will eat, besides these creatures, mealworms, cockroaches, earthworms, and the like. It jumps upon its prey from the distance of a foot, or even more. Like some other Batrachians, it can be tempted to take pieces of meat when moved before it at the end of a wire. *H. arborea* spawns from April to June, and for this purpose it leaves the trees where it chiefly dwells and takes to the water. It will spawn in captivity if it be placed in a Vivarium which possesses a large tank, well sheltered by growing plants. During the breeding season the water should not be changed if the Frogs are wished to deposit spawn. When the eggs have been extruded they should be carefully removed from the tank and placed, as already suggested, in some other vessel—a shallow one—containing soft water of the same temperature as that from which they have been taken.

During the winter these Frogs should be allowed to retire under some damp moss or pieces of cork bark. When the weather is unusually mild and bright, for that season, they will sometimes leave their hiding-places and take cockroaches, mealworms, and other small creatures which then can be procured.

These Frogs used to cost as much as 5s. each at Covent Garden Market, and now they can be bought there, I believe, at any season of the year at about 9d., or even 6d. each.

Of *H. arborea*, the tongue is almost circular, slightly nicked, and free behind; the snout is rounded, and the head is broader than long; the tympanum is distinct, and about half the size of the eye; the fingers are webbed at their base, and the toes for about two-thirds of their length; the disks are smaller than the tympanum; there is an ankle fold. The skin of this Frog is smooth above and granulated below. As a rule, the upper parts of the body are green, and the lower parts a uniform white.

The male may be known from the female by a large brown subgular vocal sac. This Batrachian is about $1\frac{1}{2}$in. long. It is a native of Europe, the temperate parts of Asia, and of North Africa. There are, owing to a difference of markings, which chiefly take the form of darkish streaks and bands, four or five varieties of this Frog.

The Leaf-green Tree-Frog (*Hyla phyllochroa*) is a very beautiful Batrachian, and a native of Eastern Australia. It is a smaller animal than *H. arborea*, but it has very similar habits. This Frog, lately introduced into England in some considerable numbers, has been sold here for so low a sum as 5s. It becomes very lively towards the evening, but during the daytime it is generally quite ready to leave its retreat on the leaf of a plant, or under a piece of cork, when some insect is placed in its Vivarium.

This Frog has an almost circular tongue, slightly nicked, and free behind; a short, broad head; the vomerine teeth placed in two small groups behind the level of the inner nostrils; a tympanum much smaller than the eye; fingers webbed at their base, and toes webbed for three-quarters of their length; there is a fold on the ankle and another on the chest. The upper parts of the body are smooth and the lower granulate. The colour above is a uniform green and below a uniform white. A very narrow black line runs from the eye, above the tympanum, and disappears at a short distance from the shoulder.

White's Tree-Frog (*Hyla cærulea*) is a large, handsome species, and a native of Australia. It is now frequently imported into this country, where it can be bought, when in the market, for 6s. or 7s. It soon grows tame. This Batrachian seems to prefer bluebottle flies for food to any other insect. It will, however, eat mealworms, young mice, and (though very rarely) cockroaches. During the daytime it is generally at rest upon some leaf, but towards evening it becomes very lively, and often very noisy, making a grunting kind of croak. *H. cærulea* has a round tongue, free and slightly notched behind; a head broader than long, and a rounded snout; a large, full eye; a very distinct tympanum, nearly as large as the eye; fingers which are webbed for one-third of their length, and toes which are webbed almost entirely; the disks at the extremities of the fingers and toes about as large as the tympanum; a slight ankle fold; and comparatively short hind limbs, showing that the animal is not so great a jumper as most of its genus; the upper parts of the body are smooth, while the lower are granulated. In full-grown specimens the parotoid glands are well developed. The colour is bluish-green above, and whitish underneath. The shade of colour, however, varies a good deal according to whether the creature's position is in the light or dark, damp or dry. During the breeding season there are some brown rugosities on the inner side of the first finger. There are two varieties of this Frog, which are distinguished by the presence or absence of spots and streaks. *H. cærulea* is sometimes nearly 4½in. in length from the snout to the vent.

Peron's Tree-Frog (*Hyla peronii*) is chiefly remarkable because of the change of its colours. Dr. Günther ("Proc. Zool. Soc., 1863," p. 250) describes this change in the following words: "When awake it is brownish-olive, covered all over with blackish-brown spots, between which small green dots are scattered; the anterior and posterior sides of the thigh and loin are bright yellow, with irregular reticulated black spots. The pupil is open, horizontally elliptic, and crossed by a very distinct blackish vertical band. When asleep the dark spots disappear entirely, the ground-colour becomes lighter . . . the green dots are very indistinct, and the numerous tubercles with which the skin is covered are whitish at the top. The pupil is contracted in a minute square opening, from which four black lines radiate."

This Frog is very active and able to jump long distances. It has lately been brought into England in some numbers, and, when in the market, may be bought for a few shillings. In size it is a little larger than the European Tree-Frog (*H. arborea*), and may be associated with it in the same case, and treated in a like manner. It is a native of New South Wales and Tasmania.

Of *H. peronii*, the upper surfaces are tuberculate, and the lower granulate; there is a fold from the eye to the shoulder, another across the chest, and a third on the ankle. The male has an internal subgular vocal sac, and is provided, during the breeding season, with brown roughnesses on the inner side of the first finger.

Ewing's Tree-Frog (*Hyla ewingii*) has been lately sold in England for so low a sum as 5s. each. It is a native of New South Wales and Tasmania. It is a smaller Batrachian than the European Tree-Frog (*H. arborea*) and may be treated while in confinement in the same way.

H. ewingii has a heart-shaped tongue which is free behind; a moderately sized head, a little broader than it is long; a rounded snout and a distinct tympanum, about half the size of the eye; fingers with only the signs of a web, and toes webbed for about two-thirds of their length; the disks of both the fingers and toes smaller in size than the tympanum; and a fold on the ankle. The upper surfaces of this Batrachian's body are either smooth or covered with small tubercles; the lower parts are granulated. According to Mr. Boulenger the colour of *H. ewingii* is as follows: " Brownish or greyish above; a dark streak on the canthus rostralis and the temporal region; below this, a whitish streak runs from below the eye to the shoulder; a large well-defined dark spot commences between the eyes and covers the middle of the back; besides, the head and back are often speckled all over with blackish; the lower surfaces are whitish, immaculate." The male has an external subgular vocal sac, and during the breeding season the black roughnesses before spoken of.

Krefft's Tree-Frog (*Hyla krefftii*) is very like *H. ewingii*, but chiefly differs from it by the greater webbing of the fingers and toes. It is also rather larger than its near relative. This Frog is marked on the upper parts of its body with a broad brown band, which commences between the eyes, runs along the back, and terminates at the vent. There is also another brown mark which runs from the eye to the shoulder, the sides are a light olive, covered with very small dark brown spots. This Frog has also lately been brought into England and sold for a few shillings. It is a native of New South Wales.

The Yellow-foot Tree-Frog (*Hyla citropus*) is a pretty little Australian species, being about 2¼in. in length from the snout to the vent. In shape it is very like the two Batrachians described last, but it has no webbing between the fingers, and the toes are only half webbed. The disks are smaller than the tympanum, which is distinct. The skin is generally smooth above and granulated underneath. There is a fold from the eye to the shoulder, and there is also another on the ankle. Its colour above is purplish, and there is a black, light-edged streak along the sides of the body. The lower parts are a yellowish-white, without spots. There is a dark streak on the snout.

The Common Golden Tree-Frog (*Hyla aurea*) is a most beautiful little creature, and one which is sure to become a great favourite of those who keep it. Personally, there is no Batrachian which I admire more than this. It is very hardy, a good feeder, and is readily tamed. Frequently, it may be bought in England for a few shillings. I believe quantities of these beautiful Frogs were brought into this country in 1895.

The Golden Tree-Frog is very widely distributed in Australia, and is there one of the commonest of Batrachians. It is said that the natives catch these creatures for food, obtaining them, as the French and Chinese peasants procure their Frogs, by means of a lighted torch. This Tree-Frog, unlike *H. cærulea*, will eagerly eat almost any number of cockroaches, and seems to suffer no ill effects therefrom. It may be associated with other Tree-Frogs of similar size and habits.

In shape *H. aurea* has a close resemblance to the common English Frog (*Rana temporaria*). The tympanum is very distinct, and nearly as large as the eye ; the fingers are free, and the toes almost entirely webbed. The disks are comparatively small. There is an ankle fold. The skin is either smooth or warty above, and granulate below. The colour above is bluish or olive, spotted with blue or brown. There is often a golden band on each side of the back, and occasionally there is also a vertebral band of the same beautiful colour. The lower parts are a bluish white. The male has two internal vocal sacs, and during the breeding season is distinguished from the female by the possession of brown roughnesses on the inner side of the first finger. This Tree-frog is about 4in. long from snout to vent. When in the market, it may be bought for from 3s. 6d. to 7s.

CHAPTER XII.

TOAD-FROGS AND DISC-TONGUED FROGS.

THE Brown Mud Frog (*Pelobates fuscus*) is a member of the family *Pelobatidæ*, or Toad-Frogs, Batrachians which are in some respects like Toads, and in others similar to Frogs. The genus *Pelobates* numbers only two species, both of which are natives of Europe, but are not found in Britain. They have neither tympanums nor vocal sacs. Their bodies are smooth, their fingers free, and their toes are very fully webbed, but are unprovided with disks. As a rule these Toad-Frogs only enter the water during the breeding season, and their eggs, like those of the Common Toad, are deposited in strings, which the male is said to take from the female and wind round the aquatic plants growing at the water's edge. The tadpoles appear in about a week, and, though the hatching of the eggs is rapid, the animals spend a comparatively long time in their tadpole-hood—from four to five months. These Toad-Frogs have a curious means of defence. For example, when they are seized or handled roughly, they make a cry like the mewing of a small kitten, and at the same time emit an odour similar to that of garlic, sometimes so powerful as to affect the eyes.

These Batrachians are great burrowers, being assisted in their labours of excavation by the formation of their feet. They seem to prefer a sandy soil. They generally leave an opening to their burrows, and seem careful to make them so deep that the rays of the sun cannot reach them while they are in these places of retirement.

P. fuscus has an eye with an erect pupil; a circular tongue, slightly nicked and free behind; vomerine teeth (unlike a true Toad); a horny tubercle beneath the fifth toe, which forms a kind of shovel-shaped spur. The colour of the animal above is brown, marbled with dark brown, and the spur is yellowish-brown. On the upper surface of the fore-leg or arm of the male there is a large oval-shaped gland which is pierced by many small holes. There are no parotoid glands.

This Batrachian, when fully grown, is from the snout to the vent about 4in. in length, and, while in captivity, may be associated with other Frogs and Toads of its size. Opportunity should be given it of making its burrow. The croak or cry of *P. fuscus* has no little resemblance to that of the Edible Frog (*Rana esculenta*). The Brown Mud Frog is occasionally brought to England, where, when in the market, it may be bought for from 6d. to 2s. There are generally specimens of this animal at the Reptile House, Regent's Park, London.

P. cultripes, the only other member of the genus, is chiefly distinguished by the flatness of its head and the deep blackness of its metatarsal spur. It is found in the South of France, and in Spain and Portugal.

The Painted Frog (*Discoglossus pictus*) is a typical representative of the family *Discoglossidæ*, or the Disc-tongued Frogs. It is the only species of its genus. The tadpoles of this Frog are distinguished by having the spiraculum, or breathing aperture, situated in the middle of the thoracic region, while in all the tadpoles of the rest of the *Phaneroglossa*, or tongued tailless Batrachia, it is placed on the left side.

The Painted Frog has a very depressed body; an outline which is almost oval; vomerine teeth in almost a straight line across the palate, behind the inner opening of the nostrils; a tympanum either hidden or partially visible; a circular tongue, without nick, and only free at its hinder margin; the fingers free, the toes of the males fully webbed, while those of the female only webbed at their base, no discs; a rather prominent snout; and three tubercles (the inner, in the males, much developed) on the palm of the hands. The upper surfaces of the body are either smooth or covered with small tubercles. The colour above is brownish or olive, marbled with black or brown light-edged spots, and sometimes there are three white stripes running along the back; the legs have transverse bands of brown or black; on the head there is a triangular mark, occasionally divided. The lower parts are either white or yellowish. The male has no vocal sac, but during the breeding season it is distinguished by the possession

FIG. 86.—THE FIRE-BELLIED TOAD (*Bombinator igneus* .

of small, rough, closely-set, dark brown roughnesses on the chin, on the palms, the inner digits, and on the free margin of the webbing of the toes. This Batrachian is a native of S. Europe and N.W. Africa. When fully grown it measures about 2½in· from the snout to the vent. *D. pictus* is sometimes brought to England and sold for a few shillings. In its native country it is found in small streams, and in salt and fresh-water marshes, frequently in the company of the Edible Frog (*R. esculenta*).

The Fire-bellied Toad (*Bombinator igneus*), Fig. 86. is also a member of the *Discoglossidæ*. Though the English name of this Batrachian is not very euphonious, the creature itself is very interesting. It is extremely hardy, and soon becomes perfectly tame. *B. igneus* is now brought into England in considerable numbers, and may be generally bought for sums ranging from 6d. to 1s. 6d. each. It will eat worms, flies, slugs, tadpoles, and mealworms greedily. It is also fond of spending its time in water, keeping only its eyes and nostrils above the surface, ready at the slightest sign of danger to dive below. Its movements on land are unusually clumsy. Lord Clermont says that this Batrachian, "when frightened and unable to escape, raises its legs towards its head, throwing the latter back in a ridiculous manner, and squirting from the vent a frothy acrid fluid." Though I have kept these frogs for several years, I have never noticed this habit of which the author speaks. *B. igneus* spawns during May and June, and its tadpoles are remarkable for their size in comparison with that of their parents, and also for the development of their tail-fin. I believe that the Fire-bellied Toad would breed in captivity if provided with a large tank. It is a native of Europe and Asia, but it is not found at liberty in Britain.

B. igneus has an eye with a triangular pupil; a tongue which is circular, entire, and adherent to the bottom of the mouth; vomerine teeth; no tympanum; a stout build, a short, rounded snout; the fingers free, the toes webbed, and no discs. The upper parts of the body are covered with warts of different sizes; the lower parts are smooth, or nearly so. The colour above is olive, pleasingly marbled with black, or uniform; below it is a rich orange colour, marbled with black. The male has no vocal sac, but it is provided during the breeding season with black rugosities on the inner side of the forearm, the inner metacarpal tubercle, and the two inner fingers.

There is a variety of *B. igneus*, or perhaps it may be a distinct species altogether, known as the Yellow-bellied Toad (*B. bombinus*), which is yellow below, marbled with black. This Batrachian is said to be found at higher elevations than is its near relative *B. igneus*. Both the varieties or species are easily purchased in London during the spring and summer months.

The Midwife Frog (*Alytes obstetricans*) has received its very extraordinary name because of the strange conduct of the male during the breeding season, who, at that time, takes charge of the eggs as they are deposited in strings by the female, and winds them round his own legs, where, owing to a glutinous secretion, they firmly adhere. He then retires to a rather deep burrow made by himself, or to some convenient hole in the bank near the water's edge, in which he spends all, or nearly all, his time until the eggs are just on the point of being hatched. When the eyes of the larvæ can be seen through their envelope, the parent Frog enters the water and immediately the tadpoles break their surroundings and swim away. The eggs are about as large as grains of sago. Midwife Frogs are sometimes brought to this country with the spawn still attached to their thighs. One female will deposit as many as sixty or more eggs.

This Batrachian is also known as the Bell Frog, owing to its curious croak, which has some resemblance to the sound made by a small bell.

The Midwife Frog is chiefly distinguished from the Fire-bellied Toad by a distinct tympanum and an eye having an erect pupil.

A. obstetricans has a circular tongue, not nicked, and hardly free behind; a row of vomerine teeth placed in a straight but interrupted line behind the inner opening of the nostrils; a flat head, with a rounded snout; a stout body; three metacarpal tubercles; and short toes, webbed at their base and fringed. The upper surfaces of the body are covered with small warts. There is a small parotoid gland. The under parts are granular. The colour above is grey or olive spotted with darker shades of the same colour. White underneath. The male has no vocal sac. This Batrachian, which from the snout to the vent is about 1½in. long, is a native of France, Switzerland, Belgium, and the western parts of Germany. It may occasionally be bought in England for 3s. or 4s.

There is a variety of the Frog, found in Spain and Portugal, which is known as *A. boscæ*. It is recognised by its larger head, and the greater and more distinct spots on the upper parts of its body.

2 A

CHAPTER XIII.

TONGUELESS FROGS.

THE Smooth Spur-toed Frog (*Xenopus lævis*) is a member of the sub-order *Aglossa*, or Tongueless Frogs. This sub-order numbers only two families and four species altogether.

Though the Smooth-clawed Frog is almost entirely aquatic, it is a suitable inmate of a properly-constructed Vivarium, as it is hardy, easily fed, and will breed freely while in captivity. It soon becomes tame. Unlike other Frogs, it will readily eat pieces of raw meat, after which it will dive, and seize them with its slender and sharply-pointed fingers. During the months of July and August it deposits its large eggs singly among the aquatic plants.

The tadpole comes into the world without external gills, but is provided with two spiracula, one on each side of the body, and in about three days after its birth develops a pair of long barbels, one at either corner of the mouth. The tadpole is very large in comparison to the size of its parent.

As soon as the eggs have been deposited, they should be removed to an aquarium containing water of the same temperature as that of the tank from which they have been taken. Neither the eggs nor the tadpoles would be safe in the company of the old Frogs.

The Smooth Spur-toed Frog (*X. lævis*), which measures 2in. from snout to vent, is found from Abyssinia to the Cape of Good Hope. It has a small head, an eye with round pupil, teeth in the upper jaw, a smooth palate, and a short, rounded snout ;. no tympanum ; free fingers, and toes which are broadly webbed, the first three inner ones being furnished with a sharp spur-like nail; the nostrils, as well as the small eyes, pointing upwards; the skin smooth and marked round the body with more or less distinct tube-like lines. The colour above is dark brown, and below white, either immaculate or spotted with brown. The females are distinguished by the possession of three flaps which close the vent.

The Surinam Toad (*Pipa Americana*) is chiefly famous because of its extraordinary manner of reproduction. It is the only representative of its family (*Pipidæ*). Marie Sibille Merian was one of the first to describe this strange Batrachian. This lady wrote a book, which was published in 1726, on the "Insects of Surinam," and in it she speaks of *P. Americana*. The Toad is a native of the forests of the Guianas and Brazil. About two years ago some specimens of this creature were brought to England, and were exhibited at the Reptile House, Regent's Park, London, where they excited a great deal of interest. There I saw them, and learnt what I could concerning them. It is hardly necessary to say that I have never been the fortunate possessor of a Surinam Toad; but as this animal is so curious in its habits, so extraordinary in its appearance, and will probably be imported into this country from time to time, a short description of it here will not be, I hope, out of place.

At the commencement of the breeding season the skin of the back of the female Surinam Toad becomes very soft and very thick. She deposits her eggs singly in the water, and then the male, it is supposed, takes them one by one and embeds them in this softened skin, which presently covers them, and so each egg is enclosed, as it were, in a separate cell, where they remain until the metamorphosis is completed.

The eggs are said to number from sixty to 120. In about eighty-two days, from the time the egg was laid, the little *Pipa*, perfectly formed like its parent, leaves its cell, having first protruded either a limb or its head.

When the female has got all her family out in the world, she frees herself of the superficial layer of her skin by rubbing it off against stones or aquatic plants. Nevertheless, little pits are still left to mark the positions occupied by the cells.

The Surinam Toad while in captivity in this country should be kept in a large tank filled with warm water, and containing suitable aquatic weed. These Toads, helped by their colour, are very clever at hiding themselves. It is, therefore, by no means an easy matter, very often, to find them in their Vivarium. Owing to the fully-developed webbing of their toes they are fast swimmers.

The Surinam Toad has a flat, triangular head, a very small eye with round pupil, one or two short tentacles on the upper lip, in front of the eye; no teeth, a smooth palate, no tympanum, a large flap of skin at each angle of the mouth, and sometimes another at the end of the snout; very slender, free fingers of unequal lengths, each ending with four radiating appendages; toes very fully webbed, and devoid of nails; the skin is covered with small tubercles. The colour of the animal above is olive-brown, and below a lighter shade of the same colour, sometimes spotted with white, and sometimes there is a black stripe along the middle of the belly.

It is said that the natives of the countries in which this strange Toad is found are accustomed to eat it, and to say that its flesh is very good. Though it is, when fully grown, of large size, I cannot believe that some authorities are correct in asserting that it "sometimes grows to a length of nearly 1ft."

Besides the Frogs and Toads already described in these articles there are many others which no doubt would be equally interesting and suitable for confinement in the Vivarium, but which are not so easily procured in this country as those mentioned. Therefore, because of their rarity here, nothing has been said, for instance, of the Bornean Flying Frog (*Rhacophorus pardalis*), a Batrachian which is reported to have the power, owing to the great development of the webbing of both feet and toes, of sailing or gliding through the air from the top of a lofty tree to the ground. Or of the short-headed Frogs of the family *Breviceps*, animals which are able to puff out their bodies to such an extent as to resemble india-rubber balls rather than Frogs at all. Or, except the briefest reference, of the Marsupial Frog (*Nototrema marsupiatum*) from Ecuador, a creature which is provided with a pouch on its back, into which the male is supposed to place the ova as soon as they are deposited by the female, and where they remain until they are hatched.

CHAPTER XIV.

SALAMANDERS.

THE order *Caudata* (*Urodela*), or the Tailed Batrachians, includes such animals as Salamanders and Newts, which are chiefly distinguished from Frogs and Toads by their elongated body, and by the retention of the tail throughout their life. Generally, these creatures possess four legs, but sometimes the hind pair is wanting. Like the members of the order *Ecaudata*, or Tailless Batrachians, they undergo a metamorphosis, though not so complete a one. Some never lose their external gills at all.

Most of the *Caudata* during a portion of their lives are inhabitants of the water. Some live in it altogether, others, when mature, only visit it during the breeding season. The *Caudata* are chiefly nocturnal in their habits, spending the daytime under stones, among aquatic weeds, in holes, or in crevices in trees and in rocks. When not in the water they frequent damp situations. As a rule, they all shun the direct rays of the sun. Most of them, more or less, under certain circumstances, exhibit wonderful tenacity of life. They are able to survive desiccation in parched mud or being frozen in blocks of ice, reviving in the one case after sufficient rain, and in the other after gradual heat. They have also the capability of reproducing lost limbs. This I have more than once witnessed. It is also recorded that certain will even replace a lost head. This feat I have not witnessed, and do not expect I ever shall.

These Batrachians are very interesting, and owing to the manner of their life and consequent difficulties of observation, a great deal still remains to be learnt concerning their habits. Most of them undergo their metamorphosis after they have left the egg, *e.g.*, the Common Newt (*Molge vulgaris*), but others complete the process before their existence is separated from that of the parent, *e.g.*, the Black Salamander (*Salamandra atra*). A few break the envelope of the egg in which they have been confined directly the egg has been deposited, *e.g.*, the Spotted Salamander (*S. maculosa*). Some die if born in the water, *e.g.*, *S. atra*, and others die if born on the land, *e.g.*, *S. maculosa*. The tadpoles of all the species have a great resemblance to each other, and unlike those of Frogs and Toads produce the fore limbs before they produce the hind ones.

The *Caudata* number about 120 species. Since they are found in the Northern Hemisphere—for example, in Europe, temperate Asia, North Africa, and North and Central America—and are altogether absent from the Southern Hemisphere, their geographical distribution is certainly curious and interesting. They are divided into the four following families: (1) *Salamandridæ*, (2) *Amphiumidæ*, (3) *Proteidæ*, and (4) *Sirenidæ*.

The Spotted Salamander (*Salamandra maculosa*, Fig. 87) is very common over nearly the whole of Europe and in Northern Africa. I have often heard people who have been looking at my specimens of this species exclaim, " Oh ! isn't that the beast which can pass unharmed through fire, and even put it out," or similar words. Poor thing ! it can do nothing of the kind. I should imagine that few animals could dread the fire more. The heat of one's hands seems to distress this Batrachian.

The fable concerning the Salamander's power over fire is a very old one indeed. Pliny, the elder, who died in A.D. 79, says in his famous Natural History, that he tested the animal's supposed capability, and found that the creature was soon burnt to powder when thrown into a fire. And yet the fable still lives and is believed in ! It is reported that François I. of France adopted " a lizard in the midst of flames " as his badge, with the inscription '

"*Nutrisco et extinguo*" (I nourish, and I extinguish). The idea of this creature's influence over flames may have risen from the seemingly remarkable chilliness of its body when taken in the hands. The derivation of the very old word *Salamandra* (Greek) is uncertain. For many centuries the animal was considered to be a lizard. And even now, if one looks out the above word in his Greek Lexicon he will find "a kind of lizard, supposed to put out fire."

The Spotted Salamander has most attractive and popular colouring, being of a bright rich yellow, and a perfectly jet-black. Its association with history, its hardiness, gentleness, and readi

FIG. 87.—THE SPOTTED SALAMANDER (*Salamandra maculosa*).

ness to breed while in captivity, altogether make it an interesting animal, and very suitable for confinement in a Vivarium.

The Batrachian is ovo-viviparous; that is, as the egg is deposited by the female, its envelope breaks and the young tadpole becomes free. The tadpole has no little resemblance to that of the Common Triton and other members of the same family.

When Spotted Salamanders seem about to produce young, they should have easy access to some shallow soft water. If the young of this species are brought forth on land, they are sure to die; at least, such has been my own experience.

The Spotted Salamander is most prolific, and I have found that it will give birth to from nineteen to twenty-nine at one time; that is, in the course of about six hours. The young should at once be removed to a suitable vessel containing clean soft water, or the old ones will be tempted to devour their offspring. They must not be crowded, for under such a condition they have a tendency, in their eagerness to feed, to seize each other's limbs, and even to eat one another.

With a little care, the Tadpoles easily accomplish their metamorphosis. The growth of the small Salamanders to maturity is very interesting to watch. The young creatures do not assume the beautiful colouring of their parents until they have attained the mature form. If the animals are properly cared for, they arrive at their full size when they are about three years old.

The Tadpoles, at first, are about 1in. long, of a brownish colour, covered with darker spots. They then require very minute food, which should consist of the tiny freshwater crustaceans, known as *Entomostraca*, or "shelled insects," such as water-fleas and the like. These small animals can generally be procured very easily, as they may be found at the time the young Salamanders are produced, in almost any soft water—cask, tank, pool, pond, or slowly-running stream.

FIG. 88.—A CONTRIVANCE FOR PROCURING ENTOMOSTRACA.

Fig. 88 represents a very simple arrangement by which these small and useful inhabitants of fresh water may be procured in great numbers without difficulty. The contrivance, as may be seen from the illustration, consists of a large glass vessel (tin will do, but then the captures cannot be so easily observed), a funnel, covered with fine muslin, attached to a piece of slender indiarubber tubing, which is used as a siphon. The muslin is of course to prevent the small crustaceans from passing up the siphon. This arrangement of vessel and funnel is carried to some water (either in cask, pond, or stream), which is seen to contain *Entomostraca*. The water holding these creatures is then ladled into the vessel, and when the latter is full, the siphon is set running. It will readily be seen that as the water flows out of the bottle, it leaves the water-fleas and their relatives behind. When the water has thus been kept running for, say a quarter-of-an-hour, a great number of small crustaceans will be found in the vessel, sufficient to last many young Salamanders several days. The vessel, deprived of the siphon, may be kept near the tadpoles—and as they need food a small quantity of the water in the vessel, which is now alive with innumerable crustaceans, is emptied carefully into the dish or tray containing the tadpoles. As the little Batrachians grow they will eat tiny pieces of meat or small garden worms.

The fore-legs of the tadpoles will be produced first, then the hind ones, and lastly, the external gills are absorbed. When it is seen that the young Salamanders are assuming the adult form, the vessel in which they are confined should be so arranged that they can leave the water. It must, however, have a perforated cover of some kind, or the young Salamanders will be certain to escape. At this age, like young Frogs and Toads, they are wonderful climbers.

As soon as the Salamanders cease to be purely aquatic animals they will eat nothing but live food, such as garden worms, slugs, mealworms, cockroaches, and woodlice. Their metamorphosis is accomplished in from three to five months, according to the quantity and suitability of their food, and to the care which has been bestowed upon them.

It is wise to keep the young Salamanders in a Vivarium by themselves until they are nearly fully grown; for these creatures are prone to act the part of cannibals. The Vivarium for Salamanders should be out of the reach of the rays of the sun, and it ought to contain an easily accessible vessel holding a shallow quantity of soft water, some growing plants, such as ferns, *Tradescantia*, and the like, and pieces of cork, stones, or tiles under which the Batrachians can hide.

The Salamanders, like toads, have a bitter, and, to a certain extent, poisonous secretion which acts as a means of defence against the attacks of carnivorous animals.

Spotted Salamanders would live at liberty in England. Specimens of my own have from time to time escaped, and have been found again, after various intervals of time, in perfect condition and health. One animal I know had had freedom for at least two years.

The Spotted Salamander, like all the members of its sub-family (*Salamandrinæ*), has no gills in its adult condition; but teeth on the palate, as well as in both the upper and lower jaws; and eyelids. Like the rest of its genus the Batrachian possesses a large sub-oval tongue, free at its edges, and partially free behind, and four toes on each fore-foot, and five on each hind foot, unprovided with webbing. Besides, *S. maculosa* may be described as having a flat, broad head, a rounded snout, large prominent eyes, a stout, flattish body, stout limbs and no crest, a sub-cylindrical tail nearly as long as the body, a skin smooth and polished-looking, pores on the upper parts of the body, large parotoids, a series of larger pores along the back, and large warts along the sides. The length of the animal when fully grown, including the tail, is from 7in. to 9in. The female is generally larger than the male.

These creatures may be purchased in London, at almost any season, for from 9d. to 1s. 6d.

The Black or Alpine Salamander (*Salamandra atra*), is a native of the Alps at a height of 2,500ft. to 10,000ft. It is found therefore near the limits of perpetual snow. In shape it much resembles the Spotted Salamander (Fig. 86), but it is smaller in size and perfectly black in colour.

The Black Salamander is a terrestrial Batrachian, and only enters the water for a few hours during the breeding season. The young are born fully developed. Though many eggs may be found in the oviducts of the females, never more than two young ones are produced at a time. The tadpoles feed upon the unfertile eggs and complete their metamorphoses within the body of the parent. Their gills at a certain part of their existence before their birth are very large indeed—about equalling in length half of that of their body. These in course of time are absorbed.

Mlle. Marie de Chauvin made some interesting experiments upon the Black Salamander. She took some young tadpoles, before they had completed their metamorphoses, from the body of their parents and placed them in water in order that she might watch their gradual development. In one instance only was she rewarded for her trouble and enterprise. This particular tadpole lived for fifteen weeks at the bottom of the water, and then its gills atrophied, its tail and skin altered, it shed its skin, and the animal left the water, having thus in this way attained the adult form.

Young Black Salamanders, I have found, may be easily reared upon small slugs and tiny garden worms. They should be kept in a small Vivarium by themselves, the bottom of which ought to be covered with damp mould. There must also be a very shallow vessel containing some soft water. A few pieces of a broken flower-pot will provide the little Batrachians with suitable hiding-places. Slugs' eggs placed in the Vivarium will, in course of time, supply the young Salamanders with plenty of the right kind and size of food.

Young Black Salamanders grow very quickly; sometimes, in a little over a year, if well fed, they will attain their full size. When in the market, they may be bought at prices ranging from 2s. to 4s.

In *S. atra* the parotoids and lateral glands are more developed than in *S. maculosa*, and the body is not quite so stout or so long. In other respects, with the exception of the colour, the animals are identical.

The Caucasian Salamander (*Salamandra caucasica*) is rarer than either the Spotted or the Black Salamander, from which it is chiefly distinguished by the tail being much longer than the head and body. It may be treated, while in confinement, in the same way as has been suggested for its near relatives just mentioned, and associated with them.

S. caucasica has a depressed head, rather longer than broad, a rounded snout, and large, prominent eyes, a long body with weak limbs, fingers and toes which are free, a smooth skin, parotoids which are distinct and elliptical in shape, no warts on the sides. The colour of the animal above is black marked with round yellow spots arranged in two longitudinal rows. The under parts are black, slightly speckled with grey. The entire length of this Batrachian is about 7in. It is a native of the Caucasus.

The Spanish Salamander (*Chioglossa lusitanica*) is the only representative of its genus which is distinguished from the genus *Salamandra*, according to M. Boulenger, by a large oval tongue, "supported by a protractile median pedicle," and is consequently free everywhere "except on the anterior half of the median line." The members of this genus possess a tail which is cylindrical at its base and compressed at its end.

The Spanish Salamander is a rarer animal than either *S. maculosa* or *S. atra*, but when obtained it may be kept in the same Vivarium as the three members of the genus *Salamandra*.

C. lusitanica, which is a native of the north-western parts of Spain and Portugal, has a depressed head, longer than broad, its greatest width being just behind the eyes, which are large and prominent; a slender body and weak limbs; fingers and toes which are fairly long and free; a tail which is very long, sometimes twice as long as the head and body; a skin which is smooth and shining; a fold of skin across the throat, which extends from parotoid to parotoid; like the other Salamanders, vertical grooves on the sides of the body, also vertical grooves on the sides of the tail. The colour of the animal above is dark brown, marked by two golden-reddish bands along each of the back and tail. The lower parts are of a lighter uniform brown. The Spanish Salamander, when fully grown, is about 6in. long from the snout to the end of the tail.

The Spectacled Salamander (*Salamandrina perspicillata*) is a tiny Batrachian, and almost as active as a small lizard. It is the only representative of its genus, and a native of Italy. Its chief distinctive features are slenderness of form, a large tongue free behind, a strong bony fronto-squamosal arch to the skull, and four toes on each foot. In Italy this pretty little creature is commonly called the Tarantolina. It is found on all the Tuscan Appennines, and perhaps throughout the whole range. It also inhabits other mountains of Italy, and it is reported to have been taken on Mount Vesuvius.

This lively little Salamander is generally active for the greater part of the year, and, like other Salamanders, prefers shade to sunshine. It feeds upon ants, spiders, and small worms. While in captivity, the Tarantolina should be confined in a Vivarium with no other associates but those of its own species. If properly tended it will live for a long time. It should be provided with a very shallow vessel containing soft water; and some moss, stones, and pieces of cork, under which it can hide, and over which it will like to climb.

This Batrachian is said to pair upon the land, and then afterwards to retire to some shallow and sheltered place in the water for the purpose of depositing its eggs. The young are supposed to be hatched in about three weeks, and to leave the water in June and July. Probably the Spectacled Salamander only enters the water at the breeding-season. I once, however, found, in the winter, a specimen of my own drowned in the very shallow water to which it always had access.

S. perspicillata has a long head, very distinct from the neck; a short and rounded snout; large and prominent eyes; the ribs and vertebræ showing distinctly through the skin; a tail much longer than the head and body, slender, slightly compressed, and keeled above and below; the skin tuberculated; no parotoids, and no fold on the throat. The upper surfaces of this animal's body are black; on the head there is a yellow triangular or horse-shoe like marking, the point of which is directed backwards between the eyes, hence the specific name; the throat is black and the chin white. The lower parts are whitish, marked, usually, with black spots. The lower half of the tail and the anal region are of a blood-red colour. The entire length of this Salamander, when fully grown, is about four inches. Healthy specimens may occasionally be bought in London at prices which range from 3s. to 7s. 6d.

No Salamander is a native of Great Britain.

CHAPTER XV.

NEWTS.

THE most apparent difference between Newts and Salamanders is that the former possess a compressed or rudder-like tail, while that of the latter is sub-cylindrical. The males of many of the Newts, during the breeding season, are distinguished by well-developed dorsal and caudal crests.

Comparatively recently Newts have received the generic name of *Molge*, a Greek word meaning *slow*. The animals seem well deserving of this title, because they are slow both in their movements on land and in their development.

Newts are hardy, intelligent (*i.e.*, for Batrachians), easily fed, and interesting. They are therefore very suitable inmates of a Vivarium. They are natives of Europe, Asia, and North America. Three species of them are the only members of their family (*Salamandridæ*) which are found in Great Britain. These three species are the Great Crested Newt (*Molge cristata*), the Common or Smooth Newt (*M. vulgaris*), and the Webbed or Palmate Newt (*M. palmata*). The genus *Molge* numbers altogether about nineteen species.

During spring-time Newts may be found in almost any pond, pool, lake, or slowly-running river, and as they are obliged to come to the surface of the water periodically for air, a few minutes' watching will generally be sufficient to discover whether any particular portion of water is inhabited by them or not, and when seen ascending to breathe, they can be caught by means of a hand-net, which, generally, may easily be placed under them as they begin to descend. When a worm is used as a means of capture it should, tied to a string, be allowed to sink to the bottom of the water, and a movement of the string from below will show that a Newt has commenced to attack the worm. Then, before the Batrachian has had time to disgorge what it has swallowed, it may be quickly and gently landed on the bank.

Though Newts are usually caught in water, it will almost invariably be found that they make every attempt to leave that in which they are placed during their captivity. It is not kind, therefore, to keep them constantly in water. If put into an aquarium, they should always be provided with something like an island upon which they can land. Most of the Newts, as a rule, only enter the water during the breeding-season.

A Vivarium made like that represented by Fig. 13 is a very suitable dwelling-place for Newts, for, when confined in it, their graceful movements in the water may easily be seen, and also their curious and interesting methods of depositing their eggs. At the same time they are at liberty to leave the water and seek retirement on land whenever they feel inclined to do so. They cannot, though wonderful climbers, escape from this kind of Vivarium, which, if properly made and tended, is ornamental.

As the Newts come to the surface for fresh air, they frequently make a distinct " popping " sound. Sometimes they will float by extending their limbs at right angles to their bodies. They occasionally maintain such a position for hours.

Whatever their movements may be described as being on land, they are not slow nor ungraceful in the water. They swim quickly by the help of their powerful and compressed tail, carrying their limbs pressed closely backwards to the sides of their body. The manner of progression of a Newt in the water is therefore exactly the reverse of that of a Frog.

The breeding season of Newts generally extends from the end of April to the end of June. The eggs of these Batrachians are deposited singly and apparently with great care. The female seems to hunt about for the leaf of some water weed suited to her needs. Sometimes she is not contented to simply see, touch, and smell the leaf under her observation, but she must bend it, too, as if to test its pliancy. When she is satisfied that a particular leaf will answer her purpose, she backs towards it as if to sit on its edge, and then, holding it with her feet, folds it, and deposits an egg within the fold. Having accomplished this part of her task, she presses, sometimes with her mouth, the leaf gently to the egg, so that every part of the folded leaf adheres to the egg.

After a short period of rest the female Newt looks for another suitable leaf, and repeats the operation just described. She will generally choose for this purpose leaves of the following plants: The Canadian Water-Weed (*Anacharis alsinastrum*), the Starwort (*Callitriche verna*), the Water Speedwell (*Veronica anagallis*), and, in captivity, the Italian Water-Weed (*Vallisneria spiralis*). Sometimes the Newt will utilise, for the protection and hiding of her eggs, any blade of grass which may be dipping in the water.

Fig. 89 shows leaves of the Starwort folded round some Newts' eggs in different stages of development. The egg, at first very small, is surrounded with a glutinous envelope, in which it floats or rotates. As the embryo within the egg begins to grow, and becomes elongated, the leaf in which the egg is wrapped gradually unfolds. In the course of a few days, more or less, according to the temperature of the water, the embryo becomes folded upon itself, and the gills gradually appear on each side of the neck of the future Newt.

FIG. 89. — LEAVES OF VERNAL GREATER STARWORT ENFOLDING EGGS OF NEWT IN VARIOUS STAGES OF DEVELOPMENT.

The little tadpole, when first hatched, is so very slender and transparent that in even a small vessel it is no easy matter to find it; indeed, it would often escape observation altogether were it not for its brilliant eyes and its apparently aimless dartings from spot to spot. By means of claspers it can cling to almost any object against which it happens to strike during these short and rapid journeys. In from two to three weeks, according to circumstances, the claspers are absorbed, and are replaced by the forelimbs, which quickly develop. "At this time" (*f*, Fig. 90), says the late Mr. Thomas Bell in his "British Reptiles," "the branchiæ offer one of the most beautiful and elegant objects in nature, as well as one of the most interesting. Observed even

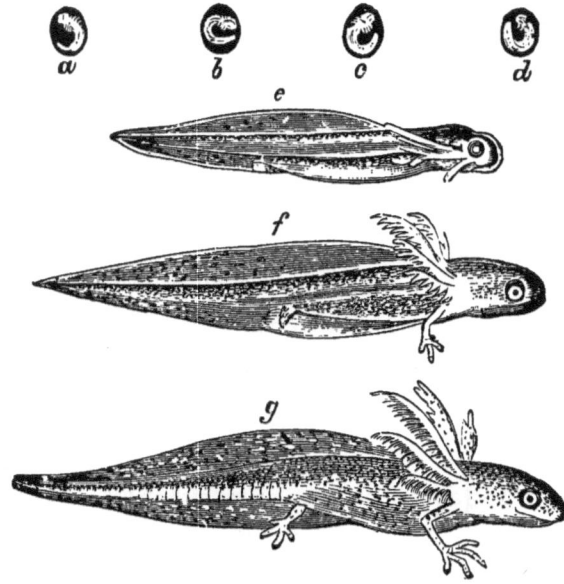

FIG. 90.—METAMORPHOSES OF THE NEWT.

with the naked eye, the leaf-like division of these organs presents a most pleasing subject of contemplation; but, viewed in the microscope, the branchial circulation excites the greatest delight and surprise."

A short time after the appearance of the hind limbs the gills begin to diminish in size, and the lungs begin to develop until by the end of the autumn, as a rule, the young Newt has attained the shape, but not the size, of its parents. It has then passed from the condition of a fish to that of a Batrachian.

When a young Newt has not, for some reason or other, completed its metamorphosis by the autumn, it spends the winter in the water, generally at the bottom, in the mud. As a rule, most of the Newts leave their aquatic life at the end of the breeding season, and find, for hiding and hibernation, such places as cavities under stones, small holes in banks, hollows in trees, and crevices in walls. A Newt may, therefore, be described as more of a terrestrial animal than an aquatic one.

At the commencement of the breeding season the males of many species assume very gaudy colours and a handsome crest, which, however, gradually disappear as the autumn advances, until, in the winter, these Batrachians once more bear a close resemblance to their females.

Several times during the year Newts shed their sloughs, which are cast either entire or in pieces. A complete slough is an interesting object, the portions which covered the feet or hands appearing like tiny gloves when filled with water. If such a slough be carefully lifted, at the end of a camel's-hair brush, from the water and placed upon a piece of white paper, it will adhere there and dry, leaving a mark, for such is the frailness and fineness of the skin, like a painting in sepia. The slough, as that of Snakes, begins to leave the animal at the mouth. Newts, sometimes, as Toads do, eat their discarded garments. Immediately before the cuticle is cast, the Batrachians are dull in colour and listless in movement, but quite the reverse is the case when the operation has been successfully performed.

Newts are intelligent enough to learn to know those who tend them, and soon become so tame as to feed from the hand. The most suitable food to give these creatures is worms, over which they will sometimes fight fiercely.

The Molge, however, is a cannibal, and ever ready to devour a diminutive brother in the form of a tadpole, or a smaller relative of another species. When Newts are kept in a Vivarium with Salamanders, Toads, and Frogs, it will be noticed that, like their comrades, they seek their food chiefly at night. They will, however, feed readily at any time during the aquatic periods of their lives.

There are many superstitions concerning the poisonous properties of these harmless creatures, country people often refusing to touch at any price what they call an ask or a water-effet. Some of these Batrachians, the Great Warty Newt (*M. cristata*), for instance, have the power of defending themselves, like Toads, against the attacks of carnivorous animals, by discharging from their skin an acrid and, in a certain sense, hurtful secretion.

The following quotation taken from an article by Mr. Higginbottom in "Annals and Magazine of Natural History," for 1853, p. 378, will show the great tenacity of life which these animals possess: "I put two Tritons into some water, and exposed them to a freezing temperature during the night; in the morning I found the water frozen firmly, with the Tritons enclosed in its centre. On thawing, they were lively and flexible. In the second experiment there was a piece of ice at the bottom of a circular vessel. I placed two Tritons upon it, and then another covering of ice, and filled the vessel with water. I exposed it during the night in the open air to a temperature of 28deg. Fahr. In the morning the whole had become a solid mass of ice 12in. in circumference, with the animals in the centre. On breaking the ice carefully, they were found completely encased in the ice. I had some difficulty in separating the extremity of one; but, being liberated, it used its arms and legs equally well."

A Newt (*Molge cristata*) of my own, attacked by a pike, lost one of its fore-limbs, and, within a few weeks after the accident, produced another arm and hand in all appearance similar to the one it had lost.

The Prince of Musignano says "that it is a wonderful circumstance, that an animal so tenacious of life should die with the most violent convulsions on having a little salt sprinkled upon it." The above quotation is taken from Mr. Bell's "British Reptiles," p. 131, second edition.

The Great Warty or Crested Newt (*Molge cristata*, Figs. 91 and 92) is one of the handsomest and largest of its genus, and from the rest of which it differs in the formation of its skull, having no fronto-squamosal arch. It is found in the ponds of many parts of Great Britain, but not everywhere. It is not nearly so common here as *Molge vulgaris*. The Great Warty Newt is also a native of France, Belgium, Holland, Switzerland,

Sweden, Denmark, Germany, Austria, Greece, Turkey, and parts of Russia. It feeds upon almost any aquatic animal smaller than itself.

This Newt has palatine teeth; a small, elliptical tongue, having its sides free; a rounded, convex snout; a rounded body, which,

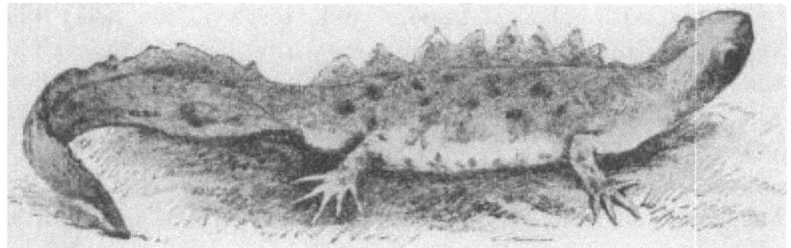

FIG. 91.—A MALE GREAT WARTY OR CRESTED NEWT (*Molge cristata*).

in the case of the male during the breeding season, is ornamented by a very deeply-toothed crest running along the back and tail (there is a considerable sinking in of the crest at the junction of the tail and body); the female, in place of a crest, has a longitudinal groove; the fingers (4) and toes (5) free; the tail about as long

FIG. 92.—A FEMALE GREAT WARTY OR CRESTED NEWT (*Molge cristata*).

as the head and body; a crest on the lower part of the tail (of the male) during the breeding season, as well as on the upper part; the skin more or less tuberculate both above and below; pores on the head and parotoid region, and a fold on the throat. The colour of this Newt is very variable. The following is the description given by Mr. Boulenger in his catalogue of *Batrachia gradientia*: "Brown, blackish, or olive above, with more or less distinct black spots; sides with white punctulation; the breeding male's head elegantly marbled with black and white; female sometimes with a yellow vertebral line; orange beneath, spotted or marbled with black; fingers and toes yellow, with black annuli; breeding male with a silvery-white band along the side of the tail; female with lower edge of the tail orange, immaculate."

The male is about six inches in length. These Batrachians may be bought for a few pence each during the spring and summer in any of our large towns.

The Marbled Newt (*Molge marmorata*, Fig. 93) is one of the handsomest members of its genus. It is a native of France, Spain, and Portugal. It is, however, rather rare in the first-mentioned country.

This Newt has a rounded, broad, and depressed snout; well-developed labial lobes during the breeding season; a rounded body, which, in the case of the males, during the spring and summer, is ornamented by a large, straight-edged dorsal crest which sinks suddenly at the junction of the tail and body; the female, instead of a crest, possesses a longitudinal groove; fingers and toes free, those of the males being longer and more slender than those of the female; the tail a little longer than the head and body, much compressed during the breeding season, and in the case of the males is provided above and below with a well-developed straight-edged crest; the skin tuberculated; distinct pores on the head and parotoid regions; and a fully developed fold on the throat.

As this species varies greatly in colouring and marking, I venture to quote the description given by Mr. Boulenger in his Catalogue of *Batrachia gradientia*: "Green above, marbled with black; dorsal and upper caudal crest with vertical, alternately black and white bars; female with an orange vertebral line; a silvery-white band along the side of the tail most distinct in the breeding male; fingers and toes green, with black annuli; lower surfaces brown or greyish, with more or less distinct darker spots, punctulated with white."

This Newt when fully grown is nearly as long as *M. cristata*. It can be bought in England occasionally for a few shillings, and

FIG. 93.—THE MARBLED NEWT (*Molge marmorata*)

may be associated in the Vivarium with other large Newts and Salamanders, and treated in the same way, as already suggested.

The Alpine Newt (*Molge alpestris*) is, especially in the breeding season, a beautifully marked little creature. In size it is comparatively small, varying from 4in. to 4½in. in length. It is a native of France, Belgium, Holland, Germany, Switzerland, Austria, and Italy. *M. cristata* is often found associated with this Newt, upon which it frequently feeds.

M. alpestris has a head a little longer than broad; in the case of the male, during the breeding season, a long, low, straight-edged crest which runs from behind the eyes to the tip of the tail; the fingers and toes free; a tail about as long as the head and body, and which possesses a well-developed lower crest, ending in a point; the skin tuberculated above and smooth below: pores about the head and parotoid regions; and a fold on the throat.

FIG. 94.—FEMALE SMOOTH NEWT (*Molge vulgaris*).

This Newt, like many others of its genus, varies greatly in colouring, of which the following is the description given by Mr. Boulenger: "Upper parts brown, blackish, greyish, or purplish, uniform or marbled with darker; a lateral series of small black spots, on whitish ground, this being bordered inferiorly in the breeding male by a sky-blue band; dorsal and caudal crests white, with round, black spots; fingers and toes with black annuli; belly orange or red, immaculate; throat, frequently black-dotted; the lower edge of the female's tail orange, with round black spots."

This beautiful Newt, which may occasionally be bought in London for a shilling or two, should be associated with other members of the *Salamandridæ* of its own size.

The Common or Smooth Newt (*M. vulgaris*, Fig. 94) is in Britain by far the most plentiful of its genus, being found in pools, ponds, ditches, and pits, during spring and summer, nearly everywhere. The young ones, that is those which have left their tadpole condition, but have not yet arrived at maturity, may generally be found some distance from the water's edge, beneath stones, or under logs and the like. They do not, as a rule, at any period of their lives, become inhabitants of the water again, after having completed their metamorphosis, until they are fully grown or nearly so, and able to assist in the reproduction of their species. The Common Newt, like other members of its genus, has the habit of giving a plaintive cry when handled.

M. vulgaris has three longitudinal grooves on its head, which is longer than broad; during the breeding season labial lobes, those of the females being more developed than those of the males; a rounded body, which in the spring and summer is adorned with a crest, that of the males being well raised and festooned, and running from behind the eyes without interruption to the end of the tail, where it ends in a point, that of the females being much lower and straight edged; in the case of the breeding males, lobated toes; a tail rather longer than the head and body, and provided during the breeding period with a lower crest, that of the male being festooned; the skin quite smooth or nearly so; and two rows of pores on the head.

The colouring and marking of *M. vulgaris* are perhaps more variable than those of any other species of Newt. I have just been looking closely at some forty of these Newts swimming about in a large glass vessel full of clear water, and I could not discover any two of the Batrachians marked and coloured quite alike. The following is the description of this Newt, as given by Mr. Boulenger in his catalogue, already often referred to: "Upper parts brown or olive, with darker spots; these are large and rounded in the male, small, and sometimes confluent into a lateral band in the female and young; head with five longitudinal dark streaks, most distinct in the male; lower surfaces yellowish with a median orange or reddish zone, and large round black spots in the male, or small black dots in the female, the latter frequently confluent into a line along each side of the belly; lower edge of the tail uniform orange in the female, red bordered above with blue interrupted by vertical black spots in the male."

This Batrachian is often called, especially by the British peasants, an "Eft," or "Evet," which comes from the Anglo-

Saxon "Efete." "An Evet" has clearly been shortened into "A Newt," the "v," as is frequently the case in our language, becoming "w." The creature is also known in different parts of Britain as the "Water Evet or Eft," the "Ask," the "Dry-Ask," the "Man-Eater" and "Man-Keeper" (these last two titles are owing to Irish superstitions concerning this animal), the "Lewker," and the "Asgal."

Smooth Newts are very suitable inmates of a fernery, for liking dampness and shade, they do well there, and keep the plants free of hurtful insects. They are, indeed, far more fitted for this purpose than even Lizards, as these Reptiles really require such an

FIG. 95.—THE PALMATE NEWT (*Molge palmata*).

amount of sunshine that it is apt to be injurious to the ferns. Smooth Newts feed upon small aquatic and other animals and earth-worms; in confinement the annelids will form its most convenient food.

M. vulgaris is found in Great Britain and in most of the other parts of Europe, with the exception of the South of France, Spain, and Portugal. It is also a native of the temperate portions of Asia. When fully grown, this Batrachian is about 4in. in length.

The Palmated Newt (*Molge palmata*, Fig. 95), which is only found in certain parts of Britain, is a very pretty little creature. It is the smallest of all the Newts, and is distinguished from those which have already been described by the possession of a bony fronto-squamosal arch to the skull instead of a ligamentous one, except *M. cristata*, which has not one at all. It has gained its specific name from the fact that the male, during the breeding-season, is provided with toes which are fully webbed.

Until comparatively recently, this interesting Newt was confused with *M. vulgaris*. Mr. W. Baker, of Bridgwater, in 1843, was, I believe, the first to discover that the Palmate Newt was a native of Great Britain. About five years later, Mr. J. Wooley gave an account in the *Zoologist* (p. 2,149) of his finding this Batrachian in the neighbourhood of Edinburgh. Since then it has been taken in many other parts of Scotland, and also in numerous localities of England. Mr. Bell, in his "British Reptiles," says that "the first intimation we have of this species as distinct is in the 'Histoire Naturelle du Jorat' of M. Razoumowski."

I have found this species of Newt to be very common in Devonshire, particularly in the neighbourhood of Dartmoor. I have generally taken it in the company of the Common Newt (*M. vulgaris*), but I have no charge of cannibalism to bring against the larger animal.

The Palmate Newt lives exceedingly well in confinement, and will often feed readily, even upon the day of its capture.

In England, *M. palmata* has been taken in the West of Lancashire, in Cheshire, in South-west of Yorkshire, in Nottinghamshire, in Hereford, in Dorsetshire, in Devonshire, in Cornwall, and in other parts. It is also a native of the Isle of Wight. On the Continent it is found in France, Belgium, Holland, Switzerland, West Germany, and the North of Spain.

M. palmata has the "body quadrangular in the breeding male, a more or less developed cutaneous fold bordering each side; a low, entire, vertebral crest; in the female the body is nearly round, with low vertebral ridge, as in *M. vulgaris*. Limbs moderate; fingers and toes depressed, the latter fully webbed in the breeding male; two small carpal and tarsal tubercles; tail a little longer than head and body, strongly compressed during the breeding season, and with an upper and lower crest; the male's tail truncate and ending in a filament, this filament scarcely distinct in the female. Skin smooth, or nearly so; head with distinct series of pores; gular fold generally distinct, upper parts brown or olive, with small darker spots; head with longitudinal dark streaks, the outer (those passing through the eyes) being constant; in the male the head is minutely speckled with dark brown, and the dorsal and upper caudal crest and feet are blackish; lower surfaces not coloured, except the medium zone of the belly, which is orange; a few small blackish dots are generally scattered on the belly; inferior caudal crest immaculate, orange in the female, bluish-grey in the male; a series of spots, sometimes confluent, along the upper and lower border of the tail." (From Mr. Boulenger's Catalogue of the *Batrachia Gradientia*).

Before the winter the tail of the male of *M. palmata* has lost its filament and has become slightly rounded. The webbing of the toes has also been absorbed, and the crest has almost entirely disappeared.

As there is a likelihood of *M. vulgaris* and *M. palmata* being confounded by the novice in Batrachian matters, I give the comparison of the two species, as drawn up by M. Derby and quoted by Dr. Cooke, in "Our Reptiles Batrachians."

M. vulgaris.

1. Tail generally tapering to a point.

2. Hind feet having the toes free, only edged by a membrane.

3. Back with a very large festooned, undulating crest, which extends from the nape of the neck to the end of the tail. No lateral elevated ridges.

4. Length much greater than *M. palmata.*

M. palmata.

1. Tail suddenly truncate before the apex, and terminating in a slender filament three lines in length.

2. Hind feet perfectly palmate, all the toes united by a membrane.

3. Back flattened, with two elevated lateral lines passing above the eyes, and extending to the base of the tail. The dorsal crest small and simple.

4. Size much smaller than *M. vulgaris.*

The Palmate Newt is about 3in. in length when fully grown. During the season it may be bought for a few pence of dealers in aquarium and vivarium requisites.

The Banded Newt (*Molge vittata*) is rather a handsome Batrachian, and when fully grown is about 4in. in length. It is a native of Asia Minor and Syria, while all of the other Newts which have now been described are inhabitants of Europe.

M. vittata has a head which is longer than broad; a rounded snout; in the case of the male during the breeding season a feebly-toothed crest which sinks abruptly at the junction of the body and tail; in that of the female at the same period of the year, a slight ridge along the back; the toes of the male in the spring and summer webbed at their bases; the tail a little larger than the head and body, compressed and furnished above and below with a crest terminating in a point; the skin either smooth or only slightly tuberculated; pores on the head and parotoid regions, and no fold on the throat. The colour above is brown or grey, spotted with black. The dorsal crest is marked with upright black bars, which are broad and narrow alternately. On the side of the body and tail there is a white band having black edges. There are small black dots on the throat, and the under parts are immaculate.

During the breeding season, the adult males of all the Newts which have now been described are furnished with dorsal crests, but all the other members of the genus, at every season of the year, are crestless on their back.

The Greenish Newt (*Molge viridescens*) has a head longer than broad, and bearing three longitudinal grooves; a truncated snout; in the place of a dorsal crest, a small ridge; very strong hind limbs, much dilated and furnished on their inner surfaces, in the case of the male, during the breeding season, with black roughnesses; fingers and toes which are depressed and free, the outer and inner toes on each foot being very short; a tail longer than the head and body, much compressed, and provided above and below with a crest; the skin either quite smooth or slightly tuberculated; three large pores on each side of the head, behind the eyes, and no fold on the throat. The upper parts of the body are reddish or greenish-brown, often spotted with black. On each side of the back there are several dark-edged red spots. There is a dark stripe on either side of the head, which passes through the eye. The under parts are red or orange spotted with black.

This Newt is a native of North America, and is, when fully grown, about 3½in. in length.

Ruscon's Newt (*Molge rusconii*) has a flat and very long head, in length equally about a third of that of the body; a rounded body, without crest; fingers and toes which are long, slender, and free; a tail about as long as the head and body, rounded at its base, and then keeled above and beneath, and furnished with a small upper and lower crest. The colour above is dark olive marked with large, almost indistinct, spots; below, the animal is of a reddish or yellowish colour, spotted with black. The entire length of this Batrachian is about 5in. It is said to be chiefly found in the hilly districts of Corsica and Sardinia. It has also been taken in the Pyrenees and in Spain. During the breeding season it lives in standing water.

The Rough or Pyrenean Newt (*Molge aspera*, Fig. 96) is chiefly remarkable because of its rugged skin. It is a native of the Pyrenees, and its entire length is about 3½in. *M. aspera* has a long and flat head, with rather prominent eyes; a rounded body without a crest; fingers and toes which are free; a tail which is without crest, and keeled above, and about as long as the head and body (that of the male is, however, a little shorter and thicker than that of the female); and the skin strongly tuberculated above, while that below is smooth. The upper parts of the body are blackish, uniform, spotted with yellow, or marked with a yellow line, which runs along the back and tail; the under parts and the tips of the fingers are reddish-yellow; and the lower edge of the tail reddish-yellow, spotted with black.

Waltli's, or the Pleurodele Newt (*Molge waltlii*), is perhaps the most interesting member of its genus. It lives extremely well in confinement, where it breeds freely. It is a native of Spain, Portugal, and Tangiers. This creature is chiefly remarkable for its very long ribs, each provided with a sharp point, which frequently perforates the skin, and helps to form on either side of the body that which has the appearance of a row of small bony spines. *M. waltlii* has a large flat head, with a short rounded snout, rather prominent eyes, depressed, and free fingers and toes; a tail much compressed, keeled above and below, and longer than the head and body; a skin which is strongly tuberculated, and a large fold on the throat. The colour above is brown, or blackish-grey, below yellowish, with dark markings, and the lower edge of the tail is yellowish-red. This Newt sometimes grows to the length of about 8in. The young of this and of all the other

FIG. 96.—THE ROUGH OR PYRENEAN NEWT (*Molge aspera*).

Newts may be treated according to the directions which have been given for the rearing of the larvæ of Salamanders, and should be fed upon the same kind of food.

CHAPTER XVI.

AXOLOTLS AND AMBLYSTOMES.

THE Axolotl (*Amblystoma tigrinum*, Figs. 97 and 98) is, I think, the most interesting and remarkable of all the Batrachians. "Axolotl" is the name which has been given by the natives of Mexico to the animal when it is in its larval state. In England, however, the word Axolotl is now

FIG. 97.—THE AXOLOTL OR LARVA OF *Amblystoma tigrinum*.

commonly used to describe the creature when either in its immature or mature condition.

For a long time this Batrachian has been a great puzzle to naturalists. Formerly, it was regarded as a member of those genera of the *Batrachia caudata*, which, like the *Proteidæ*, retained their external gills throughout their life, and it was therefore classed among the *Perennibranchiata*, or perpetual bearers of external gills. However, in 1865, this classification was proved to be a wrong one; for in January of that year some Axolotls which had been for several months in the Reptilium of the Musée d'Histoire Naturelle, at Paris, began to breed. The eggs which were deposited hatched in about four weeks, and the growth of the larvæ was carefully watched by Professor A. Duméril. In the early part of September, when the young Axolotls had grown almost as large as their parents, it was noticed that one of them had commenced to pass through a metamorphosis similar to that which is experienced by a young Newt before it arrives at maturity. In a few weeks the branchiæ were gradually absorbed, the gill openings closed up, the large dorsal and caudal fin disappeared, the tail assumed the appear-

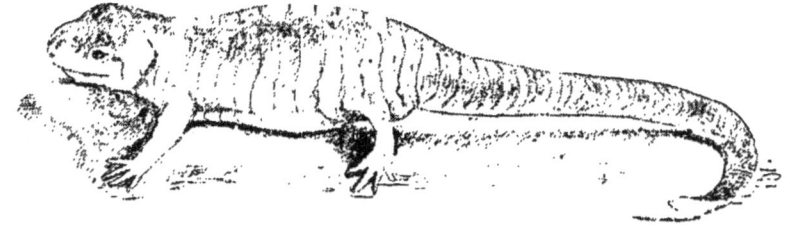

FIG. 98.—AN AMBLYSTOME (*Amblystoma tigrinum*).

ance of that of an ordinary Salamander, the toes became narrowed and lost their appendages, yellow spots appeared upon the skin, changes took place in regard to the skull and dentition, and the animal commenced to breathe altogether by means of its lungs, and ultimately left the water.

In the early part of the October following others of the young Axolotls underwent a like metamorphosis, until finally, out of several hundreds of Tadpoles, about thirty became apparently perfect Amblystomes. The parents, however, passed through no such change at all.

The account which Professor Duméril published of these unexpected metamorphoses excited a great deal of interest among naturalists, and many of them procured Axolotls for the purpose of observation and experiment.

When these creatures, which had changed, seemingly, from Axolotls into Amblystomes, under the eyes of Professor Duméril, were carefully examined as to their structure, they were found to possess characteristics identical with the members of the genus *Amblystoma*, which numbers about seventeen species, inhabiting different parts of North America and Mexico.

For ten years after their birth the Amblystomes which had been born in the Musée d'Histoire Naturelle at Paris did not breed, and it was thought by many naturalists that transformed Axolotls were sterile. Many efforts were made to encourage them to reproduce their kind, but without success. Their food was repeatedly changed. They were paired in different ways, *e.g.* male Amblystomes were associated with female Amblystomes, female Axolotls with male Amblystomes, and female Amblystomes with male Axolotls. And yet, Axolotls with Axolotls continued to bring forth young in considerable numbers, and apparently with no extraordinary care on the part of those who tended for them.

However, in 1874, the Batrachians were removed from the Musée d'Histoire Naturelle at Paris to new and far more suitable quarters, where the Amblystomes almost immediately produced fertile eggs.

The Axolotl is not the only Batrachian which is capable of reproducing its species while in a larval state; for example, Alpine Newts (*Molge alpestris*) have been found still bearing branchiæ, and yet possessing fully-developed ova and spermatozoa.

Fraülein von Chauvin, at Freiburg, on the suggestion of Professor Weissmann, attempted to bring about the transformation of young Axolotls by gradually depriving them of water. Her endeavours were quite successful. Axolotls between six and nine months of age were placed in a vessel containing water, and a small island upon which the Batrachians could climb. A small quantity of water was withdrawn daily from this vivarium, and almost immediately the branchiæ of the Axolotls began to decrease in size, and gradually, after living for some time surrounded by damp moss, most of them became perfect Amblystomes.

Mr. Tegetmeier, the well-known naturalist, has seen an Axolotl of his own, from the Lake of Mexico, undergo the metamorphosis just described, an account of which was published in the Proceedings of the Zoological Society of London for 1870, p. 160.

The attempt to obtain the transformation of Axolotls should be made while the Batrachians are young, say between six and twelve months of age, and before they have bred.

A year or two ago I tried to bring about the transformation of some old Axolotls which had reproduced their species, and was only partially successful. I placed the animals in a large aquarium containing some sand, gravel, an island gradually sloping into the water, which at its greatest depth was about 4in. The water was not removed daily by hand, but allowed simply to evaporate. In course of time the Axolotls lost much of their branchiæ, most of the median fin, the appendages of their feet, and yellow spots slowly appeared on different parts of their body, but when they arrived at this condition they made no other progress in their metamorphosis. The water slowly evaporated until only a depth of about ½in. remained at the deepest part of the tank, and in this scanty quantity of water the creatures lived for something like a year. I did not venture to deprive them of all the water, lest they should die for want of it. A little was occasionally added to make up for the loss through evaporation.

Ultimately I replaced these partially-transformed Axolotls with the other Axolotls from whose company I had taken them. Their removal was made as an experiment, but unfortunately it was a fatal one. They died. Their death, however, I did not expect, for I was careful to see that they had access to an island which gradually sloped into the water. They, therefore, could choose water of any depth up to 6in. or 8in. to live in. Sometimes I found them in the deepest water they could get to, and sometimes in the shallowest.

The Axolotl is a native of the lakes near the city of Mexico. It is there so plentiful that it is frequently sold in the markets of Mexico, its flesh being highly esteemed by the natives of that country. I believe that it is only the lakes of Mexico which contain Axolotls, or larvæ of the *Amblystoma tigrinum*, capable of reproducing their species while still in an immature condition. In other parts of America where this species occurs, the tadpoles go through their metamorphosis in the same regular way as do the rest of the members of the *Salamandridæ*. And I think I am correct in saying that, in their native lakes near the city of Mexico, the Axolotls never now become transformed into Amblystomes.

Professor Weissmann explains this peculiar and uncertain metamorphosis of the Axolotl by remarking that when the ancestors of the Axolotls passed through the ordinary changes which occur in the usual life-history of *A. tigrinum*, the climate in the neighbourhood of Mexico was sufficiently moist to allow members of the *Salamandridæ* to live while in a mature condition upon the land. But now, since the climate, for reasons, has become too dry for these creatures to live as terrestrial animals, they remain throughout their lives in the water, where they breed while still in a larval state.

The change, therefore, which takes place under certain conditions in confinement is really what is called *atavism*, i.e., the resemblance of offspring to some remote ancestors, instead of to immediate parents.

Axolotls are very easily kept in captivity, where they will live for a great many years. They feed readily upon worms, tadpoles, small fish, newts, and raw meat. If properly cared for, they are almost sure to breed regularly every year, depositing their eggs among the weeds, or on stones and pieces of rocks, which should be placed in the water in which they live.

Directly the eggs are noticed, either they or the parent Axolotls should be removed from the tank. The eggs will hatch in about a month, or even much sooner than this, if they are kept in water of a high temperature. When the tiny tadpoles are hatched, they should be treated exactly according to those directions which have been given for the rearing of young Newts and Salamanders. An Axolotl is very like a Newt while in its branchiate state, and the early development of the two animals is almost identical.

Axolotls of different sizes and ages ought never to be associated together, or the larger Batrachians are certain to prey upon the smaller ones. When fully grown, several Axolotls may be kept together.

Axolotls soon become quite tame, and are intelligent enough to know their fosterer. In colour, roughly speaking, they are either black or white. The white ones are beautiful, and used to be very rare, but now they are so common that nice specimens may be bought in Covent Garden for a few shillings. The eggs of the Axolotl, in the season, may also be purchased there.

Axolotls, like Newts, have the power of reproducing lost limbs. The Axolotl, or larva of *A. tigrinum* (Fig. 97), has four pairs of gill slits and three pairs of external branchiæ; a cylindrical body; a broad flat head; a large straight-edged fin which runs along the back and tail and round the end of and under the latter, terminating ventrally at the anus; four short legs, the fore-limbs possessing four toes, and the hind ones five, all of which are furnished with web-like appendages; and distinct costal grooves. It sometimes grows to a length of about 10in.

The Amblystome, or transformed Axolotl (*Amblystoma tigrinum*, Fig. 98), has a large flat head with broad rounded snout; stout body and limbs, short fingers, and toes depressed and pointed; a tail about as long as the head and body, compressed, keeled towards the end, which ends in a point; a shining, finely granulated skin; large, flat parotoids, and twelve distinct costal grooves. The colour above is black or dark brown, marked with yellow spots; the animal is of a lighter shade underneath. The entire length is from 8in. to 10in. There are about seventeen species in the genus *Amblystoma*.

CHAPTER XVII.

FISH-LIKE SALAMANDERS, OLMS, &c.

AS the following very interesting Batrachians are almost entirely aquatic in their habits they should be kept in Vivaria which are provided with a considerable quantity of water, and to which they can have easy access: for example, in such cases as those which are represented by Figs. 10, 12, 23, or in any ordinary fresh-water aquarium.

The *Amphiumidæ*, or, as they are sometimes called, the Fishlike Salamanders, are chiefly distinguished from the *Salamandridæ* by the want of eyelids. Although they lose their gills during metamorphosis they live almost entirely in the water. This family (*Amphiumidæ*) is divided into three genera—*Megalobatrachus*, *Cryptobranchus*, and *Amphiuma*, which contain altogether only four species.

The Gigantic Salamander (*Megalobatrachus maximus*) is the largest of all existing Batrachians, measuring when fully grown about 4ft. in length, and weighing nearly 50lb. It is the living representative of the fossil Salamander of Œningen, in Basle, Switzerland, the remains of which when found in the Upper Miocene beds were regarded by Dr. Scheuchzer, in 1726, as those of a man buried by the flood, and consequently received the name *Homo diluvii testis*.

The Gigantic Salamander was discovered in Japan by Dr. D. Siebold in the year 1820. Since that time it has been found in

China. It is therefore now known to be an inhabitant of some of the lakes, rivers, and streams of Japan and China. It is nowhere very abundant. It seems to prefer for its breeding-places small mountain streams at considerable elevation above the sea.

The older Batrachians generally live under water among rocks and tangles of aquatic weeds, while the younger ones take refuge in holes in the banks.

For so large an animal, the female of the *M. maximus* lays very small eggs, which are supposed to be deposited during the months of August and September. The Tadpoles lose their branchiæ before they (the Tadpoles) are 6in. in length. And when the gill openings have become closed the young resemble their parents in almost every particular.

Dr. Siebold started for Europe in 1829, bringing with him two living specimens of the Gigantic Salamander, a male and a female. After a time the supply of fresh-water fish which had been procured as food for the Salamanders was consumed, and the male, under the influence of hunger, devoured his mate. The survivor ultimately arrived safely in Holland, where it lived in captivity for more than half a century. It died at Amsterdam in the year 1881.

Since then many of these huge Batrachians have been brought to Europe, and have lived in the various zoological gardens for numbers of years. There is at the present moment, I believe, a fine specimen in the Reptile House, Regent's Park, London, which has been in confinement since 1884.

These Salamanders, while in captivity, may be kept in a tank of fresh water. The tank, of course, should be of such dimensions as are suited to the size of its occupants. No island or landing-place need be prepared, as these creatures seldom voluntarily leave the water. The bottom of the tank ought to be covered with a layer of coarse and clean river sand to a depth of about 6in.; over this there should be water of at least 1ft. in depth. If the water reaches within a few inches of the top edges of the tank, there should be a cover of perforated zinc or glass, for these Batrachians may climb out of the tank and hurt themselves by falling upon the floor of the building in which their aquarium stands.

While in confinement, these Salamanders generally choose for their resting-place during the daytime the darkest and most retired part of the tank, coming up to the surface of the water for the purpose of respiration at intervals of from five minutes to half-an-hour, protruding, as they do so, only the end of the snout. Towards evening the creatures exhibit what little activity they possess, and take exercise or hunt for food.

They may be fed upon frogs, worms, fish, and raw meat, when they can be persuaded to accept this last-mentioned article as food. They prefer fish, especially smelts.

The members of the genus *Megalobatrachus* are characterised by the possession of a tongue which covers the floor of the mouth, to which it is entirely adherent; strong vomerine teeth, placed between the inner openings of the nostrils, and parallel with the intermaxillary and maxillary teeth; four fingers on each hand; and five toes on each foot. There are no gill-openings, but there are two internal gill-arches.

M. maximus has a very stout body; a large, broad, very depressed head, with rounded snout; extremely small eyes and nostrils; a depressed body; short, stout limbs, fingers, and toes; a short, much compressed finned tail, with rounded end; a very porous skin, covered with tubercles, the largest of which are placed on the head. The colour is dark brown, spotted with black. These huge Salamanders may, from time to time, be bought of the larger dealers in wild animals, at prices, according to size, which range from £10 downwards.

The Hell Bender, or Mississippian Salamander (*Cryptobranchus alleghaniensis*), is in many respects very like its gigantic relative of China and Japan. The chief differences between the two animals are that the former possesses gill-openings (at any rate upon the left side), four branchial arches instead of two, and a tongue which is free at its anterior border.

The Hell Bender is found in all the tributaries of the Mississippi and the Alleghany rivers, in which waters it is occasionally taken on the hook of the angler, and is frequently erroneously regarded by him as poisonous. It does not often of its own accord leave the water.

Since 1869 it has been frequently brought to Europe, where it has lived in captivity for a great many years. It should be treated, while in confinement, in the same way as has been suggested for the management of the Gigantic Salamander. It is a very free feeder.

C. alleghaniensis has a very stout body; a large, broad, and very depressed head; a rounded snout; very small nostrils, and tiny black eyes; a much depressed body; short and stout limbs, and short, flat fingers and toes, the outer fingers and toes being bordered with well-developed membranes; a short, compressed, finned tail, with a round end; a skin which is porous and fairly smooth; tubercles on the head, and a fold of skin on the sides of the body. The colour of the animal is brownish-grey, with darker spots. Its fingers and toes are yellow. When fully grown, the Hell Bender sometimes reaches a length of 18in.

The Amphiuma, or Three-toed Salamander (*Amphiuma tridactyla*), is a strange, very eel-like looking animal, possessing two pairs of very small limbs, the fore-limbs being placed very wide apart from the hind ones. Each limb is provided with three digits.

The Amphiuma will live for a great many years in captivity. The large, blind specimen which is now in the Reptile House, Regent's Park, London, has been in the Zoological Gardens there since, I think, 1870. When fully grown, *A. tridactyla* sometimes reaches a length of 2½ft. Like an eel, it will frequently bury itself in the mud at the bottom of the water in which it lives. In a state of nature it feeds upon young fish, small crustaceans, worms, and almost any aquatic animal it may happen to meet with. It occasionally leaves the water, out of which it can live without injury for at least twenty-four hours.

While in captivity, it should be provided with a large tank of fresh water, having a good depth at its bottom of coarse and clean river sand. Its food may consist of fish, worms, and pieces of meat. The Amphiuma is a native of the River Mississippi and its tributaries, and the streams of the State of Louisiana.

A. tridactyla has, in addition to the limbs already mentioned, a tongue which is entirely adherent to the floor of the mouth; large vomerine teeth; a gill opening on each side of the neck, partly covered with a fold of thin skin; four branchial arches; a small head with a long snout; small nostrils and eyes; well developed upper and lower labial lobes; a short tail, compressed, and keeled above; and a smooth, slimy skin. The colour above is bluish-black; underneath it is of a lighter shade.

Amphiuma means is exactly like the Batrachian which has just been described, except that it possesses two digits at the extremity of each limb instead of three. It is found from North Carolina to the Mississippi.

The Proteus (*Proteus anguinus*) is a representative of the family *Proteidæ*, or permanently-gilled Salamanders, which includes the two genera *Necturus* and *Proteus*. The members of the latter genus have their eyes concealed under the skin.

For the last two hundred years the Proteus, or Olm, as it is sometimes called, has excited the greatest interest among naturalists, both from its singular structure and from the strange situations in which it is found. It is an inhabitant of the dark subterranean lakes of the Alps of Carniola, in Austria.

Though the eyes of this creature are very small and hidden under the skin, they are of a certain amount of use to the owner. This can be shown by the animal's anxiety, while in captivity, to withdraw itself into the darkest part of its tank.

The Proteus has been called a double-breathing animal, because it is possessed of both lungs and gills. It has been proved, by depriving the Batrachian of its branchiæ, that its lungs are not merely rudimentary, for thus mutilated it has continued to live for a very considerable time. I am not aware that a Proteus has ever been able to grow new branchiæ in the place of those which have been taken from it.

The Olm will live for many years in confinement, even, it is said, without food. When the water of its tank is regularly changed, the Batrachian remains at the bottom of the water, breathing only by means of its gills. But when the water in which it lives is not renewed from time to time, and consequently (if comparatively of small expanse) is gradually deprived of much of the oxygen it contained, the Proteus is obliged to come to its surface periodically, for the purpose of breathing by the help of its lungs.

The Proteus, when in captivity, should always be provided with a dark place of retirement, or the whole tank ought to be covered with green baize. For food it may be supplied with garden worms, river worms (*Tubifex rivulorum*), fresh-water shrimps (*Gammarus fluviatilis*), water-fleas (*Entomostraca*), and the like.

The Olm is caught by the Austrian peasants, placed in vessels of water, and, when opportunity offers, sold to tourists. It is also occasionally brought into this country, and may be bought at prices which vary from 7s. 6d. to 10s. 6d.

It has sometimes, while in confinement, deposited eggs, which, after a period of about three months, have produced Tadpoles. The larvæ are very like their parents, except that the tail fins and the eyes are much larger in proportion to the size of the body than those of the adult. The legs during the tadpole-hood are represented by what may be called small knobs. One adult female has been known to lay as many as seventy-six eggs.

The blood corpuscles, or disks, of the Proteus are immense, being about fifteen times larger than those of man.

P. anguinus has a narrow head, with a long snout, narrowed and the tip truncate; a small tongue, free in front; feeble vomerine teeth; a small mouth; well-developed labial lobes; a long slender body; two pairs of very weak limbs; three fingers on each hand, and two toes on each foot; a short, compressed, finned tail, having a rounded end; a smooth skin; about twenty-six costal grooves. The colour is pinkish-white, without spots or markings. The colour becomes gradually darker upon constant exposure to light.

The Proteus sometimes reaches a length of about 1ft.

The Siren (*Siren lacertina*) is a representative of the family *Sirenidæ*, which is divided into the two genera, and *Siren* and *Pseudo-branchus*, each containing only one species, viz., *S. lacertina* and *P. striatus*. The chief differences between the Batrachians of these two genera are that the members of the former possess three gill-openings on either side of the neck, and two four-fingered hands, while those of the latter have only one gill-opening on each side of the neck, and three fingers on each hand.

The Siren is a native of the South Eastern part of the United States of America. It is often found in the rice fields there. The slaves in days gone by looked upon this Salamander as poisonous, and killed it whenever they had the opportunity of doing so, calling it, I believe, the Congo Snake. It is hardly necessary, however, to say that the animal is perfectly harmless.

The Siren is not seldom thrown with the mud on the land when ditches and ponds are being cleared out. It will live for a long time in captivity if provided with a suitable Vivarium, which should be arranged so that a bed of fine sand slopes into rather deep water. There also ought to be a small quantity of moss under which the Salamander can hide. It will feed upon garden worms and mealworms, eating several at a meal.

S. lacertina has a tongue which covers the floor of its mouth and is free in front; jaws with a bony sheath like a beak; vomerine teeth; a long eel-like body; a short head; a broad snout; tiny eyes; well-developed labial lobes; two short fore limbs, and no hind limbs; a tail shorter than the body, much compressed, finned, and ending in a joint; a smooth skin, blackish in colour, occasionally finely spotted with white. This Batrachian sometimes grows to a length of three feet.

The Siren retains its gills throughout life—and, like the Proteus, has enormous blood corpuscles.

CHAPTER XVIII.

CŒCILIANS.

THE Cœcilians, or worm-like Batrachians, have been placed in the order *Apoda*, and in the family *Cœciliidæ*. These creatures are characterised by a worm-like, or, in some cases, a snake-like appearance, by the total want of limbs, and by the tail being either rudimentary or altogether wanting. Some have overlapping scales embedded in the skin, and others are scaleless. The eyes of these Batrachians are either under the skin or below the cranial bones. Their vertebræ are bi-concave. Their mouth is small and situated on the lower surface of the head. These animals possess tentacles, either above or below the nostrils.

In the family *Cœciliidæ* there are eleven genera and about thirty-five species. The Cœcilians, when fully grown, are terrestrial, and chiefly spend their time in burrows underground, leading a life similar to that of a worm.

Certain of these Batrachians are ovo-viviparous, while others deposit their eggs in damp earth, near water, the mother coiling herself about them, after the manner of a female Python. The young, while within the egg, develop large external gills, which, in course of time, are absorbed, and the gill-openings become closed. Some little time after their birth the larvæ, for a short period, take to the water.

The size of different species of the Cœcilians varies considerably. For example, some of them have a diameter of ¾in., while others do not exceed ¼in. One species (*Cæcilia gracilis*) grows to a length of more than 2ft.

These strange animals are natives of India, Africa, south of the Sahara Desert, and North and South America.

When in captivity they should be provided with plenty of damp mould, water, and, as food, earthworms.

INDEX.

A.

Acontias meleagris, 129
Acris gryllus, 340
Acrochordinæ, 214
Adder, 223
  Chequered, 271
  Spreading, 271
Adiantums for vivaria, 31
Adjigar, 203
Æsculapian Snake, 260
Agamidæ, 130, 133
Aglossa, 354
Aglypha, 213
Ahætulla liocercus, 269
Aldrovandi's Skink, 123, 125
Algiroides nigropunctatus, 105
All-green Tree Snake, 285
Alligatoridæ, 60
ALLIGATORS, 58, and Frontispiece. See Crocodiles.
Alpine Newt, 377
  Salamander, 363
Alytes boscæ, 353
  obstetricans, 353
Amblyrhynchus, 137, 138
Amblystoma, 385, 390
  tigrinum, 385
AMBLYSTOMES, 385, 390. See Axolotls
Ameiva dorsalis, 83

American Black Snake, 253
Bull Frog, 307
Glass Snake, 111
Green Frog, 315
Pouched Tree-Frog, 295, 357
Toad, 337
Amphibians, 5
Amphibolurus barbatus, 134
Amphisbæna alba, 148
  Grey, 148
  White, 148
Amphisbænidæ, 148
Amphiuma means, 395
  tridactyla, 394
Amphiumidæ, 359, 391
Anacharis Alsinastrum, 369
Anaconda, 187, 199, 206
Angiostomata, 175
Angry Snake, 244
Anguidæ, 107
Anguis cerastes, 213
  fragilis, 112
Anodon, 282
Anoles, 140
  colour-changing in, 141
  food of, 141
  vivaria for, 142
Anolis, 140
  grahami, 142
Anomalepis, 186
Anomodontia, 4
Aponogeton distachyon, 340

INDEX.

Aquarium converted into a vivarium, 35
Aquatic plants for vivaria, 37. See Plants
Arch for vivaria, 18
Arcifera, 303
Asgal, 379. See Newts
Ask, 379. See Newts
Asp, Cleopatra's, 213
Aspleniums, 31
Aulic Lycodon, 242
Australian Carpet Snake, 197
Frog, 324
AXOLOTLS, 385
atavism in, 389
eggs of, 389
metamorphosis of, 386
reproduction of lost limbs by, 390
reproduction of, while in larval state, 387
tadpoles of, 386
tameness of, 390
transformation into Amblystomes, 386
vivaria for, 38

B.

Ball Snake, 204
Banded-tail Tree-Snake, 269
Basiliscus, 138
americanus, 140
Basilisk, 139
Banded Newt, 382
Batagurs, 49
BATRACHIANS, 294-399
Aglossa, 296, 354
Amblystomes, 385
Amphiumidæ, 359, 391
Anoura, 294
Apoda, 5, 294, 398
Axolotls, 385
bath for, 299
Bufonidæ, 325
Caudata, 5, 294, 358
characteristics of, 294
classification of, 4, 294

BATRACHIANS—
Cœcilians, 398
Cœciliidæ, 398
Discoglossidæ, 350
Disc-tongued Frogs, 349, 350
distribution of, 295
Ecaudata, 5, 294
eggs of, 295
Fish-like Salamanders, 391
food of, 101, 296, 300
Frogs, 303
Gradientia, catalogue of, 374, 381
hibernation of, 300
Hylidæ, 339
Labyrinthodonta, 5, 294
largest of, 391
metamorphosis of, 295
Molge, 367
Newts, 367
Olms, 391
Ophiomorpha, 5, 294
Pelobatidæ, 349
Perennibranchiata, 386
Phaneroglossa, 296, 303
plants for vivaria of, 299
popular ideas of, 3
Proteidæ, 359, 395
Ranidæ, 303
Salamanders, 358
Salamandridæ, 359, 367, 389
Sirenidæ, 359
sounds emitted by, 295
Stegocephala, 294
tailed, 294, 358. See Newts, Salamanders, etc.
tailless, 294, 296. See Frogs, Toads, etc.
Toads, 325
Toad-frogs, 349
Tongueless Frogs, 354
Tree-frogs, 339
Urodela, 294, 358
vivaria for, 8, 298, 306
Worm-like, 398
Beak-headed Lizards, 156
Bearded Lizard, 134
Bell Frog, 353

2 D

Bipes, 129
Black Iguana, 144
  Salamander, 363
  Snake, 248
    American, 253
Black-marked Snake, 264
Black-spotted Lizard, 103
Black-and-white Blind Snake, 185
  Snake, 267
Black-and-yellow Cyclodus, 120
Bladder Frog, 324
Blanus einereus, 148
Blind Snakes, 184
  Worm, 112, 117
Blood ejected by Horned Lizard, 145
Bloodsucker, 134
Blowing Viper, 271
BOAS, 197, 208, 210
  bath for, 210
  classification of, 196
  Common, 208
  Constrictor, 187, 208
  feeding, 194
  Jamaica Yellow, 205, 206
  Pale-headed Tree, 205
  tameness of, 208
  vivaria for, 187, 210
  Water, 206
  Yellow, 205, 206
Boidæ, 186, 197
Boiler for vivaria, 15, 19
Boinæ, 196
Bombinator bombinus, 352
  igneus, 351
Boodon infernalis, 241
  lineatus, 242
Bordeaux Snake, 279
Bornean Flying Frog, 356
Boss Ferns, 32
Box Tortoise, Carolina, 54
Brachylophus, 138
Brachysoma diadema, 197
Brackens, 32
Breviceps, 356
Broad-leaved Pond-weed, 340
Brookesia, 152
Brooklime, 38

Brown Mud Frog, 349
Bucephalus capensis, 286
Buck-bean, 38
Buckered Reptiles, 42
Bufo calamita, 325
  lentiginosus, 336
  marinus, 337
  mauritanicus, 330
  regularis, 330
  viridis, 329
  vulgaris, 330
Bufonidæ, 325
BULL-FROGS, 306
  American, 307
  bellowing of, 307, 309
  food of, 310
  Indian, 306
  Occipital, 307
Bull-killer, 206
Bull Snake, 265
Burrowing Snakes, 182
Bush Snakes, 285
  Snake, variegated, 268

C.

Caiman, 60
Californian Toad, 106, 144
Calitriche verna, 369
Calotes versicolor, 134
" Cambridgeshire Nightingales," 313
Canadian Water-weed, 369
Canvas for vivaria, 9
Cape Bucephalus, 286
  Fragrant Water Lily, 340
Carolina Box Tortoise, 54
Carpet Snake, 197
  Viper, 197
Cases, making, 8
Caspian Terrapin, 54
Cat Snake, 284
Caucasian Salamander, 364
Caudata (Batrachians), 358
Cement for vivaria, 13
Cenchris piscivora, 239
Cerastes hasselquistii, 213

Ceratophrys, 320
  Adorned, 323
  cornuta, 321, 322
  Horned, 322
  ornata, 321
  voice of, 322
Chalcides ocellatus, 124
  tridactylus, 128
  viridanus, 127
Chamæleon vulgaris, 149
Chamæleontidæ, 155
CHAMELEONS, colour-changing in, 149, 152
  eggs of, 155
  eyes of, 150
  fasting power of, 149
  food of, 151, 154
  tongue of, 150
  vivaria for, 21, 153
  water supply for, 153
Chameleon-Lizards, 142
Changeable Tree-frog, 340
Chelodina longicollis, 57
Chelonia, 5
Chelonians, 42
Cheloniidæ, 43
Chequered Adder, 271
Chicken Snake, 259
  Tortoise, 54, 57
Chilabothrus inornatus, 205, 206
Chioglossa lusitanica, 365
Chirotes canaliculatus, 148
Chlamydosaurus kingi, 133
Chrysopelea ornata, 287
Cistudo Carolina, 54
Classification, general, 4
Climbing Ferns, 32
Club Mosses, 34
Cockroaches as food, 300
Cæcilia gracilis, 399
CŒCILIANS, 398
  food of, 399
Cæciliidæ, 398
Cælopeltis lacertina, 286
Cold-blooded animals, 5
Coluber æsculapii, 260
  alleghaniensis, 260
  dumfrisiensis, 273
  eximius, 281

Coluber guttatus, 253
  leopardinus, 254
  lindheimeri, 2
  longissimus, 260
  melanoleucus, 265
  obsoletus, 259, 260
  quadrilineatus, 257, 259
  quadristriatus, 259
  quadrivittatus, 259, 260
  quaterradiatus, 259
  quatuor-lineatus, 257, 261
  sauromates, 259
  scalaris, 264
  spiloides, 260
Colubridæ, 213
Colubrinæ, 214
Colubrine Xenodon, 270
Congo Snake, 397
Conolophus, 138
Constrictor, Boa, 187, 208
  formosissimus, 208
  rex-serpentum, 208
Corn Snake, 253
Coronella, 279
  austriaca, 273
  Boylii, 280
  californiæ, 280
  cana, 243
  getula, 280
  g. Boylii, 280
  g. californiæ, 280
  g. Sayi, 280
  girondica, 279
  lævis, 273
  Sayi, 280
  triangulum, 281
Coryphodon constrictor, 248
  c. flaviventris, 251
Crested Newt, 372
Cripple, Long, 253
CROCODILES, 58 and Frontispiece
  and Alligators, difference between, 60
  Caiman, 60
  classification of, 60
  Crocodilus, 60
    porosus, 63
  eggs of, 62

CROCODILES—
  food for, 65
  Garialis, 60
  hatching, 63
  in history, 59
  intelligence of, 65
  Jacare, 60
  Land, 78
  leeches in mouth of, 59
  omnivorous appetite of, 61
  Tomistoma, 60
  vivaria for, 19, 64
Crocodilia, 4, 60
Crocodilidæ, 60
Cross-marked Snake, 285
Crowfoots, 37
Crustaceans, freshwater, contrivance for procuring, 361
Cryptobranchus alleghanicnsis, 393
Ctenosaura, 138
Cyclodus, Black-and-yellow, 120
  gigas, 120
  Great, 120
  nigroluteus, 120
Cyrtomium, Large-leaved, 32
Cystignathidæ, 320

D.

Dahl's Snake, 249, 251
Dark Green Snake, 244
Dasypeltis scabra, 281
  s. fasciolata, 283
  s. inornata, 283
  s. medici, 283
  s. palmarum, 283
Davallias, 32
Deer-swallower, 206
Deirodon scaber, 281
Delaland's Gecko, 75
Dendrophis pictus, 267
  punctulatus, 268
Derbian Lizard, 106
Dermatemys, 49
Devil, Mountain, 136
  Thorn, 136

Dhabb, 136
Diamond Snake, 197
Dice Snake, 234
Dinosauria, 4
Discoglossus pictus, 350
DISC-TONGUED FROGS, 349, 350
  Alytes boscæ, 353
    obstctricans, 353
  Bell Frog, 353
  Bombinator bombinus, 352
    igneus, 351
  Dictyoglossus pictus, 350
  eggs of, 353
  Fire-bellied Toad, 351
  fluid discharged by, 352
  food of, 352
  Midwife Frog, 353
  Painted Frog, 350
  spawning of, 352
  tadpoles of, 350, 352, 353
  Yellow-bellied Toad, 352
Disinfectants, care required in using, 233
Dorsal Lizard, 83
Dragons, 130
Dry Ask, 379. See Newts
Dryinus fuscus, 289
Dryophidæ, 288
Duck-weeds, 38
Dusky Toad, 336

E.

Earwigs as food, 302
Echis carinata, 197
Edible Frogs, 307, 311, 317
  Frogs, decrease in numbers of, 314
Eft, 378. See Newts
Egg-eaters, 214
Egg-eating Snake, 281
Egyptian Eryx, 212
  Mastigure, 135
Elaphis quaterradiatus, 184, 185, 259
Elk's-horn Fern, 32
Emydidæ, 43, 49
Emys caspica, 54

Emys lutaria, 50
  reticulata, 54, 57
  sigriz, 54
Entomostraca, contrivance for procuring, 361
Epicrates angulifer, 205
  inornatus, 205, 206
  striatus, 205
Eryx cerastes, 213
  Egyptian, 212
  Indian, 213
  jaculus, 212
  johnii, 212
  Shielded, 213
  thebaicus, 213
Escorpion, 81
Eumeces schneideri, 123
Eunectes murinus, 187, 197, 199, 206
European Green Tree-frog, 342
Phyllodactyle, 75
Eurystomata, 175
Evet, 378. See Newts
Ewing's Tree-frog, 346
Eye, median, 161
  parietal, 161
  pineal, 161
Eyed Lizard, 84. See also Ocellated
Eyervreter, 283

F.

Fan-foot, 75
Fernery and vivarium combined, 17, 28
  for Frogs, etc., 11
  gravel, etc., for, 28
  soil for, 31
Ferns, 28. See Plants
Filmy Ferns, 33. See Plants
Fire-bellied Toad, 351
Firmisternia, 303
FISH-LIKE SALAMANDERS, 391
  Amphiuma means, 395
    tridactyla, 394
  classification of, 391
  Congo "Snake," 397

FISH-LIKE SALAMANDERS—
  Cryptobranchus alleghaniensis, 393
  eggs of, 392, 396
  food of, 393, 394, 396
  Gigantic, 391
  Hell Bender, 393
  Megalobotrachus maximus, 391
  Mississippian, 393
  Olm, 395
  Proteidæ, 395
  Proteus anguinus, 395
  Pseudo-branchus striatus, 396
  Siren lacertina, 396
  Sirenidæ, 396
  tadpoles of, 392, 396
  Three-toed, 394
  vivaria for, 391, 392, 394
Fly-catcher, 301
Flying Frog, Bornean, 356
Gecko, 71
Lizards, 130
Four-rayed Snake, 257, 261
Fragrant Water Lily, 340
Freshwater Snakes, 183
  Tortoises, 43, 49. See Tortoises
  Turtles, 43
Frilled Lizard, 133
FROGS, 303
  Acris gryllus, 340
  Adorned Ceratophrys, 323
  Alytes boscæ, 353
    obstetricans, 353
  American Bull, 307
    Green, 315
  Arch-jawed, 320
  Arcifera, 303
  Australian, 324
  Bell, 353
  Bladder, 324
  Bornean Flying, 356
  Breviceps, 356
  Brown Mud, 349
  Bull, 306
    bellowing of, 307, 309
    food of, 310

INDEX.

FROGS—
Bull, Indian, 306
"Cambridgeshire Nightingales," 313
Ceratophrys, 320
 cornuta, 321
 ornata, 323
Changeable Tree, 340
colour-changing in, 306, 319, 345
Common, 316
 Golden Tree, 347
croaking of, 305
Cystignathidæ, 320
Dictyoglossus pictus, 350
Disc-tongued, 349, 350. See Disc-tongued Frogs
Edible, 307, 311, 317
 decrease in numbers of, 314
eggs of, 296
enemies of, 317
Esquerzo, 323
European Green Tree, 342
Ewing's Tree, 346
farming, 307
Firmisternia, 303
fluid discharged by, 305
Flying, 356
Golden Tree, 347
Graceful, 307
Grasshopper, 340
Green, 315, 343
 Tree, 342
Horned, 320, 321
Hyla arborea, 342
 aurea, 347
 cærulea, 345
 citropus, 347
 ewingii, 346
 krefftii, 346
 peronii, 345
 phyllochroa, 344
 versicolor, 340
Indian Bull, 306
Krefft's Tree, 346
Laubfrosch, 343
Leaf, 343
Leaf-green Tree, 344

FROGS—
leaping powers of, 306
legs of, like those of man, 305
Leptodactylus ocellatus, 324
 pentadactylus, 323
life of, 296
Marsupial, 357
metamorphosis of, 296
Midwife, 353
Mud, 349
Noisy, 310
Nototrema marsupiatum, 357
Occipital Bull, 307
Ocellated Piping, 324
Painted, 350
Pelobates cultripes, 350
 fuscus, 349
Pelobatidæ, 349
Peron's Tree, 345
Phaneroglossa, 303
Pipa americana, 355
Pipidæ, 355
Piping, 323
Pseudophryne australis, 324
Rana Catesbiana, 307
 clamata, 310
 esculenta, 311
 gracilis, 307
 halecina, 315
 occipitalis, 307
 temporaria, 316
 tigrina, 306
Ranidæ, 303
rearing, 319
remaining under water, 305
respiration of, 304
Rhacophorus pardalis, 356
scientific interest in, 303
Short-headed, 356
skin of, 304
Slender-fingered, 323
sloughing of, 319
Smooth-clawed, 354
Smooth Spur-toed, 354
spawn of, 296
Spur-toed, 354
tadpoles of, 297

FROGS—
Toad, 349. See Toad-frogs
tongue of, 304
Tongueless, 354. See
Tongueless Frogs
Tree, 339. See Tree-frogs
true, 303
uses of, 318
Versicolor, 341
vitality of, 319
vivaria for, 11, 300, 306
" Whaddon Organs," 313
White's Tree, 345
Yellow-foot Tree, 347
Xenopus lœvis, 354
Frog-bit, 37
Funaria hygrometrica, 34

G.

Gallot's Lizard, 105
Garialidœ, 60
Garialis, 60
Garter Snake, Green-spotted, 214
Gecko verus, 75
GECKOS, 69
adhesive feet of, 71
brittle tails of, 71
changeable colours of, 72
climbing powers of, 71
cry of, 70
Delaland's 75
European Phyllodactyle, 75
Fan-foot, 75
flying, 71
food of, 70, 73
Hemidactylus verruculatus, 75
Ocellated, 75
Phyllodactylus europœus, 75
Platydactylus muralis, 73
Ptyodactylus Gecko, 75
Tarentola, 73
vivaria for, 25, 72
Wall, 73
Warty Hemidactyle, 75

Geckotidœ, 69
Giant Toad, 337
Gigantic Salamander, 391
Gila Monster, 81
Glass " Snakes," 107, 111
Glauconia, 186
Glauconiidœ, 186
Golden Tree-frog, Common, 347
Gongylus ocellatus, 124
Gould's Monitor, 80
Graceful Frog, 307
Grass Snake, 217
Grasshopper Frog, 340
Great Cyclodus, 120
" Sea Serpent," 187
Warty or Crested Newt, 372
Greek Tortoise, 43
Green Frog, American, 315
Lizard, 90
Great, 87
Snake, Dark, 244
Toad, 329
Tree-Frog, European, 342
Tree-Snake, 285
Greenish Newt, 382
Sand-Skink, 127
Green-spotted Garter Snake, 214
Grey Amphisbæna, 148
Ground Snakes, 182

H.

Hamadryas, 173
Hard Fern, 32
Hardwicke's Mastigure, 135
Hare's-foot Ferns, 32
Harlequin Snake, 208
Hart's-tongues, 32
Hatteria punctata, 155
Heating vivaria, 15, 19
Hederas, 35
Hell Bender, 393
Helminthophis, 185
Heloderm, 81
Heloderma horridum, 81
Hemidactyle, Warty, 73

Hemidactylus verruculatus, 75
Heterodon, 272
   nasicus, 272
   platyrhinus, 271
   simus, 272
Hibernation, 6
Hissing Sand Snake, 285
   Snake, 271
Hoary Snake, 243
Hog-nosed Snake, 271
Hoop Snake, 173
Hoplocephalus curtus, 197
Hoplopterus spinosus, 59
Horned Frogs, 320
   Lizards, 106, 135, 144
      blood ejected by, 145
      vivarium for, 147
   Snake, 213
   Toad, 144
Horseshoe Snake, 251
Houseleeks, 34
Hydrocharis morsus-ranæ, 37
Hyla arborea, 342
   aurea, 347
   cærulea, 345
   citropus, 347
   ewingii, 346
   krefftii, 346
   peronii, 345
   phyllochroa, 344
   versicolor, 340
Hylidæ, 339
Hylodes, 295
Hymenophyllums, 33

I.

Ichthyopteridia, 4
Iguana, 138
   Black, 144
   delicatissima, 144
   Naked-necked, 144
   tuberculata, 143
Iguanidæ, 77, 130, 137
   Anoles, 140
   colour-changing in, 138
   eggs of, 138
   size of, 137

Incubator for Lizards' eggs, 89
Indian Bull Frog, 306
   Eryx, 213
   Gecko, 75
   Python, 199, 200, 202
   Rat Snake, 247
Infernal Snake, 241
Italian Water-weed, 369
Ivies, 35

J.

Jacare, 60
Jamaica Yellow Boa, 205, 206

K.

King Snake, 208, 280
Knob-nosed Lizard, 133
Krefft's Tree-frog, 346

L.

Lace Monitor, Gigantic, 80
Lacerta, 84
   agilis, 94
   a. exigua, 98
   galloti, 105
   lævis, 104
   muralis, 103
   m. filfolensis, 103
   m. lilfordii, 103
   m. tiliguerta, 103
   nigropunctata, 105
   ocellata, 84
   oxycephala, 104
   rubra, 98
   taurica, 104
   viridis, 90
   v. major, 93
   v. schreiberi, 90
   v. strigata, 93
   vivipara, 95, 98
Lacertidæ, 84
Lacertilia, 5
Lacertine Snake, 286

INDEX.

Land Crocodile, 78
Monitors, 77, 78. See Monitors.
Tortoises, 43. See Tortoises
Lastreas, 32
Laubfrosch, 343
Leaf Frog, 343
Leaf-green Tree-frog, 344
Lemnas, 38
Leopard Snake, 254
Leptodactylus ocellatus, 324
   pentadactylus, 323
Leptophis liocercus, 269
Lewker, 379. See Newts
Liasis, 197
Lineated Boodon, 242
Liophis Merremi, 269
   pœcilogyrus, 269
   reginæ, 270
LIZARDS, 67
   Acontias meleagris, 129
   Agamidæ, 130, 133
   Aldrovandi's Skink, 123, 125
   Algiroides nigropunctatus, 105
   Amblyrhynchus, 138
   Ameiva dorsalis, 83
   American Glass "Snake," 111
   Amphibolurus barbatus, 134
   Amphisbæna alba, 148
   Amphisbænidæ, 148
   Anguidæ, 107
   Anoles, 140
   Basiliscus, 138
   americanus, 139, 140
   Basilisk, 139
   Beak-headed, 156
   Bearded, 134
   Bipes, 129
   Black Iguana, 144
   Black-and-yellow Cyclodus, 120
   Black-spotted, 105
   Blanus cinereus, 148
   Blind-worm, 112, 117
   blood ejected by, 145
   Bloodsucker, 134
   Brachylophus, 138

LIZARDS—
   Brookesia, 152
   Californian "Toad," 106, 135, 144
   Calotes versicolor, 134
   catalogue of, 87, 137
   catching, 99
   Chalcides ocellatus, 124
      tridactylus, 128
      viridanus, 127
   Chamæleon vulgaris, 149
   Chamæleontidæ, 155
   Chameleons, 142, 149. See Chameleons
   Chirotes canaliculatus, 148
   Chlamydosaurus kingi, 133
   Conolophus, 138
   Ctenosauria, 138
   Cyclodus gigas, 120
      nigroluteus, 120
   definition of, 67
   Delaland's Gecko, 75
   Derbian, 106
   desquamation of, 68
   Dhabb, 136
   Dorsal, 83
   Dragons, 130
   eggs of, 68
   Eumeces schneideri, 123, 125
   European Phyllodactyle, 75
   Eyed, 84
   Fan-foot, 75
   feeding, 87
   Flying, 130
   Gecko, 71
   Frilled, 133
   Gallot's, 105
   Geckos, 69
   Geckotidæ, 69
   Gigantic Lace Monitor, 80
   Glass "Snakes," 107, 111
   Gongylus ocellatus, 124
   Gould's Monitor, 80
   Graham's Anolis, 143
   Great Cyclodus, 120
   Green, 90
      Great, 87
   Greenish Sand-skink, 127
   Grey Amphisbæna, 148

LIZARDS—
Hardwicke's Mastigure, 135
hatching eggs of, 89, 101
Hatteria punctata, 155
Heloderma horridum, 81
Hemidactyle, Warty, 75
Hemidactylus verruculatus, 75
Horned, 106, 135, 144
" Toad," 106, 135, 144
Iguana, 138
delicatissima, 144
tuberculata, 143
Iguanidæ, 77, 130, 137
Indian Gecko, 75
Knob-nosed, 133
Lace Monitor, Gigantic, 80
Lacerta, 84
agilis, 94
a. exigua, 98
galloti, 105
lævis, 104
muralis, 103
m. filfolensis, 103
m. lilfordii, 103
m. tiliguerta, 103
nigropunctata, 105
ocellata, 84
oxycephala, 104
rubra, 98
taurica, 104
viridis, 90
v. major, 93
v. schreiberi, 90
v. strigata, 93
vivipara, 95, 98
Lacertidæ, 84
Land Monitors, 77, 78
large, 137
localities for, 99
Lord Derby's, 166
Lycodon, 242
aulicus, 242
Lyriocephalus scutatus, 133
Mastigures, 135
Metopoceros cornutus, 144
Moloch horridus, 136
Monitoridæ, 76
Monitors, 76. See Monitors.

LIZARDS—
Mountain Devil, 136
Naked-necked Iguana, 144
Narara, 156
Nile Monitor, 78
Ocellated, 84
  Gecko, 75
  Monitor, 79
  Sand-skink, 124
Ophisaurus apus, 107
  ventralis, 111
Ouaran Monitor, 78
Pachydactylus ocellatus, 75
Phrynosoma, 135, 148
  blainvillii, 146
  cornutum, 144
Phyllodactylus europæus, 75
  muralis, 73
Phymaturus, 138
Plestiodon auratus, 123, 125
poisonous, 81
Psammodromus hispanicus, 105
Pseudopus pallasii, 107
Ptychozoon homalocephalum, 71
Ptyodactylus Gecko, 75
Red Teguexin, 83
Rhampholeon, 152
Rhiptoglossa, 151
Rhynchocephalia, 156
Rough-scaled Zonure, 107
Salamanders, 358. See Salamanders
Sand, 94, 105
Sand-skinks, 124, 127
Sauromalus, 138
Sauvegarde, South American, 83
Scelotes bipes, 129
Scheltopusik, 108
Scincidæ, 119
Scincus officinalis, 123
sea, 138
Seps tridactylus, 128, 131
  viridanus, 127
Sharp-headed, 104
Short-toed Monitor, 79
Skinks, 119

LIZARDS—
  Sleeping, 119
  Slow-worm, 112
  Spotted, 129
  Smooth, 104
  Snake-like, 107, 111
  South American Sauvegarde, 83
  Spanish Sand, 105
  Spotted Slow-worm, 129
  Stagyrite, 144
  Stump-tailed, 119
  swiftness of, 68
  Tapayaxin, 144
  Tarentola Delalandii, 75
  Taurian, 104
  Teguexins, 82
  Teiidæ, 81
  Thorn Devil, 136
  Three-toed Sand-skink, 128, 131
  Tiliqua nigrolutea, 120
    scincoides, 120
  "Toad," Californian, 144
    Horned, 144
  Trachysaurus rugosus, 119
  Tuatera, 135, 155
  Tuberculated Iguana, 143
  Tupinambis rufescens, 83
    teguexin, 82
  Two-banded Monitor, 79
  Two-headed, 119
  Uromastix Hardwickii, 135
    spinipes, 135
  Varanidæ, 75
  Varanus albigularis, 78
    flavescens, 79
    giganteus, 80
    Gouldii, 80
    griseus, 78
    niloticus, 78
    salvator, 76, 79
  Variegated, 83
  vivaria for, 8, 88
  Viviparous, 98
  Wall, 103
    Gecko, 73
  Waran, 78
  Warty Hemidactyle, 75

LIZARDS—
  White Amphisbæna, 148
  White-throated Monitor, 78
    young, 101
  Zonure, Rough-scaled, 107
  Zonurus cordylus, 107
    derbianus, 106
    giganteus, 106
Lomaria alpina, 32
London Pride, 35
Long Cripple, 253
Long-headed Snake, 271
Long-necked Tortoise, 57
Long-snouted Whip Snake, 288
Lord Derby's Lizard, 106
Loxocemus, 197
Lycodon aulicus, 242
Lycopodiums, 34
Lygodiums, 32
Lyriocephalus scutatus, 133

M.

Maggots as food, 301
Maidenhair Ferns, 31
Man-eater, 379. See Newts
Man-keeper, 379. See Newts
Marbled Newt, 374
Margined Tortoise, 48
Marsh Tortoises, 43
Marsupial Frog, 357
Mastigures, Egyptian, 135
  Hardwicke's, 135
  torpidity of, in low temperatures, 135
Matatoro, 206
Mealworms as food, 302
Median eye, 101
Megalobatrachus maximus, 391
Mentha sylvestris, 38
Menyanthes trifoliata, 38
Merrem's Snake, 269
Metopoceros cornutus, 144
Midwife Frog, 353
Milk Snake, 281
Mississippian Alligator, 58 and Frontispiece
  Salamander, 393

Mocassin Snake, 239
  Water, 239
Molge, 367
  alpestris, 377
  aspera, 383
  cristata, 372
  marmorata, 374
  palmata, 379
  rusconii, 383
  viridescens, 382
  vittata, 382
  vulgaris, 377, 380
  waltlii, 383
Moloch horridus, 136
  Lizard, 136
MONITORS, 76. See also Lizards.
  food of, 77
  Gigantic Lace, 80
  Gould's, 80
  Lace, 80
  Land, 77, 78
  Nile, 78
  Ocellated, 79
  Ouaran, 78
  pugnaciousness of, 78
  remaining under water, 77
  Short-toed, 79
  Two-banded, 76, 79
  Water, 80
  White-throated, 78
Monitoridæ, 76
Moorish Toad, 330
  Tortoise, 48
Morelia spilotes, 197
  variegata, 197
Mosses, 34
Mountain Devil, 136
Mud Frog, Brown, 349
  Tortoise, 50

N.

Naked-necked Iguana, 144
Narara, 156
Nardoa, 197
Nasturtium officinale, 38
NATTERJACK TOAD, 325
  colour-changing in, 327

NATTERJACK TOAD—
  croak of, 327
  eggs of, 328
  food of, 328
  smell emitted by, 326
  superstition regarding, 328
Necturus, 395
NEWTS, 367
  Alpine, 377
  Asgal, 379
  Ask, 379
  Banded, 382
  collecting, 367
  colour-changing in, 371
  Common, 377, 380
  Crested, 372
  Dry-Ask, 379
  Eft, 378
  eggs of, 368
  Evet, 379
  food of, 371, 379, 384
  Great Warty or Crested, 372
  Greenish, 382
  habits of, 367, 377
  intelligence of, 371
  Lewker, 379
  Man-eater, 379
  Man-keeper, 379
  Marbled, 374
  metamorphosis of, 369
  Molge, 367
    alpestris, 377
    aspera, 383
    cristata, 372
    marmorata, 374
    palmata, 379
    rusconii, 383
    viridescens, 382
    vittata, 382
    vulgaris, 377, 380
    waltlii, 383
  movements of, 368
  Palmated, 379
  plants for, 369
  Pleurodele, 383
  poisonous secretion of, 372
  Pyrenean, 383
  reproduction of lost limbs of, 372

NEWTS—
  Rough, 383
  Ruscon's, 383
  sloughing of, 371
  Smooth, 377, 380
  sound emitted by, 368
  superstitions regarding, 371
  tadpoles of, 369
  tenacity of life of, 372
  vivaria for, 11, 21, 368
  Waltli's, 383
  Warty, 372
  Water Eft or Evet, 379
  young, feeding, 384
Nightingales, Cambridgeshire, 313
Nile Monitor, 78
Noisy Frog, 310
None so Pretty, 35
Nototrema marsupiatum, 357

O.

Occipital Bull Frog, 307
Ocellated Gecko, 75
  Lizard, 84
  Monitor, 79
  Piping Frog, 324
  Sand-Skink, 124
OLMS, 391, 395
Ophidia, 5
Ophidians, 5, 162. See Snakes
Ophisaurus apus, 107
  ventralis, 111
Opisthoglypha, 213
Organs, Whaddon, 313
Ornamented Tree Snake, 287
Ornithosauria, 5
Ouaran Monitor, 78

P.

Pachydactylus ocellatus, 75
Painted Frog, 350
  Tree Snake, 267
Pale-headed Tree Boa, 205
Palmated Newt, 379

Parietal eye, 161
Passerita mycterizans, 288
Pelias berus, 223, 273
Pelobates cultripes, 350
  fuscus, 349
Pelobatidæ, 349
Perennibranchiata, 386
Peron's Tree-frog, 345
Phaneroglossa, 303
Philodryas viridissimus, 285
Philothamnus semivaricgatus, 268
Phrynosoma, 135
  blainvillii, 146
  cornutum, 144
Phyllodactylus europæus, 75
Phymaturus, 138
Pilot Snake, 267
Pine Snake, 267
Pineal eye, 161
Pipa americana, 355
Pipidæ, 355
Piping Frogs, 323
Pituophis Sayi, 265
PLANTS FOR VIVARIA, 28, 299, 369
  Anacharis alsinastrum, 369
  Aponogeton distachyon, 340
  Aquatics, 37
  Aspleniums, 31
  Boss Ferns, 32
  Brackens, 32
  Broad-leaved Pond-weed, 340
  Brooklime, 38
  Buck-bean, 38
  Callitriche verna, 369
  Canadian Water-weed, 369
  Cape Fragrant Water Lily, 340
  Climbing Ferns, 32
  Club Mosses, 34
  Crowfoots, 37
  Cyrtomium, Large-leaved, 32
  Davallias, 32
  Duck-weeds, 38
  Elk's-horn Fern, 32
  Ferns, 28

PLANTS FOR VIVARIA—
Filmy Ferns, 33
for Batrachians, 299
for Newts, 369
for Tree Frogs, 340
Fragrant Water Lily, 340
Frog-bit, 37
Funaria hygrometrica, 34
Hard Fern, 32
Hare's-foot Ferns, 32
Hart"s-tongues, 32
Hederas, 35
Houseleeks, 34
Hydrocharis morsus-ranæ, 37
Hymenophyllums, 33
Italian Water-weed, 369
Ivies, 35
Lastreas, 32
Lemnas, 38
Lomaria alpina, 32
London Pride, 35
Lycopodiums, 34
Lygodiums, 32
Maidenhair Ferns, 31
Mentha sylvestris, 38
Menyanthes trifoliata, 38
Mosses, 34
Nasturtium officinale, 38
None so Pretty, 35
Platycerium grande, 32
Polypodies, 32
Pond-weed, Broad-leaved, 340
Potamogeton natans, 340
Pterises, 32
Ranunculuses, 37
Saxifrages, 34
Scolopendriums, 32
Sedums, 35
Selaginellas, 33
Sempervivums, 34
Shrubs, 35
Speedwell, Water, 369
Sphagnums, 34
Spiderworts, 35
Spleenworts, 31
Starwort, 37, 369
with Newts' eggs, 369

PLANTS FOR VIVARIA—
Stonecrops, 35
Stratiotes aloides, 37
Todeas, 33
Tortula muralis, 34
Tradescantias, 35
Trees, 35
Trichomanes radicans, 33
Vallisneria spiralis, 369
Vernal Greater Starwort, 369
Veronica anagallis, 369
beccabunga, 38
Wall Rue, 32
Water Cress, 38
Lily, Cape Fragrant, 340
Mint, 38
Soldier, 37
Speedwell, 369
Weed, Canadian, 369
Weed, Italian, 369
Platycerium grande, 32
Platydactylus muralis, 73
Plestiodon auratus, 123, 125
Pleurodele Newt, 383
Plover, Spur-winged, and Crocodiles, 59
Polypodies, 32
Pond-weed, Broad-leaved, 340
Potamogeton natans, 340
Pouched Tree-Frog, American, 295, 357
Proteidæ, 359, 395
Proteroglypha, 213
Proteus anguinus, 395
Psammodromus hispanicus, 105
Psammophidæ, 285
Psammophis crucifer, 285
sibilans, 285
Psammophylax rhombeatus, 285
Pseudaspis cana, 243
Pseudo-branchus striatus, 396
Pseudophryne australis, 324
Pseudopus pallasii, 107
Pterises, 32
Ptyas mucosus, 247
Ptychozoon homalocephalum, 71
Ptyodactylus Gecko, 75

Punctulated Tree Snake, 268
Pyrenean Newt, 383
Pythoninæ, 196
PYTHONS, 197, 204
　eggs of, 200, 202
　feeding, 194
　incubation of, 200, 202
　Indian, 199, 200, 202
　jaws of, 175
　Python molurus, 199, 200, 202
　　regius, 204
　　sebæ, 199, 200
　　spilotes, 197
　Reticulated, 198
　Royal, 204
　size of, 166
　vivaria for, 187
　West African, 199, 200

R.

Racer, 248
Rana Catesbiana, 307
　clamata, 310
　esculenta, 311
　gracilis, 307
　halecina, 315
　occipitalis, 307
　temporaria, 316
　tigrina, 306
Ranidæ, 303
Ranunculuses, 37
Rat Snake, Indian, 247
　Snake, South American, 252
Rat-tail, 252
Red Teguexin, 83
Reptiles, British, 313
　Bucklered, 42
　classification of, 4
　European, Guide to, 313
　feeding, 100
　largest, 199
　poisonous, 80
　popular ideas of, 3
　repugnance for, 2
　starving, 100

Reptiles, superstitions regarding, 4, 112, 163, 170, 172, 174, 186, 218, 328, 331, 371
Reticulated Python, 198
Rhachiodontinæ, 214, 282
Rhacophorus pardalis, 356
Rhampholeon, 152
Rhinechis scalaris, 264
Rhinoderma darwinii, 295
Rhiptoglossa, 151
Rhomb-marked Snake, 285
Rhynchocephalia, 5, 156
Ribbon Snake, 233
Ringed Snake, 217
River Tortoises, 43
Rock Snake, Indian, 202
Rough Newt, 383
Rough-scaled Zonure, 107
Royal Python, 204
　Snake, 270
Ruscon's Newt, 383

S.

SALAMANDERS, 358
　Alpine, 363
　Amphiuma means, 395
　　tridactyla, 394
　Black, 363
　Caucasian, 364
　Chioglossa lusitanica, 365
　Congo "Snake," 397
　Cryptobranchus alleghaniensis, 393
　eggs of, 360
　fabulous power of, over fire, 359
　Fish-like, 391. See Fish-like Salamanders
　food of, 362, 364, 365
　　for young, 361
　fossil, at Œningen, 391
　Gigantic, 391
　habits of, 358
　Hell Bender, 393
　Megalobotrachus maximus, 391

SALAMANDERS—
  metamorphosis of, 361, 363
  Mississippian, 393
  Necturus, 395
  Olm, 395
  poisonous secretion of, 362
  Proteidæ, 395
  Proteus anguinus, 395
  Pseudo-branchus striatus, 396
  reproduction of lost limbs by, 358
  Salamandra atra, 363
    caucasica, 364
    maculosa, 359
    perspicillata, 365
  Siren lacertina, 396
  Sirenidæ, 396
  Spanish, 365
  Spectacled, 365
  Spotted, 359
  tadpoles of, 360, 363
  Tarantolina, 365
  tenacity of life of, 358
  Three-toed, 394
  vivaria for, 23, 362, 364
  young of, 361
Salamandridæ, 359, 367, 389
Sand-Lizard, 84
  Spanish, 105
Sand-Skink, Greenish, 127
  Ocellated, 124
  Three-toed, 128, 131
Sand-Snakes, 212
  Hissing, 285
Sauromalus, 138
Sauropsida, 4
Saaropterygia, 4
Sauvegarde, South American, 83
Saxifrages, 34
Scelotes bipes, 129
  tridactylus, 128, 131
Scheltopusik, 108
Scincidæ, 119
Scincus officinalis, 123
Scolopendriums, 32
Sea Lizard, 138
  Serpent, the "Great," 187

Sea Snakes, 183
Turtles, 43
Sedums, 35
Selaginellas, 33
Selection of animals, 27, 53
Sempervivums, 34
Seps tridactylus, 128, 131
  viridanus, 127
Serpent, "Great" Sea, 187
SERPENTS, 162. See Snakes
Seven-banded Snake, 238
Sharp-headed Lizard, 104
Shielded Eryx, 213
Short-headed Frogs, 356
Short-toed Monitor, 79
Shrubs for vivaria, 35
Siren lacertina, 396
Sirenidæ, 359, 396
SKINKS, 119
  Aldrovandi's, 123, 125
  Common, 123
  food for, 124
  Greenish Sand, 127
  Ocellated Sand, 124
  Sand, 124, 127
  Three-toed, 128, 131
  vivaria for, 25, 124
Sleeping Lizard, 119
Slender-fingered Frog, 323
SLOW-WORMS, 112, 115, 129
  brittleness of, 114
  food of, 117
  median eye of, 114
  Spotted, 129
  superstitions regarding, 112
  vivaria for, 11, 117
Slugs and their eggs as food, 302
Smooth Lizard, 104
  Newt, 377, 380
  Snake, 273
Spur-toed Frog, 354
SNAKES, 162
  Acrochordinæ, 214
  Adder, 223
    Chequered, 271
    Spreading, 271
  Ahætulla liocercus, 269
  Adjigar, 203
  Æsculapian, 260

INDEX.

SNAKES—
affectionate nature of, 208
Aglypha, 213
All-green Tree, 285
American Black, 253
  Glass, not a true Snake, 111
Anaconda, 187, 199, 206
Angiostomata, 175
Angry, 244
Anguis cerastes, 213
Anodon, 282
Anomalepis, 186
artificial feeding of, 290
Asp, 213
Aulic Lycodon, 242
Australian Carpet Snake, 197
Ball, 204
Banded-tail Tree, 269
Black, 248, 253
Black-marked, 264
Black-and-white, 267
  Blind, 185
Blind, 184
Blowing Viper, 271
Boas, 186, 208, 211. See Boas
Boa constrictor, 208
Boidæ, 186, 197
Boinæ, 196
Boodon infernalis, 241
  lineatus, 242
Bordeaux, 279
Brachysoma diadema, 197
Brown Water Viper, 239
Bucephalus capensis, 286
Bull, 265
Bull-killer, 206
Burrowing, 182
Bush, 268, 285
buying, 200
Cape Bucephalus, 286
capricious feeders, 289
Carpet, 197
Cat, 284
catalogue of, 197
catching, 221
charmers, frauds perpetrated by, 173, 212, 213

SNAKES—
Chequered Adder, 271
Chicken, 259
Chilabothrus inornatus, 206
Chrysopelea ornata, 287
classification of, 182
Cœlopeltis lacertina, 286
Coluber æsculapii, 260
  alleghaniensis, 260
  dumfrisiensis, 273
  eximius, 281
  guttatus, 253
  leopardinus, 254
  lindheimeri, 260
  longissimus, 260
  melanoleucus, 265
  obsoletus, 259, 260
  quadrilineatus, 257, 259
  quadristriatus, 259
  quadrivittatus, 259, 260
  quaterradiatus, 259
  quatuor-lineatus, 257, 261
  sauromates, 259
  scalaris, 264
  spiloides, 260
Colubridæ, 213
Colubrinæ, 214
Colubrine Xenodon, 270
Common, 217
  distinguishing from the Viper, 221
  eggs of, 230
  tameness of, 231
  vivaria for, 226
Congo, 397
Constrictors, 186, 208. See Boas
Constrictor formosissimus, 208
  rex-serpentum, 208
Corn, 253
Coronella, 279
  austriaca, 273
  Boylii, 280
  californiæ, 280
  cana, 243
  getula, 280
  g. Boylii, 280

2 E

SNAKES—
Coronella getula californiæ, 280
  g. Sayi, 280
  girondica, 279
  lævis, 273
  Sayi, 280
  triangulum, 281
Coryphodon constrictor, 248
  c. flaviventris, 251
Crebo, 252
Cripple, 253
Cross-marked, 285
Dahl's, 249, 251
Dark Green, 244
Dasypeltis fasciolata, 283
  inornata, 283
  medici, 283
  palmarum, 283
  scabra, 281
Deer-swallower, 206
definition of a, 174
deglutition of, 176
Deirodon, 281
  fasciolata, 283
  inornata, 283
  medici, 283
  palmarum, 283
  scaber, 281
Dendrophis pictus, 267
  punctulatus, 268
desquamation of, 179
Diamond, 197
Dice, 234
distribution of, 184
Dryinus fuscus, 289
Dryophidæ, 288
Echis carinata, 197
Egg-eating, 281
Egyptian Eryx, 212
Elaphis quaterradiatus, 259
English Smooth, 273
Epicrates angulifer, 205
  inornatus, 206
  striatus, 205
Eryx, 212, 213
  cerastes, 213
  jaculus, 212
  johnii, 212, 213

SNAKES—
Eryx thebaicus, 213
Eunectes murinus, 187, 199, 206
Eurystomata, 175
Eyervreter, 283
fabulous, 186
fascinating power of (supposed) 164
feeding, 194, 228, 289
Four-rayed, 257, 261
Freshwater, 183
Garter, 214
Glass, not a true Snake, 107
Glauconia, 186
Glauconiidæ, 186
Grass, 217
Green, 244
Green-spotted Garter, 214
Ground, 182
Harlequin, 208
head-shields of, 184
Helminthophis, 185
Heterodon nasicus, 272
  platyrhinus, 271
  simus, 272
Hissing, 271, 285
  Sand, 285
hissing of, 164
Hoary, 243
Hog-nosed, 271
Hoop, 173
Hoplocephalus curtus, 197
Horned, 213
horsehair ropes and, 174
Horseshoe, 251
incubation of, 200, 202
Indian Eryx, 213
  Python, 199, 203
  Rat, 247
  Rock, 202
Infernal, 241
in history, 162, 260
insect pests on, 191
intelligence of, 208
Jamaica Yellow Boa, 206
jaws of, 175, 178
King (Boa), 208
King (Coronella), 280

SNAKES—
Lacertine, 286
large, 186, 199, 206
vivaria for, 187
Leopard, 254
Leptophis liocercus, 269
Liasis, 197
Liophis, 270
Merremi, 269
pœcilogyrus, 269
reginæ, 270
Lizards so called, 175
Long Cripple, 253
Long-headed, 271
Long-snouted Whip, 288
Loxocemus, 197
Matatoro, 206
measuring, 182
Merrem's, 269
Milk, 281
Mocassin, 239
Morelia spilotes, 197
variegata, 197
Mosses, 34
mouth of, 178
movements of, 166, 173
Nardoa, 197
Opisthoglypha, 213
Ornamented Tree, 287
Painted Tree, 267
Pale-headed Tree Boa, 205
parasites on, 191
Passerita mycterizans, 288
Philodryas viridissimus, 285
Philothamnus semivariega-
tus, 268
Pilot, 267
Pine, 267
Pituophis Sayi, 265
poisonous, distinguishing, 170
Proteroglypha, 213
Psammophidæ, 285
Psammophilax rhombeatus, 285
Psammophis crucifer, 285,
sibilans, 285
Pseudaspis cana, 243
Ptyas mucosus, 247

SNAKES—
Punctulated Tree, 268
purchasing, 200
puzzling names of, 253
Python molurus, 199, 203
regius, 204
reticulatus, 198
sebæ, 199, 200
spilotes, 197
Pythoninæ, 196
Racer, 248
Rat, 247, 252
Rat-tail, 252
Reticulated Python, 198
Rhachiodontinæ, 214, 282
Rhinecis scalaris, 264
Rhomb-marked, 285
Ribbon, 233
ribs of, 167
Ringed, 217
Rock, 202
Royal, 270
Python, 204
Sand, 212
Hissing, 285
scales of, 168
Sea, 183
Seven-banded, 238
sheltering their young, 170
Shielded Eryx, 213
size of, 166, 186
skinning or sloughing of, 174, 179
Slow-worms mistaken for, 113
small-mouthed, 175
Smooth, 273
South American Rat, 252
"spears" of, 4, 163, 218
Spilotes pullatus, 252
variabilis, 253
Spread Head, 271
Spreading Adder, 271
Stoled, 241
Striped, 241
superstitions regarding, 163, 170, 172, 174, 186, 218
swallowing powers of, 176
Tachymenis vivax, 284

2 E 2

SNAKES—
  tameness of, 208
  teeth of, 178
  teeth-marks of poisonous and non-poisonous, 224
  Tigrine, 240
  tongue of, 163
  Tree, 183, 267, 269, 285, 287
    Boa, Pale-headed, 205
  Troga Venado, El, 206
  Tropidonotus, 214
    ater, 232
    fasciatus, 239
    f. erythrogaster, 240
    f. rhombifer, 240
    f. sipedon, 240
    natrix, 217, 240
    n. astreptophorus, 232
    n. torquata, 273
    n. vars., 232
    ordinatus, 214
    o. sirtalis, 217
    saurita, 233
    septemvittatus, 238
    sirtalis, 217, 241
    stolatus, 241
    tessellatus, 234
    tigrinus, 240
    viperinus, 237
    v. aurolineatus, 238
    v. ocellatus, 238
  tubes for feeding, 290
  Two-headed (supposed), 212
  Typhlophis, 185
  Typhlopidæ, 185
  Typhlops, 185
    nigroalbus, 185
  typical, 213
  Ular Sawa, 198
  Variegated Bush, 268
  venomous, distinguishing, 170
    proportionate number of, 172
  ventral scales of, 168
  vertebræ of, 167, 169
  Vipera berus, 223
  Viper, Blowing, 271

SNAKES—
  Viper, Carpet, 197
  Viperine, 237
  Vivacious, 284
  vivaria for, 8, 187, 226
  Wart, 214
  Water Boa, 206
    Mocassin, 239
    Viper, 239
  West African Python, 199, 200
  Whip, 288
  wide-mouthed, 175
  Xenodon colubrinus, 270
    rhabdocephalus, 271
  Yellow Boa, Jamaica, 206
  Zamenis atrovirens, 244
    a. asianus, 247
    a. caspius, 247
    a. erythrogaster, 247
    a. trabalis, 247
    constrictor, 248
    c. flaviventris, 251
    dahlii, 249, 251
    flaviventris, 251
    gemonensis, 244
    g. asianus, 247
    g. caspius, 247
    g. erythrogaster, 247
    g. trabalis, 247
    hippocrepis, 251
    korros, 248
    mucosus, 247
Soft Tortoises, 43
Soil for fernery, 31
South American Rat Snake, 252
Spanish Salamander, 365
  Sand Lizard, 105
" Spears " of Snakes, 163, 218
Spectacled Salamander, 365
Speedwell, Water, 369
Sphagnums, 34
Spiderworts, 35
Spilotes pullatus, 252
  variabilis, 252
Spleenworts, 31
Spotted Salamander, 359
  Slow-worm, 129
Spread Head, 271

Spreading Adder, 271
Spur-toed Frog, Smooth, 354.
Spur-winged Plover and Crocodiles, 59
Square-marked Toad, 330
Stagyrite, 144
Starving Reptiles, 100
Starwort, 37, 369
   with Newts' eggs, 369
Stoled Snake, 241
Stonecrops, 35
Stratiotes aloides, 37
Striped Snake, 241
Stump-tailed Lizard, 119
Superstitions regarding Reptiles,
    etc., 4, 112, 163, 170,
    172, 174, 186, 218,
    328, 331, 371
Surinam Toad, 355

T.

Tachymenis vivax, 284
Tadpoles, 297
   feeding, 319
Tailed Batrachians, 358. See
    Newts, Salamanders,
    etc.
Tailless Batrachians, 294. See
    Frogs, Toads, etc.
Tapayaxin, 144
Tarentola, 73
   Delalandii, 75
Taurian Lizard, 104
Teguexins, 82
   Common, 82
   Red, 83
   vivaria for, 83
Teiidæ, 81
   eggs of, 82
   food of, 82
Terrapins, 43, 49
   Caspian, 54
   edible, 50
Testudinidæ, 43
Testudo græca, 45
   marginata, 48
   mauritanica, 48

Thorn Devil, 136
Three-toed Salamander, 394
   Sand-Skink, 128, 131
Tigrine Snake, 240
Tiliqua nigrolutea, 120
   scincoides, 120
TOADS, 325
   American, 337
   Bombinator bombinus, 352
      igneus, 351
   Bufo calamita, 325
      lentiginosus, 336
      marinus, 337
      mauritanicus, 330
      regularis, 330
      viridis, 329
      vulgaris, 330
   Californian, 144
   climbing powers of, 336
   colour-changing in, 327
   Common, 330
   croaking of, 327, 333
   Dusky, 336
   eggs of, 296, 328, 336
   embedded in stone, etc., 333
   endurance, power of, 332
   fasting powers of, 335
   Fire-bellied, 351
   "fire-eaters," 334
   fluid discharged by, 337
   food of, 328, 334, 338
   Giant, 337
   Green, 329
   Horned, 144
   hot cinders swallowed by, 335
   largest, 337
   life of, 296
   Lizards miscalled, 144
   longevity of, 333
   metamorphosis of, 296
   Moorish, 330
   Natterjack, 325. See Natterjack
   Pipa americana, 355
   size of, 337
   skin, change of, 335
   sloughing of, 335
   spawning of, 296, 336

TOADS—
  Square-marked, 330
  superstitions regarding, 328, 331
  Surinam, 355
  tadpoles of, 297
  tameness of, 325, 332
  true, 325
  venomous exudation of, 338
  vivaria for, 11, 23
  Walking, 326
  water for, 335
  Yellow-bellied, 352
TOAD-FROGS, 349
  burrows of, 349
  croak of, 350
  eggs of, 349
  odour emitted by, 349
  Pelobates cultripes, 350
      fuscus, 349
  tadpoles of, 349
Todeas, 33
Tomistoma, 60
TONGUELESS FROGS, 354
  eggs of, 354, 355
  food of, 354
  Pipa americana, 355
  size of, 356
  sloughing of, 355
  Smooth Spur-toed Frog, 354
  Surinam Toad, 355
  tadpoles of, 354
  tank for, 356
  Xenopus lævis, 354
Torpor, winter, 6
TORTOISES, 42
  breeding, 47
  "Bucklered Reptiles," 42
  Carolina Box, 54
  Chelodina longicollis, 57
  Cheloniidæ, 43
  Chicken, 54, 57
  Cistudo Carolina, 54
  classification of, 43
  eggs of, 42
  Emydidæ, 49
  Emys caspica, 54
      lutaria, 50
      reticulata, 54, 57

TORTOISES—
  Emys sigriz, 54
  food of, 47
  Freshwater, 43, 49
  Greek, 43
  hibernation of, 48, 50
  Land, 43
  longevity of, 44
  Long-necked, 57
  Margined, 48
  Marsh, 43
  Moorish, 48
  Mud, 50
  River, 43
  shelter for, 49
  Soft, 43
  tenacity of life of, 42
  Terrapins, 49
  Testudinidæ, 43
  Testudo Græca, 48
      marginata, 48
      mauritanica, 48
  Trionychidæ, 43
  vivaria for, 19
Tortula muralis, 34
Trachysaurus rugosus, 119
Tradescantias, 35
Trees for vivaria, 35
Tree-Boa, Pale-headed, 205
TREE-FROGS, 339
  Acris gryllus, 340
  Changeable, 340
  colour-changing in, 345
  Common Golden, 347
  eggs of, 343
  European Green, 342
  Ewing's, 346
  food of, 343, 347
  Golden, 347
  Grasshopper, 340
  Green, 342
  Hyla arborea, 342
      aurea, 347
      cærulea, 345
      citropus, 347
      ewingii, 346
      krefftii, 346
      peronii, 345
      phyllochroa, 344

TREE-FROGS—
  Hyla versicolor, 340
  Krefft's, 346
  Laubfrosch, 343
  Leaf-green, 344
  noise emitted by, 342, 343, 345
  Peron's, 345
  plants for, 340
  spawning of, 343
  tadpoles of, 340
  Versicolor, 341
  vivaria for, 339, 343
  White's, 345
  winter quarters for, 343
  Yellow-foot, 347
TREE-SNAKES, 183, 286, 287
  All-green, 285
  Banded-tail, 269
  Ornamented, 287
  Painted, 267
  Punctulated, 268
Trichomanes radicans, 33
Trionychidæ, 43
Tritons, 367. See Newts
Troga Venado, 206
Tropidonotus, 214
  ater, 232
  fasciatus, 239
  f. erythrogaster, 240
  f. rhombifer, 240
  f. sipedon, 240
  natrix, 217, 240
  n. astreptophorus, 232
  n. torquata, 273
  n. vars., 232
  ordinatus, 214
  o. sirtalis, 217
  saurita, 233
  septemvittatus, 238
  sirtalis, 217, 241
  stolatus, 241
  tessellatus, 234
  tigrinus, 240
  viperinus, 237
  v. aurolineatus, 238
  v. ocellatus, 238
Tuateras, 135, 155
  food of, 160

Tuateras, vivaria for, 160
Tuberculated Iguana, 143
Tubes for feeding Snakes, 290
Tupinambis rufescens, 83
  teguixin, 82
Turtles, Freshwater, 43
  Sea, 43
Two-banded Monitor, 76, 79
Two-headed Lizard, 119
  Snake (supposed), 212
Typhlophis, 185
Typhlopidæ, 185
Typhlops, 185
  nigroalbus, 185

U.

Ular Sawa, 198
"*Una lagarta*," 66
Urodela, 358
Uromastix Hardwickii, 135
  spinipes, 135

V.

Vallisneria spiralis, 369
Varanidæ, 75. See Monitors
Varanus albigularis, 78
  flavescens, 79
  giganteus, 80
  Gouldii, 80
  griseus, 78
  niloticus, 78
  salvator, 76, 79
Variegated Bush Snake, 268
  Lizard, 83
Vernal Greater Starwort, 369
Veronica anagallis, 369
  beccabunga, 38
Vertebrata, 4
Villarsia nymphæoides, 340
Viper, Blowing, 271
  distinguishing, 221
  Water, 239
Vipera berus, 223, 273
Viperine Snake, 237
Vivacious Snake, 284

VIVARIA, 8
  and ferneries, 17
  arch for, 18
  canvas for, 9
  cement for, 13
  fastening glass sides of, 13
  Ferns for, 28
  heating, 15, 19
  making, 8
  plants for, 28
Viviparous Lizard, 98

W.

Walking Toad, 326
Wall Gecko, 73
  Lizard, 103
  Rue, 32
Waltli's Newt, 383
Waran, 78
Warming vivaria, 15, 19
Wart Snakes, 214
Warty Hemidactyle, 75
  Newt, 372
  or Crested Newt, 372
Water Boa, 206
  Cress, 38
  Eft or Evet, 379. See
    Newts
  Lily, Cape Fragrant, 340
  Mint, 38
  Mocassin, 239
  Monitors, 80
  Soldier, 37
  Speedwell, 369
  Weed, Canadian, 369
    Italian, 369
Water-tortoises, vivaria for, 23, 38
  Viper, 239
West African Python, 199, 200
Whaddon Organs, 313
Whip Snake, Long-snouted, 288
White Amphisbæna, 148
White's Tree-frog, 345
White-throated Monitor, 78

Worm, Blind, 112, 117
  Slow, 112
  Spotted Slow, 129
Worm-like Batrachians, 398
Worms as food, 101

X.

Xenodon colubrinus, 270
  rhabdocephalus, 271
Xenopus lævis, 354

Y.

Yellow-bellied Toad, 352
Yellow-foot Tree-frog, 347

Z.

Zamenis atrovirens, 244
  a. asianus, 247
  a. caspius, 247
  a. erythrogaster, 247
  a. trabalis, 247
  constrictor, 248
  c. flaviventris, 251
  dahlii, 249, 251
  flaviventris, 251
  gemonensis, 244
  g. asianus, 247
  g. caspius, 247
  g. erythrogaster, 247
  g. trabalis, 247
  hippocrepis, 251
  korros, 248
  mucosus, 247
Zic-zac and Crocodiles, 59
Zinc for vivaria, 12
Zonure, Derbian, 106
  Rough-scaled, 107
Zonurus cordylus, 107
  derbianus, 106
  giganteus, 106

www.ingramcontent.com/pod-product-compliance
Lightning Source LLC
Chambersburg PA
CBHW030601230426
43661CB00053B/1797